ADVANCE PRAISE FOR
THE BEAUTIFUL SNOW

"*The Beautiful Snow* is a thoroughly engrossing read. Cindy Wilson's impeccable research resulted in an exciting, panoramic account of the infamous winter of 1880–1881 and its effect on Minnesota and the Dakota Territory. With a dual focus on weather and railroads, this book is a perfect companion volume to Laura Ingalls Wilder's *The Long Winter*. The book's scope and content will fascinate a wide audience of readers."

—William Anderson, historian and author of
The Selected Letters of Laura Ingalls Wilder;
Laura Ingalls Wilder Country; and many other titles

"*The Long Winter*, one of Laura Ingalls Wilder's most beloved children's novels, portrays the harsh realities of life on the late-nineteenth-century agricultural frontier. In a heroic piece of historical detective work, Cindy Wilson has written a book placing Wilder's fictional narrative in broad and detailed historical context. She emphasizes the challenges, obstacles, and hardships settlers on the Dakota prairie faced along with the energy, ingenuity, and tenacity they exhibited during the Hard Winter of 1880–1881. This book provides eloquent evidence of the hardiness and vision of these pioneers as well as testimony to the human spirit."

—John E. Miller, professor emeritus, South Dakota State University,
and author of *Becoming Laura Ingalls Wilder: The Woman Behind the
Legend*; *Laura Ingalls Wilder and Rose Wilder Lane: Authorship,
Place, Time, and Culture*; and *Laura Ingalls Wilder's Little Town:
Where History and Literature Meet*

"Cindy Wilson's *The Beautiful Snow* is an impressive and immersive look at the Hard Winter of 1880–1881 in Minnesota and South Dakota. Wilson builds on Laura Ingalls Wilder's memories and her novel based on this historical winter by mining information from contemporary newspapers, railroad archives, and other primary sources. Her detailed study not only helps explain how settlers managed to weather the storms but also offers fresh insight into the expansion of the railroads into Dakota Territory, a massive undertaking that would transform the Northern Great Plains. *The Beautiful Snow* is wonderful, a true gift to Wilder scholarship."

—Nancy Tystad Koupal, director of the *Pioneer Girl Project*, South Dakota Historical Society Press

"*The Beautiful Snow* is the story of the trials, tribulations, and triumphs of the people who stood up against the worst that nature could throw against them. It is also a fine study of the region's railroads. Indeed, without the railroads there would have been no story to tell concerning this terrible winter. They facilitated the settlement of the area and with this came the responsibility for maintaining the vital supply lines that were the life-blood of the new communities throughout the region. In the face of the unimaginable wrath of the winter storms, the railroad companies did their level best to keep the supply routes open, going to great and expensive lengths to accomplish this end. Eventually, however, they were forced to surrender and retire from the field of battle in the face of an opponent that commanded infinitely superior forces in a tactically superior manner. The campaign against the elements during the winter of 1880-81 represented the best and the worst of times for the railroads. Despite their ultimate defeat, the story of their efforts is a wonder in and of itself. The railroads learned from their experiences and took prompt measures to ensure that they would be able to counter attack in force when next nature took aim at their systems.

The Beautiful Snow is a must read for any student of railroad history!"

—John C. Luecke, railroad historian and author of *The Chicago and Northwestern in Minnesota*; *More Chicago & North Western in Minnesota*; *Dreams, Disasters and Demise: The Milwaukee Road in Minnesota*; and *More Milwaukee Road in Minnesota*

"In *The Beautiful Snow*, following the railroad lines of the Upper Midwest, Cindy Wilson journeys through the Hard Winter of 1880–1881 and tells the stories of families who survived the blizzards. Kudos to Wilson for placing this extraordinary book in our hands."

—Lynn Jarrett, freelance writer in central Oklahoma

"*The Long Winter* by Laura Ingalls Wilder is a claustrophobic book, written to show how frontier life could be a struggle against the elements. Cindy Wilson's *The Beautiful Snow* views Ingalls's story through a wider lens. Using primary sources from railroad archives and newspapers printed during that long winter, Wilson reveals how the 'beautiful snow' affected every community it fell on. This book could be read in tandem with *The Long Winter* or by anyone interested in how pioneers survived on the early frontier during one of the snowiest winters ever to occur."

—Sara Pfannkuche, archaeologist and specialist in
frontier interactions and museum curation

The Beautiful SNOW

THE INGALLS FAMILY, THE RAILROADS, AND THE HARD WINTER OF 1880-81

CINDY WILSON

Softcover ISBN 13: 978-1-64343-905-1
ebook ISBN 13: 978-1-64343-871-9

Library of Congress Catalog Number: 2019906472

Printed in the United States of America
First Printing: 2020
24 23 22 21 20   5 4 3 2 1

Cover and interior design by James Monroe Design, LLC.

Illustrations by Margarita Sikorskaia

BEAVER'S
POND
PRESS

939 Seventh Street West
Saint Paul, Minnesota 55102

(952) 829-8818
www.BeaversPondPress.com

"Oh the snow ! the beautiful snow,
Filling the cuts so the trains can't go."

Clipping from the *Murray County Pioneer*, Currie, Minnesota, January 20, 1881.

Contents

Author's Note

The Long Winter is my favorite of the Little House books. To me, it is a perfect novel. A hot September of haying plunges into the depths of hunger, brutal cold, and despair until the crucible is finally lifted by the whistle of the train and the return of spring—the dramatic arc is thrilling! You might even want to read it before beginning this book, to set the mood.

Having lived in southern Minnesota my whole life, I've spent countless hours wandering the area between Walnut Grove, Minnesota, and De Smet, South Dakota. In October 2016, I selected *The Long Winter* for my neighborhood book club. While preparing to immerse my fellow readers in the world of the novel, I wondered, *Where, exactly, is the Tracy Cut?*—a pivotal setting in the plot.

That thought eventually led to nearly two years of my own immersion in that winter and the railroad development that preceded it. My initial goal was simply to find the Tracy Cut, where "the Superintendent from the East" admitted defeat and called off all further attempts to clear the tracks until the sunshine itself melted the snow.

Once the cut was located, what began as curiosity became a quest to find the identity of the superintendent. Once his name was found, verifying the story became a near obsession. After all, the story appeared in *Pioneer Girl*, Wilder's earliest autobiography. She believed the story was true, so evidence of it had to be out there, somewhere.

I am excited to guide you through what became known historically as the Hard Winter of 1880–81, as well as through tangent "sidetrack" subjects that further enrich the narrative. The more one learns about that particular winter, the more fascinating and impressive it becomes.

The Friction Between Fact and Fiction

Interestingly, Wilder struggled to find a plot while writing *The Long Winter*. Writing to her daughter, Rose Wilder Lane, she confessed,

> Here is what is bothering me and holding me up. I can't seem to find a plot, or pattern as you call it. There seems to be nothing to it only the struggle to live, through the winter, until spring comes again. This of course they all did. But is it strong enough, or can it be made strong enough to supply the necessary thread running all through the book.[1]

Of course, Wilder did a wonderful job crafting a plot and finding the necessary thread. That thread is part of a magnificent tapestry that links the novel to the history as reflected in the newspaper record. In the book you hold now, I interweave Wilder's plot with the various voices and perspectives of editors and correspondents throughout the region to shine a light on that "struggle to live."

That said, this book does not fact-check the novel. The novel is indeed fiction, though heavily influenced by Wilder's experience. For that matter, there are even a few places where Wilder's autobiography does not necessarily line up with verifiable fact nor follow a reliable chronology. It is not always possible to identify the specific time that an event took place or when one month became another.

I have attempted to provide context to each month from the perspective of the Ingalls family and what they experienced. Throughout the book, I identify this information as coming from one of the versions of Wilder's autobiography, correspondence between Wilder and others, the manuscript of the novel, or the published novel. Using clues within the various documents, I have made "best-guess" decisions to link actions to a specific month. I may not have chosen perfectly, but it should suffice for our purposes.

Let us remember that Wilder was in her early teenage years during the winter covered here, and that she led a sheltered and relatively isolated life up to that point. Therefore, this book offers an opportunity to view the events from windows other than those that young Laura looked out from.

The Railroad System as a Whole

The railroad lines and companies became intricately entwined in the events of the Hard Winter. I spent several months at the beginning of the project simply determining the progress of the rails from the Mississippi River westward and how towns were linked and founded. This was done to determine how established—or not—some of the shipping and warehouse centers were along the various railroad lines and whether there might have been storehouses of food and fuel close to De Smet. This exercise also helped me visualize the location of rail systems and towns in relation to one another. It was a critical part of the research that helped create the map on the next page.

Looking at the map, you can see the tracks as they ran from the established towns of eastern and central Minnesota to the newer communities of southwestern Minnesota and southeastern Dakota Territory (as of the end of 1880). The year noted near each segment of track indicates when the rails reached the westernmost town on that segment. The impact of the Panic of 1873—a financial crisis that caused, among other things, the stagnation of railroad expansion—is highly visible.

The years used on the map occasionally differ from published railroad history books (by one or two years). Where newspaper articles from the towns involved indicated that a railroad bed was prepared but rails had not yet reached them, those were the years used, rather than those recorded in the railroad histories, which may have had other criteria for establishing completion. For the purposes of this book, I've considered a segment complete as of the year that trains could reach a town. As an additional reference while you read, the inside cover of this book features a version of the map showing distances between towns.

Most of the towns west of the 1878–79 resumption of railroad construction were no older than the tracks that stretched across the prairie. Some were barely months old as the first storm hit in October 1880, making them particularly vulnerable. Construction of houses and businesses had been rapid, sometimes even haphazard, and supply chains were still being established.

This book originally had a first half that followed in detail the construction of the Winona & St. Peter and Dakota Central Railroads, with the Ingalls family woven in among the milestones. For many reasons, I decided to split it apart, and that fascinating story will appear as a second book, which will be similar to this one but focus on *By the Shores of Silver Lake* instead of *The Long Winter*.

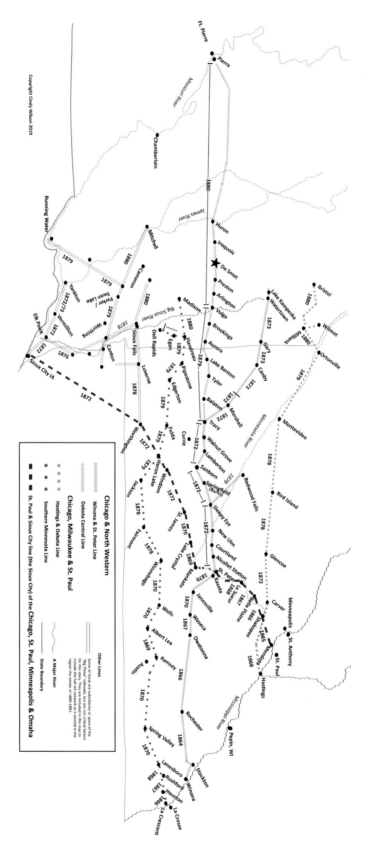

Editorial Notes

Below is a quick list of editorial choices used throughout the book.

Names

The Little House series is fictional though also autobiographical; throughout the book, I reference the same people as characters in the novels and also as real-life historical figures. To aid with this distinction, I use first names or familiar names when referring to characters in the novels: Laura, Ma, Pa, etc. I primarily refer to real-life people by last name. However, because many people share the Ingalls and Wilder family names, some first names must be used for clarity: Charles, Caroline, Almanzo, etc. As the one exception, I will consistently refer to the real Laura Ingalls Wilder as "Wilder," even in contexts where other Wilders are referenced.

Quotes and Spellings

Quotes from Wilder's writing and from newspaper articles are included as originally written or published, with only occasional bracketed edits or notations in extreme cases of potential misreading. Also, the names of newspapers, which often include the name of a town/city, were italicized to help distinguish them from the surrounding text. In addition, a couple of discrepancies from current nomenclature should be explained:

The town of Flandreau (pronounced FLAN-droo), currently spelled with the *e*, was named for US Indian Agent Charles E. Flandrau, and that is how the town's name was spelled throughout the Hard Winter. Since the town officially calls itself Flandreau, I spelled it that way when outside of quotes from the era.

Similarly, the modern spelling of the town of De Smet includes a space. However, in the era discussed, it was commonly written as *DeSmet* (without a space). Where I reference the town, I use the modern spelling. And to avoid confusion, I use Pierre instead of East Pierre, which was inconsistently used in the newspapers. In keeping with my aforementioned hands-off treatment of quotes throughout this book, in all cases where a town name appears in a quote, I reproduce it as published.

The treatment of the names of railroad companies can be contentious for rail fans. For the purposes of this work, I settled on name treatments that mirror the annual reports put out by each company in their respective fiscal years ending in 1881 or 1882. For example, I use "Chicago and North Western Railway Company" for the initial mention, as that is how it is written in that company's annual report for the fiscal year (FY) ending May 31, 1881, though I shorten it to "the Chicago &

North Western" for simplicity throughout most of the text. Many of the names of these parent companies' subsidiary lines are also shortened throughout most of the text.

The newspaper editors of the era used a wide variety of name treatments, abbreviations, and initialisms, making standardization for the purposes of this book difficult. As a result, in quoted material, all variations of the railroad companies' names were left unchanged unless likely to cause confusion. In most cases, the context should provide sufficient clarity.

Finally, while considerable research helped me ferret out many answers and details, there are still many unknowns. There are places where I muse on possibilities. These are not final answers nor all-inclusive sets of hypotheses. There are things we might never know, and there are mysteries that someone else might solve in the years to come. But hopefully there is a good amount of new, in-depth information in these pages to paint a fuller picture of the conditions with which the settlers contended as the blizzards raged around them during this early winter of their residency.

Endnotes

I enjoy finding extra information hidden within endnotes. Therefore, I have added little nuggets of information to the endnotes in this work. Sometimes they are simply my own observations, and other times they provide extra details that didn't fit as well within the main text.

Newspaper Archives

Researching historical newspaper archives sent me on a journey across Minnesota and South Dakota. Most Minnesota newspapers were accessed via microfilm at the Gale Family Library at the Minnesota Historical Society in St. Paul, Minnesota. The *Janesville Argus* was accessed via microfilm at the Waseca County Historical Society in Waseca, Minnesota, and the *Marshall Messenger* was accessed via microfilm at the Lyon County Historical Society in Marshall, Minnesota. Most South Dakota newspapers were accessed via microfilm at the South Dakota State Historical Society archives in Pierre, South Dakota. The linen editions of the *Dakota Pantagraph and Sioux Falls Independent* were viewed in person at the Minnehaha Historical Society in Sioux Falls, South Dakota.

Units of Measurement

For readers outside of the United States, appendix VI contains a conversion chart for temperature (Fahrenheit to Celsius) and distance (miles to kilometers).

Regarding temperature accuracy, due to ideal thermometer placement and standardized calibration guidelines, official temperature readings are usually more reliable than readings taken by "backyard" thermometers, and temperature readings between thermometers can vary by several degrees in general. Also, according to Dr. Barbara Mayes Boustead, a meteorologist with the National Weather Service, "the range of accuracy for any thermometer depends on the type of thermometer being used, which is true of thermometers from the 1800s through today."[2]

Financial Buying Power Conversions

Throughout the newspaper record are references to costs and expenses. As a simple comparison, $1 in 1881 had the buying power of $25.15 in 2019, according to the US Bureau of Labor Statistics.[3] You may find that conversion useful as you read about the price of a dozen eggs or a cord of wood, the daily pay for a snow shoveler, or the overall cost to the railroad companies as they tried to keep the roads clear.

Charles and Caroline Ingalls, ca. 1879–1881. From the Laura Ingalls Wilder Home and Museum, Mansfield, Missouri.

Introductions and Background

Before beginning, we must become acquainted with people, places, and railroad lines in order to better understand the saga we are about to embark upon.

People from *The Long Winter*

The Ingalls Family

The core family consisted of parents Charles ("Pa," age 45) and Caroline ("Ma," age 41) and their four daughters: Mary (16), Laura (14), Carrie (10), and Grace (4). (The numbers listed represent their ages by the end of the winter.)

Mary lost her sight at age fourteen, between late June and mid-July 1879. The novel *The Long Winter*, published in 1940, takes place in De Smet, Dakota Territory, and is highly autobiographical, though fictionalized conversations and situations were added for literary purposes.

The Masters Family

Though it's not included in the novel, the Ingalls family spent the winter boarding George and Maggie Masters and their infant son. Acknowledging their presence here, I won't mention them again. The reader should remember, though, that there were three additional mouths to feed in the household beyond those of the six Ingalls family members.

Carrie, Mary, and Laura Ingalls, ca. 1879–1881. From the Laura Ingalls Wilder Home and Museum, Mansfield, Missouri.

The Wilder Family

Royal and Almanzo ("the Wilders") and their sister Eliza Jane took homesteads near De Smet in 1879, though they spent the winter of 1879–80 in Minnesota. In the spring of 1880, Almanzo planted a wheat crop near Marshall, Minnesota, then moved west to work for the railroad in Dakota Territory. As harvest time approached, he left his railroad work to return to Marshall, harvested his crop, and then moved west to De Smet—weeks before the Hard Winter began. Eliza Jane left De Smet after the first storm in October. Royal and Almanzo operated a feed store on De Smet's main street, where they spent the winter. As two bachelors, they had food resources beyond what the Ingalls family had. Almanzo was friends with another resident of De Smet, Cap Garland, who was a school friend of Laura's.

Almanzo Wilder, Laura Ingalls Wilder, and Rose Wilder Lane

In August 1885, Laura Ingalls married Almanzo Wilder. Their daughter, Rose Wilder Lane, was born in December 1886 on Almanzo's homestead property, north of De Smet. Rose went on to become a famous author and served as a writing mentor for her mother. Following some deaths in the family, Wilder (Laura) began to record her childhood memories and her father's stories. Rose helped her mother expand and polish her writing, with one result being the Little House book series. Four of those books take place in De Smet, and a fifth book set in De Smet was published from a draft manuscript after Wilder's death. *The Long Winter* is the second of the De Smet novels.

The Town of De Smet

The setting for *The Long Winter*, De Smet was officially founded in the spring of 1880, when the Western Town Lot Company, a subsidiary of the Chicago and North Western Railway Company, marked out the streets and lots.

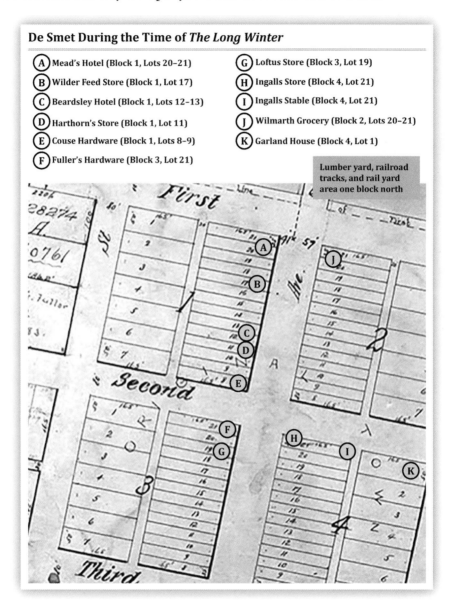

De Smet During the Time of *The Long Winter*

(A) Mead's Hotel (Block 1, Lots 20–21)

(B) Wilder Feed Store (Block 1, Lot 17)

(C) Beardsley Hotel (Block 1, Lots 12–13)

(D) Harthorn's Store (Block 1, Lot 11)

(E) Couse Hardware (Block 1, Lots 8–9)

(F) Fuller's Hardware (Block 3, Lot 21)

(G) Loftus Store (Block 3, Lot 19)

(H) Ingalls Store (Block 4, Lot 21)

(I) Ingalls Stable (Block 4, Lot 21)

(J) Wilmarth Grocery (Block 2, Lots 20–21)

(K) Garland House (Block 4, Lot 1)

Lumber yard, railroad tracks, and rail yard area one block north

Original plat map of De Smet, created March 27, 1880. Block 1, Lots 8–9 (E) were purchased by T. Maguire of Volga and housed Couse Hardware, which was closed for the winter. Block 1, Lot 8 is where Charles Ingalls constructed his first building and where the Ingalls family lived briefly in April 1880. They spent the Hard Winter diagonally across the street at Block 4, Lot 21 (H). Courtesy of the Chicago & North Western Historical Society. Business locations verified using the land purchase records.

When exactly the town's name was decided upon is unknown, but lead surveyor Charles Wood Irish wrote in his diary on Saturday, October 25, 1879, that he stopped in De Smet for the night. The next day's entry noted that he had stayed "at Engineers house."[4] That engineer's house was the surveyor's house that sheltered the Ingalls family through the winter of 1879–80, as related in *By the Shores of Silver Lake*. This places Mr. Irish at the Silver Lake camp at the same time as the Ingalls family. The original plat map of the town is shown on the previous page. Location maps throughout this book include De Smet for context.

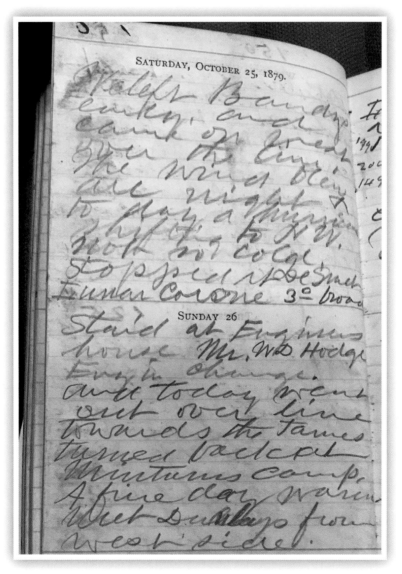

Photo of diary, from the Charles Wood Irish Papers, courtesy of the University of Iowa Libraries, Iowa City, Iowa. Photo by Mac Gill.

The Railroad Lines

In order to follow the five major rail lines throughout the Hard Winter, let's take a moment to get familiar with each. (Again, maps appear on page x and the inside cover.) The superintendents of each line will be further introduced later in the book as we meet them via their duties.

The Hastings & Dakota Railroad (the Hastings & Dakota)
Superintendent Charles Prior

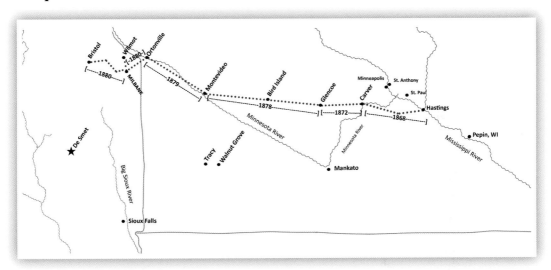

The northernmost east–west route included in this book was the Hastings & Dakota line of the Chicago, Milwaukee and St. Paul Railway Company. Running westward from Hastings, on the Mississippi River, to the Minnesota River and then northwest to the border of Dakota Territory, construction of this line pushed past the Minneapolis–St. Paul area in 1872 but did not expand beyond Glencoe, Minnesota, until 1878. In 1880, as the line reached a few dozen erratic miles into Dakota Territory, the town of Milbank formed. Around the same time, De Smet was founded to the south.

The Winona & St. Peter Railroad (the Winona & St. Peter)
Superintendent Sherburne Sanborn

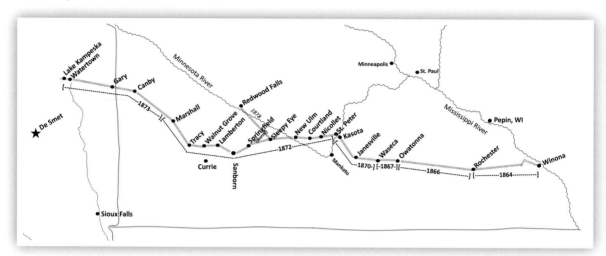

Roughly paralleling the Hastings & Dakota, and approximately forty to fifty miles to the south, was the Winona & St. Peter line, controlled through stock ownership by the Chicago and North Western Railway Company. This track stretched slowly (over nearly two decades) across the southern portion of Minnesota—from Winona, on the Mississippi River, to St. Peter, on the Minnesota River, then westward to Lake Kampeska (the founding site of Watertown, Dakota Territory, in 1879). This line of track was the most developed east–west route in the region—the company having spent a decade or more establishing freight warehouses, supply depots, and well-practiced processes for transport.

The Dakota Central Railroad (the Dakota Central)
Superintendent T. J. Nicholl

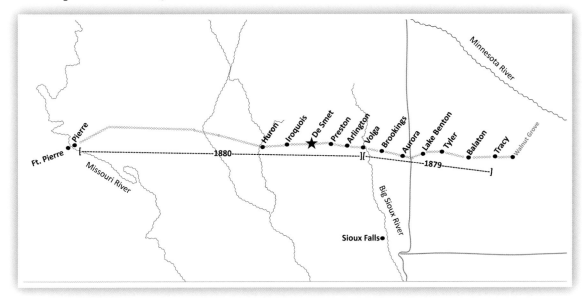

The Dakota Central Railroad began in Tracy, Minnesota, and pushed westward through the Prairie Pothole region of southwestern Minnesota and into eastern Dakota Territory. Marshes, small lakes, and rolling hills were, and remain, a major feature of the landscape from Tracy to just west of De Smet. This was the railroad line that Charles Ingalls worked for via a contractor and that led the Ingalls family, in search of a homestead, to what became De Smet.

The Southern Minnesota Railroad (the Southern Minnesota)
Superintendent John M. Egan

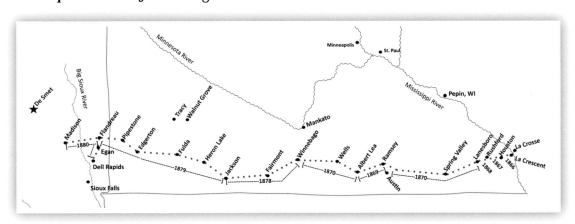

Twenty or so miles south of the Winona & St. Peter and the Dakota Central was the fourth main east–west line, the Southern Minnesota branch of the Chicago, Milwaukee & St. Paul. It, too, wended its way across the prairie in the late 1860s and early 1870s. Then, after a several-factor period of dormancy (we'll get into that later), the company resumed building it into Dakota Territory in the late 1870s.

The St. Paul & Sioux City Railroad (the Sioux City)
Superintendent John F. Lincoln

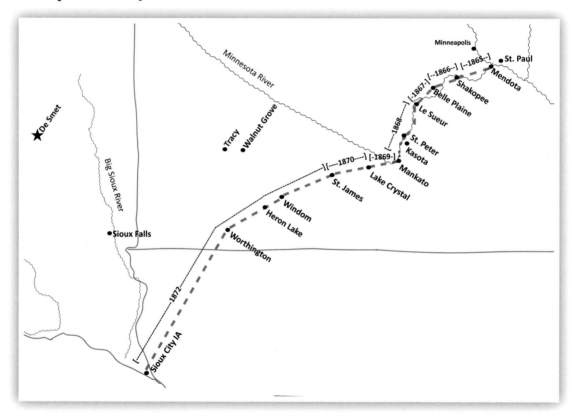

This line of the Chicago, St. Paul, Minneapolis & Omaha Railway Company cut a diagonal path from Minneapolis southwestward along the Minnesota River to Mankato, Minnesota, then traveled through southwestern Minnesota until it shadowed the Missouri River as it separated Dakota Territory from Iowa on its way into Nebraska. The towns along this line were older river towns until the line reached Mankato in the late 1860s, at which point new towns sprung up along the rails like plants in a furrow. These towns had a nearly eight-year start on the settlements of the Dakota Central. From 1867 to 1880, John F. Lincoln served as superintendent of this well-established line. It appears that his official duties as superintendent ended before the winter began, although newspaper articles mentioned him during the winter as if he were still acting in that capacity. These details are provided here because I do not mention him again, though he is mentioned in a quotation in the chapter covering January.

The Railroad Cuts and Blockades

In the context used here, a railroad blockade refers to drifted snow and, eventually, compacted ice that made it impossible for a train to move forward. Usually—but not always—these blockades were located in a cut, where a hill or undulation in the landscape was "cut out" to make way for the track and maintain a steadier grade of incline or decline. The narrower the cut, the more likely it was to capture snow. In the years following the Hard Winter, the railroad companies expended great effort to widen the more notorious cuts and make them less susceptible to drifting. But before the first snow of the Hard Winter descended on the prairie in 1880, those cuts were often relatively narrow—yet wide enough for the snow to drift in and become trapped.

A railroad cut through the prairie. This is wider than it would have been in 1880–81. The wider the cut, the less compressed and compacted the snow became. Photo by author.

The Tracy Cut

Throughout *The Long Winter*, the "big cut west of Tracy" was the focus of considerable attention, effort, and angst. The cut itself was barely a year and a half old at the time the story takes place (1880–81).

After the surveyors did their work in the spring of 1879, graders came along to prepare the roadbed. Four and a half miles west of Tracy, the workers began to cut through a long, sloping hill that would one day be immortalized by Laura Ingalls Wilder.

The grid below shows the elevation and grade map prepared by principal surveyor Charles Wood Irish in the spring of 1879. The straight line represents the steady grade of the roadbed. The undulating line above and below the grade shows the varying elevation of the terrain along the planned route. The land above the grade needed to be cut through, and the land below the grade needed to be filled in. The photographs below show the area as it appears today, clearly illustrating both the cut and fill.

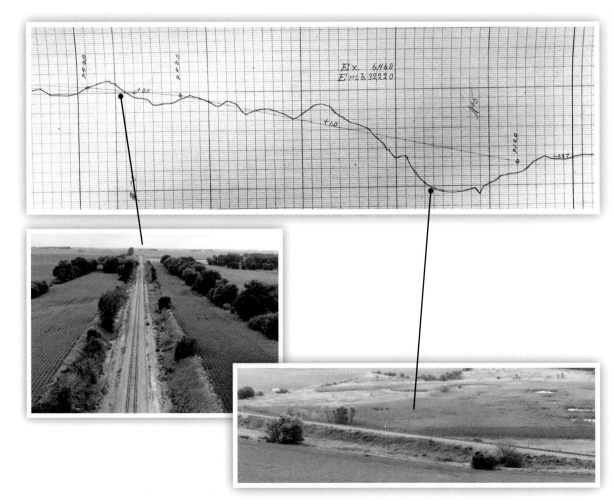

Elevation and grade map from the Charles Wood Irish Papers, photographed by Mac Gill, courtesy of the University of Iowa Libraries, Iowa City, Iowa (*top*). Drone photographs by Steve Devore (*bottom*).

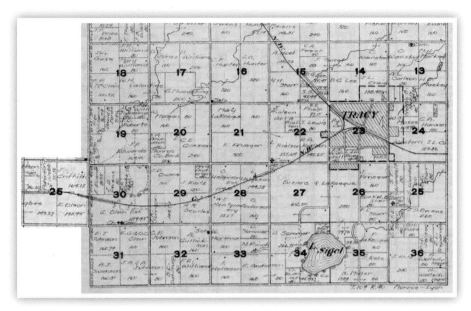

This 1916 Lyon County plat map shows the cuts to the west of Tracy. (Cuts are represented by lengths of thinner lines running parallel to the thicker line of the track.) The smaller cut straddling the line between Sections 27 and 28 was shown in the earlier photograph illustrating a railroad cut through a prairie. The long cut on the left edge of Section 30 is the probable Tracy Cut.[5]

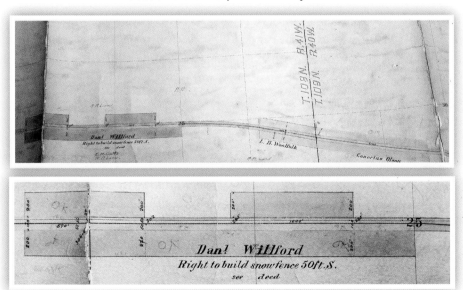

A linen right-of-way map from 1879 shows an area to the west containing a *siding*, a length of track that allows one train to pull over and wait while another train passes. A notation on the map (visible in the zoomed-in view, *bottom image*) indicates the landowner had granted permission to construct fifty feet of snow fence along the siding. The shaded area on the right (*top image*) matches with the cut notation on the west edge of Section 30 on the 1916 Lyon County plat map above. Right-of-way map photos courtesy of the Chicago & North Western Historical Society.

Brief Railroad History

It took the Winona & St. Peter (and its predecessors) over eighteen *years*, from 1855 to 1873, to stretch the approximately three hundred miles from the western bank of the Mississippi River at Winona, Minnesota, to the marshy banks of Lake Kampeska, which became Watertown, in eastern Dakota Territory. The Civil War, two financial panics, a region-clearing Indian war, the Grange movement, and a grasshopper scourge all contributed to the difficulties establishing the route that ran through the towns of Walnut Grove and Tracy in western Minnesota and beyond into Dakota Territory.

In contrast, it only took the Dakota Central approximately eighteen *months*, during 1879 and 1880, to traverse the prairies from Tracy, Minnesota, to the breaks of the Missouri River at Pierre, Dakota Territory—a distance of roughly 240 miles. Nearly every possible condition had been different, even favorable, when the Dakota Central was planned and executed. The Panic of 1873 had ended, the lingering economic depression had dissolved, and a gold rush was imminent following a discovery in the Black Hills during the Custer Expedition of 1874. Optimism and capital were running rampant.

Railroad companies looked at their maps and saw that, for the most part, they'd caught up with settlement. What to do? Beyond those horizons were dreamed-of opportunities. Dakota Territory promised bounties of gold and—possibly even more reliably—bountiful crops year after year into forever. Big dollar signs flashed before the eyes of enterprising executives and financiers. The railroad companies saw the opportune moment and pounced. Tracks soon followed.

In 1877, Marvin Hughitt, director of the Chicago & North Western, envisioned riches on the fertile prairies of Dakota Territory and set a plan in motion to obtain them. Surveying of the Dakota Central began in early 1879, and by the end of 1880, the tracks had reached the Missouri River. Indeed, surveyors were well west of the river by then, looking for a route to the Black Hills. Hughitt was a hands-on leader, shadowing the path of the surveyors to confirm route choices, even finding himself snowed in at the western terminus of the Dakota Central during a November 1880 storm.

The difference in time frames is staggering. Tens of thousands of people answered the call to settle on the prairies of Dakota Territory. They were promised mythically wondrous wheat-growing soils and a life of happy prosperity among people who were likewise willing to work hard to create new communities out upon the waving grasses. The messaging—boosterism—was effective. If you'd like to see the results, appendix III has population records for the region.

The Panic of 1873

In the years between the close of the Civil War and 1873, railroad construction increased significantly. While the expansion of railroad tracks spurred development wherever they reached, it was an expensive endeavor. Banks and financiers were heavily invested—and heavily in debt due to slow returns.

A second transcontinental railroad was under development in the early 1870s, with Jay Cooke & Company being the major investor. In September 1873, the company collapsed due to overextension. This failure spawned others, and a financial panic ensued that impacted the economy not only in the United States but in Europe as well. The economy entered a depression, and most investments stopped. Railroads and other industries and businesses of all kinds failed, and unemployment climbed.

The railroad system map on page x of the Introduction clearly shows the impact, as there was little expansion of tracks in Minnesota and Dakota Territory between 1873 and the end of the depression more than five years later. This is an extreme simplification. The topic is a large one, and I encourage you to explore it on your own.

The Railroads and the Snow

Winter brought additional challenges to railroad operations. Cold weather caused rails to become brittle and break under the weight of passing trains, and frost heave buckled the railbed during thaw cycles. Steam locomotives required water, which could be obtained from melted snow, though the process of melting snow required more fuel than was needed in warmer weather.

Farmers and townspeople alike had long depended on merchants for obtaining staples such as cornmeal, sugar, tea, spices, and other basic items.[6] In these newly railroad-settled areas, farmers who had previously relied mostly upon their own crops, gardens, and animals to feed their families were more able and apt to depend upon groceries being available via local merchants.

Similarly, merchants counted on the trains running regularly to provide goods for their shelves and did not necessarily keep their storerooms heavily stocked. Coal, kerosene, and lumber were likewise assumed to be no further away than the next train or two. In *The Long Winter*, the merchants Loftus and Harthorn both mention they had been counting on the trains running to keep their shelves stocked, waiting on their orders as much as their customers were.[7] It was a cultural change in expectations for the availability of the necessary items of life—and it coincided with what became known as one of the worst winters in American history.

Similar to modern air traffic backing up across a wide area when an airport is shut down, the clogging of railroad cars across hundreds of miles of railroad lines, sidetracks, and sidings caused significant logistical issues. Like airplanes that have to be repositioned to realign routes, locomotives and train cars found themselves out of place due to weather delays. Freight and mail, like luggage at baggage claims, piled up and had to await retrieval.

Described simplistically, a *siding* is an additional, parallel length of track— often constructed using lighter-duty rails—connected to the main line of track and used to allow one train to pass another. *Sidetracks* are found in rail yards and allow the repositioning of individual cars or locomotives. Some towns had neither. Some towns had both. Some sidings were located between towns, out on the prairie, so that one train could "pull over" to allow an oncoming train to pass. Larger towns and cities with major rail yards had miles of sidings and sidetracks, but as the Hard Winter progressed, that extra space was utilized as parking lots for trains with loaded cars that found themselves unable to proceed westward.

The winter of 1872–73, the first experienced by the Winona & St. Peter west of the Minnesota River, was an eye-opener. Cuts west of Sleepy Eye, Minnesota, were reported to be packed with snow eight to twelve feet deep. Eight locomotives were stranded along the line following a November 1872 storm, and attempts to retrieve them were hindered by more blizzards. Five of the locomotives were eventually retrieved and repaired, though the other three, located west of Marshall, remained snowbound until after the spring thaw.

Subsequent winters were problematic too. During the winter of 1874–75, trains did not run at all between February 16 and April 8.[8] The railroads weren't completely without recourse, though. By the winter of 1882–83, there were a total of seventeen wedge plows being used between Winona and Pierre. Despite this, February 5, 1883, still brought an official stop to operations west of St. Peter.[9]

As you read, keep in mind the astounding complexity of unraveling snowbound rail cars parked on sidings and sidetracks along hundreds of miles of track, buried amidst thousands of other snowbound railcars.

Editors and Their Newspapers

One of the benefits of a small-town newspaper—to historians, at least—is that just about everything finds its way into print at some point. As a result, we can look back nearly a century and a half and see who visited whom, and when. The role of a small-town newspaper editor often included functioning as the town's booster in chief, an endeavor particularly important in the new communities. This role complicates the newspaper record but also provides a gold mine of details about the hopes, dreams, and aspirations of the little towns that were waiting to blossom with the melting of the snow. Appendix II features short biographies of a few of the editors whose work will guide us through the winter.

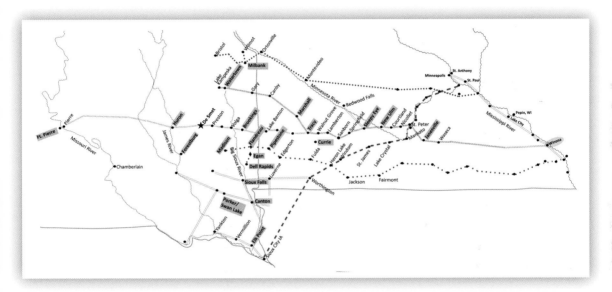

The towns with names highlighted in gray published the newspapers most frequently cited throughout this book. Input from across the region helped provide a broader perspective.

The Evolution of Boosterism

Part of the tragedy of the Hard Winter was that the towns—full of hopeful citizens and area farmers—were barely established, many just months old as winter descended. The larger story of how the towns came to be is just as interesting as the thousands of smaller stories and dreams of the people that settled the region.

The railroad companies needed to attract and persuade farmers, merchants, and other business owners to move farther west, creating a market for rail services and filling out the supply chain.

Whereas in previous decades it could take settlers weeks to travel a few hundred miles with only what could fit into a wagon, railroads could now transport people, equipment, and supplies the same distance in just hours. That enticing western horizon no longer seemed so out of reach.

The poster shown below feels like an early version of clickbait, where an enticing headline lures the reader in, then latches on with an entirely different message. It reads:

A MILLION DOLLARS A MINUTE
Cannot be made even by going to CENTRAL DAKOTA, but you can get, virtually free of cost, a farm that, if you expend one-half the time and labor upon it that you are doing upon the farm in the East, that you are paying large rent for, and never will own, you will reap twenty times the reward, in sure and abundant crops, and in a prosperous and contented future.

Several of the larger railroad companies sent promoters as far afield as Europe to wax poetic about the lands along their main and branch lines. Individual railroad lines advertised similarly, encouraging people to move west. For instance, the Western Town Lot Company, a subsidiary of the Winona & St. Peter, marketed the land as a "farmer's paradise" that awaited the adventurous settler. Brochures tempted the hopeful with statistics (both real and embellished) and hyperbolic entreaties about the quality of life and prosperity to be found at the end of the rails.[10]

Photos courtesy of the Chicago & North Western Historical Society.

Railroad-organized land excursions took prospective settlers to inspect western lands. The tickets were often discounted, or they included free or discounted transportation of household goods, should the traveler have decided to move west. People boarded the excursion trains, looked around, and returned home to pack for their golden futures.

Town boosters tended to focus on their individual burgs, shouting the benefits of location, climate, and culture as well as the extraordinary quality and friendliness of the people already settled there. As practiced, boosterism most often played out via the local newspaper and letters sent back east to friends and family.

Those efforts were having an impact. In Marshall, the *Lyon County News* noted that the first four months of 1879 had brought 342 emigrant families through the depot, and suggested that the stations on either side of them were experiencing a similar influx.[11] People were on the move.

The Local News

With limited communication channels, local news editors depended upon regional publications and other resources for their own news items. As newspapers arrived via mail, local editors examined them for information to share with their own readers, interspersed with their own local content. Additionally, they asked correspondents from other area communities to provide news that the editor was unable to obtain on his own.[12]

Winona Republican, Winona, Minnesota, September 5, 1870.

In many towns, the postmaster was also one of the proprietors, or the sole proprietor/editor, of the local newspaper. Due to franking laws, newspapers were able to mail their papers for free within a certain distance of their business, making the dissemination of news easy and cheap. It was also helpful that townspeople had to pick up their mail at the newspaper office, where the editor could extract newsy items from the customers.

News sharing was also done via telegraph. Telegraph operators in different towns communicated with each other over the wires, keeping information flowing even when the mail stopped. Newspapers in larger cities often had at least one tele-graph operator in the newsroom, who would send out requests for things like weather updates and railroad status reports from the surrounding towns and settlements and then share the gathered information with readers. Among those readers, of course, were the editors of other newspapers, and in this way, reports were spread across the region.

The most frequent complaint among editors during the Hard Winter was the lack of mail service, which meant they were not receiving correspondence or news-papers from other locations, severely limiting the amount of news they could include within their own pages.

Some local papers were printed entirely in-house, though most papers purchased weekly "patents." These were preprinted pages full of national and international news, which local editors would supplement with their own pages focusing on local news.

Unfortunately, these patents were shipped from bigger cities like Milwaukee and Chicago. If blockades lingered and the trains couldn't get through, neither could the patents. Editors were forced to improvise. To save on paper, they made half-size editions and even printed issues on butcher paper and, in a few lovely examples, colored linen—all in an attempt to keep the people informed of what was happening. The editors were certainly giving it a gallant try. (More on this later.)

The Beautiful Snow

"The beautiful snow" is a phrase that appeared frequently throughout the regional newspapers. Used both as a descriptor and as a derisive, sarcastic term, the phrase lends itself to visions of the typesetter gritting his teeth as he placed each. Individual. Letter. Into. Place. to relay the phrase. It was so prevalent and catchy that it inspired the title of this book.

A New Look at the Hard Winter

Five railroad lines, nearly a quarter of a million southwestern Minnesota residents, the Ingalls family, and approaching eighty thousand other new settlers in eastern Dakota Territory[13] all found themselves contending with what became known as the historic Hard Winter of 1880–81. You may have learned about it by reading *The Long Winter* or through exposure to local or regional history—possibly both. We have a sense of that winter as a nearly six-month blizzard with mythically cold air. Of settlers huddled around their stoves, burning whatever they could, trying not to freeze to death. Of hollow eyes and weak limbs due to lack of nutrition.

There is a reason for this. That perspective was borne of historical documentary efforts made after the fact. Most histories contained at least a few sentences about the winter. Some reached back into the newspaper record and published articles as they had appeared at the time, adding narrative to the flow. Others slipped into generalized, poetic, and sometimes hyperbolic prose. Most fell somewhere in between.

What We've Been Taught through *The Long Winter*

The novel *The Long Winter* follows the deprivations experienced by the Ingalls family of newly founded De Smet, Dakota Territory, throughout the winter of 1880–81. Beginning with the hot, sweaty work of cutting hay and the sweet smells and sounds of the autumnal prairie, the book's narrative quickly descended into a hellacious winter. The family endured months of snowstorms, strong winds that resculpted the already-fallen snow, and deadly cold temperatures that altered the patterns of life and essentially trapped them in their home.

Food and fuel supplies dwindled dangerously. The family was isolated from most of the townspeople, although patriarch Charles, between blizzards, went out to converse with other men about the news. Nearly starving, minds numbed—the constant twisting of hay to feed the feeble fires consumed almost seven bleak months.

Describing the weather, Wilder wrote in her autobiography, "It gave the impression of a malignant power of destruction wreaking havoc as long as possible, then pausing for breath to go on with the work."[14] That sense of menace informed the tone of the novel; the cyclical blizzard became one of the antagonists.

The railroad company was depicted as having abandoned the new towns it had founded, leaving the townspeople to fend for themselves on the frozen prairie. Only the bravery of a few townsmen kept the residents alive.

What We've Been Taught through County and State Histories

As noted, *The Long Winter* is fiction, despite being autobiographical. Official history books, however, *should* be trustworthy as closer to fact than fiction. As we move through the winter, however, we'll see that this is not always the case. Regardless, those histories, combined with the novel, comprise most of what has informed our view of that winter.

Arthur P. Rose wrote of the winter as experienced in Lyon County (which includes Marshall, Minnesota) as "one of the dates from which time is reckoned" and as a "season of Siberian frigidity." He admits to experiencing other, shorter periods of equally extreme blizzards and other winter weather but adds that "never was a winter to compare with this one in duration, continued severity, depth of snow, and damage to property." The unrelenting blizzards caused blockades lasting weeks, even months, at a time. With no trains to replenish fuel and food, supplies were nearly exhausted. At night, the only light came from the fires keeping people warm. "People burned green wood, fences, lumber, hay and grain . . . and the farmers obtained their supplies from the villages by means of handsleds."[15]

In *History of Dakota Territory*, George Washington Kingsbury wrote that "a pitiable condition existed. At DeSmet the people were living on flour and potatoes, with nothing but hay for fuel." The boarding houses and hotels in Volga had been closed. Worse, there was reportedly a cut between the Minnesota cities Sleepy Eye and Tracy "where the snow was sixty-five feet deep" and others buried in "twenty to forty feet." The railroads "had abandoned the work in these large cuts as useless" and were making every effort to send mail, coal, and other provisions through on horseback to "the people imprisoned in the towns along the line."[16]

The History of Southeastern Dakota was more poetic than historical in its summary. For the entire season from mid-October until the final storm,

> it seemed as though all the moisture then in the atmosphere, or likely to be in the atmosphere for years to come, had been inspired with an instinct to form itself into snow and precipitate itself on the prairies.... Not only were the snow falls immense in volume, but they followed each other with provoking promptness, and a strife for ascendancy, worthy of a better cause.[17]

The summary ended by sharing that by the start of 1881, the mail, food, and fuel were becoming scarce due to the inability of trains to get through—and the depletion grew worse as the months progressed.

A 1911 history of Pipestone County made use of newspaper articles to document the winter, adding this summary to the record: "A book could be filled with the adventures and unpleasant features of the long winter of deep snow, 1880–81." On top of reports of over twelve and a half feet of snow, it went on to say that "for months some farmers entered their stables through the roofs; others tunneled passageways through the snow from their houses to the stables and for weeks at a time did not go above the surface to do their chores. In places the snow remained on the ground until late in the spring."[18]

Of the eastern edge of the region, a 1901 history of Blue Earth County (which includes Mankato, Minnesota) made only cursory mention: "The winter of 1880–1 was very long, cold and snowy. The snow came about November 2nd and did not leave until about the 20th of April."[19]

Most of these county histories fail to match the newspaper record. A 1949 history of Minnehaha County claimed that trains could not reach Sioux Falls between December 1880 and June 1881, which we will see is inaccurate. The history stated, "The winter of 1880–81 is still referred to by the remaining 'Old Timers' as 'the winter of the deep snow.' The railway cuts became effectively blockaded in December and there was no more train service into Sioux Falls until June."[20] But within the core of the story is the truth of deprivation.

A 1916 history of Nicollet and Le Sueur Counties in Minnesota, including the town of St. Peter, bypassed the winter altogether, except to mention the April flooding. The Hard Winter thirty-six years prior to the book's publication must have been distant enough to no longer warrant a section of its own.[21]

While the collective county histories may have embellished the hardships of the winter to help formulate the "hardy settler" persona, the railroad companies had more at stake in painting the winter as beyond extraordinary. Having lured settlers by the tens of thousands to the prairies, the railroads knew that many blamed them for the destitutions; they needed the messaging to be dire and heroic in order to explain why supplies had dwindled on the western prairies.

In his official history of the Chicago & North Western, longtime employee William Stennett summarized the winter, gleaning information from the post-winter annual report for the fiscal year. He wrote:

> Such a storm was nearly or quite unprecedented in the Northwest. Thousands of settlers had, in the summer and fall of 1880, flocked to Minnesota and Dakota and settled along the lines of this road; and everyone of them was dependent on the trains of this company for fuel and food and light, as all were pioneers and had no accumulated stores to draw from. Hence it seemed absolutely incumbent on the company to open its lines and keep them open. Its snow plows were kept moving day and night and thousands of men were hired to shovel snow.

Having established the situation, Stennett went on to acknowledge the company's responsibilities towards the settlers, stating,

> Literally hundreds of thousands of dollars were spent in paying for shoveling snow in these six months; and when spring came nothing was to be seen as a return for it. The road that was cleared in the day would be covered again in the night . . . and so the fight was kept up day and night for practically six months.

In regard to feeding the settlers, he added, "Though many had to live on wheat or corn ground in coffee mills or pounded in a mortar, none was allowed to starve."

Stennett then brought the readers down to the individual cuts: "The weather was intensely cold and the snow was so granular that it rolled on the surface like shot might on a level floor. . . ." This aggravating behavior resulted in compacted cuts measuring twenty to forty feet deep. As a result, they needed shoveling crews standing in six or seven ranks on a slope to move the snow out of the cut and far enough back that it wouldn't roll back in.

Finishing his summary, he noted that one particular storm in March added another four feet on top of the level snow, and also stated, "It is said, and probably truly, that over fourteen feet of snow fell that winter 'on a level' [or 'on *the* level'— the snow depth out in the open] in Central Minnesota and in what is now South

Dakota." He then claimed that the "last snowstorm and snow blockade did not occur until May 5, 1881."[22] However, the newspaper record indicates the last snowstorm ended about three weeks earlier, on April 12. The lingering and newly reinforced blockades that kept trains from returning were, indeed, cleared by early May, and the trains did, in fact, reappear in Dakota Territory in around the same time. This is just another example of the many contradictions in the records from this period.

What We'll Find through the Newspaper Record

The newspaper record of the region paints a picture that both reflects the paths of the histories and novel and shows marked differences. There were pockets that suffered deep deprivations, and De Smet appears to have been one of those locations. It was also a winter of flourishing social engagement, including masquerades, oyster parties, and other events held in communities within relatively easy reach of those who were huddled together in their not-entirely-ready-for-winter structures.

The story as revealed through the newspapers, while full of contradictions, is as interesting as the one experienced by the Ingalls family, and much livelier than what was recorded in official history books. As we will see, where one town reported sufficient food and/or fuel, another may have been utterly without. Location was a critical difference between the haves and have-nots, in terms of both distance from the more established towns to the east and proximity to the many storms.

By following the stories and vignettes, the flat statements and flowery prose, the probably factual and probably boosterish, and the frustrations and all-out tantrums of the editors of the region's newspapers, we can establish a broader canvas upon which to place the darkness and hunger described by Laura Ingalls Wilder.

A New Look at the Winter of 1880–81

The winter of 1880–81 remains one of the historically iconic episodes of the American story. The storms are legendary, and the hardships suffered sowed regional identity. It's a fascinating story of optimism, stoicism, and, for some, the threat of starvation.

The book you are holding explores the situations in multiple communities along several railroad lines. All but one or two of those towns were within a day's horse ride (in good weather) of at least one, and in most cases several, other communities. Telegraph lines were available to coordinate provisioning efforts. Did these efforts happen? Where were the closest provisions? What did things look like, logistically, around the region during those months? These questions led me to the newspaper archives in Minnesota and South Dakota.

Some of the impacted towns had been established for less than six months when the first blizzard hit. Around the newest towns, roads were barely more than tracks across the prairie. Houses and stores were not well insulated. Relationships between townspeople were still forming, and citizenship roles still evolving.

The newspaper record reveals an amazing story of perseverance, stubbornness, patience, impatience, humor, sarcasm, community, survival, frustration, and optimism. There are even stories of old-timers being angry that their tales of yore had been eclipsed and that the newcomers could now do the bragging.

Book Flow

We will now walk through the winter month by month, covering the topics of weather, railroads, food, fuel, getting out and about, mail, newspapers, and boosterism. Within each main topic section, we will present key information chronologically, from the beginning of the month to the end. For some topics, we will further break into subsections, which will also be presented chronologically. Looking at the table of contents may help readers get a better sense of this structure.

Chapter by chapter, month by month, a story of blizzards waging their assault will unfold. But so too will a story of those who were determined not to let the snow—the beautiful snow—beat them or their towns.

OCTOBER 1880

Sunday	Monday	Tuesday	Wednesday	Thursday	Friday	Saturday
					1	2
3	4	5	6	7	8	9
10	11	12	13	14	15	16 northwest wind cold
17 northwest wind cold	18	19 drifts 10′–12′	20	21 delightful snow melting sloppy	22 pleasant	23
24	25 balmy	26	27	28 cloudy wintry/blustery light snowfall	29	30
31						

▬▬▬ Blizzard or significant snow event

/////////// Lighter snow or mixed precipitation

This calendar shows weather reports gleaned from the various newspaper articles. If the weather was significantly different in one portion of the region versus another, that is noted.

The surprise early-season blizzard caught the settlers unprepared for snow in a myriad of different ways. Though trains got stuck in drifts along the tracks, several days of shoveling cleared them, and by month's end the weather was again delightful, pleasant, and even muddy.

Those warmer temperatures allowed farmers to resume their fall-harvest activities, and the newspaper editors rallied around the issue of fuel, which had run dangerously low during the poststorm railroad blockades.

All in all, the impact of the blizzard was short, though the event itself was somewhat shocking. After the fact, the whole affair seemed to be viewed as an anomaly, something to impress distant friends and family. As such, it inspired initial accounts that would morph into the mythic tales that still appear in local history books.

The Month for the Ingalls Family

"Then the sun peeped cautiously over the edge of the prairie and the whole world glittered. Every tiniest thing glittered rosy toward the sun and pale blue toward the sky, and all along every blade of grass ran twinkling rainbow-sparkles."[23]

—Manuscript, *The Long Winter*

According to Wilder's autobiography, her father spent the spring, summer, and early fall of 1880 working on two store buildings, establishing the claim shanty, digging a well, breaking ground for crops, planting turnips, haying to feed the animals over the coming months, and doing carpentry work in town—"earning money to last [them] through the winter."[24] In *The Long Winter*, the family harvested turnips, potatoes, corn, beans, tomatoes, and pumpkins from their homestead garden.[25] These made a relatively small yield, but the family seemed pleased with their first year's crop.

Wilder noted that prior to the shortages spawned by the winter, she'd noticed her father leaving the table without eating his entire share, letting the others have it. Following his example, she also began leaving food for others, quieting her appetite with raw turnips between meals,[26] illustrating a concern for the family's nutritional security prior to the beginning of winter.

In the novel, Pa expressed concern about the many signs provided by nature that the coming winter would be especially difficult. He became fidgety and nervous, though Ma was dismissive of his worries.

The store building where the Ingalls family lived during the winter. The building had been moved by the time of this photo. From the South Dakota State Historical Society, South Dakota Digital Archives, 2009-07-14-028.

In each version of her autobiography, Wilder mentioned that the family had planned to move from their homestead shanty, one mile south of town, to the store building in town for the winter, only to be delayed by the unexpected October blizzard.[27] Instead, they stuck out the storm on the homestead. In the novel, Wilder described how the winds shredded the tar paper that wrapped the tiny house and how as a result, "icy-cold breezes sucked and fluttered the curtains around the beds. The little shanty quivered in the storm."[28] The Ingalls would eventually build onto the shanty to create a larger home.

Wilder noted in the autobiographies that after the worst of the storm, the "still blowing snow was rolling along close to the ground instead of filling the air. We could see over it."[29] In the novel, she expanded on this poetically: "Outdoors the sun-glitter hurt her eyes. She breathed a deep breath of the tingling cold and squinted her eyes to look around her. The sky was hugely blue and all the land was blowing white. The straight, strong wind did not lift the snow, but drove it scudding across the prairie."[30]

The visitation of such an early blizzard, combined with the warning from an elderly Indian that this would be an especially difficult winter,[31] solidified Pa's worry, and the family moved into his store building in town in late October. The Indian's warning took place in Harthorn's Grocery, perhaps a providential omen—or intentional literary device—about the hunger to come.

Before and after the move, Pa remained concerned about signs of a bad winter, admitting in the novel's manuscript, "If you must have the truth, I'm afraid of it."[32] Ma was almost cheerfully dismissive of his concerns, confident that all would be well in town.

In a bit of foreshadowing after the move, Pa optimistically noted, "It's a satisfaction to me to be where we're sure of getting coal and supplies. . . . We'll keep enough coal in the lean-to to outlast any blizzard, and I can get more from the lumberyard. Living in town, we're in no danger of running short of any kind of supplies."[33]

The Weather

"The storm continuing to increase throughout Friday night, by daylight immense mountains of snow was heaped about all buildings exposed to retain the snow, and by Saturday night locomotion of all kinds was impossible."[34]

—*Murray County Pioneer*, October 21, 1880

And So It Begins: The First Blizzard

The harbinger storm began in eastern Dakota Territory as a cold rain on Wednesday, October 13; turned to snow on Thursday; transformed into a blizzard on Friday; then whipped into a fury that scoured eastward at least as far as Lake Michigan. It didn't subside in the towns of western Minnesota until Sunday, October 17. The wind fell silent, the snow settled to the ground, the skies cleared, and the settlers stepped out to compare experiences. The people who assembled the area newspapers began to flex their creative muscles, incidentally preparing to escort their readers through a particularly trying winter.

Along the Winona & St. Peter

Marshall was fortunate enough to have a photographer in residence, and a new opportunity presented itself. The *Marshall Messenger* enthused, "Never were such snow drifts seen in town as were after the late storm. Magandy [a photographer] has some views of the storm for sale."[35] These photographs were mailed to friends and family back east to awe them with the hardiness of those on the prairies.

New Ulm, spread out along the Minnesota River valley 117 miles east of Brookings, Dakota Territory, had a delayed time frame for the storm. According to the *New Ulm Weekly Review*, "Friday evening a cold rain set in, which before morning changed into snow accompanied by a strong wind that made the snow fly about at a lively rate considering the large amount of moisture contained in the flakes."[36]

Temperatures plummeted in the wake of the storm, and young local boys were quick to test the ice that had formed on the area lakes. The ice was thick enough to hold their weight, an unusual occurrence for October.[37]

Winds blew the snow around almost unabated across the open prairie. Where they encountered a prairie town, snow piled up in huge drifts, trapped by the buildings. The October 27 issue of the *New Ulm Weekly Review* reported, "A correspondent . . . from Marshall says that during the storm of week before last, the snow drifted to a height of fifteen feet on the business streets. A large wind mill wheel was torn to shreds and one wall of a brick building in process of erection was blown down."[38]

Along the Dakota Central

In Fort Pierre, Dakota Territory, safely nestled along the western bank of the Missouri River, the editor of the *Fort Pierre Weekly Signal* shared that "the eastern and southward portions of the territory were submerged in snow and sleet week before last. Trains were blocked, boats driven to the banks, cattle frozen to death, and various other damage done. In this portion of the territory, while we had severe winds, no snow nor rain fell."[39] The assertion that they were free of snow may not have been entirely accurate.

The weather ahead of the October storm was fickle, as recorded in the diary of Dakota Central lead surveyor Charles Wood Irish, who was in the general vicinity of Fort Pierre at the time. On Tuesday, October 12, temperatures dropped to around twelve degrees, and a "canteen of coffee froze solid" beside him in bed. The next day was windy, and the air reached a balmy eighty degrees at two o'clock in the afternoon. Overnight, a weather system swept in, and snow began to fall. Thursday it "snowed all day," and the wind blew "a perfect gale." Temperatures were in the low twenties, and the conditions of four of his workers, who had been ill earlier in the week, became worse. "The camp is comfortless," he wrote as the crew did all they could "to keep warm in this gale."[40]

Surveyor Charles Wood Irish

Mr. Irish played a significant role in the construction of the Dakota Central, having been the lead surveyor of its route. His story will be told in deeper detail in a companion book, which will weave the construction of the Dakota Central through the events portrayed in *By the Shores of Silver Lake*. His diaries are a gold mine of fascinating information about the Dakota Central's construction.

The June 12, 1879, issue of the *Brookings County Press* described Mr. Irish as the "intelligent and entertaining leader" of the surveyors. [41] He was also an engineer, geologist, botanist, and astronomer. Irish met up with Dakota Central superintendent T. J. Nicholl on a stormy May 23, 1880, near the surveyor's work camp. Despite the weather, the men had a good time.[42]

On Friday, October 15, three inches of snow fell and was then blown around by a high wind. Saturday and Sunday's entries similarly noted snowfall and strong winds. Irish set the men to use tent flaps to construct a tepee, which, along with a sod bank to protect it, was "a success." By the morning of Monday, October 18, he recorded, "the ground is hard frozen 4 inches deep." Thus, his diary entries differ somewhat from the article from Fort Pierre.[43]

The weather quickly improved. By October 20, Irish's team had resumed their surveying work, though the men were feeling tired and sick, and the entries for the following week are plagued with tallies of illness and remedies. Their work was conducted in severe conditions, sometimes without tents, with only blankets and robes to warm them. Note that Irish recorded an eighty-degree temperature on Wednesday afternoon, a high of twenty-two on Thursday, and snow beginning to fall on Friday.

Approximately 180 miles to the east, the *Brookings County Press* reported that Wednesday's rain had turned to snow by Thursday night, and on Friday night, the "wind, which had hitherto been quiet, commenced blowing a gale." The storm "continued to slowly get better until Sunday afternoon when it ceased entirely, and no finer evening could be asked for than that of Sunday."[44] The storm had caught people by surprise, and "numerous storm-bound persons gathered around the fires at . . . hotels and told about the hard winters they had seen and made the best of bad circumstances."[45]

As the first storm of the season, it elicited excitement and amusement, even bonding. "The town on Monday morning was a picture of desolation. Everything was covered with snow. It had blown into every crack and crevice which air could get into, and snow banks from two to twenty feet high were the only scenery."[46] If you've ever experienced a subzero day with bright blue skies and sparkling snow, then it's possible to imagine feeling and smelling this scene and squinting your eyes against the brilliance.

Despite a midautumn sun beating down on the snow, stubborn drifts and piles held on. Ten days after the final flakes, there was still snow on the ground—probably more ice than snow after the melt-freeze cycles. The *Brookings County Press* published correspondence from a town northeast of Sioux Falls bantering, "We have long desired to see a real genuine blizzard, but this one is enough, we are more than satisfied that Dakota can and does take the lead first, last and all the time."[47]

Along the Southern Minnesota

Approximately twenty-two miles to the southeast of Brookings, reporting from the *Egan Express* was much more understated: "Last Friday morning it commenced snowing, and continued until Saturday night. The storm Friday was accompanied by a stiff breeze from the north, but no one contemplated that it would amount to much . . ." (ellipsis in original).[48]

The town of Pipestone, Minnesota, sits less than twenty miles east of Egan (Dakota Territory, now South Dakota) and about thirty-two miles southeast of Brookings. The *Pipestone Star* emerged as a regular source of weather information throughout the winter. Of this storm, it noted,

> The wind veered around into the northwest and snow began falling thick and fast. With the rising of the sun on Saturday morning, the wind began to blow a perfect hurricane from the northwest, driving the snow in every direction, piling it up in some places to the height of eighteen and twenty feet . . . and its suddenness and severity took all by surprise. Fortunately the weather was not very cold or many people would have frozen to death.[49]

A resident near Pipestone took most of a day to get into town following the storm, a distance of only four miles. Upon reaching Pipestone, he reported that he had "encountered snow drifts mountains high"[50] on the open prairies.

Along the Sioux City

We have something better than written articles to illustrate the situation along the Sioux City line southwest of Mankato. Photographer J. W. Palmer captured a series of images at the town of St. James, providing visual evidence of the snowfall. Two of those photos are included below. The second photo shows a bit of ingenuity: the rail yard was cleared by workers filling open cars with snow, which were then hauled onto the open prairie and unceremoniously dumped, allowing the yard workers room to resume their duties.

The aftermath of the October 1880 blizzard at the train yard in St. James, Minnesota, along the Sioux City southwest of Mankato. Photographs by J. W. Palmer. Top photo courtesy of the Chicago & North Western Historical Society. Bottom photo from the Minnesota Historical Society.

The Railroad Superintendents

The responsibilities of a railroad's superintendent included overseeing the flow of traffic over the line, managing repairs and upkeep of the physical tracks and equipment, and managing employees. His office and storage rooms contained maps, as well as detailed schematics of all the various structures and pieces—bridges, trestles, spikes, etc.—that made up the entire operation. Essentially, he was responsible for making sure that everything ran smoothly.[51]

People

Eventually, a few stories of human deaths drifted in. An emigrant family was reportedly caught out on the open prairie near Springfield, Minnesota, and was overtaken by the weather in their camping place.[52] Farther west, in Tyler, Minnesota, a farmer was out threshing when the storm blew up. He ran to his house, but just as he reached safety, his hat blew off. He turned to chase it, lost his way, and was found coatless and hatless after the storm ended.[53] According to *An Illustrated History of Lyon County, Minnesota*, the man's name was Samuel Kile, and his friends, who had been with him at the time, searched for three weeks before finding his body less than one-fifth of a mile from his barn. The hat was found one and a half miles to the southeast.[54] A nameless Swede was also reported to have frozen to death.

Sometimes these harrowing stories combined humans and animals, as in this story from Brookings: Prior to the storm, several friends from Wisconsin, their families in tow, arrived at the sod home of a local resident. The storm caused the house to cave in, and the seventeen people "took refuge in the barn, which was also made of sod. That also caved in, forcing the people to shelter themselves in the straw stack, from Saturday night to Sunday morning." While the people in the collapsed barn escaped, six horses were left behind, and five of those perished. The article finished with a quip, saying that "we do not wonder that these men are discouraged with their Dakota experience, and are anxious to return to Wisconsin."[55]

The *Murray County Pioneer* shared that a traveler—returning to his home in Currie, Minnesota—was stuck on the road, a few miles from town, and sheltered with another settler. The next evening, the settler went out to the stable and discovered that not only had two of his cows died, so had the traveler's horse. Another horse was struggling to survive, and the homeowner brought it into the house in an attempt to save it.[56]

As the month drew to a close, the newspapers were still expressing awe at the impact of this out-of-season storm. Some of the articles foreshadowed the phenomenon that would torment the region—drifting.

The Railroads

"In Dakota we learn that the storm was even more severe than in Murray County, and the fact that no trains reached Tracy over the Chicago & Northwestern railroad on Saturday, and not until late on Tuesday, shows that the storm extended for some distance towards the east."[57]

—*Murray County Pioneer*, October 21, 1880

Stuck Along the Rails

Stories about travelers stranded on trains were common following the October storm. Some were tales of mere inconvenience, while others were vague on specifics but contained enough worrisome details to let the readers' imaginations fill in the rest.

Along the Southern Minnesota, several freight and passenger trains were stuck in drifts reported to be ten to twelve feet deep, with passengers "suffering for want of food and fuel."[58]

Along the Dakota Central, many trains were impacted. According to the *Brookings County Press*, a westbound train was "so hindered by the storm" that it became stuck in the snow in a cut east of Brookings. The train's conductor walked into town and rounded up volunteers to help shovel out the train. After liberation, the train became stuck again at Volga, unable to proceed farther west. Meanwhile, an engine and caboose were sent eastward and became stuck in the cut that had originally plagued the train that was now mired at Volga.

Likewise, a westbound freight train became stuck just west of Aurora, Dakota Territory, remaining for nearly a week. Farther west, an eastbound freight train got stuck near De Smet, taking several days to clear. After taking a final account, the article from Brookings summed up the situation:

On Saturday morning there was only one live engine between Huron and Sleepy Eye, and that was the engine of the west bound passenger which went into quarters at Volga. . . . All day Sunday and from that time on men had been at work in every direction getting the track clear.[59]

The *Mankato Free Press* had someone on staff with a skill for dramatic description, composing this tale of snowbound passengers along the Southern Minnesota: Snowdrifts over the tracks were reported to be ten to twelve feet deep, as shared by a resident who experienced the stalling of the passenger train "out upon the bleak prairie" of western Minnesota, "with not a house or tree in [sight] to afford shelter or grub . . . and eighteen defenceless, hungry and uncomfortable passengers in the car." While the story says their limited rations from Friday morning until Sunday night consisted only of "what few apples and other small fruit the newsboy was in possession of," the very next sentence contradicts that, saying a conductor and passenger had raided a nearby chicken coop Sunday morning, then "hurried back to the besieged passengers, who at once organized themselves into a culinary department and relieved their gnawing hunger."[60] The tale was shared in multiple newspapers across the region.

After the drifts were cleared and trains resumed operations, this piece of wit in the *Brookings County Press* brought this particular snowbound situation to a humorous conclusion:

> The train on which our worthy P. M. [postmaster], J. W. Shannon went to Dakota, was caught in the heavy storm of the 15th and for fifty hours was in a snow drift. There not being much to eat on the train, the people were obliged to follow the example of Dr. Tanner, and obstain [sic] from eating. That is where J. W.'s experience as a country editor came into play. He had so long been used to living on promises, that he was not at all inconvenienced.[61]

Postmaster Shannon and Dr. Tanner

J. W. Shannon came to Huron, Dakota Territory, in October 1880. After spending time snowbound in a train car during the big storm, he established the *Huron Tribune* on June 2, 1881, under the firm Shannon & Hopp. He partnered with one of the Hopp brothers, founders of the *Brookings County Press*, the *Kingsbury County News* (in De Smet), and several other newspapers in the area. Shannon also served on the Huron Board of Trade, organized in August 1881 and presided over by T. J. Nicholl, superintendent of the Dakota Central division of the Winona & St. Peter Railroad.[62]

The referenced Dr. Tanner had become a pop culture phenomenon, partially due to him conducting a highly publicized experiment: On June 28, 1880, forty-nine-year-old Dr. Henry S. Tanner left Minnesota and headed to New York City, where he embarked on a forty-day fast. While his plan had been a full food-and-water fast, he did relent to taking water. Newspapers around the world spread the story of this spectacular attempt, along with lessons in biology, nutrition, physiology, chemistry, physical fitness, the tempering of mood and irritability, and how the human body processes food.[63]

While the excitement of the storm waned and the weather warmed, small armies of people were working to clear snow from score upon score of cuts along the various lines. Railroad employees and volunteers headed to trouble spots with shovels, picks, jackets, gloves, and packed lunches to speed along the arrival of the next train.

The Winona & St. Peter was running to Tracy by Tuesday, October 19,[64] and the Southern Minnesota was operating by October 20. The *Pipestone Star* proudly noted that "a lot of our town boys turned out . . . and helped the railroad boys shovel snow between here and Edgerton." As a result of the work, the blockade ended, and the trains were able to resupply the area.[65]

Back along the Winona & St. Peter, the rails going northwest to Marshall were open by Saturday, October 23.[66] Trains along the Hastings & Dakota were back on schedule by the time the October 28 issue of the *Grant County Review* out of Milbank, Dakota Territory, was published.

Heading west out of Tracy, however, shovelers along the Dakota Central were still working to clear the tracks near Lake Benton, Minnesota, as of Tuesday, October 26.[67] The Dakota Central branch was especially vexed by the snow and wind, in part because the terrain through which it passed had many challenging geological features such as gently rolling hills both large and small, all seemingly designed specifically to trap snow.

Food and Fuel

"A large majority of the farmers have most of their potatoes and other vegetables still in the ground, and of course a large portion of them will become entirely worthless when overtaken by such hard frost as the one now had."[68]

—*New Ulm Weekly Review*, October 20, 1880

An Early Warning

The early storm not only interrupted the arrival of supplies from the east but also hindered the harvesting of crops and root vegetables on farms across the region. A perceptive editor from the *Murray County Pioneer* wrote,

> The suffering and loss to the settlers cannot be imagined, as nearly all have their threshing yet to do, and [t]he fury of the wind with the rain and snow will make it almost impossible unless a warm spell follows; many had dug but a small portion of their crop of potatoes and only a few had husked their corn. These facts of themselves do not give evidence of any suffering, but when we consider that many are greatly in debt and rely on the late crop to satisfy the claims of those who have furnished them, in some instances, with their summer's supplies, it is impossible for them to do so without making greater sacrifices than would otherwise have been necessary, it is evident it is a great misfortune to all who are within reach of its unwelcome visit.[69]

With just a few exceptions, the only mentions of food shortage during this particular storm and its aftermath came from stories about passengers stranded on trains, who were fed by the meager rations on board or taken care of by local farmers. More commonly mentioned was the shortage of food for animals, as when the *Brookings County Press* noted that for the duration of the storm, hay was a precious commodity.[70]

Aside from the wonder at the weather, the biggest topic was concern over fuel for heat and lighting. Towns all along the major railroad lines in southwestern Minnesota and southeastern Dakota Territory found themselves unexpectedly without fuel for their stoves and lamps—in October.

Not surprisingly, the treeless prairie was not equipped to provide firewood except in a handful of lush floodplains. The Camden Woods near Marshall, the

Dakota Hills west of Milbank, and some parts of the James River Valley (Dakota Territory) were among the few exceptions. The newspapers alternately scolded and cajoled merchants and citizens alike to prepare for the next inevitable blizzard.

Watertown merchants quickly placed orders for fuel, then advertised to the settlers: "The recent blockade of trains shows that it is the duty of every man to provide ahead for fuel. Therefore order your coal ahead, of Kemp Bros. / We expect ten car loads of soft coal on the 1st train. Will book orders for same."[71] A merchant in Pipestone ordered an entire carload of kerosene, anticipating a rush of concerned customers.[72]

The editor of the *Dakota News* out of Watertown took things to the next step, passionately pleading the case for a Coal and Wood Association to facilitate maintaining supplies and reasonable pricing for members; chastising those who blamed the railroads for causing their shortages; and giving several insights into the larger issues of settlement, supply, transportation, and costs. Once the association's business structure was established, the processes would go into place, including the practice of buying the winter's fuel when it was cheapest—in July or August. After reassuring the readers that careful and thoughtful planning around the topic of fuel could overcome the circumstances that led to the late shortage, he then reminded them that "fuel is a necessity. People need it as much as bread; they cannot survive without it."[73] (This article's full text further articulates the wider context of this important topic; it is available to read at thebeautifulsnow.com.)

The scarcity of fuel was not a new concern. In its end-of-year annual report for 1861, the Chicago & North Western noted that "this important element in railway operations has demanded the serious attention of the board. The country upon either side of the Mississippi is essentially destitute of timber." While not entirely accurate, this concern was noted in the context of feeding the locomotives, not the hungry stoves of newly arrived settlers, and the report went on to discuss the methods of obtaining coal to lessen the expense. It would certainly have been no surprise to the railroad that the treeless prairies would offer as little or less fuel in the early 1880s than the regions along the relatively timbered Mississippi River Valley in the early 1860s.[74]

The October blizzard lasted a couple of days in any given spot as it moved from southeastern Dakota Territory into southwestern Minnesota, but the impact of running out of fuel—heat—remained on the minds of most until the last frozen pebbles of slushy snow melted with the spring floods.

Stock Losses

Similar to Wilder's story about the cattle whose breath froze them to the ground[75] were stories of stock dying—often by being smothered "in the immense heaps of snow"[76]—that passed from town to town. Near Currie, one resident "lost a valuable cow, which, with others, strayed from the stable and was found buried in a snow drift, almost dead."[77] The names of the unfortunate farmers were published along with lists of the valued animals they'd lost.

Nearly all newspapers throughout the region listed the tally: forty head of cattle here, thirty to sixty head of sheep there, large numbers of horses, three oxen, two cows, etc. "Stock...suffered badly," wrote one *Pipestone Star* editor, with "many head being smothered to death in the huge drifts that piled up all over the prairie.... The loss to the farmers in this regard is very large and very severe just at this time."[78]

One report from Janesville included a name familiar to Little House readers: "Mr. Bedal of Walnut Grove, lost forty head of cattle, valued at $1,000 in the late storm. Many others have lost more or less stock in that section."[79] (For the 1881 to 2019 conversion rate, see the Financial Buying Power Conversions section in the Editorial Notes at the beginning of this book, on page xiii). Even wild animals were included in the reports, as when the paper in Forestburg, Dakota Territory, noted, "Quite a number of antelope were killed in this vicinity during the storm of last week."[80] As these fledgling towns were still taking root, the impact of losing so many animals at the beginning of the winter—whether work animals or wild animals hunted for food—should not be underestimated.

Crops and Gardens

Today, the average first-frost date for this region is mid-September. It is likely that by the time the mid-October storm hit, most garden crops had already been preserved for the coming winter, though any unharvested root vegetables may have survived the blizzard. One paper confidently declared that the garden crops were indeed lost due to the recent "heavy frost" and warned of a hungry winter.[81]

There was also a great deal of optimism. Field stubble had caught the snow, which melted in the moderate poststorm temperatures and provided moisture for the soil—and bumper crops were predicted for the coming season. According to newspaper reports, farmers were soon back in the fields harvesting the year's corn and wheat, plodding through the mud they hoped would bring bounty for the next cycle.[82]

Out and About

"Why can't we have club dances here this winter.
Let the young folks talk it up."[83]
—*Brookings County Press*, October 28, 1880

Despite the depth of the snow immediately following the blizzard, and what must have been very muddy roads as the melt began in the aftermath, people were moving about not only within their own towns but from town to town and even state to state.

Within the first ten days following the storm's end, there were numerous reports of people traveling between towns—Volga to Brookings, Brookings to De Smet, Egan to Mitchell, and similar treks.

Travelers went farther afield, too. People left Fort Pierre for points such as Rochester, Minnesota, to the east and the Black Hills on the western edge of Dakota Territory. No tracks crossed the Missouri River yet, but the Chicago & North Western worked with the Northwestern Stage Company to complete the westward journey.[84]

One businessman left Milbank for the winter and traveled to Wisconsin to oversee winter work at his logging firm there.[85] While others were exiting the area, the *Forestburg Miner County Mercury* announced that one gentleman "will be a Miner countyite hereafter. He has come to stay and stand the storm."[86]

Newspapers and Mail

"On account of the storm, which has delayed us in several ways, an unusual amount of job work, and a failure to find the Editor, the News will not be of much interest to its readers this week.
Will try and do better in the future."[87]
—*The Dakota News*, November 1, 1880

Editors knew that mail delay was important enough to devote the space and labor it took to write and typeset each sentence about it. Even at this early point in the winter, there were notations of how long it had been since a mail delivery had come through not only to their own towns but to neighboring burgs as well. It became a common tally included in most editions.

In the first week following the October storm and blockades, the Pipestone mail was five days overdue; Brookings received its first mail via horseback from Flandreau; Watertown was devoid of mail for over a week; and Fort Pierre, which had not experienced the blizzard, noted that their mail was delayed on account of the snow farther east.[88] The storm had been severe enough that telegraph lines were also down.

When the newspaper reported a train arriving in Brookings on Tuesday, October 26, it was the mail that was mentioned. Not fuel, not food, but mail. And passengers—it was crowded with passengers, apparently undeterred by the recent blizzard.[89]

By the second week after the storm, weather had warmed considerably, and most of the snow had melted across the region. However, a few locations remained impacted by snow-packed cuts. As of Tuesday, October 26, Lake Benton had gone ten days without mail due to a continued blockade on the Dakota Central.[90] When the trains resumed running, they were bringing a considerable backlog of mail. In Brookings, after eleven days without a mail delivery, one finally arrived, and "it was an immense one."[91]

The Resumption of "Normal"

By the end of the month, trains had resumed normal operations, and freight was again flowing freely along the various railroad lines.[92] As the snow melted and trains returned, newspapers across the region reported that their towns' clever merchants had ordered kerosene to be prepared for the next blizzard, that threshing machines had been liberated from the snowbanks, and that farmers were again in their fields.

The blizzard did not significantly affect the most western portion of the Dakota Central, and work and life continued there as usual. In late October, the Chicago & North Western announced that tracks would reach Pierre by November 1, at which point a stagecoaches would carry passengers the final 170 miles to Deadwood, on the western border of Dakota Territory.[93] Some of the passengers who rolled into Brookings on that first through train on October 26 may well have been headed there. Never mind that there was no bridge in place yet to carry passengers from one side of the Missouri River to the other; ferryboats were ready to collect fees for that service.

Pierre and Fort Pierre found the storm to be an irritant, as it had led to "stacks of freight [being] piled up around the warehouses."[94] It also delayed needed lumber, and building was proceeding rapidly—or trying to—in anticipation of the business that the arriving trains would bring.

The path that materials had to take was complicated. For example, according to the Fort Pierre newspaper, the anxiously awaited lumber had been ordered from sources in Minneapolis and Winona. The lumber from Minneapolis then had to be transported to Winona via train (and/or possibly riverboat), at which point it boarded another train headed toward Pierre on the Winona & St. Peter. The car(s) would go west to the division point at Tracy, then possibly switch to a different train to proceed west on the Dakota Central.[95]

The Chicago & North Western was investing heavily in Pierre overall, erecting a large hotel in town to house passengers. Merchants were likewise busy establishing storefronts.[96] Winter may have been approaching, but the inhabitants where the Dakota Central met the Missouri River were enjoying a financial springtime and foresaw a bright summer ahead.

All of this building was happening in yearning for the arrival of the first train and the promise of all the trains to follow. As the tracks inched closer and closer, approaching the bluffs that would deliver trains to the once-far-off Missouri River, the train whistle could "be heard in East Pierre when the wind [was] favorable." Settlers would soon "see Pierre connected with the outside world by telegraph and rail."[97]

This early in the season, the nuisance of the October blizzard seems to have been experienced, survived, looked back upon with amusement, and then packed away to be pulled out as a badge of honor at some future point. No one yet expected that the trains would be cut off for more than a day or two at a time, here and there, now and then.

November 1880

Sunday	Monday	Tuesday	Wednesday	Thursday	Friday	Saturday
	1 beautiful warm springlike	2 magnificent no wind, clear springlike	3 cooler rain	4 beautiful	5 ////////// "tried to stir up a blizzard"	6
7	8	9	10 6–8 inches snow strong N wind cold (west)	11 cold good sleighing	12 ////////// cold brisk NW wind	13 cold brisk NW wind
14 cold brisk NW wind	15 cold, –5F brisk NW wind	16 cold brisk NW wind pleasant (east)	17 cold	18 ////////// pleasant	19	20 cold
21 cold fair	22	23 ////////// N/NW wind good plowing (east)	24 good plowing nice winter weather	25 //////////	26 ////// good plowing (east)	27 good plowing nice weather
28 good plowing nice weather	29 good plowing nice weather	30 //////////				

▬▬▬ Blizzard or significant snow event

////////// Lighter snow or mixed precipitation

Prairie fires reported widely in entire region up until the storm of November 10.

This calendar shows weather reports gleaned from the various newspaper articles.
If the weather was significantly different in one portion of the region versus another, that is noted.

November was mostly warm, though punctuated by two storms and some smaller wind events, which triggered short blockades. Weather was pleasant enough that tracklayers continued to work westward, and a few communities even welcomed their very first trains. As an additional preventive measure, snow fences were hastily and strategically placed alongside the tracks at points that had already proven to be trouble spots during the October storm.

The first hints of concern that the railroad companies might not invest the effort it would take to keep the tracks clear, should the storms continue all winter, surfaced. While shortages appeared now and then, trains were usually able to replenish stocks before actual need was reported, and though fuel could not be described as plentiful, complaints against the railroads certainly were. Nonetheless, editors throughout the region reminded their readers that humans could not be held responsible for the vagaries of the weather, even if those humans represented the railroads.

In new towns across the region, residents, who were still getting to know each other, began to plan for winter entertainments, including literary societies, masquerades, and oyster parties. Despite minor disruptions in mail delivery, the newspaper editors were generally happy, and their efforts at boosterism remained generally positive in nature, though there remained an undercurrent of worry over fuel.

The Month for the Ingalls Family

"When Laura's eyes opened in the morning she saw that every clinched nail in the roof overhead was furry-white with frost. Thick frost covered every windowpane to its very top. The daylight was still and dim inside the stout walls that kept out the howling blizzard."[98]

—*The Long Winter*

In her autobiography, *Pioneer Girl*, we learn that Wilder and her sister Carrie—and through them, Mary—began school on the first of November.[99] Not long after, just as the two girls were getting more familiar with their new schoolmates, a dangerous blizzard hit. Leaving the schoolhouse to head home in low-visibility conditions, the students risked getting lost on the prairie.[100]

In the aftermath of the storm, the first of many mentions of the big cut west of Tracy and the "men with shovels"[101] appear in all versions of the autobiography, the manuscript, and the novel. The novel embellishes with the optimistic conviction that they'd "shovel through it in a couple of days."[102]

Smaller cuts between De Smet and Volga also needed work; in *The Long Winter*, Pa rode to Volga on a handcar with other townsmen to help shovel out the tracks.[103] School resumed, and life returned to relative normal, at least for a while.

At this point in the novel, even as the first indications of scarcity were beginning to appear (the lack of salt pork and milk being the first), the family enjoyed hearty meals for at least the first few weeks of November. Pa focused on hauling hay from the homestead to feed the stock, and Ma continued to chide him for worrying about the winter. In the evenings, Pa played the fiddle, once even mimicking the sounds of the storm that followed the schoolhouse blizzard until his startled wife reminded him that the weather would provide enough of that sound, thank you.[104] A third November blizzard coupled with tumbling temperatures resulted in the school closing until coal could be replenished. (School sessions may not have ceased, though, as we'll learn later.)

Throughout the autobiographies and novel, Charles was the conduit for news of what was going on outside the store building where the family lived. He visited with others in town, gathered the news, and shared it at home, keeping the family apprised of progress along the rails, reports of which included information telegraphed to Woodworth, the station agent at the depot. Between reports of human shoveling crews and locomotive snowplows, the Tracy Cut was the focus of concern and considerable effort.

With the trains not running, mail delivery was also cut off. As happened in many communities throughout the region, alternative arrangements were made. In De Smet, resident David Gilbert, who was eighteen at the time, became part of a relay team, running mail to and from Preston to the immediate east.

In the novel, as the month progressed, the family made generous use of coal the first few weeks,[105] but their supplies of coal and kerosene ran low by late November. The town had, by this time, run out of coal, kerosene, meat, and most other provisions.[106]

Meanwhile, the novel has Royal and Almanzo Wilder enjoying plenty of food in their feedstore. While Almanzo, a farmer, worried that they hadn't cut enough hay, Royal, a merchant, felt confident in the running of the trains, though he did foreshadow by speculating what would happen if the trains, indeed, failed to get through.[107]

Royal wasn't the only one banking on the trains. During the storm that sent the girls home from school, Ma answered Pa's concern about the weather by saying, "Here we are in town where we can get what we need from the stores even in a storm."[108]

The Weather

> The weather is beautiful once more, and will undoubtedly
> remain so for several weeks.[109]
>
> —*The Dakota News*, November 1, 1880

The weather was reported as beautiful, mild, balmy, and magnificent. People quickly returned to harvesting their crops and shoring up their homes and businesses.

In fact, as the snow melted off, the grasses dried enough that prairie fires became a problem in both Dakota Territory and southwestern Minnesota. Similar reports appeared in newspapers across the entire region.

The November 3 issue of the *Fort Pierre Weekly Signal* printed that "every day brings new reports of prairie fires in Minnesota and Dakota. So far the loss has been contained to property, and no lives have been sacrificed; but the destruction of all his crops and hard-earned improvements is serious enough for the farmer settler to face."[110]

The Storm of November 10:
The Long Winter's Schoolhouse Blizzard?

According to newspaper reports, there were few weather events during November. However, there was an early storm variously described as a one-to-three-day blizzard as it moved across the region. It began on Wednesday, November 10; dropped approximately six to ten inches of snow, depending on exact location; and had a strong northwest wind. It appears to have been focused on the region along the Winona & St. Peter, Dakota Central, and Southern Minnesota railroads.

In each extant version of her autobiography, Wilder shares the story of being at her desk when "the school house cracked and shook from a blow of the wind that struck the northwest corner like a mighty sledge. The sun was blotted out and all we could see from the windows was a white blur for all outside was a whirling chaos of snow."[111]

As the episode unfolded in *The Long Winter*, the students and their teacher, Miss Garland, left the school. Their intent was to walk the two blocks east to town, but as was common in the blinding, swirling snow, they inadvertently headed off course. Cap Garland broke off from the group, found a storefront, and alerted the men in town to the situation. Meanwhile, Laura bumped into Mead's Hotel just as the group of students was about to wander out onto the prairie. Knowing their location, they were able to reorient and soon found their way safely home.[112]

Wilder consistently noted the storm as happening soon after "the first of November," the start of the school term, while the students were still becoming acquainted. The storm of Wednesday, November 10, appears to be a good candidate for the blizzard that drove the students from school, despite having a Monday start in the novel.[113]

Wilder appears to have experienced frustration trying to get her daughter, Rose, to understand the situation, expending several handwritten pages explaining the stoicism of the people of the time. She began the letter, "Rose Dearest, No! The people in the hard winter were not 'monsters.'" Wilder then defended her teacher's decision to get the children home and Cap's choice to break away from the group while the snow swirled around them: "In one of those storms where it is a struggle to even breathe one does not think much. If Cap thought at all I suppose he thought we would come to one of the long line of buildings along main street, which we did. It was no place to stop and argue. Get the cold and the confusion of it."

Wilder continued extolling, writing, "Cap and Miss Garland were nice, friendly, ordinary persons. I wish I could explain how I mean about the stoicism of the people." The writing went on for several more pages, likely working to solidify her own sense of the novel's plot as much as trying to illustrate the emotional baseline of the residents for Rose.[114]

While it was a significant memory for Wilder, the newspapers did not spend much column space on this storm. The *Egan Express* described it as having been "rather winterish." It continued, "Some snow fell accompanied by a strong north wind, which made it very disagreeable."[115] Six to eight inches of snow were reported to have fallen,[116] with the result that the roads were again blockaded.[117]

The *New Ulm Weekly Review* put a little more effort into the description: "Last week our locality was visited by another storm, but it was far less severe than the October blizzard." Beginning early on Wednesday, snow fell most of the day but "melted nearly as fast as it came down." The weather turned colder overnight, and on Thursday, "the air was pretty well filled with snow which was flung through the air at a lively rate by a strong wind . . . Enough snow fell to afford fair sleighing in many places."[118]

Following the storm of November 10, below-zero temperatures spread across the region with scattered reports of light snows.

The Storm of November 20

The *New Ulm Weekly Review* reported "quite a storm" on November 20, followed by fair weather.[119] The next day, approximately 120 miles to the west, in Egan, it "was a very disagreeable day. Snow fell nearly the entire day, and was accompanied by a stiff north wind."[120]

At this early point in the winter, specific weather reports became less numerous than stories of railroad blockades. There were relatively few reports focusing on this particular storm, though there were multiple reports about the hardships resulting from it—trains stuck in various locations along the tracks in the southern portions of Minnesota.

Despite the cold, phrases such as "good weather for plowing," "nice weather," and "comfortable" appeared over and over as November transitioned to December. Farmers took advantage of the lack of stormy weather to resume the work of threshing and plowing.

During the thaw, roads had become muddy and difficult to travel. Beginning with the storm of November 10, temperatures plummeted, and the ground froze, making travel much easier and enabling farmers to get their harvests to the elevators in town and thus to the railroad.

The Railroads

"The trains which were delayed on account of the snow blockade made their appearance at the depot in this city Tuesday for the first time in eleven days."[121]

—*Dakota News*, November 1, 1880

Superintendents Inspect the Tracks

With just a few exceptions, both freight and passenger trains were running more or less unimpeded throughout most of November, and life settled back into a normal routine. Along the Hastings & Dakota, Superintendent Prior checked in with station agents to make sure the rails were in good shape.[122]

Superintendent Prior of the Hastings & Dakota

Superintendent Charles Henry Prior oversaw the Hastings & Dakota line. Born in 1833, he was forty-seven years old as the winter began. Educated as a civil engineer, he held multiple railroad positions over his career, including considerable survey work. He was described as being courteous, efficient, and official, and he is the eponym of Prior Lake, Minnesota.[123]

The newspaper record does not include specifics about the efforts of the Dakota Central's superintendent in November, except to mention—with excitement and approval—the promotion of T. J. Nicholl to general manager, effective November 15:

Mr. Nicholl is a young man who has won his way to the position he now holds not by influential friends, but by showing himself worthy of confidence. Although Dakota is a young men's country, few men of Mr. Nicholl's age can boast of having made their way to so high a position of responsibility and trust as the one now held by him. Mr. Nicholl has reason to be proud of his success and Dakota is proud of so rising a young man.[124]

Superintendent Nicholl of the Dakota Central

T. J. Nicholl, who was thirty-four when winter began, served as superintendent for the Dakota Central from 1880 until 1883. According to an 1881 published history, he worked at the division offices in Huron and was listed as one of Huron's "first settlers to come and remain." Additionally, he was a member of the Episcopal Church Society of Huron, its first worship service being held in his home in September 1880. He was also director of the school board; justice of the peace; a founding officer of the Lodge of the Order of Free and Accepted Masons, which was established in August 1881; and, that same month, became president of the Huron Board of Trade.[125]

In the same publication, a probable typo appears when, in the biography section, this listing appears: "I. J. Nicholl—Superintendent Dakota Central Railroad; born in England in 1846; came to America in 1852; located in Chicago in 1857." It further noted that he was a civil engineer and had helped to construct "nearly 700 miles of railway in different states and territories." The bio also lets us know that he moved to Huron in June 1880, was married, and had four children.[126]

His work during the winter of 1880–81, however, proved to be more elusive. Few mentions of him appear in the newspaper record, though they were appreciative ones. He would also have been the man responsible for operations at the Tracy Cut.

Farther south along the Southern Minnesota, the Egan paper noted that the town's eponym, Superintendent J. M. Egan, had swept through town while carrying out his responsibilities and that "he was no sooner here than he was gone again. He never stops long in a place."[127]

Superintendent Egan of the Southern Minnesota

John M. Egan was born in 1848, making him thirty-three years old as of March 1881. He entered railway service in 1863 at the age of fifteen, apprenticing and serving as a message boy, clerking in the freight office, and then moving into the engineering office. Various opportunities and promotions followed, and by March 1880 he was serving as the superintendent on the Southern Minnesota line. In 1890, he became president of the Chicago, St. Paul & Kansas City Railroad.[128] Many of the articles used in this book, from the winter months at least, come from the town of Egan, Dakota Territory, named for the superintendent.

It wasn't just the superintendents that were traveling and inspecting the lines. Along the Dakota Central extension of the Winona & St. Peter, officers of the Chicago & North Western headed to Fort Pierre on Tuesday, November 9, to check on progress. The storm of November 10 hit behind them. As a result, executive Marvin Hughitt and two other managers, riding in their "special train," were stranded for a few days and experienced firsthand the perils of travel in central Dakota.[129]

Trains Stream into the Region

As the weather warmed and the October blockades lifted, life returned to normal while still vibrating with that type of energy that follows an exceptional experience. In Brookings, "immense freight trains" were passing through daily.[130]

The editor of the *Grant County Review* composed this bit of optimistic exuberance on the very eve of the storm of November 10:

> The sight of the regular passenger trains coming into Milbank, bringing a new stir of life and activity to our rapidly growing town, makes us old settlers that came here three to six months ago feel all the more venerable when we contrast the present lively situation of affairs with that of the early summer when nothing could be seen on the open prairie for a mile either side of us save the growing grain that waved before the wind, and when our only resting places were in the box cars and lumber sheds that commenced to make their appearance about the first of August. Now, with our regular passenger trains, elevators, stock yards, lumber yards, hotels, blocks of business stores, and, of course, the Review, we feel that we have a good right to hold up our heads and feel proud upon viewing the evidences of prosperity all around us.[131]

While trains with freight had just begun to replenish supplies days before the second storm hit Milbank, merchants such as Watertown's Kemp Bros. Hardware and Farm Machinery leveraged the recent discomforts to remind people to invest in fuel, because the trains could stop running again at any moment . . . so come in and buy now, ahead of time![132]

Railroad Blockades

"The roads are good at present and will probably remain so until spring."[133]

—*Brookings County Press*, November 18, 1880

After the Storm of November 10

The storm of November 10 deposited six to eight inches of snow, which was enough to cause mischief. Blockades formed west of New Ulm on the Winona & St. Peter; west of Wells, Minnesota, on the Southern Minnesota; and southwest of

Lake Crystal, Minnesota, on the Sioux City.[134] The snowfall was nothing monumental, but enough to stop three engines and blockade five trains along the Dakota Central between Huron and Tracy.[135]

Shovels, picks, and possibly plows were employed in earnest, and the blockades were cleared after a few days. The *Brookings County Press* of November 18 reported that "long freight trains have been running both ways lately and all the towns along the road from Tracy to Huron seem to be booming."[136]

These first two storms of the winter had already troubled the railroad companies. As a result, attempts were made to shore things up around the notorious cuts, as was written by an editor in Janesville: "The Chicago & North Western company are shipping car load after car lord [*sic*] of snow fence into Dakota. Snow fences we fear will hardly save them."[137] Prophetic words, those.

With trains running again, depleted stocks of supplies were replenished. In Watertown, along the Winona & St. Peter, Fowler & Hersey's announced that it again had a full carload of fresh groceries, ready for purchase.[138] That announcement was published as the third major storm was whirling outside. The blockades had been cleared for about a week.

In her autobiography, Wilder noted that a train came through De Smet on November 20.[139] That is also the day that the next storm whipped up.

Snow Fences

To divert snow and curb its drifting across the tracks, "snow fences were erected at short distances from the cuts to divert the drifts around the end so that they would cross the track and be distributed in the open prairie. But the snow, after two or three days of drifting, would generally pile up over the snow fence."[140] Eventually, rows of trees were planted near some of the cuts to replace snow fences, which demanded ongoing maintenance and were, as we'll see, tempting sources of firewood for cold settlers.

Following the Storm of November 20

November's second storm brought the winter's third set of blockades, and the snows that began on November 20 caused trains in Pipestone to arrive a full day late.[141]

Meanwhile, on the eastern edge of the region, a Janesville editor wrote that "trains and mails were sadly demoralized. . . . They came at all hours except when they didn't come at all. This winter does begin old fashioned."[142]

The October blockades were ancient history, and hopes had seemed high that the entire winter would follow along as November had—a few nuisance snows, a handful of trainless days, but mostly business as usual. Yet it was also in this time frame that a few alarming articles began to appear in assorted newspapers, setting in motion an insecurity among the settlers: *If things get bad, will the railroads abandon us?*

The First Hints

Rumors began to surface that the railroad companies were going to give up trying to keep the tracks clear. This concern was especially ardent among the communities to the west of the usual blockade spots. The editor of the *Grant County Review* took time to reassure his readers in the November 25 issue:

> Some little uneasiness has been entertained by a few individuals over a report in the St. Paul *Pioneer Press* a couple of weeks ago, to the effect that the H. & D. Division would be closed west of Glencoe, by reason of the difficulty in keeping the road open and clear from snow, but we apprehend that all such fears will prove groundless. The snow this season has been unprecedently [*sic*] heavy, but the company has used all possible means to keep the road open, and we understand that it is the intention to run trains as regularly as "men and money will permit." No sane person would believe for a moment that the company would be foolish enough to think of discontinuing operating the road at this juncture of affairs, especially when it is known the company must necessarily keep the road open for the purpose of pushing through its own material for the construction of the road to the Jim river.[143]

This piece reveals a couple of interesting tidbits: The phrase "as regularly as men and money will permit" suggested a gaping loophole. On the other hand, the editor did a good job of leveraging people's opinions of the driving force that was "the railroad"; as long as the railroad's profits required a push forward, they would continue keeping the tracks clear, if not for the sake of the settlers, then for the fiscal heartiness of their annual reports and everything those documents represented. The settlers would benefit from the aspirations of the railroad companies.

This very message was thinly veiled in those posters that encouraged settlers to follow the railroads in the first place.

Other Railroad Work

"The Chicago and Northwestern company have neglected nothing to make the Dakota Central road a first class one in every particular, and to render a trip from Chicago to Pierre a luxurious one, and to be remembered pleasantly. Regular passenger trains are now running between Pierre and Chicago, carrying the mail."[144]

—*Volga Gazette*, reprinted in the *Fort Pierre Weekly Signal*, November 17, 1880

Expansion Work / Business as Usual

Despite the somewhat volatile weather situation, work on the various railroads—ranging from the physical establishment of the tracks themselves to bolstering the services at stops along the lines—continued with little interruption throughout November:

Along the Hastings & Dakota

The storm of November 20 seemed barely an annoyance to the tracklayers on the Hastings & Dakota. As the storm died down, workers resumed laying track at a rate of one mile a day, reaching a point twenty-nine miles east of the James River. The grade was prepared an additional twelve miles west of the river.[145]

Along the Winona & St. Peter

The business managers of the railroad were certainly planning on a full and busy winter, and work wasn't just focused on expanding into new territories or setting up facilities in new towns. For railroads that expanded as part of a land grant, the original construction was often the result of a rush to create railed beds as quickly and as cheaply as possible. This sometimes meant using rails made of low-cost materials such as iron (softer and more prone to breakage) instead of steel (harder and stronger) and using foundations that were less than solid.[146]

A handful of specific locations became notorious for having derailments due to structural failure, as we will see later. During mid-November, the Winona & St.

Peter was busy replacing old railroad ties and upgrading the rails to steel along certain stretches, and new time cards went into effect as expansion stations, such as Pierre, were folded into the train schedules.[147]

An extension line to connect Watertown and Volga to the south along the Dakota Central was graded but not yet railed. Work stopped for the winter in late November with plans to resume as soon as spring weather allowed.[148] Over the months to come, graded or completed railbeds around the region were sometimes used by teams and sleighs to move goods. This, unfortunately, compounded the problems of compressed snow later in the season.

Teams are mentioned throughout the winter. A team could be made up of horses, mules, or even oxen, pulling a wagon, sleigh, or similar conveyance. It is also possible that a "team" comprised one animal pulling a vehicle with a driver. Such references were as common in the newspapers then as a car or truck would be mentioned today, as they were used for both personal and business purposes.

Along the Dakota Central

As trains reached the Missouri River in the central part of Dakota Territory, the editor of the *Volga Gazette* took a moment to marvel at the accomplishment:

> We cannot refrain from noting the remarkable celerity with which this road has been pushed through to completion to the Missouri river. One year ago in March last the surveys were started from Tracy, ... and to-day we have 257 miles of road built and equipped in the most superb manner. ... The bridges, culverts and roadbed are solidly and substantially constructed. The ties and the steel rails are of the best throughout, and the station buildings are models of neatness and convenience.[149]

Indeed, in approximately one and a half years, the Dakota Central had successfully surveyed a path the full distance from Tracy to the Missouri River, cut through hills and filled in low spots, prepared the rail bed, laid ties and rails, located towns to be near good water sources for the locomotives, platted the located towns, sold lots to eager purchasers, and run trains over the tracks. Additionally, in nearly all towns, they built depots, telegraph stations, and sidetracks, and in some cases, built warehouses, coal houses, roundhouses, or other railroad operation accoutrements. In comparison to the fits and starts experienced by the Winona & St. Peter, which took ninety-two months to rail its first eleven miles, the success of the Dakota Central was nothing short of astonishing.[150]

A sidetrack to store cars was finished and put into use in Brookings.[151] In Pierre, telegraph lines, freight trains, and passenger trains all made their first appearance. A roundhouse and passenger depot were under construction, and the local freight depot was nearly completed.[152] The Northwestern Transportation Company began running stagecoaches from Fort Pierre to Deadwood, in the Black Hills, with the first coach departing Deadwood on November 1. And the Northwestern Stage Company began to advertise direct routes from Chicago to the Black Hills using a combination of rail and coach.[153]

The fact that trains had reached the Missouri River continued to be mentioned in newspapers with great enthusiasm, not just in towns along the Dakota Central but along other railroad lines as well. This connection between the entire eastern part of the country and the expanding towns of Dakota Territory brought dreams of great prosperity throughout the entire region.[154]

Crossing the Sioux Reservation Land

There was a complicating factor in the plans to get to the Black Hills from the Missouri River. The land that the Chicago & North Western wanted to traverse was owned by the Sioux, who, quite rightly, were hesitant to trust agreements made with officials of the United States government or officers of a railroad company. Those officials knew it would take a while to negotiate access to the lands for a physical railroad. In the meanwhile, an agreement was made to allow a road for stage and team traffic, and in November, the Dakota Central announced a two-year contract with the Northwestern Stage Company to take train passengers from Fort Pierre onward to the Black Hills.[155]

Along the Southern Minnesota

A stockyard was installed in Egan, and nearby, a bridge across the Big Sioux River was under construction, with several of the supports having been pounded into the bed of the river by a pile driver. It was hoped that with good weather, teams would be able to cross by mid-November. A later article noted that due to inclement weather, progress had been slow. Rather than guessing at a completion date, the later article assured readers that it would be completed "as soon as possible."[156]

As the weather cooled, so did the work to expand roadbeds and tracklaying. In Egan, the Southern Minnesota was putting in a *wye*. A Y-shaped configuration of track, it was an alternative to a turntable for rotating locomotives. Essentially, this allows the equipment to reverse direction by making a three-point turn.

In Parker, southwest of Sioux Falls, along an extension of the Chicago, Milwaukee & St. Paul, a coal house was built. The railroad owned a coal mine at Oskaloosa, Iowa, southeast of Des Moines, which helped supply the coal needed for stations along the line.[157]

The Coalfields around Oskaloosa, Iowa

As eastern land was deforested and wood became less common, its price increased. Coal offered an alternative heat source, especially on the prairies, where wood was scarce to begin with.

Mahaska County, Iowa, southeast of Des Moines, was known as early as 1843 to hold coal deposits. While local blacksmiths made use of the resource, it was several years before serious mining was underway. Various operations harvested the veins of bituminous coal, and by 1878, Consolidation Coal Company was the largest employer in the county, employing four hundred men. As the railroads resumed expansion in the late 1870s, sources of wood and coal became targets of purchase. In 1880, the Chicago and North Western Railroad Company purchased the holdings of the Consolidation Coal Company and held them until the veins ran out in 1890. Operations then moved to a new location. The Chicago, Milwaukee & St. Paul also operated coal mines in Oskaloosa.[158]

In its annual report for the fiscal year ending May 31, 1881, the Chicago & North Western noted that "the importance of this purchase may be readily seen from the statistics . . . which show an aggregate consumption of 507,786 tons of coal, at an expenditure of $1,196,330.08 during the year; an amount far in excess of the cost of this valuable property."[159]

Wrecks and Accidents

In *By the Shores of Silver Lake*, as the train approached the depot at Walnut Grove, Laura was apprehensive, both excited for her first train ride and hesitant about being near the tracks. She wrote, "The roaring thing came rushing straight at them all, swelling bigger and bigger, enormous, shaking everything with noise. Then the worst was over. It had not hit them."[160]

It was not an unrealistic fear. According to the *Janesville Argus* of March 15, 1881, a passenger train destroyed one end of the depot at La Crosse, Wisconsin, when it left the tracks while bucking snow, plowing into the building instead.[161] (There is more about snow bucking in the January chapter.)

Wrecks were all too common, primarily due to the fragility of iron rails and the sometimes-dubious quality of construction. Newspaper editors often embellished the stories with exasperated phrases about the dangers of rail travel and/or how miraculous it was that things weren't worse. The *Brookings County Press* reported that the eastbound train was delayed at Volga due to a freight train wrecked by a misplaced switch that allowed the train to run past the tracks.[162] Human error, as well as failures in infrastructure and mechanical components, will appear many more times before the end of winter.

This Benjamin Franklin Upton photo of construction along the Hastings & Dakota in 1868 illustrates the dubious quality that was sometimes employed along stretches of the rapidly built rail lines. These tracks appear to be laid across field grass without the benefit of a well-prepared roadbed. Photograph from the Minnesota Historical Society.

Train wrecks and mountainous snow piles were not the only things that afflicted the railroad. On November 1, the coal sheds of the Southern Minnesota in Lanesboro, Minnesota, were destroyed by fire. The 850 tons of coal housed there were consumed, along with two flatcars and a pile driver. The culprit was believed to have been sparks created by a passing locomotive, a common occupational hazard. The financial loss was estimated at $5,000.[163] The practical loss of 850 tons of coal seems, in hindsight, more disastrous.

Accidents were not limited to moving trains. An unknown laborer suffered a broken leg when a "large clump of frozen earth" rolled down the embankment while he was working in a big cut near Big Stone City, Dakota Territory, southwest of Ortonville, Minnesota.[164]

Some accidents are head-scratchers. Numerous articles from the following months mention accidents caused by "a removed rail." That a rail could be removed from a track without an oncoming train being notified seems baffling, yet it occurred—frequently.

On November 19, the *Marshall Messenger* let its readers know that a freight engine and two cars of wheat had derailed near Walnut Grove the previous week due to "a removed rail."[165]

This harrowing story from the "trouble zone" along the Winona & St. Peter had nothing to do with snow:

> Last Sunday conductor Rowley ran a wild freight train from Sleepy Eye
> to Tracy. He started on his return trip with only the engine and caboose
> and when near the bridge this side of Walnut Grove, a broken rail threw
> the caboose from the track, it ran over the bridge bumping its way across
> on the ties and then made a fearful plunge down the grade wrecking the
> caboose completely. Mr. Rowley and his two brakemen were seriously
> but not dangerously injured.[166]

The Lure of the Train Wreck

Popular periodicals such as *Harper's Weekly* published lurid, frightening accounts of train wrecks, even printing elaborate drawings of the anguished faces of passengers tangled amid the debris. The stories were breathless in their descriptions, and it is a wonder that anyone still dared to step aboard the rail-bound impending disasters called trains. The Ingalls family would have been exposed to these emotional renderings in words and pictures, in addition to having lived near a track and knowing about various local wrecks and accidents.

This photo from a 1918 Wisconsin wreck illustrates how fragile the boxcars were. If one toppled from the tracks and separated from its wheel truck assembly, chances were good they were deemed salvage material, not worth repairing. It was common for the public to pose among the wreckage, as shown here. Photo courtesy of the Chicago & North Western Historical Society.

Food

"2000 pounds of fresh and choice butter just received."[167]
—*Dakota News*, November 8, 1880

Food Remains Plentiful

Despite the October blockade and the shorter blockades in November, food remained a nonconcern. Watertown's newspaper was especially prolific at listing the various food options available in town. Just before Thanksgiving, it reported that Fowler & Hersey's had received a full carload of fresh groceries, while an ad for a competing merchant tempted buyers with promises of not only fresh groceries but coffee, fresh and cured meat, sugar, salt, flour, corn, oats, coal, fruits, and canned goods.[168]

A week later, an entire carload of flour was announced as having arrived in Watertown, completing the production cycle where farmers provided wheat to the mills farther east, and the mills shipped white flour back to the settlements out west.[169]

Wheat Everywhere

One of the main factors in settling the region was the dangling carrot of near-miraculous wheat-growing land, and most newspaper issues mentioned some aspect of the process. According to a Lyon County history, the harvest of 1880 was very successful throughout all of southwestern Minnesota.[170]

It is unclear how the crop fared around De Smet. While gathering material for her own fiction, Rose Wilder Lane asked her father a series of questions. Sometimes his answers were comically short, as when she asked, "What were the early saloons like?" and he answered, "Saloons." To other questions, he added detailed information beyond the answer to the question asked. When asked about the crops and weather in the early days of De Smet, he answered that the best crop year was in 1881, but that 1885 was "nearly as good."

Mixed in with his answer about the crops, he added several sentences about the blizzard of January 1888, known historically as the Children's Blizzard due to the number of children who perished on their way home from school as the storm raged. He did not, however, provide any clues as to how the crop of 1880 in the vicinity of De Smet fared.[171] This makes sense, considering Almanzo's crop that year, which generated the seed wheat he harbored and which would play a dramatic role later in the winter, had been raised in Marshall, Minnesota. More about this later.

In Brookings, wheat had been rolling in "since the freeze up," attesting to a solid crop.[172] By the end of November, elevators in Brookings were overflowing and unable to take in all of the regional wheat.

Buyers in Egan, south of Brookings, reported "considerable grain [arriving] from the south portions of Brookings County," even on stormy days.[173] Southwest of Egan, Madison had over thirty-five thousand bushels awaiting shipment. Frustrated farmers were forced to travel farther from home to find buyers for their wheat.[174]

With a bountiful harvest and trains running regularly, food and funds were likely free-flowing within the region. And while family gardens had been harmed by the early storm, that did not seem to be a topic of concern to the newspapers, considering that grocers were within easy reach.

Fuel

> "It is said the people of the newly settled western districts
> on the tree-less prairies are suffering terribly for fuel....
> People have not only pulled down and burned their fences,
> but have also burned their machinery to keep from freezing.
> Costly warmth that must be."[175]
>
> —*Janesville Argus*, November 30, 1880

While food was not a scarcity at this early stage of the winter, the topic of fuel remained a high priority for citizens, railroad companies, and newspapers. Despite the return of the trains, concern about coal and wood for fuel continued to take up column space, with little reprieve.

In the eastern portion of the region, articles about fuel were more general, pointing farther west and absent specific details. The ability to obtain wood was a cardinal concern, and coal seemed to be a good option. In *The Long Winter*, Pa remarked that "coal beats brushwood all hollow, for giving a good, steady heat."[176] But coal proved to be no easier to obtain on the prairie than wood.

Along the Hastings & Dakota

Conditions were reported to be most serious along the Hastings & Dakota, despite the railroad making "strenuous efforts" to get fuel to the settlers. As the editor of the *Janesville Argus* noted while reporting on conditions along this line, "Shipping wood out there is said to be like pouring water into a rat hole, so great is the demand and so limited was the stock to commence the winter on."[177]

The Hastings & Dakota was indeed providing fuel along its line, both intentionally and inadvertently. In at least one town, "there was neither wood nor coal to be had," and "many [people] were being supplied from or helping themselves to the short wood used by the engines."[178]

In Milbank, the November 11 paper reminded people again that "the stocks of goods, lumber, etc., of most of our merchants was well-nigh exhausted during the snow blockade, and when freight commenced to move in last Saturday . . . there was a general feeling of relief and satisfaction all around."[179]

Along the Winona & St. Peter

Not wanting the residents to forget about the idea of the formation of a Fuel Association, the *Dakota News* continued to remind readers that, despite it being "rather late in the season," the concept seemed to be acceptable to the populace, expressing hope that it would be organized yet.[180] The situation was serious. The editor of the *New Ulm Weekly Review* noted that towns along even major rail lines were suffering from "a remarkable scarcity of fuel."[181]

Along the Dakota Central

An otherwise uninteresting story, the report in the *Brookings County Press* that "a small shipment of coal arrived" was news worth sharing, given the circumstances.[182] The town had been devoid of fuel for twelve days during the October blockade, and every arrival of fuel was greeted with relief, not just in Brookings but throughout the region.[183]

This is also when the first newspaper mentions of hay being used for fuel appeared. In the absence of coal and wood, residents had to get creative. The November 18 issue of the *Brookings County Press* wrote that "bean, corn, hay, and in fact every thing except wood and coal" were utilized, and that "almost every town in Dakota and Minnesota [was] howling about the shortness of fuel supplies." They further prompted, "What is the matter with the railroads?"[184]

Although many complained that the railroad companies were at fault for the shortage of fuel, the Dakota Central "dealt out coal freely at DeSmet, during the late snow blockade, which in that vicinity lasted two weeks lacking two days."[185]

Out and About

"The country has once more settled down
to its regular business."[186]

—*Brookings County Press*, November 18, 1880

Reports of citizens snowbound somewhere other than their homes continued to appear during "the late unpleasantness" of the big storm. Since most of November's weather was agreeable, with little new snowfall to interrupt travel plans, people moved about the region with relative ease.

Among the travelers were Almanzo Wilder's sister Eliza Jane Wilder (E. J.), his brother Perley Day Wilder, and their mother, Angeline Day Wilder, who had been visiting her offspring in De Smet when the October blizzard struck. E. J.'s written account of the storm closely mirrors those of others. She wrote that "the storm raged with unabated fury three days," that hay was twisted for heat when fuel ran out, and that some of her chickens and hens perished.

Following the storm, her mother insisted that E. J. return to Spring Valley, Minnesota, for the winter. The return of three members of the Wilder family was not mentioned in the Spring Valley newspaper prior to the November 7 issue (the next available issue was from January 21), nor did their return appear in newspapers from towns within a fifteen-mile radius of Spring Valley. Therefore, a date for their departure from De Smet could not be established. However, as E. J. does not describe the second storm, which took place on November 10, they likely returned within the first few weeks after the blockade lifted.[187]

In Milbank, the new station agent and his family, having arrived early in the month, were now ready to set up a home, evidently unconcerned about the oncoming winter.[188] Brookings was reported as being "very lively"[189] prior to the November 10 storm. In Watertown, the "streets were crowded with teams, and our business houses enjoyed a splendid trade."[190] Life wasn't all about business, however. Plans were afoot in Watertown, fully supported by the newspaper, to form a debating society to provide entertainment throughout the winter.[191] This concept was displayed in most newspapers throughout the region as new towns started to evolve into communities.

Despite good weather, travel still came at a risk. From Sioux Falls came this dramatic report of a local stagecoach that went off its own rails, so to speak, with the apparent help of its driver:

> In crossing the river between here and Dell Rapids, it was upset and the passengers promiscuously dumped out on the bank, severely injuring some of them. The cover was completely smashed and left to mark the spot where the catastrophe occurred. [One passenger] says he never saw such a mixed up mess in his life. A little more care on the part of the driver might prevent a like occurrence in the future.[192]

Land Seekers Continue to Arrive

The enthusiasm that had pulled people into the region continued. In Watertown, every train brought land seekers.[193] In fact, the entire region was being besieged despite the excitable onset of winter.

One article, appearing in multiple papers, noted that upwards of six thousand people went through Chicago daily on their way west to "look at valuable lands along the line of the various land grant railways." It continued,

> [They] are spreading themselves all over this portion of the west in their effort to see as much as possible for the money invested in cheap railroad

fare. A great many of them cross the Dakota line and extend their investigations into the interior. While the season is not the best for sight seeing, the mammoth excursions will result in adding several hundred to Dakota's population.[194]

The Far West

It is always interesting to step back from the events experienced by the Ingalls family and place them in a context of time and history. One of these historical incidents, the Battle of the Little Bighorn, was not quite four and a half years past as winter set in.

One of the participants in the events of late June 1876 was a stern-wheel steamboat named the *Far West*. She was under contract to the army that summer and served as General Terry's headquarters for the expedition. Major and minor US military players of that campaign trod upon her decks as plans were worked and reworked.

On June 21, the leaders held a meeting onboard that finalized the impending campaign, which, despite their plans, resulted in a victory for the Lakota Sioux, Northern Cheyenne, and Arapaho tribes over Lieutenant Colonel Custer and most of those under his command.[195]

Following the battle, the *Far West* moved upriver to retrieve wounded soldiers, then returned to bring first word of the event. The news was telegraphed to Bismarck and then the world. The loss fueled an animosity that eventually led to the 1890 massacre at Wounded Knee and what is considered the historical end of the horrific Indian Wars.

After her military service in 1876, the *Far West* resumed an adventurous civilian life, moving passengers and freight and reinforcing a reputation for breaking speed records. A summary of the vessel will bring a hint of recognition to those familiar with various descriptions of young Laura Ingalls: "The *Far West* was neither graceful nor grand in appearance, but she was strong, powerful, fast, durable and had an enormous capacity for hard work."[196]

Due to her fame, the *Far West* remained a bit of an attraction throughout the rest of her days. Newspaper accounts frequently reported her location in towns up and down the Missouri and Yellowstone rivers, and during the cold snap of mid-November, the *Far West* found herself frozen in place on the Missouri River. Yankton's *Press and Daily Dakotaian* of November 17 reported that the river had frozen and that, based on a telegram dated November 15, "the *Far West* was last heard from at the foot of Big Bend [meander], bound for Pierre."

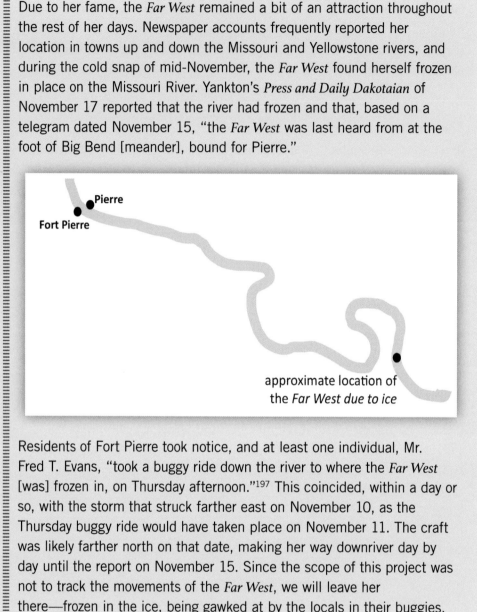

Pierre

Fort Pierre

approximate location of
the *Far West due to ice*

Residents of Fort Pierre took notice, and at least one individual, Mr. Fred T. Evans, "took a buggy ride down the river to where the *Far West* [was] frozen in, on Thursday afternoon."[197] This coincided, within a day or so, with the storm that struck farther east on November 10, as the Thursday buggy ride would have taken place on November 11. The craft was likely farther north on that date, making her way downriver day by day until the report on November 15. Since the scope of this project was not to track the movements of the *Far West*, we will leave her there—frozen in the ice, being gawked at by the locals in their buggies.

Newspapers and Mail

"For several days past the United States mail has been delivered regularly at the Egan post office, and the average Eganite is accordingly happy. May it ever be thus."[198]

—*Egan Express*, November 25, 1880

In terms of being able to complete their duties and distribution, there were very few complaints from the editors in November. A notable exception occurred once the worst of the October storm had melted away, when settlers expected a return to normalcy. This piece gives some insight into the various options that existed for mail delivery at the time:

For the past week the mail has been received at the Egan post office very irregularly, and we can conceive of no reason for it. We understand the stage driver says the river is too high and the water too cold to put his horse through it. Now it may be that the water is a little cold, but we know that there has not been a day for the past two weeks that teams have not crossed the river, and where other teams have crossed the stage could cross, too. It is well known to all of our citizens that this postoffice [sic] has been given the 'go-by' on the smallest pretext, and that very few, if any, extra efforts have been made to supply this office with mail. We are just as much entitled to our regular mail as any office on the route, and when there is nothing to hinder getting it here we should have it, or the contractor be made to suffer for his negligence—or cussedness.[199]

Boosterism

"A few years of patient battle with the privations and discomforts of pioneer life, will be rewarded by rich possessions that will place them beyond the reach of want during the balance of their years."[200]

—*Dakota News*, November 29, 1880

Sometimes the editors wrote their own enthusiasms about their town or region. At other times, they reprinted pieces found within the pages of another paper. In one instance—a particularly good example of boosterism that applied to the wider region—the *Volga Gazette* covered a speech by Territorial Governor Ordway, which was then picked up and reprinted by other papers.

Winters in the region were already known to be the thing of legend. Yet here, on the brink of a Dakota winter, with near breathless excitement, Ordway used the prepared railbed (neither ties nor rails yet laid) between Volga and Watertown as a metaphor for the promise, based on what he called "somewhat authentic sources,"[201] to link this tiny corner of Dakota Territory to the great markets of both coasts, creating boundless prosperity for the future.

After Ordway established the golden opportunities that lay before his listeners and noted that he had visited "nearly all the principal cities and towns in Dakota," he then boasted "that a more energetic, wide awake, and intelligent population does not exist in this broad land." He evangelized that "the dry and bracing atmosphere sharpens the intellect of this people, and the life of the pioneer trains him for the struggles of life, and prepares him for any emergency."[202] (One wonders what young Laura Ingalls would have thought of that sentiment, considering she would, in the months to come, find her mind numb and unable to focus due to one of those "emergencies.")

Progressive for the era, Ordway touted not only the male settlers but the women of Dakota as well:

It is not man alone who is taking possession of the beautiful prairies of Dakota, for among the settlers on public lands may be found many aspiring and spirited women. . . . We egotistical men are very apt to forget what we owe to woman. . . . All honor to the brave women who, single handed and alone, are building up homes in Dakota.[203]

Newspapers also expended considerable energy promoting the benefits of their individual towns and regions, and some of them went to extraordinary lengths. One extended saga was a project by the editor of the *Dakota News*; he dreamed of an "Extra Edition," designed to lure new settlers and businessmen to the Watertown region.

In stoking the fires for support of his pet project, he noted that he had attempted his venture the year prior but had not found "sufficient encouragement" among his fellow townspeople to make it worth the effort. A year had passed, and there had been significant expansion and an influx of emigrants. He revived the idea and, in a single day, "secured a sufficient subscription to warrant . . . commencing the work of getting out such an edition," to be issued the second Monday of the following January. Various businesses in town subscribed to receive between 100 and 500 copies, at five cents per copy.[204]

The editor realized that this was, by nature, a serious undertaking involving "a large amount of extra labor and expense." He assured readers that "no pains will be spared to make this edition an encyclopedia of News of that class that the people east are wanting."[205]

Noting that prospective settlers wrote innumerable letters, mostly asking the same set of questions, he stated that in the name of efficiency, the Extra Edition would answer those questions, then be "mailed by subscribers to those of their acquaintances most likely to desire to come west."[206]

Shifting ever so slightly from town booster to newspaper businessman, he then told the businessmen in town that each should "reserve at least 200 copies to mail from time to time during the coming year, in answer to the inquiries [they would] be sure to receive." Local farmers were likewise encouraged to send in orders for a more modest "10 to 25 copies each."[207]

Finishing up the article, the editor assured his readers that after a mere half day of canvassing, he'd accumulated "4,000 subscribers" for the Extra, with a goal of 10,000. Likely, those 4,000 subscribers meant 4,000 copies of the Extra, not 4,000 individual people who had subscribed for a certain number of copies each. The large numbers, however, probably helped him stimulate excitement among the readers.[208] (The full text of this article is available at thebeautifulsnow.com. We will pick up the story of Watertown's Extra Edition in the January chapter.)

December 1880

Sunday	Monday	Tuesday	Wednesday	Thursday	Friday	Saturday
			1 "devilish cold" (west) comfortable (east)	2 comfortable	3 comfortable	4 −26F windy fierce blizzard
5 cold,−26F windy ice 18" thick	6 calm, sunny cold, −22F	7 windy snow squalls	8 −20F	9 −12 to −20F	10	11 delightful (west) cold (east)
12 delightful mild and soft	13 springlike (west) −18, clear, cold, rain, mild (east)	14 springlike (west) clear, cold, mild (east)	15 springlike (west) clear, cold, mild (east)	16 mild changeable moonlight	17 snows at intervals	18 cold
19	20	21 cold, bright foggy	22 foggy	23 good sleighing bright and beautiful	24	25 very windy cold
26 cold −30 to−34F blizzardous	27 cold −28 to −34F blizzardous	28 cold, windy −32F blizzardous	29 cold, windy −25 to −40F stormy	30 drifting, cold −25 to −40F	31 drifting, cold −25 to −40F	

▬▬▬▬ Blizzard or significant snow event

//////////// Lighter snow or mixed precipitation

December 1: Brookings reported "little snow on ground."

December 4: Brookings reported "slight fall of snow" while Milbank reported a blizzard.

December 6: Missouri River reported as frozen.

December 9: Brookings claimed no snow, insisting all snowfall had been in Minnesota.

December 31: Marshall paper stops using the word "blizzard."

This calendar shows weather reports gleaned from the various newspaper articles.
If the weather was significantly different in one portion of the region versus another, that is noted.

Most of December was cold, with relatively minor wind events sprinkled throughout. Things changed considerably the day after Christmas, however. As festivities wound down, the atmosphere let loose with one of the most crushing storms of the winter, providing a healthy taste of what was to come.

Early in the month, articles reassured residents that the railroad companies had strategically placed snowplows of such capacity that it was inconceivable that mere snow could stop them.

Meanwhile, the results of the fall harvest were brought to local granaries in such quantities that there were not enough railcars available to move them all to eastern markets. While food was still reported as plentiful, the railroad companies were concerned about fuel availability, even lowering freight charges for moving coal and wood out to the western settlements.

Mail delays became more common later in the month, and the first of the half-sheet newspapers were published as a result of not having enough paper—or news—to publish full-sheet editions. Additionally, winter activities began in earnest, as new neighbors deepened relationships.

The Month for the Ingalls Family

"These times are too progressive. Everything has changed too fast. Railroads and telegraph and kerosene and coal stoves— they're good things to have but the trouble is, folks get to depend on 'em."[209]
—*The Long Winter*

As supported in the newspaper record, towns up and down the railroad lines had organized, via the telegraph, relay systems to get mail from one town to another. De Smet, through David Gilbert, was a part of one such relay.

In the novel, upon hearing there was an opportunity to send a letter back to Wisconsin, Ma and the girls excitedly gathered to write updates, which were sent along with Gilbert,[210] but a blizzard hit before he had a chance to return to De Smet with replies. With their meat supply gone and kerosene running low, the Ingalls rationed what food they had and tried to conserve their energy.

For the Wilder brothers, the storm prompted Almanzo to hide his seed wheat, fearful that, should the trains fail to return, the townspeople would pressure Royal, a merchant at heart, to sell the seed for a nice profit and leave Almanzo without the means to plant his crop come spring.[211] While this preventive measure takes place during December in the novel, it is not possible to pinpoint actual timing based on the autobiographies, again due to lack of chronology.[212] Unless noted, the rest of this section covers the story as presented in the novel.

As the blizzard cleared, Pa gathered news from town. Gilbert had succeeded in retrieving the mail, and the Ingalls family was excited to receive copies of several newspapers and periodicals, including the *Youth's Companion*. There was also a letter telling them that a Christmas barrel containing gifts, including a frozen turkey, had been shipped to them. Anticipation for Christmas built.[213]

Pa also told the family that double crews and snowplows had been set to task along the Tracy Cut.[214] He then announced he would be shoveling for the railroad,[215] becoming part of a crew, as so many other men did that winter. He, like many others, came home with red, puffy eyes,[216] a condition that would become common later in the winter. He was optimistic that the work train would be through the blockade the next day, followed by the regular train.[217]

The family's meals throughout the month continued to reflect relative diversity, including potatoes, bread, beans, turnips, tea, and some flour. The bread, however, changed—ground wheat instead of white flour.[218]

With Christmas approaching, Laura and Carrie visited local stores to shop for a pair of suspenders for Pa. They stopped at the stores run by Harthorn (bare shelves, dull suspenders), then Loftus (bare shelves, bright suspenders), opting to purchase the bright ones.[219] Laura woke the next morning excited that a train would arrive, but a blizzard arrived first.

When Ma suggested they wait until Christmas to read their coveted copy of the *Youth's Companion*, Laura was less than enthusiastic. Carrie went along with it. Mary, however, basked in the goodness of the wait.[220]

Despite the hardships, Christmas itself was a joyous affair, made special by oyster soup and the reading of stories from the periodicals that Gilbert had delivered. The day ended with another storm slamming into town. When that blizzard cleared, Pa again crossed the street to gather news, returning with a sack of wheat from the Wilder store. He informed the family that snow had again filled the Tracy Cut, but a crew was working to clear the tracks.

Their coal supply ran out, and twisted hay was employed for heat.[221] Kerosene was depleted, but Ma dug into her basket of ingenuity and assembled a button lamp (tallow lamp)—using axle grease, cloth, and a large coat button—to provide light.[222] The year was ending dimly.

The Weather

*"The weather the present week has been bright and beautiful—
just keen and bracing enough to make one feel like stepping out
on a brisk and lively pace."*[223]

—*Grant County Review*, December 23, 1880

In a slight contradiction to the action in *The Long Winter,* the majority of the month was free of blizzards, with the exception of a storm on December 4. There were days with winds, days with lighter snows, and even days with rain and fog. The temperature fluctuated as much as the precipitation, ranging in description from a "devilish cold" of twenty-six below zero to delightful, mild, and soft. At midmonth, several editors waxed poetic about the beautiful, clear moonlit nights.

The Storm of December 4

This storm ushered in a period of cold weather. It started on Saturday with wind and snow, following a path southeast from Milbank to at least Springfield, and lasted until Sunday, when the wind died down and the temperature dropped to –26 degrees. Monday brought a bright blue, sunny sky.[224] While short in duration, the storm was enough to block the tracks of the Winona & St. Peter in the vicinity of Springfield until Thursday, when trains resumed.[225]

Watertown's *Dakota News* of December 6 claimed that while it was cold, there was "not even enough 'of the beautiful' to make for good sleighing."[226] This could be an accurate assessment of the snow cover, or it could be the dry sarcasm that was in abundant supply among the editors, as when the *Egan Express* of December 9 noted that the –20s that had afflicted the region of late were "somewhat chilly."[227] When the warm-up began, reaching a balmy –12, the Janesville paper of December 14 quipped that "one felt the need of a fan and a chip hat" while also noting that "the oldest inhabitant never before saw such continued, severe, cold weather so early in the season."[228]

Mid-December brought warmer temperatures and, in Egan, "delightful days. The nicest we have had this winter."[229] With inspiration, the *Pipestone Star* described the weather as having "put new life in to everybody, and made them feel as though Minnesota was not such a bad place to live after all."[230]

Snows of December 17

Along with the milder weather came a handful of minor snows, which brought sleighing to a "passably good" state in Egan.[231] There was even fog in Brookings on December 21 as the temperatures fluctuated towards warm.[232]

Christmas cheer also infused the tone, as when the Milbank editor playfully noted that the "fall of snow" made for "good sleighing," a wonderful entertainment at holiday time.[233]

The Christmas Blizzard: December 26

The warmer temperatures of mid-December began to recede as Christmas approached, with reports of cold winds becoming more common. The winds picked up on Christmas Day, and what followed was one of the most significant blizzards of the season. The newspapers dedicated more column space to it than any weather event since October.

Sun dog photo courtesy of Carl Morsching, January 31, 2019.

Just prior to the storm, sun dogs were reported in Milbank, on the northern edge of the region,[234] and in Janesville, on the eastern edge.[235] Sun dogs, a type of sun halo (an atmospheric optical phenomenon) often seen during cold weather, occur when hexagonal ice crystals in the atmosphere refract sunlight. They appear as bright spots on one or both sides of the sun, twenty-two degrees out, often with pillars of light cast up and down.

A bit south of Milbank, the *Brookings County Press* reported that "Sunday was a terror. It snowed, and it blowed, and it drifted, until it seemed as though the whole country was to be inundated, but Monday it let up somewhat, and now all is serene once more."[236]

Southeast of Brookings, the *Egan Express* shared that the moderate weather of the previous several weeks had come to a violent end: A strong northwest wind continued for days "with increased velocity, and the air was filled with snow, so that it was very disagreeable traveling." The article recounted the winds, snows, and below-zero temperatures of Saturday, Sunday, Monday, and Tuesday, but reserved its best prose for Wednesday: "Yesterday was a stunner. From early morn till late at night the wind blew a perfect gale, and the air was so full of snow that it was next to impossible to be out for any length of time." It finally began to calm down on Thursday, being "not quite so bad as yesterday."[237]

Moving a bit eastward, the *Marshall Messenger* was a bit more philosophical:

The old year has very persistently refused all the week to die a peaceful death, but to-morrow will usher in the new one in spite of wind or weather. This is about the time of the year when there exists all through this region a more or less suppressed suspicion that civilization has gotten too far north. . . . But all this will soon pass. Spring will soon thaw out your love of home, and by July you will be talking of Manitoba, as a country where people don't roast in summer.[238]

A few dozen miles south of Marshall, the *Murray County Pioneer* shared that "on Sunday we were favored with weather approaching what might be termed as blizzardous." The temperature dropped to 30 degrees below zero by Monday morning, and the deep cold remained until the paper went to press on Thursday. The writer added that the frigid air was "sandwiched now and then by a small hurricane by way of variation."[239]

One oddly poignant result of the storm was that, near Marshall, "Mrs. C. B. Tyler had the misfortune to lose all her house plants during the late meteorological unpleasantness."[240] That "late meteorological unpleasantness" delivered impending doom for the railroads.

The Railroads

"The *Lyon County News* says trains were running regularly all the time of the blockage, on the west end from Tracy to Watertown. The blockade was between Tracy and Sleepy Eye."[241]

—*Janesville Argus*, December 21, 1880

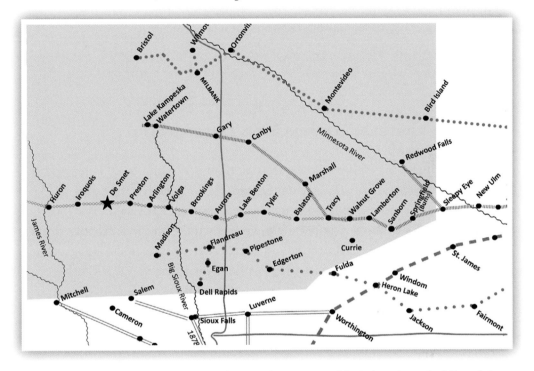

The gray area generally represents where trains were unable to travel most of the winter.

While trains were able to operate on the eastern end of the systems just before the end of the year, the tracks west of an approximate north–south line at Sleepy Eye, Minnesota, would remain mostly blocked for the next several months.

The storm of December 4 brought blockades along the Winona & St. Peter and the Dakota Central, which were cleared by December 9. The blockades were mostly between Sleepy Eye and Tracy in Minnesota, but with trains unable to travel west of Sleepy Eye, hardship spread into Dakota Territory as well.

Accident and Injury Statistics

Year-end summaries included statistics for accidents and injuries. The *Marshall Messenger* noted that "according to an official estimate, the total number of train accidents in this country for the year ending November 30 was 1,012, in which 304 persons were killed and 1,103 injured. The mortality and injuries were about 45 percent greater this year than the preceding year."[242]

Another article extracted from the Chicago, Milwaukee & St. Paul's annual report shared that overall, "the company employs 10,824 men; killed no passengers during the year; employe[e]s killed, 22; others killed, 22; passengers injured, 10; employe[e]s injured, 76; others injured, 14."[243]

Snowplows along the Winona & St. Peter and the Dakota Central

The first mentions of snowplows used along the Winona & St. Peter and the Dakota Central appear in the December papers. So effective that they are still occasionally used today, wedge plows were a common sight at the various rail yards. (The rotary plow would not be employed by the Chicago & North Western until 1888 and, according to its annual report for that year, rivaled a locomotive in terms of price.)[244]

This Elmer & Tenney photo was captured on March 22, 1881, a quarter mile west of Sleepy Eye. It shows one of the plows in use along the Winona & St. Peter during the winter. Photo courtesy of the Chicago & North Western Historical Society.

Because articles were printed and reprinted across multiple newspapers, it can be difficult to ascertain their precise origins, but it appears that by mid-December, plows were stationed in New Ulm, Tracy, and probably some points farther west.

Residents of New Ulm likely believed that winter would be vanquished with ease when they read, "We have taken a view of the mammoth snowplow which is lying at the depot. It is a big one, and none need fear of being deluged by snow storms. From appearances we should think that the monster might go through a mountain of snow, let alone a 16-foot drift."[245]

Westward along the tracks, Tracy harbored "A Monster Snow Plow!" which was not meant to be attached to a locomotive, as the others were. A reprinted article described it further:

[It] stands on two pairs of trucks [wheel assemblies] the same as those of a box car. The rear end is built something like a box car with room inside for tools, &c. The front end is just simply a [huge] plow. It is about as wide as a box car and is about twelve feet in perpendicular height. It is heavily built and when propelled by three or four locomotives, is a terror to a snow bank.[246]

The editor of the *Dakota News* was more matter of fact, letting his readers know that "the railroad company have now a thorough bred snow plow, one of the effective kind, which will scoop the snow high and far when called upon to do service."[247]

This uncredited photo was tentatively identified via markings on the reverse side as having been taken at Waseca, Minnesota, on the Winona & St. Peter in 1880. It shows a behemoth of a snowplow, possibly matching the description of the equipment stationed at Tracy. Photo courtesy of the Chicago & North Western Historical Society.

This uncredited photo of a wedge plow was identified via markings on the reverse side as having been taken at Sleepy Eye on the Winona & St. Peter in 1887. Photo courtesy of the Chicago & North Western Historical Society.

Rumors

A few articles published in December may have caused concern among the settlers. The December 9 issue of the *Grant County Review* reprinted an article from the *Glencoe Register* reporting that the Hastings & Dakota line "will keep the road open just as long as it is possible to do so, but if the elements continued to pile the snow upon the track for a few weeks longer as they have for three weeks past, they will be completely snowed under and may be obliged to suspend."

Following the Christmas storm, when it was dangerously cold, the *Murray County Pioneer* of December 30 noted that "as a natural consequence the trains were all 'hung up' since Saturday and railroad employees instructed to await more favorable signs in the elements."[248]

After reading articles such as these, it is easy to imagine how citizens, while chatting along main streets throughout the region, would gossip amongst themselves that the railroads were going to abandon them to the elements. Neither article above indicates a long-term suspension, but it would not be much of a leap for the discouraged, worried citizens to interpret them that way.

Railroad Blockades

"The R. R. is in a continual struggle with the snow drifts."[249]
—*New Ulm Weekly Review*, December 8, 1880

Along the Winona & St. Peter and Dakota Central

Even without significant snowfall, the situation was becoming frustrating due to the winds blowing around the existing snow. This string of short news items (called *squibs* in the newspaper industry) in the *Brookings County Press* has the ring of an irritated editor:

- Trains were snow-bound in Minnesota last week.
- The delays of trains are too numerous to mention.
- The water tanks along the railroad freeze up and give the engineers much trouble these days.
- No mail last Saturday. A wreck and too much snow in Minnesota caused the delay. No snow here. The snow blockade on the Winona & St. Peter, between Sleepy Eye and Tracy was broken Wednesday night. Trains are running on time again. No snow in Dakota and trains running every day. Dakota is evidently west of the storm belt.[250]

The stretch of track between Sleepy Eye and Tracy became problematic early on, and it continued that way throughout the winter. Trains had been unable to run west of Sleepy Eye for several days prior to mid-December due to heavy snow.[251]

Despite frustrations expressed up and down the line, the Watertown newspaper reassured its readers that "Supt. Sanborn is putting forth herculean efforts to keep the road open."[252]

Superintendent Sanborn of the Winona & St. Peter

Sherburne Sanborn was born in September 1834, making him forty-six years old during the winter of 1880–81, during which he led operations along the Winona & St. Peter. The town of Sanborn, Minnesota, between Springfield and Lamberton, was named in his honor. In August 1887, he was appointed general superintendent of the entire Chicago & North Western railway system, operating out of Chicago.[253]

On the eastern edge of the region, the Janesville paper reassured its readers they had it easy compared to farther west, where it was "all snowed up, jam[m]ed in and drifted over"—especially between Tracy and Sleepy Eye—and admitted, "How it was beyond that no man knows or can find out."[254] Of course, the telegraph was available to provide ready updates, but pointing that out would not keep the readers from moving west or be as entertaining as the drama of thinking those "out west" were beyond reach.

Meanwhile, the *Brookings County Press* reported the reappearance of trains in town, where nine tons of freight were unloaded. Additionally, "five or six car loads of coal and wood" arrived. The issue also mused whether the arrival of a train heralded another blizzard, quipping, "P. S.—The blizzard is here."[255] The blizzard mentioned may not have been a true storm, as other areas reported spotty snow at the time, and no blockages resulted. But the fear that each snowfall would result in a blizzard was palpable.

The frustration on the western side of the blockades was apparent and continued for weeks after the trains were again running. Numerous articles noted that while "trains were running regularly all the time of the blockage, on the west end from Tracy to Watertown," the source of the problem was the stretch of track from Tracy to Sleepy Eye.[256]

Along the Southern Minnesota

Outside Madison, Dakota Territory, the end of track was still several miles short of town. There was already a station agent employed and working in Madison, however, and he did not let the absence of tracks hinder him in his duties. The *Egan Express* lauded his efforts accordingly:

> W. A. Conrad, our station agent, went out to the end of the track, four
> miles this side of Madison, last Sunday, with two cars of emigrants, two
> cars of lumber, and three cars of merchandise, for the Madison
> merchants. This action on the part of the agent will be appreciated by the
> people of Madison. By the way, Mr. Conrad is one of the most efficient and
> obliging agents on this line of road, always willing to do all in his power
> for the patrons of the road, and we hope he may be retained at this station,
> until through his own merits, he is called to fill a more exalted position.
> Then, and not till then will we willingly part with him.[257]

To those who dared compare the hardworking local superintendents to the pampered officers riding in their opulent cars, the *Egan Express* offered this humorous retort: "Supt. Egan went through town last Saturday on a special train consisting of a hand car and three men, bound for Dell Rapids."[258]

With trains running and Christmas approaching, moods were high. Articles talked of gift purchases, outings, parties, and travel. However, one of the biggest storms of the winter was on the region's doorstep.

The Christmas Storm

The storm that began after Christmas lasted several days, blocking the major railroad lines in southwestern Minnesota into January and impacting the towns in eastern Dakota Territory as well.

New Ulm reported the difficulties experienced by the railroads following the storm: "It took three engines and a force of men all day Monday to clear the track between Sleepy Eye and New Ulm [16 miles] and at the time of going to press they are still bucking snow between this city and Nicollet Station [13 miles]." It would take them several days to get the trains running again. The storm was especially unsympathetic between Watertown and Sleepy Eye. The writer then speculated that the severity of the storm "has no doubt caused much suffering among the settlers."[259]

Marshall, northwest of the junction at Tracy, was frustrated but trying to be patient: "Just when we will have [a train] again is a matter still under discussion. There are more or less drifts down the road. Spring time is coming, gentle Annie. So are other blessings in the sweet bye and bye."[260]

Gentle Annie

The phrase "gentle Annie" appeared in a handful of articles during the winter, usually as a calming reassurance that things would improve. This is likely a cultural reference to the song "Gentle Annie," which was written by Stephen Foster in 1856. The inspiration for the song is in dispute, as several women have been suggested as possible models for Annie. After the song was released, the saying fell into popular usage until at least the mid-1890s. The lyrics do not include "in the sweet bye and bye"; these words were added by the writer of the article, borrowed from the beloved hymn "The Sweet Bye-and-Bye" (lyrics by S. Fillmore Bennett), a favorite of Charles Ingalls. Stephen Foster wrote several other well-known American songs, such as "Camptown Races," "Beautiful Dreamer," "Oh! Susanna," and "Jeanie with the Light Brown Hair."

Despite evidence in the written record that the storm did indeed drop snow in eastern Dakota Territory, the towns there began to theorize that were it not for Minnesota, all would be well in Dakota. Watertown reported that its incoming passenger train was delayed by three hours due to "heavy snows in Minnesota."[261] Egan similarly noted that it had been over four days since their last train from the east and that due to the Minnesota blockades, prospects were bad for the next few days.[262]

The *Brookings County Press* sympathized with Dakota residents, placing appropriate blame eastward when it shared, "The railroad tracks in Dakota will easily be cleared. The trouble is in Minnesota, where the cuts are so deep. Snow has filled these cuts so many times this winter that it will no doubt be a difficult matter to clear them."[263]

Tracks Clogged with Cars

As early as November, articles began to discuss not having sufficient cars available to transport harvested grain out of communities or deliver wood and coal into the new settlements.

With fuel a significant concern across the region, having cars available to haul wood and coal was a high priority for the superintendents. Along the Southern Minnesota, the *Egan Express* showed residents' gratitude when its editor wrote, "Supt. Egan has done the square thing by Pipestone. . . . He has taken cars that were in demand for other purposes and loaded them with wood and coal for the prairie country, and delayed other freight so that there should be no suffering from cold. Long live Egan."[264]

While the blockades were indeed troublesome for towns awaiting the arrival of supplies and news, they also impacted farmers. Trading grain to elevators proved difficult, as noted by the Currie paper: "The warehouses and elevators . . . are filled 'chock full' of wheat awaiting shipment," and "the line cars were either all in transit or blockaded, and it was impossible to comply with [the] demand."[265]

As for the backlog of cars which caused the wheat elevators to overflow, the editor of the *Janesville Argus* simply described the situation as "bad, very bad, [with] no immediate prospects of improvement."[266] The big mills in Minneapolis were likewise unable to ship their products, further contributing to the backup of the entire supply chain.

In Dakota Territory, Milbank reported similar circumstances. The town's elevators were completely full.[267] Reinforcing how widespread the problem was, reports indicated that New Ulm was able to receive trains with relative regularity compared to Milbank, which was unable to ship eastward throughout most of the winter, yet both towns overflowed with wheat. Loaded freight cars were parked on sidetracks, becoming more and more inaccessible with each subsequent snowfall or wind event.

By the end of December, the situation fluctuated, and New Ulm was able to report that things had opened up: the railroad had begun to haul away grain, and farmers could resume bringing in their wheat.[268]

Other Railroad Business

"The Indians make it a subject of general complaint that while they have ceded the right of way to [the Chicago & North Western and the Chicago, Milwaukee & St. Paul], and they have built and have been operating their roads for some time, they have not yet received a single cent from the companies."[269]

—Annual Report of the Commissioner of Indian Affairs, 1881

The Push to Madison, Dakota Territory

The blockades also, of course, hindered construction projects. On the western end of the Southern Minnesota, the company had been working to get rails laid to reach Madison, approximately twenty-five miles west of Egan, much to the excitement of the residents. Progress was slowed by the weather, and disappointment loomed.

Despite being within a mere three or four miles of Madison, track construction stopped due to unavailability of rails to put down. Further, the contractor was planning to abandon work for the season, and the boarding cars, which housed the workers, were scheduled to be moved to the nearby town of Egan.[270]

Instead, two weeks later, the Egan paper reported that there appeared to be a flurry of activity: "A train load of iron and ties . . . passed through town yesterday morning. This looks well for the Madison folks, and we hope they will get the road without further delay."[271] The same edition was able to confirm that, indeed, track-layers were hard at work.

Finally, just days before the late-December storm, a train pulled into Madison. The December 30 edition of the *Egan Express* reported that "the people of that town are as happy as a boy with his first pair of boots; and we don't blame them, either."[272] A fitting Christmas gift, even if it would go unused much of the winter.

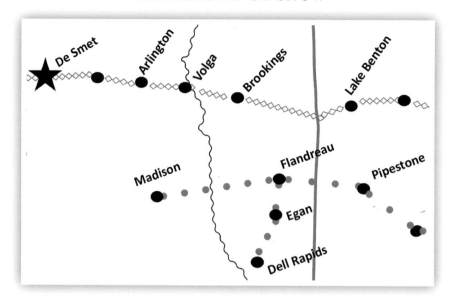

While the town of Madison celebrated the arrival of the railroad, the people of Janesville were seeking maintenance on long-established equipment. Amidst the frequent winds, the editor complained that "the Superintendent of the Chicago & North Western should send up a special agent and a special pot of oil to grease the wind mill at the water tank. Howls and grumbles like a flock of wild geese mourning for their first born. Excruciating and horrible."[273]

Dakota Leads the Nation in Tracklaying for 1880

Using a little less detail than the local newspapers to herald accomplishments, the rail industry trade journal, the *Railway Age*, published a tally of track laid in 1880. Its original numbers were published in mid-January, then updated in late March. The corrected numbers are represented here: "Dakota leads the country with 738 miles of new track, Texas as next, with 696; New Mexico, 556; Ohio, 484; and Iowa, 436."[274]

An astounding feat—2,910 miles of track established during one year in the top five states alone. According to the Chicago & North Western Historical Society archivists, an average of 2,600 ties were used per mile. In Dakota alone, that meant 1,918,800 ties. On the prairie, that likely meant added transportation costs for railroad companies to bring in wooden ties from the more timbered areas of northern Minnesota and Wisconsin. However, the railroads either owned or invested in lumber companies to help secure supplies at minimal cost.

In Minnesota, early railroads were advantageously placed to haul the harvest of vast timber supplies from the northern forests. Ties, bridges, and all manner of railroad structures required timber, so the railroads secured their supplies directly.[275]

Wrecks & Accidents

From December 9 until Christmas, things ran more or less on time, except when a broken rail, broken axle, or misaligned switch caused a wreck that had to be cleared. Some of the stories were simple and routine, while others were much more intriguing.

Newspaper reports of injured railroad workers often combined the danger of the job, the storytelling skills of those directly involved, and the dramatic flair of the newspaper writers, who crafted stories to keep the citizens both entertained and cautious about getting too close to the trains.[276]

Last Friday evening as S. S. Taylor was crossing the railroad track . . . a locomotive, which was coming to this place for coal and water, struck his buggy, knocking it all to slivers and throwing Mr. Taylor out and seriously injuring him. He was riding in a top-buggy, and as it was after dark he did not see the locomotive and not hearing any signal, he did not know there was one near him until it struck the buggy. When thrown out Mr. Taylor retained his hold on the lines, which in some way were wrapped around the telegraph pole and the team held until he got up and unhitched them from what remained of the buggy.[277]

A carpenter in the employ of the Winona and St. Peter Railroad Co., was knocked off the Red Stone bridge [just east of New Ulm] last Sunday night by a passing locomotive to which a snow plow was attached. . . . He had proceeded quite a distance onto the bridge before he encountered the engine and snow plow, but having met with similar occurrences daily he merely stepped to the outer edge of the bridge to allow the engine to pass. Just as the snow plow came along side of him a lot of snow which had accumulated on the plow fell off and swept him, off the bridge. He fell a distance of about 20 feet into a snow drift, striking several of the bridge timbers in his descent. He lay in the snow drift during the whole night and until found by some of his comrades on Monday morning. They conveyed him to his house and then summoned Dr. Berry to attend to his injuries. Had the weather been cold he would certainly have frozen to death as he was unable to move, after his fall, and when found he lay just where he had fallen.[278]

The Courtland Wreck and the Dakota Sioux

One of the most reprinted incidents of the winter involved a delegation of Sioux on their way to Washington, DC, to finalize negotiations that would grant right-of-way access to the Chicago & North Western to run tracks from the Missouri River to the Black Hills. The delegation boarded the train in Pierre and proceeded east, passing through De Smet and Walnut Grove along the way.

It appears that this was the first train to get through from the west for "four or five days" and was "loaded with 330 passengers stowed away in seven coaches. There were also two baggage cars and two engines."[279]

At half past two in the morning on Thursday, December 9, the train approached a troublesome spot near the Courtland station, approximately six miles east of New Ulm. While this area was noted as having rail problems, all reports of this wreck indicate equipment failure as the cause. A description in the *Marshall Messenger* read:

> [The] accident occurred on a level prairie and the cars tipped over into a snow bank, which broke the force of the overthrow. The passengers were badly shaken but none were seriously hurt, which is considered a miracle, as the train was running twenty miles an hour. The thermometer indicated twenty degrees below zero and there was considerable suffering from cold, but an engine was brought from New Ulm and the passengers transferred back to that place. Superintendent Sanborn . . . was on the ground and under his direction a track was built around the wreck and at 3 o'clock Thursday afternoon the road was open again. Onboard were five Indian chiefs. . . . They don't like car riding, and had to be almost forced aboard at Pierre. What their sensations were as they got out of that snow bank cannot be expressed except in Sioux."[280]

The articles varied in detail and perspective, and some left out the Sioux passengers altogether. The version that ran in the *New Ulm Weekly Review* added more detail and identified the five Cheyenne River agency chiefs: they were "Little No-Heart, Rattling Rib, Blue Coat, White Swan and Four Bear, under the charge of

U.S. Indian Agent Leonard Love. . . . While the track was being repaired and the coaches righted, the Indians were brought back to this city, and they took breakfast." While in New Ulm, the Sioux "were the centre of a great deal of attraction, especially Blue Coat who was in full costume. . . . Another had never seen a train of cars until he reached Fort Pierre, and after the accident near Courtland he expressed his disgust of the white man's mode of traveling, in strong terms."[281]

The *New Ulm Weekly Review* also described the actual wreck, giving deeper insight into the kinds of things that could occur when traveling by train in the winter:

> The baggage cars and one of the coaches fell over on their sides while the other coaches, with the exception of the sleeper, were merely thrown from the track. It was lucky for the passengers that the accident occurred on level ground, for had it happened twenty rods this side of where it did occur, at a place where the track crosses a deep ravine, the loss of life would have been great. None of the cars were damaged very much, although had the fire which caught in one of the baggage cars once got under way the whole train would have been burned."[282]

Not to be left out of all the train drama, the Janesville editor shared that "five cars of wheat spread themselves over the country two miles west of town on Wednesday morning last. Broken rail. No body hurt and no great damage done. The morning passenger west was delayed three or four hours and the mails slightly deranged."[283]

Clearing Train Wrecks and Mishaps

If a car's wheels came off the rails but the car itself remained upright, it could be as simple as employing a *rerailer* (a device similar to a small ramp) to nudge the wheels back into place, tugging the car with a locomotive. Also called "frogs," rerailers remain in use today.

This photo shows the rerailers, or frogs, hanging from the tender car behind the locomotive. Each frog has a "lip," oriented to the outside, to help guide the wheels back up onto the rails and keep

them from slipping off the frog. Photo courtesy of the Chicago & North Western Historical Society.

If a car toppled, it likely separated from its wheels, as they were held together by gravity and friction rather than nuts and bolts. In this case, the wheel assembly (called a truck) would likely be reusable as it was or after repair. The car, however, was often damaged or destroyed during the accident.

If the wreck involved multiple cars or a locomotive, a *wrecking train* would likely be called. A wrecking train consisted of a crane; multiple flatbed cars loaded with ties, rails, and specialized tools; and often a boarding car for the laborers. The crane would lift heavier elements, such as locomotives, either back onto the tracks or onto the flatbed cars for hauling away.

For severe wrecks, a *shoofly*, or temporary track, would be built around the wreckage, as Superintendent Sanborn directed following the December 9 wreck that involved the delegation of Sioux. Once the wreck was cleared and any necessary repairs made to the tracks, the shoofly was dismantled, and its pieces were returned to the wrecking train for future use.

The expense and inconvenience of a wreck wasn't the only concern. The railroad companies felt that failing to clear debris from a crash site could hurt their public image. According to Minnesota railroad historian John C. Luecke, any stray metal was collected and returned to a maintenance shop for either repair or scrap, and "it was not uncommon for [the wood] to be piled up and burned. Wreckage strewn along the right-of-way did not tend to add to the comfort and peace of mind of the traveler."[284] For a longer discussion of the topic, visit the Resources page at thebeautifulsnow.com.

This undated photo shows a wrecking train using its crane to lift a locomotive near New Ulm, Minnesota. It also shows a wheel truck assembly that disconnected from its car. Photo courtesy of the Chicago & North Western Historical Society.

This uncredited 1917 photo taken near the Nicollet station, along what in 1880–81 was called the Winona & St. Peter, illustrates how a locomotive could hit snow or ice, derail, and be held upright by the surrounding snow. Photo courtesy of the Chicago & North Western Historical Society.

Food

"We have greatly reduced the prices of most of our groceries—
Red Front Bee Hive."[285]

—Advertisement in the *Marshall Messenger*, December 17, 1880

Mostly Plentiful

Merchants in New Ulm, Watertown, and Marshall reported being stocked with every kind of necessity,[286] and reports did not change much throughout the month. As the new year approached, area farms continued supplying New Ulm with a steady supply of butter and eggs, to be sold at local merchants,[287] and in Watertown, one merchant's advertisement mentioned "nuts, candies, raisins, and figs" for holiday celebrations.[288]

Elaborate grocery ads, sometimes illustrated and almost always making use of multiple font styles and sizes, filled the pages of many newspapers. However, this did not guarantee food availability, as merchants saved significant money by purchasing ongoing ads. The pieces typeset in the local columns of the paper, however, we can assume were more current.

On the outer reaches of the Hastings & Dakota, the new town of Wilmot, Dakota Territory, celebrated its first grocery store.[289] In New Ulm, one merchant wanted residents to know that he planned to provide "delicious food" all winter at noninflated prices. One ad read, "Oysters! Oysters! Mr. R. Pfefferle wishes to inform the public that he will, during the winter months, keep on hand a splendid brand of fresh oysters. He sells them by the can only and at Chicago prices."[290]

However, a squib (short news item) included in the December 27 Watertown paper hinted that not everyone was enjoying the same access to food. It read, "Remember the poor. A sack of flour is worth many long prayers."[291] It could have been a seasonal Christmas reminder to remember those in need, or it may be that the editor knew of some who were already experiencing hunger.

Wheat Still Coming In

Despite the railroad companies pushing westward in an effort to, in part, reap the harvest of wheat, it appears that the yield was more than even they had anticipated.

December found farmers still threshing wheat and husking corn. Although bad weather delayed the activities at intervals, elevators continued to receive crops, and the railroads worked to marshal cars to carry the bounty off to eastern markets.

On the eastern edge of the region, on December 7, Janesville reported that the "elevator [was] full of wheat and sticking out the top of the smoke stack." The editor went on, stating that "the North Western better sell out. The rats will carry off more than the railroads."[292]

On December 9, the Milbank paper reported that since the first week of September, approximately 45,000 bushels of wheat had been collected by the two grain elevators in town.[293] What it didn't include was that because of a shortage of cars, much of that wheat was piling up in elevators in town after town across the region, regardless of the railroad line they sat upon.

Two weeks later, the same paper reported that due to the freight blockades, even the mills in Minneapolis had suspended operations, finding it "impossible to get cars to ship their products."[294] An additional week on, the editor further noted that "the company had not prepared for so large an increase in business over that of last year."[295]

White flour had increased in popularity during the 1860s and '70s thanks to advances in technology that made processing easier. Minnesota had many mills dedicated to creating white flour, and Minneapolis would go on to become one of the world's largest flour-producing centers, harnessing the power of St. Anthony Falls and the astronomical quantities of wheat coming in from western Minnesota and Dakota Territory. By 1880, there were at least twenty-two mills operating in Minneapolis, with more to come. With that much milling capacity sitting idle due to lack of cars for transporting the resulting flour, there was considerable pressure on the railroad companies to restore service and raise the blockades. This disruption in the wheat-flour supply chain is just one example of how the backlog of trains impacted industry in the region.

It is interesting that cars were not available on the eastern edge of the region, as the blockades had little impact there. Many cars had likely either been commandeered to haul fuel to the western prairies or, less likely at this early stage, parked in the snow on sidetracks in western Minnesota.

It appears that in mid-December, just about every grain elevator along the railroad lines was full to overflowing, proving the potential of the miraculous soil and growing conditions of the region. The vital railroad infrastructure to transport the bounty, however, was lacking.

On December 28, the *Janesville Argus* reported that the Winona & St. Peter had been able to begin emptying at least some of the elevators. "Cars began to be harvested again the past week," wrote the Janesville editor, "and the boys began taking in wheat once more. We hope the crop may yield bountifully and be well secured. Later. – Another drought."[296] In that same edition, the editor presumed,

"The western country must be improving fast. The Ortonville elevator has already received over 100,000 bushels of wheat this season."[297] It is probable that the phrase "improving fast" was not referring to the weather of the previous month or two, but to the fact that the region was being settled, plowed, planted, and harvested.

Fuel

"The railroad company reduced the freight on soft coal one dollar per ton to help the poor man. . . . The price of fuel is doing more to damn this country than all the live men in this town can do to save it. We trust the management of the northwestern company will give this question their earliest attention."[298]

—*Dakota News*, December 13, 1880

The cry for fuel continued, and the *Brookings County Press* reminded people that the superintendents of the lines were doing their best. Superintendent Egan of the Southern Minnesota was offering "free transportation to the farmers along that line if they will club together and get their wood in five or six car load lots."[299]

Prior to the storm of December 4, short articles appeared across the region encouraging residents to order their fuel early in the season,[300] an admonishment hardly useful at the time of print, but likely stored away in the memories of residents for coming years. In Egan, three newly received carloads of wood caused the editor to note, "The sight of it alone makes us feel warm."[301]

An interesting item appeared in the Milbank paper: It recorded that "storekeepers find it necessary to keep up good fires all night during this sharp weather. Last Sunday morning some of them found more or less of their bottled goods frozen, and the bottles cracked."[302]

The storm of December 4 lasted approximately two days, and the blockade along the Winona & St. Peter stood about five days. Not long, but enough to rattle the nerves of settlers and irritate the editors.

As mentioned earlier, December was cold, and "the fuel question" continued to consume column space and considerable emotional energy. The Milbank editor further chided his readers with a warning that if the residents themselves did not properly prepare by "ordering their fuel in the summer, when cars are plenty and transportation uninterrupted," they'd be at the mercy of the railroad companies who would have planned ahead by stockpiling fuel at each station, then charging "higher prices than now to pay them for the investment . . . so long ahead of the winter demand."[303]

While most editors talked about coal and wood, one looked for possible alternatives. "If some invention could be secured by which power could be converted into heat," wrote the Ortonville editor, "the fuel question would be solved. Our prairie winds will furnish the power, if Edison will furnish the machine."[304]

The editor of the *Grant County Review* in Milbank, along the Hastings & Dakota, again scolded those who continued to complain that the railroad was not doing enough to ensure that the area had fuel. "We have no doubt," he empathized, "that in many places the supply of fuel has run very short, but we are not prepared to wholly blame the railway company for such shortage. The sudden and unprecedented cold snap caught all hands unprepared."[305]

In the next issue, the Milbank paper shared a lengthy article that had appeared in the *St. Paul Globe,* further shaming those who groused:

> Mr. C. H. Prior, superintendent of the Chicago, Milwaukee, & St. Paul railway [on behalf of the Hastings & Dakota], visited [Minnesota] Governor Pillsbury. . . . Mr. Prior explained to him what the company had done and engaged to do and satisfied him that no effort or expense would be spared. . . . He stated that another wood train was sent out on the road yesterday and more would follow, and that until an ample supply has been placed at the prairie stations wood cars and wood trains will have the right of way as against any other business on the road. He stated also that the company is now in receipt at Oskaloosa, daily, fifty tons of coal of which about thirty tons will be required for operating the road, leaving twenty tons daily for distribution among the villages along the line. The extension line of the H. & D. . . . is reopened and is kept open by employing whatever force the day may require."[306]

Conditions were not much different along the Winona & St. Peter, where numerous communities experienced a scarcity of fuel, though Springfield noted that some wood arrived when the blockade from early in the month lifted.[307] On the western end, in Watertown, it was "18 degrees below zero and Van Dusen & Co., have sent 1 car load of soft coal to supply the hundreds who need it." The residents were "under great obligations to them for their foresight. They could not get along without them."[308] The town was resupplied when "four car loads of coal" rolled into town a week before Christmas.[309]

Residents were not the only ones hurting for coal. At least one railroad company was experimenting with "alternate fuels" for its locomotives: "The St. Paul & Sioux City is burning corn in their engines in some instances. Coal is scarce with railroads as well as other people it appears."[310]

While wood appeared to be piling up and pouring out of Eagle Lake (just east of Mankato) to fulfill orders along the Winona & St. Peter, it remained scarce in towns approximately sixty miles to the west. Where available, it was chopped, split, sold to a dealer, and hauled away to the waiting, hungry stoves across the prairie. A resident of Sioux Falls went as far east as Mankato to contract for wood,[311] while the newspaper in Springfield noted that wood was scarce there.[312]

Out and About

"Notwithstanding the extreme cold weather the saw and hammer of the carpenter are heard all over town."[313]

—*Fort Pierre Weekly Signal*, December 4, 1880

Travels

The number of people that were coming and going seems higher in December than in other winter months, likely due to a combination of holiday visits, vacations, and people returning east for the winter.

Building and Trading

At the Missouri River, Fort Pierre was a haven of activity throughout December despite the cold weather. The sound of hammers and saws reverberated in the subzero air as new buildings were constructed at a fever pitch. Merchants moved out of makeshift structures and into fresh buildings, and grocery stores opened and touted their own wares over those of competitors.[314]

While Fort Pierre was across the Missouri River from the western terminus of the Dakota Central and was the main gathering spot along the Missouri River between Yankton and Bismarck, people were not content to simply stop there. In early December, the Wyoming Stage Company commenced daily service between Fort Pierre and Rapid City, Dakota Territory, with plans to operate throughout the winter.[315]

Meanwhile, back in Brookings, the town was bustling. The roads were dry and good for teams and wagons to travel upon, and the editor "heard several of our merchants complain . . . that they could not wait on customers fast enough, and in many cases customers got tired of waiting and went away."[316] True to the Christmas season, packages flooded the post office with gifts headed—and received from—elsewhere.[317]

Community Building

For new towns working to build a sense of community, social activities were critical. With harvest nearing completion and December's weather relatively cooperative, there were plenty of opportunities. A New England supper was held on December 22 at the Methodist church in Watertown.[318] Dances were held in Aurora and Volga on December 23, and both "were pleasant affairs" with "a large attendance."[319] On Christmas Eve in Brookings, about twenty "young folks assembled . . . and danced until the wee hours,"[320] and oyster suppers were in vogue for all manner of gatherings.[321] These are just a small sampling of the activities across the region.

The Christmas storm impacted school attendance, though several communities noted that even if the weather hadn't been bad, the holidays would have kept students home.[322] In Egan, the Literary and Social Society cancelled its meeting scheduled for December 29, with plans to reschedule to January 5.[323]

Newspapers and Mail

"We are again compelled to issue a half sheet by reason of the non-arrival of our ready-print papers. The trials of the newspaper men along the H. & D., during the blockade are many, and most of our brethren along the line find themselves in the same unfortunate position that we are in."[324]

—*Grant County Review*, December 16, 1880

While the December storms were relatively minor overall, newspaper operations and mail delivery began to experience irregularities.

The *Murray County Pioneer* in Currie and the *Grant County Review* in Milbank both apologized for printing half-sheet editions, as their paper had not arrived via train. In Brookings, there were complaints about the mail not arriving: "A wreck and too much snow in Minnesota caused the delay. No snow here."[325]

While other towns were missing paper and news to put to print, the *Grant County Review* in Milbank was missing actual equipment: "The *Review* thinks that its troubles have been particularly annoying. One of our presses has been on the road over two months, and another is stuck in the blockade." Additionally, "our supply of paper has become almost exhausted and we consequently are obliged to issue half a sheet this week, which we trust our readers will excuse under the circumstances."[326]

Another consequence of delayed mail was that when it did come through, the postmaster had a big job to accomplish, often with anxious residents awaiting their pickup. "A huge batch of mail was received at the postoffice on Sunday morning," wrote the *Grant County Review*, "the first that had come through for a week."[327] Articles such as this appeared all winter, often with a tally of how many hours it took to get it sorted and distributed.

Boosterism

"Our citizens, as far as practicable, should support each other, and thus build up the town and its interests."[328]

—*Dakota News*, December 27, 1880

"It has been decided that the use of the word blizzard has a tendency to deter immigration, so we've dropped it."[329]

—*Marshall Messenger*, December 31, 1880

The two quotes above so perfectly sum up boosterism and how it worked that they will be allowed to stand here on their own.

January 1881

Sunday	Monday	Tuesday	Wednesday	Thursday	Friday	Saturday
						1 ///////// cold NW wind
2 ///////// cold pleasant (west) snow (east)	3 −20	4 mild sleet	5 cold blizzardous	6 cold blizzardous	cold −20F daytime −35F nighttime	7 cold −20F daytime −35F nighttime
8 cold −20F daytime −35F nighttime	9 cold −20F daytime −35F nighttime	10 cold −20F daytime −35F nighttime	11 cold −20F daytime −35F nighttime	12 cold −27F NW wind	13 −27F, −20F daytime considerable snow	14 ///////// cold
15 cold	16 /////////	17 /////////	18 ///////// rain	19 ///////// pleasant rain	20 windy cold blizzardous	21 windy
22 warmer 10F stormy	23 mild	24	25 colder, drifting pleasant (west)	26 pleasant (west) boistrous (east)	27 pleasant (west) splendid sleighing	28 ///////// pleasant (west) flurries, not cold (east)
29 pleasant (west)	30 windy 3' snowfall	31				

▬▬▬▬ Blizzard or significant snow event

///////// Lighter snow or mixed precipitation

January 17: Watertown reported ice on Lake Kampeska 3–3.5 feet thick.

January 20: Pipestone reported "4 days without a blizzard."

January 27: Pipestone reported "last Friday and Saturday were two of the most trying days."

January 28: Pipestone and "Marshall reported "snowbanks 30 or 40 feet high in spots."

Last January storm: "Heaviest fall of snow in Minnesota thus far this season."

This calendar shows weather reports gleaned from the various newspaper articles.
If the weather was significantly different in one portion of the region versus another, that is noted.

January was downright "blizzardous," to borrow a beautiful word from the editors. It was cold, it was windy, and it was snowy. As a result, the railroads began their prolonged battle against the elements. Large crews, both paid and volunteer, took up shovels and braced themselves against the elements in hopes of getting a train into their towns or to the towns of those "to the west" who were reported as destitute. This effort was successful several times during January, but freight cars were already snowed in on sidetracks up and down the lines, and accidents involving snowplows and vulnerable shoveling crews became a sad and frequent reality.

Coal and wood supplies were not yet critically short, but shortages were widespread enough that alternative fuels, such as hay, were employed. With train service becoming inconsistent, travel by wagon road, by sleigh, or on foot became the only reliable options. Community activities increased in number, though were sometimes cancelled because of snow, cold, or both.

Due to the increased unreliability of trains, alternate plans for mail delivery were established. Newspaper editors became more and more frustrated with the lack of supplies—whether paper or information—making it harder to keep their readers informed. Prior to January, most instances of boosterism were general and positive. Now, however, instances of the "angry retort" became more prevalent, even humorous.

The Month for the Ingalls Family

> "The sun was setting so red that it colored the frosted
> windowpanes. It gave a faintly rosy light to the kitchen. . . .
> But Laura thought there was a change in the sound of the wind,
> a wild and frightening note."[330]
>
> —*The Long Winter*

A herd of antelope raised the hopes of the hungry citizens, longing for some meat to supplement their diets. In the novel, the hunt was unsuccessful[331]—though in reality, Charles did shoot an antelope, which was shared among the hunters.[332] A low cloud in the northwest added a sense of urgency to the novel's events, though the menace subsided and did not develop into a storm. Nevertheless, Pa remained uneasy. He hauled more hay to replenish supplies for the stock and stove, also bringing home four pounds of beef, courtesy of a neighbor who shared a butchered oxen with the townspeople.[333]

Along with the beef, Pa also brought home a bombshell—the train would not be coming. The Tracy Cut had proven insurmountable. Efforts to clear the tracks were done for the winter. A superintendent from the East had come out to fix the situation. After making an effort and failing, he called off all future efforts until spring. This episode, which appears in the autobiographies as well as the novel, will be further explored at the end of the chapter.[334]

Only a few times throughout the entire Little House series does Ma outwardly lose her temper. More than one of those outbursts occur in *The Long Winter*. During what is arguably one of her most adamant outbursts, she vents her anger at the superintendent for abandoning them—for leaving them isolated without food or fuel—to fend for themselves against the blizzards: "'Patience?' Ma exclaimed. 'Patience! What's his patience got to do with it I'd like to know! He knows we are out here without supplies. How does he think we are going to live till spring? It isn't his business to be patient. It's his business to run the trains.'"[335] Pa calmly reassured the family that they would be able to get through the winter alright.[336]

As the next blizzard raged, life meant being confined to a small physical space with minimal warmth, food, and light. Days revolved around grinding wheat and twisting hay, heeding the howling winds and the despair they begot. Minds were becoming numb, and spirits low.

The aforementioned treat of beef aside, food for the family became more monotonous, with potatoes, brown bread, tea, and a small amount of sugar being the tally. Hay became the sole source of heat.

At this point, Wilder wrote of additional blizzards, varying in duration, without detail. A high point for the month, a tunnel formed following one of the undescribed blizzards, allowing Pa to care for the animals without exposure to the elements.[337]

Snow was described as being level with the second floor of the buildings one day, only to be scoured away by winds the next, something that appears in both the autobiographies and novel.[338] That same phenomenon was compacting the snow in the railroad cuts. But it wasn't the weather that presented the emotional low point of January. When Laura requested that Pa play a song on his fiddle to raise everyone's spirits, "every note from the fiddle was a little wrong." The narrative continued,

'My fingers are too stiff and thick from being out in the cold so much, I can't play.' Pa spoke as if he were ashamed. He laid the fiddle in its box. 'Put it away, Laura, until some other time,' he said. . . . Laura listened to the winds while she stared at the blank window without seeing it. The worst thing that had happened was that Pa could not play the fiddle. If she had not asked him to play it, he might not have known that he could not do it.[339]

A thing that had always given the family a sense of peace and security was gone. This emotional turning point in the novel mirrored this deepest, darkest time of the winter, though February would be little better. The first three months of 1881 would prove significantly more trying than the last three of 1880.

The Weather

"A telegram came raring and charging and cavortin' down the telegraph line on Friday last, from the beyond (snow blockade) . . . certainly is a great country out that way."[340]

—*Janesville Argus*, January 4, 1881

The Christmas storm marked the beginning of the end for the trains. With a few exceptions, which the various newspapers noted with excitement, January saw trains spend much less time rolling along the tracks than the railroad employees and volunteers spent travailing—and failing—to keep them clear.

January was recorded as being especially cold and windy. Reports of nighttime lows in the –20s and –30s were common across the region for much of the month, and existing snow was blown around, creating new drifts and new problems. A "wind event" causing a three-day blockade was reported on January 5. Once cleared, the track was open for four days before the storm of January 12 caused things to close up again.[341]

Blizzards and lighter snowstorms were intermittent, interspersed with rain on January 18 and 19, though a pleasant thaw brought some respite near the end of the month before yet another blizzard. A midmonth article from Watertown joked, "Still the 'oldest settler' will tell you the weather is nice and not very cold. But one thing is certain, it is dry—no mud or slush is mixed up with the other unpleasantness."[342]

True to the pioneer spirit, the "silver lining" of hard, mud-free, and frozen roads was a blessing among the rest. In addition, ice was thick on the area lakes, making the harvest of ice a productive expenditure of time. As Ma would say, "There's no great loss without some gain."[343]

On January 20, the Pipestone editor noted it had been four days since the last blizzard, giving merchants a chance to harvest the three-foot-thick ice and pack it down for summer use.[344] Ice on Lake Kampeska, on the western edge of Watertown, was similarly reported to be "three to three and a half feet thick" and "clear as a crystal."[345]

Aside from noting the cold temperatures, the papers in January contained relatively few weather-specific reports. Trains went through Brookings on January 10 and 19, hinting that the weather had been cooperative enough to allow shovelers to stay ahead of the drifted cuts for a portion of January.[346] In a poetic, tongue-in-cheek exclamation, the Brookings paper printed one of the few mentions of blizzards west of the border: "If blizzards were only beautiful streams, dotted will mill sites! With what ecstasy should we see them dammed!"[347]

The Storm of January 12

A January 19 article from New Ulm titled "Another Blizzard" began with a description of the previous week's storm but quickly spoke of the resulting blockade and a delay of mail. About the storm, it noted, "On Wednesday evening of last week the familiar northwest wind began to whirl a quantity of light snow through the air, continuing in the work during the following night and the greater part of Thursday."[348] The *Egan Express* did not describe the storm, but did share that it caused a scheduled sociable to be canceled.[349]

"The days are becoming quite perceptibly longer," wrote the Milbank editor, "and kerosene bills accordingly growing charmingly less in proportion."[350] It is unclear whether he was referring to the amount of daylight starting to extend by mid-January, or if it was more of an abstract concept referring to the monotony of the weather.

The Currie editor dramatically and poetically noted, "The weather is blizzardous again. Oh the snow! The beautiful snow! We have been blessed (?) with such stormy weather during the past week..."[351] The "(?)" was in the original article, punctuating the sarcasm.

A Mirage

On January 9 or 16 (the article, published on January 20, noted the event as taking place on "Monday morning last," which could refer to either date), the residents of Pipestone, seventeen miles south of Lake Benton, were "treated to one of those beautiful mirages [sic] for which this country is noted." They marveled that the town of Verdi, fourteen miles to the north-northwest, "seemed not more than a mile distant while the village of Lake Benton laid at our very door."[352] Mirages are "caused by the bending of light rays (refraction) in layers of air of varying density."[353] While they are most often seen at sea or over bodies of water, they can also appear on land. Under certain conditions, mirages can make distant objects appear above or below their actual locations, inverted, or even distorted—larger or taller.

The Storm of January 21

In Pipestone, January 21 and 22 were noted as "two of the most trying days we have had this winter." For both days, the "wind blew a perfect gale from the northwest, piling snow in all sorts of shapes."[354] Temperatures were above zero, a fact the editor was grateful to relay. Just a week later, on January 31, there "was a delightful breeze. . . . Only about three feet more snow."[355]

Aside from publishing the daily weather records kept by a citizen in Currie, the small-town newspapers kept fairly quiet about the storm of January 21–22. The *Minneapolis Tribune*, however, published a report that covered the entire region, stating, "The snow-storm . . . had not abated up to midnight, upwards of a foot having fallen, with the prospect of a very general blockade of all the railroads."[356] The heaviest snows appear to have fallen in southwestern Minnesota, and they were "accompanied on the prairies by a wind which was blowing it into drifts, the import of which the railroad man's imagination can best paint."[357]

By late January, Watertown was also glad to note the weather was not only warmer but even "very pleasant." The town's newspaper hinted that a January thaw attempted to make an appearance but was not quite successful.[358]

The Currie resident that kept daily weather records was named F. H. Barrows. For January, he noted fifteen days that experienced snow ranging from flurries to full-blown blizzards.[359]

The Railroads

"Not a train farther west than St. Peter for a week. Expect to get through to day, Superintendent Sanborn is out there spitting on his hands and swearing."[360]

—*Janesville Argus*, January 4, 1881

The Snowplows

As the winter wore on, the public perception of the snowplows regressed from *impressive industrial marvels* to *vessels of hope*, then to *symbols of despair*; if even the monstrous plows were incapable of conquering the insurmountable drifts, what was to bring the settlers hope and keep their fears at bay?

On the Hastings & Dakota, a snowplow cleared the tracks to Milbank (from Ortonville or more likely Montevideo, Minnesota, one might assume) on January 10, and passenger trains resumed the next day. The appearance of a train was news in itself, but the importance of mail could not be overstated, as conveyed when the Milbank paper wrote, "Mail that had accumulated along the road for a couple of weeks was received, whereat the hearts of all rejoiced with exceeding great joy."[361] Before the paper had a chance to go to press, however, another blizzard hit and blocked the line.

West of Sleepy Eye, a procession of eleven teams was needed to resupply a locomotive that ran out of coal while pushing a plow.[362] Snowplows were critical for clearing the tracks, but pushing one caused the locomotive to consume more fuel than if merely pulling a train—an added concern at a time when settlers were already struggling to maintain fuel supplies for basic survival.

Even when the blockades were opened and it wasn't storming, blowing snow drifted over the rails. A preferred method of keeping the rails clear was to keep the trains running along the tracks, preventing buildup.

A Janesville resident described his experience riding on a train doing double duty, ramming through snowdrifts, stating it "required two engines and a snow plow to snake the train. Every now and then a bank would be struck and the train stalled. Then they would back up and take a run. The cars would grind and scrape along [and the passengers would] show they weren't afraid and there was no danger."[363]

Snow Bucking

Normal operating procedure was to keep trains rolling, with or without a plow, over the tracks frequently enough to prevent the snow from piling up. But as snowdrifts across the tracks became larger, the railroads resorted to "snow bucking." This procedure consisted of running a locomotive or two (and sometimes more), with a plow in the lead, into a drift at full speed in the hope it would break through. The process was often supplemented with shovelers, who would help break up the snow.

Sometimes this worked on the first attempt, but it often required multiple. On some occasions, they had to dig locomotives out of the snowbank (as we'll see at the end of the chapter, when we explore the story about the superintendent from the East). However, the snow wasn't always so deep as to trap a locomotive. West of Marshall, in late January, "the snow plow which went up the road the other day jumped the track near Gary, and ran out on the prairie about 40 feet."[364]

Snow bucking, February 1917. The shoveling crew is standing by to help move the broken-up snow away from the tracks. Photo courtesy of the Chicago & North Western Historical Society.

The storm of January 12 caused multiple blockades between St. Peter and New Ulm, in the eastern part of the region. A plow came from the west, starting in Sleepy Eye, and after nearly two days of effort, it broke through to New Ulm (about fourteen miles). It took an additional day and a half to reach St. Peter (an additional twenty-five miles), and the first westbound train since the blockades brought "fourteen bags of mail matter which kept the assistant postmaster busy for two or three hours before the same could all be distributed."[365]

Rumors Grow

As the snow blockades lingered and access to goods from the East became more tenuous, rumors saying that the railroad companies were planning to give up fighting the snow continued to circulate. The foundation for these rumors was likely a combination of general worry among the settlers and the shortening of longer newspaper articles. When reprinting content from other newspapers, editors would often omit critical details but retain sentences that focused on the expense and effort being expended without any reward in the end. Without full context, the articles were foreboding.

In *The Long Winter*, it was the beginning or middle of January when when Pa told his family there would be no more trains until spring.[366] In each extant version of Wilder's autobiography, the time frame for this announcement lacks chronology. The newspapers throughout the region continued to publish plenty about the wasted efforts of both railroad employees and dutiful volunteers as well as the hopelessness of getting ahead of the blowing, drifting snow.

The *Marshall Messenger* published an article saying that "from St. Peter west to Tracy all trains have been suspended on the Chicago & Northwestern railway. Mr. Sanborn, the general manager has gone to St. Peter, and will hurry up matters as lively as possible."[367]

At the far western end of the Dakota Central, the *Fort Pierre Weekly Signal* told its readers that it not only held no prospects for a train reaching Pierre before the end of winter, but it wasn't entirely sure that one would arrive by summer.[368]

A careful reading of the multitude of alarming articles from mid to late January does not show a permanent suspension of work, but merely a blockage of trains while efforts to clear the tracks continued. Work may have been suspended for the duration of a storm but resumed once the conditions improved. We will examine the Tracy Cut and the incident involving the superintendent from *The Long Winter* in more detail at the end of the chapter.

Railroad Blockades

> "Oh the snow! the beautiful snow, Filling the cuts
> so the trains can't go."[369]
>
> —*Murray County Pioneer*, January 20, 1881

The post-Christmas blockade was longer than any since the October storm, and large brigades of shovelers, both volunteer and paid, trudged out of the scattered towns to battle the drifts. Trains made a brief return mid-January for one last gasp. The gray areas on the map below became the most troublesome locations along the Hastings & Dakota, the Winona & St. Peter, the Dakota Central, and the Southern Minnesota. For the most part, it would be over three months before trains could venture past them.

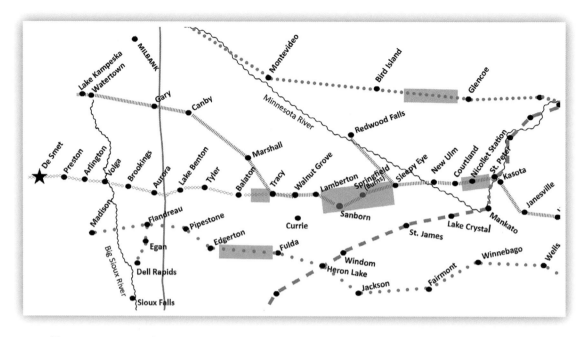

The gray areas on the map above became the most troublesome locations along each line.

Along the Hastings & Dakota

In Milbank, in an effort to prevent drifting on the tracks, nearly all cuts between there and Ortonville had snow fences installed.[370] Despite these efforts, the snow was getting around, under, over, and through the fences. Settlers were also, on occasion, poaching wood from the fences for fuel.

After the Christmas storm, Milbank had to wait a week and a half between trains. The blockade was briefly lifted on January 4;[371] then winds caused drifting that again hindered travel. Neither mail nor supplies were coming in, and the editors were unable to provide "any news from the outside world."[372] The blockade was again cleared by Monday, January 17, and trains began to run. The track was open for four days before the next blizzard came through.[373]

With appreciation, the *Grant County Review* in Milbank noted that "the officers of the H. & D. have done all in their power . . . to clear obstructions, and now that folks have found that other railroads were blockaded almost, if not quite, as badly as the H. & D., we hear less complaint against the latter."[374]

Things were starting to feel secure again. Then came the storm that initiated the final blockade. "Just as the railroad blockade had been cleared, all but a mile," wrote the Milbank editor, "the heavy snow of Monday drifted the cuts full again."[375]

Along the Winona & St. Peter

Along the Winona & St. Peter, the January papers devoted considerable column space to the blockades, which began with the Christmas storm. A major trouble spot emerged—the region starting less than a mile west of Sleepy Eye. Whether or not tracks west of the Tracy Cut were open, the trains, packed with goods, couldn't travel any farther west than Sleepy Eye, approximately fifty miles east of Tracy.

For a week after the Christmas storm, trains from the east reached no farther west than St. Peter.[376] West of Tracy, however, the tracks were "free from obstruction and trains over the Fort Pierre route were operated with regularity."

During the storm, "five engines and an east bound passenger train were snow bound at Nicollet Station, and four engines were caught at Springfield. Coal was hauled with teams from Sleepy Eye to Springfield to keep the engines at the latter named place alive." Another train was stuck at Walnut Station, showing that perhaps the heavy snow line lay between Walnut Grove and Tracy.[377]

One of the men who put together the *Dakota News* in Watertown jumped in to help shovel, as humorously reported by one of his colleagues: "The last we heard from our partner he was shoveling snow at Lamberton, Minnesota, or watching others shovel, we don't know exactly which, with prospects fair to reach Milwaukee some time in June."[378]

If the following article is to be believed, the newspaperman from Watertown mentioned above may have been battling unimaginable snowdrifts, reported to be thirty feet deep, according to a *Janesville Argus* reprint from the *Sleepy Eye Herald*. It went on to say, "To a person approaching them from a distance, the opening made by the shovels and the snow plow seems almost too narrow for a man to pass through. On the top of the snow bank, one can look down into the cut and see the train passing below him."[379]

Despite the weather's incessant hindering of progress, efforts to clear the road continued:

The Chicago & Northwestern railroad company is doing all in its power to keep the Winona & St. Peter road open, but so far the elements have been against it. The road from St. Peter west became again blockaded.... Trains at this writing are again running on regular schedule from Sleepy Eye east, but the largest portion of the western division [the Dakota Central] is still blockaded and it will be several days yet before trains will reach the terminus.[380]

The stretch from St. Peter to Sleepy Eye seemed to be as far west as the company was successful in maintaining operations. Reports were beginning to come in via telegraph and word of mouth, however, of people to the west suffering as a result of the blockades. This news brought out many civilians who were determined to get the trains through to help the destitute. From the beginning, there existed an uneasy symbiotic relationship between the settlers and the railroad, and an acknowledged kinship between the townspeople and railroad employees, who all needed to work together to get food and—possibly even more critical—fuel to the settlers beyond the blockades.

On January 26, one hundred fifty men from New Ulm took up shovels and boarded a special train outfitted for snow removal. They rode west and set to work, and by midafternoon had cleared two miles of heavy drifts. Their location put them halfway to an engine that was stuck in the snow, "patiently waiting for the gallant force to relieve [it] from the unpleasant situation." The crew was "determined not to give up before readying the engine, and thereby aiding the people who [were] suffering on the western prairies for want of fuel and other necessities."[381]

Likewise, the town of Tracy sent forth sixty-four volunteers, a crew made up of "merchants, clerks, mechanics and laborers," who worked for four arduous days. In contrast to the New Ulm brigade, whose expressed intention was to aid the settlers on the western prairies, the men from Tracy complained that their efforts were "just so much time wasted." They had believed they would receive "the first train of fuel and supplies, but the train that was started to them was ditched near Lamberton bridge and before the wreck could be cleared away the road was again blockaded by snow."[382] Empathizing with the people of Tracy, the New Ulm editor scolded the railroad company for not standing behind their promise of supplies: "When people show themselves willing to assist the railroad . . . the railroad company should leave nothing undone to keep the settlers along the line of the road supplied with the necessaries of life."[383]

Mixed in with the volunteers from Tracy were a dozen or so citizens from Currie, who responded to the call to help to alleviate the "suffering condition" of those on the western end of the Dakota Central. These "able bodied men joined the shovel brigade and marched to the front to battle with 'the beautiful snow.'"[384]

The *Marshall Messenger* reported that "snow-drifts on the Winona & St. Peter . . . extend a distance of 100 miles, between Sleepy Eye and Lake Benton. Gangs of men are shoveling out the cuts. . . . With snow banks 30 or 40 feet high in spots, it is almost a hopeless task to try to keep the railroad open." The company stated it intended to, during the coming summer, lay additional track to bypass the worst of the cuts.[385]

Reports continued to highlight the heroic efforts put forth to clear the tracks. (Imagine the calories expended—and at a time when nutritious food was harder to come by.) In Watertown, the editor noted, "The railroad employers and employees are battling with another railroad blockade, and laboring day and night to remove the snow and clear the track. The main trouble appears to be in Minnesota, between Tracy and Sleepy Eye."[386]

Along the Dakota Central

Very little specific information was found in the newspapers about efforts of the Dakota Central during January, except that it was "having a devil of a time with the snow."[387]

A piece that ran in the *Volga Gazette* and was reprinted in multiple regional newspapers in late January and early February read, "It seems to be an impossibility to keep the road open between Sleepy Eye and Tracy. They no sooner get a train through when along comes another blizzard and fills up the cuts again. The railroad company are doing all any human power can do to keep the road clear."[388] While the stretch of rail mentioned is along the Winona & St. Peter, it directly impacted the towns along the Dakota Central.

Along the Southern Minnesota

Conditions along the Southern Minnesota were just as bleak. On January 6, the *Pipestone Star* shared that four hundred shovelers were at work on various cuts along the tracks of the Southern Minnesota, though the storms were making their efforts futile. In town, twenty-five men had worked to clear the depot, and all suffered frostbite.[389]

On January 4, Egan reported its first train since the post-Christmas blockade, only to see the tracks close up again a mere two days later.[390] That blockade was cleared, but did not remain open for long, for the *Egan Express* of January 20 reported that there had been no train since January 12, and prospects were not good for the foreseeable future. The Southern Minnesota was blockaded for the better part of January, and "about half a million bushels of grain were stored in different elevators and warehouses along the road, awaiting shipment."[391]

The storm of January 21 essentially closed the roads for good, despite ongoing efforts that would continue throughout the winter. For two days in Pipestone, "the wind blew at a perfect gale . . . All cuts on the railroad are again piled full and just when we will get a train it is hard to tell."[392]

The *Egan Express* was optimistic when it printed, "As we go to press we understand the prospects are good for a train to get through sometime tomorrow."[393]

Based on the previous months, expectations were likely that snow would fall, winds would blow, cuts would fill, shovelers would shovel, and trains would roll. The possibility that there would be no trains for several months was not yet seen as realistic.

The *Volga Gazette* wasn't the only paper to publish a note of dismay at the end of January. The *Egan Express* let out its own plaintive cry when it printed, "It is said that patience and perseverance will accomplish almost everything, but thus far they have failed to raise the blockade. When, O, when will the blockade be raised and the trains be running regularly again?"[394]

January experienced several less-severe snow events that continued the cycle of blockades, efforts to clear them, and hope. An article in the January 27 *Egan Express* acknowledged the shared frustration but also reminded readers that this was a more widespread issue, extending beyond Dakota Territory:

> For the past six weeks we have had very severe winter weather, in fact the worst that has been known in this country for years. Blizzard has succeeded blizzard so closely that it has been a hard matter to determine when one ceased and another commenced. During the time mentioned, but three or four trains have reached this place owing to the blockade in Minnesota. . . . As soon as the wind would cease blowing and the snow flying, the railroad company commenced opening the road, but would scarcely get the track clear ere the wind again filled the cuts with snow, and made the operation of clearing them more difficult than before. Such has been the condition of things on this line of road, but let us assure our readers that it has been no worse here than in other parts of the country, and not near so bad as in many localities.[395]

Railroad employees often went above and beyond the call of duty that winter, as when the Pipestone station agent moved into the depot. The paper reported, "Charlie Cawley now lodges at the depot so as to be on hand for all trains day or night. His repose hasn't been broking much lately."[396] It may be that his previous lodging was not sufficient to withstand the cold—a convenient move either way. Despite efforts like this, the weather continued to overpower the railroads. Some of the worst storms were yet to come.

Along the Sioux City

It was noted that the Sioux City, which ran on a northeast–southwest diagonal, was not as prone to becoming blocked by snow as the other lines, all of which generally ran east–west. Nonetheless, the late-January storm was enough to cause a blockade on that line, too, and must have caused extra alarm among the settlers.

More and more articles talked of the futility of trying to keep the tracks clear. Editors focused on praising the railroad companies for their efforts, noting the exorbitant costs of those attempts, and further shared that some locations were out of food and fuel.

Flandreau's *Moody County Enterprise* published a winter-in-review article with details similar to those in other published summaries. However, it added the perspective that the railroad was experiencing economic hardship due to the loss of revenue-producing traffic, both passenger and freight, and the monumental cost of fighting the snow. "Business is necessarily at a stand still," wrote the Flandreau editor. The article continued,

> The elevators and warehouses are full so that no wheat can be bought and the frequent storms keep the roads bad and prevent people coming to town to trade.... The Southern Minnesota is expending over a thousand dollars a day in their efforts to keep the road open and is probably losing another thousand dollars a day in loss of business. It is safe to say that another winter will find the railroads leading into this country protected against snow by every means that can be devised.[397]

Aside from articles about wheat buyers, the article above is one of the few that mentioned the difficulties of businessmen trying to conduct business. It was also one of a small number that explicitly noted that there were towns without groceries or fuel, though again, it did not name names.

Blaming "the East" – Particularly Minnesota

Part boosterism, part reality, and part little white lie, the newspapers of Dakota Territory began to imply that the real source of the blockade problem was found to the east, that Dakota was an innocent bystander, and that, therefore, people should not hesitate to continue their plans to settle in the region (come spring). As the next few months progressed and spring travel season approached, there was an abundance of articles extolling the benefits of Dakota Territory in general and the advantages of a specific region or town in minutiae.

For the problems they were experiencing, however, someone had to be at fault. While the railroads sometimes found themselves in the blame-game crosshairs, the newspapers were much more likely to, instead, praise their local railroad employees. But during January—in the heart of a cold, dark upper-Midwest winter—the narrowed eyes of frustration and suspicion were cast upon Minnesota, which many considered the cause of all the troubles in eastern Dakota Territory. Below are some noteworthy examples:

"The Dakota tracks are all clear. It is the eastern storms that block our trains, and they are annoyingly blocked just now."[398]

—*Brookings County Press*

"Railroad travel has been quiet for several days, owing to too much now in Minnesota, and that the said Minnesota should be suppressed? / It's a fact worthy of note that thus far no railroad blockade has existed in Southern Dakota, during the present winter, while in Minnesota, Wisconsin, Iowa, Illinois, and in fact everywhere east and south, blockades have been almost perpetual."[399]

—*Egan Express*

"The blockade continues. Our Dakota line is open, but those Minnesota fellows keep up such a snowing and blowing as to keep us cut off from the east. A motion to have Minnesota suppressed is in order. Perhaps delegate Bennett can help the matter by getting congress to make Lake Michigan our eastern boundary."[400]

—*Brookings County Press*

Tracks Clogged with Cars

On January 13, the *Egan Express*, along the Southern Minnesota, reported that "there are 500 cars between Egan and La Crosse, loaded with freight for the west."[401]

Snide comments about railroad officials and their fancy cars appeared now and then throughout the winter, as in a piece from the feisty editor of the *Janesville Argus* saying that a "correspondent . . . says the wheat blockade still continues [in New Richland, Minnesota,] . . . for want of cars. The Minneapolis & St. Louis should send down that $20,000.00 president's car and haul off a few loads."[402]

When less-elegant cars could make their way westward, they could not always return. Flandreau's paper observed that "26 cars loaded with wheat" were stranded there, "awaiting shipment."[403] At midmonth, Pipestone made note that "many carloads of fuel and other stuff are lying on the side tracks east of here."[404]

By the end of January, carloads of wood were sidetracked along the Southern Minnesota. "Wood! O, would to God that the trains would get through and bring some wood. / Several car loads of wood are on the road consigned to parties at this place, but the Lord only knows when it will get here."[405] Based on articles mentioned in earlier chapters, it can be surmised that crews with sleds obtained the wood and distributed it to residents around the area.

Other Railroad Business

"The east bound train on Wednesday of last week, jumped the track four miles west of Fulda, and shook things up pretty lively."[406]

—*Pipestone Star*, January 20, 1881

Expansion Work

Reports to this point have been rather demoralizing. Lest we get too mired down, let's check in with other activities. It was not all fruitless snow throwing for the railroads.

Along the Hastings & Dakota

In Milbank, "the engine at the round elevator was started up on Monday, after having been shut down nearly a month, and a large quantity of wheat that had accumulated was shipped off."[407]

Along the Winona & St. Peter and the Dakota Central

Whether due to eternal optimism, gritty stubbornness, or plain ol' denial, the Chicago & North Western announced that around February 1, a new Lightning Train—a rapid transit service between Chicago and Tracy with a midway stop at Winona—would commence operations.[408] We can assume that the planned offering missed its inaugural run in early February.

A fancy new hotel with a first-rate eating house was planned for Tracy. It would be built between the tracks of the Winona & St. Peter and the Dakota Central so as to serve passengers on each.[409]

The *Dakota News* of January 17 announced that the railroad planned to add a large coal house and icehouse to the already-constructed railroad structures in place at Watertown.[410]

Along the Southern Minnesota

Despite the reduction in train travel, a new timetable for the Southern Minnesota was issued as the tracks to Dell Rapids, Dakota Territory, were officially opened to traffic.[411]

A boxcar being used as a temporary depot. Photo courtesy of the
Chicago & North Western Historical Society.

The increased traffic warranted the expansion of eating houses, freight houses, warehouses, and hotel space.[412] Sometimes this expansion was actual construction. Other times, it was the efficient appropriation of what was handy, as when the Southern Minnesota pulled one of its railroad cars out of rotation and turned it into a temporary depot in Egan, planning to "erect one of the nobbiest depots on the road" come spring.[413]

The residents were looking to expansion to solve problems too. The *Moody County Enterprise* of January 27 expressed,

The people of this section all hope that the Chicago Milwaukee & St. Paul Railroad Company, will next season complete the Southern Minnesota line between Dell Rapids and Sioux Falls. The line from Sioux City to Sioux Falls has not been blockaded for more than two days at any time this winter and the 75 miles of track now operated by the Southern Minnesota east of Edgerton has been practically open all the time and had the line been completed to Sioux Falls the towns of Edgerton, Pipestone, Flandrau, Dell Rapids and Madison might [have] had quite regular railroad communications all winter.[414]

Wrecks and Accidents

Serving as a snow shoveler for the railroad was dangerous on multiple fronts. It was severely cold, and clothing was often of dubious quality for the conditions. Reports of frostbitten hands and feet were plentiful. The snow was thick and heavy—and often compressed to solid ice. In many cases, the crews were miles away from towns where shelter could be sought should a storm have borne down.

While the image one may have is of the wide-open prairie, being in a cut could insulate the men from the sound and sight lines of the few oncoming trains, making them vulnerable to being run down. Sadly, this happened multiple times.

One unfortunate group of seven men was left in a narrow and deep cut by the work train that brought them out "when a passenger train came along at full speed and it is supposed the draught created by its rapid movement drew them under the wheels, and all were frightfully and fatally mangled except one, who had a leg taken off."[415]

Sometimes the wrecks merely involved cars derailing; that is, the wheels came off the rails, but the cars remained upright. *Merely*, of course, is not an appropriate term, as these cars needed to be rerailed—not a quick endeavor: "A portion of a freight car got off the track near Nicollet yesterday morning delaying the west-going train nearly three hours."[416]

It wasn't only railroad employees and volunteers who were present at the cuts, either. In one instance, a resident of New Ulm went out to a nearby cut to observe activities. J. C. Zieske, a future state representative,

took a stroll up to the track last Saturday to see if the boys were doing their duty, and if not, to set them aright. The Hon. gent placed himself alongside of a drift through which the snow plow had to go (hands in pockets) in order to be ready to give directions. While he was standing in this position the engine came along to the satisfaction of all; but Mr. Z.

who was standing on solid snow was thrown several feet over a snow fence and buried alive in the snow. After a few minutes spading he was extricated from his cool and disagreeable position when he was heard to say: "The blockade is open, boys, good-bye."[417]

In late January, a freight train became stuck in the snow four miles from Lamberton, Minnesota. Another freight train came along and hit the stuck train, "smashing up the caboose and demolishing the snow plow, pilot and headlight of the engine." (A locomotive's *pilot* is the structure mounted on its front to deflect obstacles. It has been colloquially referred to as a "cowcatcher" or "cow plow.") A worker on the stuck train swore he "had sent out a flagman with signals to the rear and the other conductor [claimed] that he did not or could not see it."[418]

Demolishing the snow plow—with just a little imagination, you can almost hear the collective gasps of the readers up and down the Winona & St. Peter and the Dakota Central as they learned of the destruction of one of the pieces of equipment vital to raising the blockades, and thus that there was one less protection against isolation.

Food

"We understand that some sneak thief stole 60 bushels of oats . . .
a short time since."[419]

—*Egan Express*, January 6, 1881

Moving west to east across the region, most communities claimed to have plenty of food, with assorted reports of shortages. When reports of true scarcity did come in, they were almost never identified to a specific location or family.

Fort Pierre was still enjoying the benefits of its location. It had experienced cold, but not much snow, the bulk of the storms having swept down just north and east of it. Its supply line remained intact, with teams filling the gap, likely running from the railhead at Sioux Falls or Yankton and carrying goods cross-country. Thus, the newspapers were full of what must have made for torturous, mouthwatering reading to those in more isolated settlements in the areas hit the hardest. A noteworthy example:

> If you are in want of a lunch or oysters at any hour of day or night
> call at Snow's restaurant.

Fresh roll butter at Sparks & Allen's.
Fresh ranch eggs at Sparks & Allen's.
Buckwheat flour, self raising at DeGraff's.
Vermont maple syrup at Sparks & Allen's.[420]

In Watertown, there were mentions of the bounties held within the walls of the various merchants, obtainable for the exchange of legal tender—or possibly whatever the merchant was willing to accept in barter. One merchant had "thirty or forty barrels of good, solid apples for sale . . . at the low rate of $1,50 per barrel. . . . for the purpose of closing them out before moving into their new quarters."[421]

A merchant in Currie, just south of Tracy, openly advertised, "Good fresh stock, and reasonable prices at Bryan's. Butter, eggs, hides, fur, grain, and, in fact, all kinds of produce, wanted in exchange for goods."[422] And grocers were not the only avenue to obtain food. "Lots of fish are being speared in the Sioux now-a-days,"[423] wrote the Egan paper. The frozen lakes and rivers near Egan offered a solid foundation for people to stand upon while fishing for their dinners.

While fuel remained the primary concern expressed in print at this point, the accessibility of food was becoming a rising issue. With that said, two weeks later, the Egan newspaper bragged about healthy trade and the prosperity of the residents. This may have been accurate, it may have been simple boosterism, or it may have gone beyond, attempting to hide from others that life in the region was becoming one of empty stomachs, with spring far out on a distant horizon.

As previously discussed, reports of deprivation "in the prairie towns to the west" inspired people from less affected towns to take part in shoveling brigades for humanitarian purposes; however, very seldom was an exact location noted. It was almost always some vague place, in a vague direction, experiencing vague destitutions.

Fuel

"Wood will be $15.00 a cord for chips out west, when the road
gets open again, but after the next storm it won't be worth
any thing because there won't be any alive to use it. Gone to a
warmer clime where they don't use wood for heating."[424]

—*Janesville Argus*, January 4, 1881

As we've seen, the fact that most of the tracks were open throughout November and December did little to alleviate concerns about having enough fuel to last through the winter. January's weather deepened those concerns. Immediately following the breaking of the Christmas storm blockade, the Brookings paper reassured its readers, "Nobody hereabouts is suffering for fuel. Don't borrow trouble.... Stations along the line of our Northwestern Railroad are all congratulating themselves on having plenty of coal.... We seem in a fair way to enjoy our evenings 'by the moonlight alone.' The kerosene supply is about exhausted in town and the oil car is on a Minnesota switch!"[425]

One gentleman left Egan "for the Mankato woods where he will remain long enough to get out a year's supply of wood."[426] It is difficult to ascertain whether *the Mankato woods* was the name of a collection of trees near a river or creek in the area of Egan, or if he indeed went as far east as Mankato, Minnesota. Regardless, he had grand plans to bring back plenty of wood.

Farther south, near Yankton, a passenger train was unable to move due to lack of fuel. An improvisational "fifty bushels of corn were purchased," and the train was able to get as far as Elk Point, where it obtained coal.[427]

The train near Yankton was not the only one experiencing fuel problems. A strike in Iowa made things difficult for the Hastings & Dakota, farther to the north:

> The fuel famine is being transferred to the railroad companies. Owing to the strike at the Iowa coal mines, the Sioux City division of the Chicago, St. Paul Minneapolis & Omaha, has run short of fuel, and Superintendent Lincoln is with difficulty obtaining a sufficient supply to keep the engines moving. The trouble is not so bad on the St. Paul division, as part of the engines in use on it are wood-burners.[428]

All lines within the region relied upon the Oskaloosa coal mines, so this strike would have impacted each.

Editors often injected humor into situations to bring levity, as in this article about people routinely stealing wood in Sleepy Eye:

> Those who were out of wood helped themselves from the loaded cars detained here on their way to western points. Our shippers who are troubled to make the cords and car loads come out as it went in, can now understand how it 'shrinks so.' A phalanx of those hungry hay burning veterans charging on a seven cord load would be apt to make it shrink two or three shrinks.[429]

There were those who were unwilling to look at the situation with honest eyes—or fair ones, at least—and instead blamed the lack of fuel on the settlers, railroad companies, and dealers. One article from the *St. Paul Globe* illustrated why there may have been some significant animosity towards those "back East" when it came to the situation "out West."

According to the article, the executive and legislative committees of the Chamber of Commerce met to discuss transportation and fuel supply issues for the prairie communities. From their cozy and warm perch in St. Paul, they declared that there was already "an abundance of cheap fuel in the State to supply all needs, present and future." They also claimed that the existing infrastructure was able to transport the fuel to those who needed it.[430]

They then came down hard on the victims of the blockade, declaring that the "scarcity of fuel, which commenced October 25 and continued to the close of November, was the result of inexcusable carelessness on the part of consumers, dealers and railroad companies, and that the railroad companies and dealers were guilty of the greater carelessness." The "carelessness" they spoke of was a failure to plan for an especially harsh winter. The executives then softened a bit, acknowledging the uncommon severity of the season, for "only once before in twenty-seven years had there been such severe weather in November, and that as it is possible such weather may occur again in November, all fuel for the winter should be at the stations for which it is destined on or before November 1st each year."[431]

The article concluded with the committee's opinion: the settlers would learn a lesson from this winter and not repeat their foolishness. It did not, however, suggest any resolutions for the current winter and the hardships it was inflicting.[432]

Whatever the St. Paul chamber thought of the fuel shortage, the railroads were working to keep the supply flowing. On January 27, the *Pipestone Star* noted, "The Northwestern road has supplied its stations pretty well with fuel. Sorry we can't say the same for our road."[433]

Grousing aside, the Southern Minnesota, the line that ran through Pipestone, was indeed providing railroad ties to residents to burn as fuel. In Flandreau, the railroad sold ties "at cost, 32 cents a piece, . . . as cheap as wood at the prices that have prevailed here this winter."[434] On the open prairie, where trees were scarce but railroad-owned ties and snow fences were handy, it is not surprising that settlers also poached those items in parallel to their willing sale.

An article from Marshall in late January is intriguing: "Coal Stolen: Last Saturday night all the coal on the railroad platform, probably 3 tons or so, was stolen. [Another merchant] . . . also had some stolen which had been placed for the night near his shop."[435] Three tons of stolen coal should not have been difficult to chase down. The density of coal varies greatly depending on type. But, to form a visual, 3 tons of coal in a container with the same footprint as a standard twin-size mattress (39 by 75 inches, or 3¼ by 6¼ feet) would measure between 6 and 7½ feet deep. Or, for another visual, consider a 5-gallon bucket. Three tons of coal would require approximately 180 such buckets, each weighing approximately 33½ pounds.[436] Man or beast, wagon or sleigh—moving that coal would have required significant effort, and its path(s) should have been trackable. Perhaps the culprit was known and shared the contraband with his neighbors, or perhaps the culprit was the collective population of Marshall, using anything from coat pockets to wagon beds.

While Fort Pierre doesn't seem to have suffered any food shortage, fuel did become a concern by late January. "Coal is again exhausted," wrote the editor, "and if there is not wood enough in town, we will commence to play freeze out from now until spring."[437]

As the long, frigid month of January came to a close, the bridge that crossed the Big Sioux in Watertown found new purpose—helping preserve the lives of those who had crossed it on their way into Dakota Territory during the previous year. "The saw was heard in the land Tuesday morning," wrote the Watertown editor on January 31, "and in consequence thereof the railroad bridge over the Sioux is not so much of a structure as it used to be. . . . If the coal famine continues much longer the entire structure will undoubtedly be taken away, and it may prove to be dear fire wood to some." The same edition, which was published early to conserve fuel, noted that coal was being obtained from a neighboring town.[438]

Whether the fuel shortage was because of failings on the part of the railroad, settlers, or some combination of both, the reality was that people were cold—and in fear of getting colder.

Out and About

"Dull holidays. Blizzards and business are no acquaintances.
A whole week of Sunday."[439]
—*Janesville Argus*, January 4, 1881

Significant travel and visiting continued during January. People left eastern Dakota Territory to visit friends and family throughout the eastern states, or they went from town to town within the region. Oyster suppers were quite popular that winter, as were masquerades, literary societies, and singing schools. Sleighing was another favorite activity, and the papers regularly noted whether people were able to get out in their cutters ... or not.

If it wasn't snowing, people continued their lives, attending community events and church activities. School sessions were slightly spottier, but most towns continued to educate their children.

Travels

The blockades were not as severe on the eastern edge of the region, but that did not mean trains ran as scheduled. Humorously, people were reportedly heading north to escape the cold. One resident left Janesville for the warmer climes of Fargo, saying that it was "too cold down here" and that "he wants to go where he can wear out his summer clothes."[440] Another gentleman left Milbank for Canada, to "remain until spring."[441]

As seen in previous months, people embarked upon significant (in both volume and distance) travel despite the lack of trains. Locally, people from Brookings visited De Smet, and "Fuller, the hardware man, and man of many initials, who hails from De Smet," traveled to Brookings."[442] Fuller's hardware store, where Charles went to collect news between blizzards, was across the street from the Ingalls' building in De Smet. A footnote in *Pioneer Girl* details that the hardware man's full name was Charleton Sumner George Fuller, or C. S. G. Fuller, leading newspapers to refer to him as "Alphabetical Fuller."[443]

A humorous article printed in the *Janesville Argus* reflects the perception "back east" (Minnesota) of the conditions on the Dakota prairies. In it, a couple from Flandreau visited their friends in Janesville. According to their friends, the couple from Flandreau looked

> as happy and prosperous as of old and twice as natural. Evidently that
> country is doing well by our fellows and heaping lots of good things up to
> them. We thought it was all snow drifts out there and frozen skeletons of
> unfortunate pioneers, who having wandered a few rods from their doors,
> lay down and died, but not one of our fellows have done that yet or
> frozen, at least if they have they are mighty lively and jocose corpses, one
> of which we wouldn't mind being.[444]

One resident of New Ulm traveled to Pierre and back during the second half of January, demonstrating that despite the weather, travel over large stretches was still possible. If he followed the railroad tracks, this trip would have taken him through both Walnut Grove and De Smet. The article out of New Ulm did not indicate how he reached Pierre, but he returned "by train and team a portion of the way, while from Sleepy Eye to [New Ulm] he employed the foot express."[445] This article also shows that trains were running somewhere between New Ulm and Pierre, but it is not specific as to exactly where.

In her autobiographies, Wilder included an incident about a De Smet lawyer named Waters, who left town on foot in order to get to his own wedding in Massachusetts. In a letter, Almanzo explained to Rose that "when he started to walk out to a train the trane [sic] came as far as Tracy 100 miles but when he got to Tracy the snow had stoped [sic] the train some 70 miles farther east to New Ulm there he had to stay for 3 or 4 weeks to doctor his feet that had been partly frozen."[446]

Community Building

On the northern edge of the region, Milbank reported a large attendance at a New Year's Eve dance.[447] Later in the month, "the weather moderated very considerably," such that "one [could] look out of the window without first being obliged to scrape the frost off." The moderate weather also allowed farmers and other residents to ride into town to do some trading and shopping, giving the streets "a very animated and stirring appearance."[448] One Milbank resident "had a staunch little sleigh built, and evidently [took] lots of pleasure going sleigh riding."[449]

Similar to events in Milbank, Brookings reported that "numerous dances were held in the county New Years night." Additionally, "a pleasant dancing party met at the Commercial House [the evening of January 4], and tripped the light fantastic for several hours."[450] Brookings residents were also entertained when a group of runaway horses broke "the monotony of blockade life."[451]

In Watertown, someone observed, "Folks seem to be enjoying themselves to their hearts' content this winter. They are having a series of concerts, dances, masquerades, etc."[452] If anyone got bored, they could always go to observe the legal wranglings of their local peace officers. In Watertown, "a law suit before [Squire] Owsley last Tuesday caused a little excitement. . . . Anything for a change during the blockade."[453]

The residents of Watertown weren't the only ones that enjoyed watching legal proceedings unfold. The January 27 *Pipestone Star* noted there had been no lawsuits the past week due to stormy weather, and also that a lyceum [public lecture] was cancelled. That did not seem to deter one Mr. Wells, however: "Stage-driver Wells made his usual trip from Luverne [Minnesota] last Saturday. He has the right kind of grit."[454]

The *Egan Express* of Friday, January 20 noted that "school commenced . . . with 44 scholars in attendance." And due to the good weather, the wheat trade was described as "quite active." Social activities, however, were less reliable: "Owing to the storm of last Wednesday evening, no sociable was held," though residents were optimistic that a "social hop" would take place the following Friday.[455]

Newspapers and Mail

> "If any person desires to try the pleasures of 'running a newspaper' we advise them to make the attempt when the mail trains make a trip once a week or thereabouts."[456]
>
> —*Murray County Pioneer*, January 13, 1881

In December, Currie's *Murray County Pioneer* had been one of the first of the regional papers to succumb to publishing a half-sheet edition, at the time due to the nonarrival of printing paper. January did not lessen the paper's inconveniences. "The weather has been so severe for the past week or two," wrote the editor, "that no dependence could be placed in the mails on railroad trains, consequently, our paper may lack some of that interest for which it is noted."[457]

The editors seemed uniformly embarrassed and frustrated by the reduced substance of their papers and let their readers know that it wasn't for lack of wanting to provide a quality product.

Midmonth, Flandreau's *Moody County Enterprise* asked its readers not to censure the editor nor the railroad company for the half-sheet size of the edition, which was printed on colored paper. Instead, they were instructed to "blame those Minnesota blizzards." The publication's paper, which was shipped from Chicago weekly, failed to arrive.[458]

Nearby, Egan was likewise without paper, which was stuck in a blockade in Minnesota. In desperation, the *Egan Express* warned its readers that the paper they were holding may have been "printed on an old 'ready print' sheet; maybe on wrapping paper, or perchance on the off side of a big placard." It was "obliged to use anything [it] could get."[459]

It was in the wake of the January storms that mail delivery systems truly began to break down. The number of articles that spoke of the disappointment of delayed mail or, conversely, the excitement of receiving a delivery increased significantly, correlating directly with the disruption of trains. The arrival of a train was often treated as a lesser priority, secondary to the arrival of mail. Of course, the newspapers depended heavily upon the arrival of other newspapers and letters to populate their pages, so their focus may have been more attuned to the situation than the casual resident's was.

Though the worst of the blockades had not yet set in, the sense of isolation was building. The *Brookings County Press* shared its disappointment, reporting that "a mail train came through from the east last evening, but it left much of the mail behind somewhere, and prospects for another train are not brilliant at this writing."[460]

Attempting to brighten the moods of his own readers in Milbank, the editor of the *Grant County Review* made note that while the neighboring settlement of Watertown had been without mail for over two weeks due to the railroad blockade, "St. Paul was in a worse strait in 1856, when there was no telegraph, and no railroad nearer than Prairie du Chien, [Wisconsin,] and eleven days passed without a mail. The four daily papers during that period were not newspapers."[461] The "back when I was young" tone of this article is amusing, given that the editor was all of three years old in 1856 and living in an entirely different part of the country. Nonetheless, it served as a reminder that winter was capable of cutting off frontier communications. Compared to those "olden days," the winter under study here was on the cutting edge of technology—rail delivery.

The recording of mail deliveries nearly became a sport as the winter progressed. Almost every issue across the region made at least some passing note about how many days had passed since the last delivery and/or how many bags arrived. When the mail did make it through, the local postmaster was under pressure and made sure to tell the readers how many hours it took to get all of the mail sorted.

Articles reporting the arrangement of alternative delivery methods, or just musing over other options, began to appear more frequently. Given that the trains had become unreliable, people became determined to pick up the reins and keep the mail moving. "From December 25th up to last Tuesday," wrote the *Pipestone Star*, "we have had but two mails. . . . We suggest to the post office authorities that our mails be sent via Luverne, and we will then get them twice a week at least, stage driver Wells not having missed a trip yet."[462] Later in the month, the town of Flandreau suggested a similar approach: "If our eastern mail could be sent to us by way of Sioux Falls it would be a blessing that would be appreciated."[463]

When the mail was stuck about forty miles to the east, the towns of Flandreau and Pipestone made a joint effort to retrieve it. Money was raised, a person hired, and a trip set in motion. Station Agent Cawley made the arrangements via telegraph, and within forty-eight hours the mail had reached Pipestone.[464] Agent Cawley was certainly busy fulfilling his duties despite the absence of trains.

Several other towns noted they were also sending out teams to retrieve mail from neighboring communities or rail locations. Watertown reported a more elaborate system—multiple teams were established under contract with the railroad company, each with a different route, spreading as far east as Sleepy Eye. In Marshall, along the mail route, they felt confident enough in their plans to say, "We can manage to get along without trains for awhile."[465]

Despite the inconveniences and isolation brought on by the lack of mail deliveries, the editors were still quick to admonish readers if they heard of grumbling toward the railroad companies. The *Pipestone Star* reminded its readers that the railroads were not legally required to get the mail into their hands:

> As we understand it—and we believe we are correctly informed—the company is paid for carrying the mail by the trip, and the report of each trip is kept by the mail clerk on the train, and upon his report the company is paid. If they do not make the trip there is no pay. Of course the company cannot help these blockades any more than the farmer could have prevented the storm of last October, which caught them with their work half done. Railroad companies have enough to answer for without being blamed for every delay which is beyond their control. And, another thing, everybody must recollect that this has been an unusually severe winter, not anticipated by any one.[466]

Boosterism

"The country round-about here is rapidly settling up with a thrifty and intelligent set of farmers, who think that the land here is just a little better than any other part of the country."[467]

—*Grant County Review*, January 13, 1881

In November, we were introduced to the Extra Edition, the brainchild of the *Dakota News* editor out of Watertown. To bring us up to date, he had been successful in selling subscriptions, and the Extra looked like it would be published. However, as appropriate to this winter, the big day came with a big blizzard and a big long blockade.

On January 17, the *Dakota News* editor provided an update to expectant subscribers. Frustrated that the necessary paper was again snowbound somewhere along the rails to the east, he wrote,

We are again obliged to put off the getting out of the extra edition for another week, and have now set the time for Monday, January 24th, and have the papers ready for delivery some time during that week. We are sorry to disappoint our readers so often in this matter, but feel that our excuse is a good one and will be so considered by our patrons.[468]

While he waited for the paper to arrive, the Watertown editor kept himself busy with a little diversion.

Little seemed to irritate the western editor more than the concerns of Easterners about the livability of the West. In the January 24 issue of the *Dakota News*, the editor included an article strewn with thinly veiled exasperation and a handful (or more) of amusing little mistruths. After reminding readers that Watertown was a mere day and a half by train from Chicago and just three from New York—when the trains were able to run, of course—things turned more toward a proud, stubborn, set-jawed exclamation that begged challenge, especially knowing that by its publication date, the railroad blockades were locked into place.[469]

Despite Watertown being a younger community, the editor proclaimed, "We have every luxury and convenience that can be found in thirty year old towns east, of four times our population." On the topic of that population, he continued, "We have no tramps, no loafers, no dead beats, no gambling dens, no houses of prostitution, no idlers, no lawlessness, no crime. Our people are intelligent, social and generous. Buds of promises adorn the present, the blossoms of hope garland all the future."[470]

He then turned his attention to the "exaggerated weather yarns" that "surpass in ridiculous improbabilities" the fantastical tales of Sinbad the Sailor. He incredulously told his readers that one eastern paper had reported that "Watertown was blown all to pieces by a blizzard. This is but a sample of a thousand wild stories floating all over the east, that have not, in fact, a shadow of foundation. Not a house, or even a shanty, has been blown down or injured in any particular. Nor has any one been frozen to death." Continuing, he entertained that while "we had one day when the thermometer marked 37 degrees below zero," in Dakota's atmosphere, that is equivalent to the more balmy "20 in Wisconsin, Michigan, or New York."[471] He then defiantly took on the stories of overwhelming snows and blockades:

As yet we have not had snow enough to make good sleighing. What little we had was dry when it fell, and drifted into the railroad cuts, and as the business is light at this season of the year, this end of the road for some

100 miles was closed for ten days. Such a blockade on an eastern road would have been considered nothing.[472]

After putting to rest concerns about the current situation, he took on the historical record, going back to 1864 to cite a few dates and locations where people had frozen to death in Wisconsin, Minnesota, or Iowa, noting that people didn't accuse those states of being unlivable, so why do they pick on Dakota? The real problem, he insisted, was "a certain class of eastern people" who were afraid to move west, who were "nerveless, cowardly stock" who painted the situation out west in as detrimental a view as possible to frame their fears as reasonable and respectable.[473]

One would think he had expended his wrath, but no. The article, along with the editor's irritation, was barely half spent. He came back around to the weather again, wondering where the notion had come from that "Dakota is away up almost among the icebergs" when, he claimed, "the growing season here is longer by two weeks at least, than southern Wisconsin. Spring is two weeks earlier here than there, and frost hangs off as late or later, in the fall. Why this is we leave to scientists to explain."[474]

Next he bestowed wondrous qualities upon the benevolent corporation that was the Chicago & North Western Railway Company, claiming its land grant to be superior to other railroad land grants, running upon and through lands superior to other nearby lands for prices superior to other railroad land prices. As for "wood, coal, lumber, shade and ornamental trees and shrubs," he reminded readers that the railroad would carry these at "greatly reduced cost"—though he failed to mention that the trains were not currently running and therefore could not charge anything. Calling out those who were against railroads out of pure principle, he argued, "Fanatics and mischievous agitators are wont to repeat and enlarge upon that old maxim of the law, 'that corporations have no soul,' and it is pleasant to have an opportunity to illustrate that while 'corporations have no souls' managers [do]" and that the local railroad employees were people of the highest character.[475]

After that, he must have run out of column space, type, energy, or perhaps all three, and the article abruptly ended without summation. But one can almost hear the gavel crack against the writing desk. A week later, he published a piece noting that fruit, though untested as a crop in Dakota Territory, should grow marvelously, as long as it was planted in the river bottoms to protect it from prairie fires.[476]

The Extra Edition of the *Dakota News*, printed in and shipped from Milwaukee, was finally published on the last day of January. The editor, delighted, shared that the Chicago & North Western Railway Company was so impressed by the contents of the Extra, it purchased a total of 20,000 copies (an initial order of 2,000 and an additional 18,000 following publication) of the paper to share with passengers on their trains and at towns in the eastern regions. The editor in turn boasted of the importance of this order to those who had had the foresight to purchase advertisements in this special edition. The article indicated that the additional copies were shipped and would arrive on the first train. The publication date was January 31, but the first train would not arrive until late April.[477]

The Tracy Cut, the Superintendent from the East, and Abandonment of the Dakota Central

"'Where's the superintendent? What happened to him?' they asked the engineer. All he said was, 'How the dickens do I know? All I know is I'm not killed. I wouldn't do that again,' he said, 'not for a million dollars in gold.'"[478]

—*The Long Winter*

In each version of the autobiography and *The Long Winter*, the superintendent from the East attempts to drive a train through the snow and ice blocking the Tracy Cut, and upon failing at that, cancels all further attempts to keep the tracks open.[479] This pivotal scene was in the first version of the autobiography, which is considered to be written from Wilder's memory before fictional aspects were added.[480] The book you are reading began partly as a hunt for that incident.

Hundreds of newspapers were carefully examined and nearly three thousand individual articles collected, covering various aspects of life during the winter. Each edition was examined for anything that could shed light on the superintendent incident. Finally, a nugget was found.

Earliest Version, from Pioneer Girl

As Wilder first wrote, the superintendent of the division was unhappy with the work to keep the tracks clear and traveled to the "deep cut west of Tracy" to oversee operations personally. The crews had been using "two snow plows hitched together." That was not enough to move the hard-packed snow, so he ordered that a third be added.[481] The engineer tasked with driving the train into the icy mountain of snow refused to do so, and the superintendent took on the task himself, saying he would not ask another to do that which he was not willing to do himself.[482] We'll now pick up the action as Wilder wrote it:

> They put the other plow on, backed the train for a mile, then came as fast as they could and struck the snow in the cut with all the power of the engines, their weight and speed. And stopped! The front engine and its plow were completely buried, even the smoke stack covered. By a miricle [sic] the enginers [sic] were not hurt and crawled and were shoveled out. The impact, the heat and steam from the engine in front melted the snow close around it and it froze again in solid ice. When the men had shoveled the snow away so they could get to it they had to use picks to cut the ice from the wheels and gearing. It took two days, with all the men that could work around them to get the engines loose. By that time another blizzard was raging and the Suprentendent [sic] ordered all work on the track stopped with the snow one hundred feet deep on the track at the Tracy cut and Twenty-five feet deep on the track in the cut just west of De Smet.[483]

Fictionalized Version, from *The Long Winter*

The scene evolved, becoming more detailed, over the subsequent autobiographies and stretched several pages in the novel, in which Pa told the story while the rest of the family interjected awe and criticism. A portion of the story as published reads,

> Those locomotives came charging down that two miles of straight track with wide-open throttles, full speed and coming faster every second. Black plumes of coal smoke rolling away far behind them, headlights glaring bigger in the sunshine, wheels blurring faster and faster, roaring up to fifty miles an hour they hit that frozen snow.... Then up rose a fountain of flying snow that fell in chunks for forty yards around. For a minute or two no one saw anything clear, nobody knew what had happened. But when the men came running to find out, there was the second locomotive buried halfway in the snow and the engineer crawling out of its hind end. He was considerably shaken up."[484]

Now that we know two versions of the story via Wilder, let's return to the historical record to see what we can find.

Rumors Confirmed? Abandonment and the Tracy Cut Story

While the time frame for this episode in the novel was during January, most coverage of efforts to clear the railways being abandoned appear later in the newspaper record. We're discussing it here based upon the novel's time frame; therefore, some of the items below jump ahead in time.

Newspaper reports did plenty to stoke fears that storms would keep the tracks covered in snow and that the railroads would eventually stop expending money and resources on the endeavor of shoveling.[485] As also mentioned earlier, newspapers edited down larger articles into smaller bites, sometimes losing important details in the process. Below are three versions of an article about the line being abandoned.

The original article in the *Minneapolis Tribune*, published February 1:

By Telegraph—The Winona & St. Peter: Inquiring at the telegraph office at midnight developed the following state of affairs: Out on the Winona & St. Peter Railroad the storm is quite severe, and all trains will be more or less delayed. West of Sleepy Eye the Fort Pierre division of the Chicago & Northwestern is entirely blocked and probably will not be open until spring. The storm seems to extend entirely across the southern part of the state and into Dakota. . . . The Winona & St. Peter west of St. Peter, and the western part of the Southern Minnesota remained out of sight under the beautiful snow. The storm promises no good to railroad operations.[486]

On February 8, the *Janesville Argus* published this extrapolation of the *Tribune*'s article, adding concern for those affected:

The *Minneapolis Tribune* of the 1st, says the Winona & St. Peter road is to be abandoned for the winter, west of Sleepy Eye. It seems horrible for those people to be shut up and no effort made for their relief, yet while this weather continues we do not see how the company can do any thing else. The road is closed in spite of all efforts and that it cannot be opened and kept open is apparent. However, the people would undoubtedly feel better over the matter if an effort was made to keep the road open.[487]

Two weeks later, the *Moody County Enterprise* in Flandreau, fifty-two miles southeast of De Smet, ran this version of the news: "It is reported that the Northwestern has virtually abandoned their efforts to open their road."[488]

The above articles are a good example of the old game Telephone—or in this case, Telegraph and Newspaper—where a message changes and degrades as it passes from person to person, turning into something not quite matching the original message. The original article did not say that an intentional decision had been made to stop work.

The article in the *Tribune* stated that the Fort Pierre division (the Dakota Central) "probably will not be open until spring." It further complicated things by referencing the umbrella corporation, the Chicago & North Western, rather than differentiating between the Winona & St. Peter and Dakota Central lines.

Stories such as these may provide the answer to what led Charles Ingalls to sit his family down and tell them that trains were not coming until spring. But what about the story of the superintendent from the East, who attempted to blow through a snow blockade in that big cut west of Tracy? That was an elaborate story to come from a simple misinterpretation or method of preparing others for a long siege. It had to have come from somewhere.

The earliest version of Wilder's autobiography included the scene, leading to the assumption that it was in her memory as a childhood event. As we've seen, there were multitudes of stories about brigades of men, both paid and volunteer, who swarmed out of communities with shovels in hand to do all in their power to clear the tracks of snow. We've read about the mighty snowplows doing battle against the drifts and often becoming casualties themselves. But no article came close to paralleling the story Pa shared with his tired, hungry, and cold household.

"Graphic Description of a Battle with Snow Drifts"

Scrolling through the microfilmed newspapers, article by article, was often tedious, much as hay twisting or wheat grinding must have been for the Ingalls family. As with the family, just as things were becoming truly monotonous, something popped up to bring relief.[489]

The *Egan Express* of February 24 delivered a moment of profound excitement.[490] Egan, a town along the Southern Minnesota line, lies just fifty-four miles southeast of De Smet. With telegraph communications, shared local newspapers, and word of mouth, this story may have made its way to De Smet in an altered format.

The *Egan Express*–reported event took place in mid-February. Wilder's autobiography provides no clue about timing for the superintendent episode. If Wilder, for literary purposes, intentionally placed the fictionalized incident in the novel in early January instead of February, the article below could represent the original story, distorted by the worried minds of the people along the telegraph line to have happened just west of Tracy.

Or perhaps Charles, an experienced storyteller, looked at the situation as it stood, considered the story below (or one similar), then transformed the events into a story his family could picture in their minds—and thus prepare themselves for the months to come.

Here is a shortened version of the incident, which took place along the Kansas Pacific railroad, near Cheyenne Wells in eastern Colorado, as told by the *Denver Tribune* and reprinted in the *Egan Express*. The items set in italics here most closely match the story as Wilder remembered it.

Graphic Description of a Battle with Snow Drifts

During Sunday night Sup't Odell made arrangements to clear the track of snow, and realizing how great a task it was, perfected plans on the most thorough and extensive scale. Four of the largest and strongest engines on the road had been sent on from the Smoky Hill division, together with construction cars and a commissary outfit, the latter containing provisions and general supplies sufficient to sustain five hundred men five days.

A gang of 100 shovelers was got together and boarded the construction cars, and Sup't Odell and his two most efficient road bosses stepped into the *Superintendent's car.* In selecting the men for the great engines Mr. Odell exercised unusual care. Summoning an engineer or fireman, he asked, "Are you afraid to go where I tell you?" Each man selected for duty on the engines was asked this question. *Only one engineer expressed hesitation, and he was quickly and kindly relieved.*

When the train was made up it consisted of an *immense snow plow, four engines,* three construction cars, the commissary car, and the *superintendent's car,* in the order named. When all was in readiness Mr. Odell said, "I've got the best crew for such work I ever had. You will see some fun."

The train, after a slight halt was ordered forward and several big banks were met and overcome and finally the largest and deepest cut on the division was reached. The Sup't knew that the most difficult place on the road had yet to be surmounted.

The train was brought up to the east end of the cut and a survey of the task to be accomplished was taken. All hands were ordered out, and the locomotives pushed the cars back for about two miles, where they were left upon the main track. The shovelers were ordered to go upon the bank and as rapidly as possible, in gangs of four men each, cut trenches across the track, as deep as could be without too much loss of time, and about five feet apart. This work was for the purpose of disturbing the solidity of the mountain of snow, and of breaking up the mass as much as possible. The shovelers went at the work with a will, and in a short time this labor had been accomplished. Then everything was made ready for the charge on the snow with the ponderous plow. All hands secured as eligible a position as possible to witness the grand sortie.

The engines went back for the distance of a mile and a half to gain a greater degree of velocity. The engineers and firemen stood at their posts firm and fast. Full head of steam had been attained, and the powerful engines fairly trembled to exhaust their strength. The word was given and the engines were thrown wide open and came rushing along the track at a rate of speed which sent the sparks flying from the flanges and shot clouds of flame from the smoke stacks. As the gigantic plow was driven with frightful and resistless force into the wall of snow, the effect upon the spectator was such as can be experienced under no other circumstances.

Balls of snow weighing 1,000 pounds were sent from the chute of the great iron plow, as the monstrous machine pushed for a distance of 600 feet into the cut. Then the wonderful force was spent, and it was known that another and perhaps several trials would be necessary before the entire 1,700 feet could be got through.

The plow and locomotives were completely buried in snow and several men walked over the smoke stacks and cabs on the snow piled upon them. The shovelers were ordered to cut out the engines and the hundred men went to work with a will to remove the snow from around them. It consumed about one hour to accomplish the task, and then another charge was made with the same terrible excitement and danger. It required four charges to cut through the snow, and then the plow was pushed through into the open plain beyond.[491]

That account has enough similarities to Wilder's to consider it a solid candidate for the source of the story, as told by skilled storyteller Charles Ingalls. It was the only article found that even remotely approached the superintendent story in content. On the other hand, it matched scores of other articles. The story essentially describes the process of snow bucking, with the added flair of the super-intendent himself encased within the locomotive.

Snow bucking was common practice for the railroads where snowplows and shoveling didn't suffice. The excitement of this brute-force tactic may have inspired Charles Ingalls to craft a narrative offering for his family, with the bonus of helping them let go of the prospect that a train would get through any time soon. (The full article can be read in the appendix, on page 305.)

The Activity inside the Locomotive

So far, we've focused on men with shovels and on trains pushing wedge plows to move snow off the tracks. But what went on inside the cab of a locomotive midbattle with a snowdrift? An 1870s-era locomotive was a complicated and impressive piece of equipment.

The January 1882 issue of the *Railway Age Monthly and Railway Service Magazine* included an extensive article about snow bucking, authored by an engineer with relevant experience.[492] The summary here provides some interesting details; reading it with the superintendent story in mind adds to the excitement.

During and after a storm, tracks tended to be inconsistently covered with snow. Some stretches would be relatively clear while others would be covered in deep, heavy snow. The routine process was to maintain speed and momentum to simply push through the snow. When the snow was deep enough that the train became stuck, the engineer was trained to "reverse the engine at once and endeavor to back the train out." And if he knew the drift was too big to push through, procedure said, "No attempt should be made to do so, for it only entails loss of time shoveling out cars that get embedded in the drifts."[493]

To attempt snow bucking, the engineer would first park the main body of the train along a clear section of track, freeing up the locomotive to make a run at the snow alone. That way, if the drift won, only the locomotive needed to be shoveled free—and only the engineer was in some immediate danger. "If it goes through," wrote the author, "the trackmen in attendance can quickly clean out a passage that will admit the train to be pulled through. If the engine sticks fast, it is shoveled out, and the operation of running at the bank is repeated till it succeeds in making a passage."[494]

Due to this "exciting and somewhat dangerous proceeding," the front windows of the cab were boarded up, and the headlight and its platform removed and put in a safe location, precautions which hopefully prevented their destruction.[495] And it wasn't just the train that needed to be prepared for battle: the snow on each side of the track had to be equidistant from the train and made relatively smooth, for when the train hit the snowdrift, the displaced snow, if pushed into uneven gaps, could itself cause tipping or "throw the engine off the track."[496] This preparatory shoveling needed to be done before each run at a snowdrift.

The next step was to back up the locomotive far enough to allow it to reach appropriate ramming speed. "Have a good fire and as much water in the boiler as can be carried comfortably," wrote the author. "As the engine rushes into the snow the engineer must depend entirely on his ear in working the engine, for a heavy cloud of snow envelops the cab, shutting out every ray of light." He further added, "A tumult of noises accompany the cloud that heralds the engine's entrance into the drift, lumps of snow and ice thunder down on the cab, steam hisses and crackles from the hot surfaces being hugged by the snow, a whirl of slipping wheels makes every joint of the machine groan and shiver."[497]

Imagine the attack on the engineer's senses at that moment—he cannot see; the powerful machine he set in motion is hurtling toward a hard bank of snow and ice; he's holding his breath, listening, anticipating the moment of impact, when he is suddenly overcome by terrifying sounds.

Whew! We can take a few moments to catch our breath, but the engineer had to stay on his game:

> He must not be appalled by violent slipping or attempt to check it unless the engine is working water so as to endanger the cylinders. Listen attentively to the exhaust and the instant it stops sounding reverse the engine if possible and endeavor to back out for she has stalled. Where an engine makes a good run of this kind the snow generally gets packed so firmly around every wheel and box that the engine will not move until some clearing out is done.[498]

At this point in the article, the author stepped back and reminded engineers that they could not buck snow during an actual storm, because once the locomotive's wheels were swallowed by snow, as would happen as a normal part of the undertaking, the snowstorm would add more snow to the mix faster than anyone could shovel it out, and the locomotive would become hopelessly stuck.[499] The author added that should a train be "overtaken by conditions of this kind, his best efforts should be directed to keeping his engine alive and in working order." He further conceded, "A violent snow storm suddenly descending upon a road already heavily banked with drifts, generally paralyzes all the trains it encounters." With a final eyebrow-raising addition, the author warned, "An imbecile engineer often proves a very expensive employee under such circumstances."[500]

Now that the reader was hopelessly embedded in a snow-encased locomotive along with the engineer, the author gave some respite, blithely adding that the steam engine could easily be kept alive with snow. Of course, using snow brought its own caveats, such as economizing so as not to run out of fuel to melt the snow to create said steam.

A Losing Battle

Concerns over train blockades were proving disquietingly valid. By the end of January, what would become winter-long stoppages had been established for a week or more, depending on specific location. (Refer to the map on page 108 for the location of the trouble zones on each railroad line.)

The rumors that the railroad companies would abandon snow-clearing efforts, however, were unfounded. While we'll see that their efforts were mostly for naught, shoveling brigades continued to work tenaciously to keep *the beautiful* off of the tracks.

FEBRUARY 1881

Sunday	Monday	Tuesday	Wednesday	Thursday	Friday	Saturday
		1	2	3 ----------Blizzard from the southeast---------- wet snow boisterous blizzardous	4 wet snow boisterous blizzardous	5 heavy snow
6 2' snow	7 snow/rain 48F	8 moderate	9 moderate	10 mild	11 −20F stormy/windy	12 blizzardous not very cold very windy
13	14 cold, cloudy no wind	15 moonlit nights cold −30F	16 moonlit nights cold −27 to 7F in five hours	17 flurries nice	18 nice	19 boistrus afternoon
20 nice pleasant	21 nice very pleasant	22 heavy snow considerable wind, cleared	23 nice, pleasant mild, foggy	24 south wind	25 south wind	26 NW wind
27	28 storm (west)					

▬▬▬▬ Blizzard or significant snow event

//////////// Lighter snow or mixed precipitation

After first storm of February, drifts reported as 8–9' deep in New Ulm.

February 4: Snow on track between Waseca and Janesville reported at two to five feet deep.

February 6: Blizzard stopped for a few hours at midday; started up again from east.

February 9: Team reported snow on the prairie west of New Ulm as three to four feet deep on the level.

February 17: Ice three feet deep on Big Stone Lake.

This calendar shows weather reports gleaned from the various newspaper articles. If the weather was significantly different in one portion of the region versus another, that is noted.

February was truly despicable, as if the storms of the previous months had been practice sessions for the real thing. While some locations had plenty of supplies on hand, others were beginning to know real suffering.

The railroads were, by this point, irreversibly blocked, despite efforts to clear the tracks, which continued unabated. Money was to be had for those with the fitness and nutritional support to do battle, and the railroad company was bleeding money as surely as the clouds were hastening snow. For every shovelful of snow tossed onto the ever-growing banks beside the tracks, the weather seemed to toss several shovelfuls right back. Despite the continuing work, rumors that the railroads would abandon efforts to keep the tracks clear became more common, further diminishing hope that a train would get through.

Mail deliveries were consistently irregular, and newspapers published less and less regional news. While the larger situation was becoming dire, people at the community level were still traveling, getting out, and engaging in activities and entertainments. They were even enjoying the beauty of the moonlight on the sparkling snow. Oh, the beautiful snow.

The Month for the Ingalls Family

"The blizzard was beating and scouring at the house, the winds were roaring and shrieking. The window was pale in the twilight and the stove pressed out its feeble heat against the cold."[501]

—*The Long Winter*

In the novel, the fictional version of the Ingalls family was realizing that not only was their survival in peril, but what little consolations remained were dwindling as well: Pa's fingers were stiff and swollen from twisting hay and working in the cold, and he was unable to play the fiddle to bring moments of musical respite; the winds had switched direction and swept away the tunnel that Pa had used to get to and from the stable in relative comfort; Laura's fourteenth birthday had come and gone—things seemed about as dark as they could get.

The family's wheat was almost gone, and Laura asked if they would starve. When Pa reassured her they could butcher the family cow and calf, Laura expressed dismay rather than relief.

Others in town were also hungry. Rumors spread of a homesteader who may have been in possession of seed wheat.[502] Pa considered going after it until Ma, in another of her uncharacteristic outbursts, forbade it.[503] The family had six potatoes left, and enough bread for the next breakfast. Pa could not go after the rumored seed wheat, but he knew where he could get some nonetheless.

He crossed the street to the Wilder Feed Store, where Royal and Almanzo were, as usual, eating an easy feast. Having calculated that there was missing space inside the building compared to the exterior dimensions, Pa put his milk pail up to the wall and pulled the plug that restrained Almanzo's seed wheat within its hiding place.

The lifesaving grain poured into the pail while Almanzo halfheartedly objected, and Royal grinned at what he must have thought was the inevitable fate of his brother's wheat. Pa insisted on purchasing the wheat despite Almanzo's contention that he just take it. The Wilders fed Pa a nourishing meal of hotcakes, ham, and coffee. When he returned home, Pa presented the pail of seed wheat to Ma, easing her mind and reassuring her that there was more, though he was bound to keep the source a secret.[504]

Up to this point, the novel's list of meals had included the last of the potatoes, bread from the ground wheat, and tea. It also featured a surprise treat: Ma unveiled a frozen codfish she had secreted away. Had a neighbor gone ice fishing and gifted the family with this treasured bit of protein? As the food supply dwindled, Laura's appetite failed her, and she had to "choke down mouthfuls of the potato that had grown cold on the cold plate."[505] The cold was pervasive, dumbing, and numbing.

The interaction was pivotal for Almanzo, who carefully observed Charles's sunken cheekbones, then began a period of contemplation. During the blizzard that struck after Charles's visit, Almanzo was somber, thinking about the dangers of embarking on the mission to retrieve the rumored seed wheat and the implications if the trip hadn't happened.

In the end, he decided he had to go after the rumored homesteader with wheat,[506] knowing that what he had hidden behind his own wall was not enough to rescue the town.[507] Cap Garland stepped up to team with Almanzo, and they made plans for their trip to bring back the wheat—*if* it could be found.

Following yet another blizzard, Almanzo and Cap began the journey predawn.[508] Air pockets in the snow-covered slough grass slowed progress and tired them early in the day; they fought to keep the horses and sleds on stable ground. By providence, they found the rumored homesteader, negotiated the sale of wheat, then headed back to town with their precious cargo. Again, the slough grass was problematic, with the sacks tipping onto the ground and having to be reloaded onto the sled. They returned to town just as another blizzard encroached upon the stars. We will explore this episode in more detail later in the chapter.

The Ingalls family, unaware of Almanzo and Cap's status, was worried and on edge. Pa's patience broke as he shook his fist and yelled at the blizzard, leaving the family to stare at him, stunned.[509]

The last grains of wheat were poured into the coffee grinder. When the blizzard ended, Pa crossed the street to Fuller's Hardware Store, where he learned of Almanzo and Cap's success, having returned to town with sixty bushels of seed wheat.[510] In a moment of bittersweet triumph, Pa purchased a 125-pound sack, but found himself weakened to the point of having to accept assistance from Almanzo to hoist the bag.[511] The wheat—and the hope it brought—held out long enough for signs of spring to bolster spirits. Despite having only twenty-eight days, February was a long, dark month.

The Weather

> "The beautiful moonlight nights that we are now having are charming. The reflection of the moon from the ice and snow gives the appearance of a myriad of glittering diamonds from every snow drift."[512]
>
> —*Grant County Review*, February 17, 1881

The Storm of February 3

While most of the inclement weather had been coming from the northwest, this unusual blizzard came in from the southeast. That situation was unique enough to be mentioned in most articles about the storm. Not only were the railroads blocked, but the wagon roads also became impassable. Janesville, on the eastern edge of the region, was the first to experience the storm.

"Everybody says the late storm was a head and shoulders taller than any previous storm they ever knew or experienced," wrote the Janesville editor. "Not for cold or remarkably strong winds, but for the amount of snow falling and its propensity to climb the fences and roost on the top rail. It was the most am[b]itious snow we ever met."[513]

A further unusual aspect of this storm, as New Ulm experienced it, was the three-to-four-hour "window of calm," like the eye of a hurricane, before it resumed. The town's editor wrote,

The worst snow storm in the recollection of the oldest settlers struck [Friday morning] and it raged with almost unabated fury until late Sunday night. The wind blew a perfect gale from the east and drove the fast descending snow in a blinding mass before it.... The storm let up for three or four hours.... Shortly before noon the storm again commenced and continued until late Sunday night, after which time it snowed and rained by spells until Monday evening.[514]

Marshall "was visited by the heaviest and worst snow storm that the oldest inhabitant, much as it [strained] him to admit it, ever saw...." The Marshall editor further asserted they rarely saw heavy snow, though wind was a common affliction. That this storm featured both "in uncommon quantities" made it noteworthy. He continued, "While not very cold for a Winter storm, the severe wind and drifting snow made it impossible for most of the time to do anything out of doors, and nearly all business was at a stand-still."[515]

In *The Long Winter*, Wilder describes a similar storm, writing, "The blizzard seemed never to end. It paused sometimes, only to roar again quickly and more furiously out of the northwest.... Then the sun shone out, from morning till noon perhaps, and the dark anger of winds and icy snow came again." The manuscript included an identical passage, except the word *fury* had been used instead of *anger*.[516]

Travel by team near Marshall was difficult in the wake of the deep snowfall. Residents found the roads to be in "the worst possible condition." The Marshall editor further wrote,

Drifts top of drifts so perfectly impeded travel that ... very few teams ventured out, although the snow was soft and melting.... [The following cold weather] froze the drifts so that ... when an attempt was made to break a road to the Camden woods, it was found that no team could be got through without first breaking the crust by tramping and shoveling."[517]

This is reminiscent of Wilder's description of horses breaking through the crust of snow formed over the slough grasses.[518]

Conditions were similar in Pipestone and Currie. "Snow to the right of us, snow to the left of us," wrote the Pipestone editor, "snow whirling all around and above us, the highways full of it the rail roads blocked up and we wonder if Winter will ever let go his frosty, cold, snowy grip." Reminiscent of how we midwesterners sometimes take a perverse pleasure in competing over weather severity, the editor added, "This partially paid back the country northwest of us for what it has been sending down this way all winter. We owe the northeast one yet."[519]

The two towns continued to comment on the storm a week after it had passed. Pipestone complained that communications had suffered amid "drifts eight and ten feet deep of solid wet snow through which no team can pass." Even the stage-coach of the ever-dependable Mr. Wells was delayed, shocking the editors who seemed to use him as a canary-in-a-coal-mine type of bellwether.[520] Currie's paper commented, "What shall we say regarding the late storm which continued with unabated force throughout nearly all of Friday, Saturday and Sunday? We hoped that the fury of the stormy weather had been previously exhausted."[521]

Across the border in eastern Dakota Territory, the *Egan Express* described the storm as "the most awe inspiring experienced thus far this winter, and that is saying a good deal."[522]

Milbank, the most northwestern of the regional newspaper towns, experienced the storm every bit as fiercely as Janesville, to the southeast, with snowfall totals similar to those reported in Pipestone and Currie. "The last blizzard swept down upon us," wrote the Milbank editor, "with a dire vengeance as though determined to engulph us. . . . The average fall, on the level, has been between 20 and 25 inches." Because the storm came in from the southeast, the snow fences installed along the north side of the tracks proved useless, resulting in the streets in town being covered in drifts up to twelve feet deep.[523]

The Milbank editor went on to describe how this storm further hindered contingency arrangements to get provisions and mail moving via wagons instead of trains:

> Travel across the prairies has been entirely suspended. Several teams
> have endeavored to break their way to . . . Ortonville, but have been
> compelled to return. The mail stage . . . due here last Friday, has not yet
> come through. . . . The town is well supplied with fuel and provisions,
> and so we are enabled to pass the time away very comfortably—but oh! If
> we could only get some freights and mails.[524]

The *Janesville Argus* noted that the storm was one of "the heaviest of the season [with] snow in the timber . . . now fully two feet in depth." While the storm was heavy, the consistency of the resulting snow was "very light, there having been no thawing weather to condense it." The light texture of the snow meant it was easily swept up and blown about by the wind. The article concluded with, "The condition of the railroads is bad and the prospect not improving."[525]

The Storm of February 11

After just a few days of respite, another blizzard struck the region along the border between Minnesota and Dakota Territory. It was mentioned specifically as a weather event in only two of the surveyed newspapers but appeared in multiple articles focused on the railroads.

Pipestone reported, "Our regular weekly blizzard occurred last Friday and Saturday; thermometer 20 degrees below zero [on Friday and 30 below on Saturday]." The editor, in passing, noted, "It has been a common thing through this country all winter for farmers to go through the roofs of their barns, instead of in at the door, to feed their stock."[526] That situation is easily relatable to a scene in *The Long Winter*—the morning that Laura awoke to discover she could look out the upper-floor window and see level with the bottoms of the sleighs whipping past the store building.[527]

Just to the west of Pipestone, the *Egan Express* described this storm as "one of the wildest days we have had this winter." The account continued, "It was not very cold, but the wind blew and the snow fell—well just a little." After the snow abated, the temperatures dropped and were "pronounced by those who were out, to be the coldest of the season."[528]

It remained cold for several days after the storm moved on. Then on Wednesday, February 16, the temperatures took a sudden upswing. In Egan, temperatures went from –27 degrees at sunrise to 7 degrees by noon, a difference of 34 degrees over five hours. The Egan editor gleefully declared, "We can assure our readers that the change was highly gratifying to everybody."[529] This was one of the livelier squibs out of Egan; a lawyer by profession, the editor tended towards dry, unemotional reporting.

The deep and troublesome drifting was not without its silver linings. In New Ulm, a clever merchant transformed a giant snowdrift into an interesting diversion:

The enormous snow bank in front of Neumann & Rosskopf's has been utilized by that enterprising firm for a grand 'cave' saloon, with all that the word implies, and a jolly party might have been seen therein playing freeze-out most any evening last week. The cavern is large enough to admit of placing therein two tables and several chairs and it has daily attracted a crowd of visitors.[530]

At some point in the winter, a similar storm allowed Charles Ingalls to create a tunnel from his back door to the stable, providing protection from the wind and cold before it was scoured away.[531]

The Storm of February 22

The next storm came ten days later but was blessedly short-lived. Despite its brief duration, it packed a punch and undid the shoveling that had taken place over the past week.

The paper in Milbank noted, "The winds blow 'some' here but they blow a good deal 'wusser' [worse] down in the region from Fulda to Fairmont in Minnesota." Digging into his vibrant vocabulary, he tempered the earlier colloquial speech and added, "It might be remarked by timorous souls that the wind blew quite vigorously last night."[532]

The *Pipestone Star* noted that the storm "bade fair to rival any . . . had this season." It also shared that a resident, while walking home, encountered a drift west of town so enormous as to "allow him to step over the telegraph wire with ease."[533]

Based on the morning's snowfall and winds, New Ulm had been bracing itself for another onslaught. But the town was relieved and grateful when the snow stopped, providing "a little more sunshine for a change."[534]

It appears that the weather was fairly good during the final week of the month, bringing an optimism that winter might be waning. The *Egan Express* of February 24 included several wistful quips, including one that offered, "In the language of the poet we are constrained to say: 'Damn such weather.'" Despite what appeared to be an exasperated harrumph, the same issue noted, "It is wonderful, but nevertheless a fact, that we have had 8 days of the nicest kind of winter weather and it has been appreciated and enjoyed by everybody." Then, as if not wanting the readers to get too hopeful, it added, "Not less than 7 feet of snow have fallen in this country since the 15th of October. There is nearly if not quite 4 feet of snow now on the level."[535] Summarizing the local morale, a correspondent southwest of Egan optimistically noted, "The good weather of the past week has made our people feel better, and it is to be hoped we will have no more blizzards."[536]

The *Marshall Messenger* also commented on the pleasantness, venturing a prediction that winter was waning. "With the exception of one day of blizzard," wrote the editor, "this week has been a pleasant one. Most of the days being attended with midday thaws. We believe old Winter is on the down grade."[537]

F. H. Barrows, the correspondent from Currie who kept daily weather records, noted fourteen days in February that were more or less stormy.[538] As the month drew to a close and the weather returned to full blow, the editor in New Ulm took an opportunity to remind his readers that others had it worse:

> To-day, as well as many of the days past, we are having extremely stormy weather, and I am only sorry to say we are not yet at the end of the chapter.... We are complaining of snow storms, cold, and what not, but are quite silent when we read about our neighbors on all sides. Look to the west, where many are destitute and patiently waiting for the Chicago & N. W. road to bring them relief, and we only trust the trains may soon come up.[539]

The Railroads

"The great storm of this month will be memorable on account both of its severity and its extent. All the lines of railroads in Minnesota, Iowa, Kansas, and Wisconsin with very few exceptions were blockaded."[540]

—*Moody County Enterprise*, February 24, 1881

Snowplows

February was a bad month for the snowplows of the Chicago & North Western. A long article ran in the February 16 edition of the *New Ulm Weekly Review*, detailing efforts to clear the tracks after the storm of February 11. Full of activity and frustration, it illustrated the difficulties, dangers, and disappointments of working with a snowplow.

The adventurous tale began by reassuring readers that the thirteen-day-long blockade between St. Peter and Sleepy Eye had finally been conquered, and a victorious train had arrived bearing thirty-nine sacks of mail. It then recounted the trials and tribulations experienced by Superintendent Sanborn and his crew of shovelers.[541]

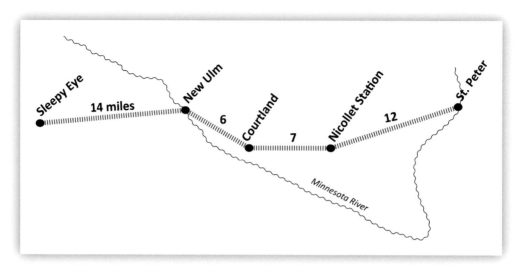

The setting of the story about Superintendent Sanborn, including the distances between each community.

Prior to the storm, Sanborn had been working with a crew of 125 shovelers to clean up and widen the cuts near Oshawa, between St. Peter and the Nicollet station. As they continued their work, another storm began, and the supply train that was sent to assist them became stuck in the snow two miles from Courtland. The article did not indicate what the shovelers, who had come from the direction of St. Peter, did for their overnight stay, but Sanborn made his way west to New Ulm, arriving nearly seven hours after starting. It was not specified whether he took the "foot express" or caught the train that had been stuck at Courtland.[542]

The next morning, he set out to continue battling the drifts. The article continued, "On the first run the snow plow struck a broken rail and was completely demolished. One of the engines was also thrown from the track, but luckily none of the train men was injured by the accident." Without the plow, the crew was completely dependent upon shovelers, and progress was slow throughout Friday.[543]

Little was accomplished the next day due to stormy weather, which lasted until after sunset, at which point the winds died down. Sanborn's crew then worked until three o'clock in the morning to remove the most recent deposits. Later that day, the rails between St. Peter and Oshawa (near Nicollet) were cleared, and three engines and a plow were sent from Sleepy Eye to clear the tracks from there to Oshawa. As was not infrequent, hopes were dashed when the plow "jumped the track" just two miles east of Sleepy Eye. It took the railroad workers "all day to get it righted again."[544]

Another day closed, and the next saw the plow from Sleepy Eye pass eastward through New Ulm on its way to assist the shovel crews working westward from St.

Peter. That night another inch of snow fell, but "as there was no wind it did no harm." The blockade was thus declared open between Sleepy Eye and St. Peter, and the force of five hundred shovelers was reassigned to the task of chipping away at the drifts to the west of Sleepy Eye.[545]

Mid-month snows continued to vex plowing efforts. Articles mentioned hundreds of men out attacking the drifts, though it is not possible to know whether these were exaggerations or accurate numbers. The depth of snow reported on the level and within the cuts is similarly impossible to confirm. Regardless, it was a frustrating and disruptive situation.

The situation was similar along the Hastings & Dakota, where one report stated, "At last accounts two of the snow plows, with the engines, were ditched, and the probability is that we won't have any mails from the old country for another week."[546] Along the Southern Minnesota, locomotives were burning snow fences and ties as they worked to clear the tracks.[547]

The plows were not, unfortunately, the invincible equipment that had been heralded with such pride and excitement in December. Instead, individual men with shovels continued to work by the hundreds along the five lines, heading into the fifth month of snow events.

Railroad Blockades

"North and South lines are something that the
big railroad companies must have out in this region.
It costs them too much to keep open their east and west lines
through the snow belt of western Minnesota in winters like this,
and the experience of the railroads this winter shows that the
most vigorous and determined efforts can not keep such . . .
open enough to supply the wants of the people or bring in
any returns for the company."[548]
—*Moody County Enterprise*, February 3, 1881

Along the Hastings & Dakota

Throughout February, the Hastings & Dakota line remained blocked. Significant man power went into clearing the tracks, but just as success was within sight, winds blew, snow whipped into the cuts, and progress was lost.

On February 17, Milbank reported that its last train had arrived on January 25, over three weeks prior. Citizens and railroad employees alike were out shoveling "in full force." Ever optimistic, the Milbank editor wrote, "Should there be no more snow or wind for the next few days, the probability is that the trains will get through by Tuesday of next week."[549]

Along the Winona & St. Peter

To the south of the Hastings & Dakota, things were not much different. Reports of shortages appeared, though lacking specific locations. It was generally out west, beyond the safety of the reporting newspaper's town, affecting unknown, unnamed people. Multiple articles about efforts to clear the tracks after the late-January storm were published in most newspapers, including the information that residents could earn thirty cents per hour by shoveling snow for the railroads.[550]

By then, residents had realized that while the expenditure of effort could bring in thirty cents an hour, it wouldn't bring in any trains. The editor of the *Janesville Argus* pointed it out plainly to his readers: "The railroad people were bragging of having broken the blockade as far west as Sleepy Eye on Sunday evening . . . but on Tuesday night old Boreas again rose up and again filled the cuts with snow." The editor further noted that while there was a great deal of snow on the ground, it was, after all, a meteorologically unstable phase of winter. "At this season of the year," he wrote, "blustering weather is common and even up to March 1st we usually have high winds from the north west. What the condition of the people up there may be we do not know but that it is bad no one can doubt."[551]

On February 2, the *New Ulm Weekly Review* chronicled the track's status for the week prior. Over the course of nine days, the road was open for a portion of one day, during which two trains arrived, bearing mail. The readers were then informed that the cuts were, yet again, drifted shut.[552] February had just begun.

Following the Storm of February 3

According to the *Janesville Argus* of February 8, the Winona & St. Peter had, "by unrelenting efforts," opened the tracks, allowing a passenger train to get as far west as Sleepy Eye. Hours later, high winds again redistributed the snows and "the snow plows, trains of shovelers, road master, Superintendent [Sanborn], [and] the passenger train"[553] all found themselves snowbound.

The same edition also shared the travels of a Dakota Territory resident who trekked to Janesville—not his final destination—by combination of train, walking, and stagecoach. The ever-spirited editor finished the article by writing, "Roads all blockaded and degraded, abandoned, approximated and absquatulated. This don't half express the size of it but it's the best we can do in our present blockaded condition."[554] By the way, *absquatulate* means to abscond or decamp. Though he seemed to imply it, the blockades were not impeding his vocabulary any.

Earlier we followed the exploits of Superintendent Sanborn as he worked to clear the tracks between Sleepy Eye and St. Peter. That episode, serving as a vignette about the snowplow, began after the storm of February 11. But on February 9, the *New Ulm Weekly Review* shared a similar article, detailing the day-to-day efforts of man and machine under Superintendent Sanborn's charge as a result of the February 3 storm. These events played out in a very similar manner to efforts following the February 11 plow story, but without the destruction of the snowplow—just one of the locomotives:

> The first snow east of here was encountered in the Redstone cut [within three miles of New Ulm] where it was about five feet deep, but the plow and engines went through it nobly, and on the third run they went through Courtland into the long cut one and a half miles east of Courtland. This cut is from eight to ten feet deep and in trying to back out of it after the second run one of the engines on the plow was disabled and had to be sent to Sleepy Eye to be repaired. The force working from St. Peter west got five miles yesterday, which at dusk left the two crews about 15 miles apart. Supt. Sanborn, who stayed here last night with his crew, expects to get his road open to-day, but as all the cuts are even full, we fear his hopes will not be realized.[555]

Due to the unavailability of trains, there were numerous reports of people walking to their destinations, sometimes stopping at farms for protection at night. One article shared, via the dramatic flair and understated humor of the era, the dangers of trying to walk to a destination fourteen miles or so distant. Railroad employee Julius Kirschstein left Sleepy Eye on foot about noon on Sunday, February 6. He stopped at a farm overnight, then continued on toward New Ulm, arriving midafternoon on Monday. The account, printed in the New Ulm paper, continued,

> Those who saw Mr. Kirschstein when he came into town say that he did not proceed with his usual rapid and firm step; on the contrary, he moved as though he had been heavily overloaded with barley juice or some other weighty stimulant. But as there was no dram shop on the route, and, besides, Julius being one of the kind that does not indulge in the luxury of getting an unsteady step from such a source, it must be

concluded that the deep snow was what produced his faltering tread. We have not seen Julius around since his pedestrian tour was accomplished, and he is probably laid up for repairs.[556]

When a train could not proceed west of New Ulm due to snow, those lacking Mr. Kirschstein's singular resolve had yet another transportation option: "Teams were engaged to take some passengers . . . to Tracy," wrote the New Ulm editor. "It must be a cold excursion for man, woman and child to cross the large prairies at such times."[557]

Gratitude for the railroad companies' efforts to clear the tracks in the face of futility appeared more frequently, along with continued optimism that things would improve before long. A correspondent from Springfield stated that, as a result of the deep snow, it took much ingenuity to get around, and he further said, "We cannot pass this opportunity by, without expressing our gratitude to the railroad company for their untiring efforts in keeping the track open at such enormous expenses to them. It must be very discouraging to be continually working to keep the road open, and almost as soon as opened to have it filled up again."[558]

One of the truly hopeful items of the winter appeared in the February 11 edition of the *Marshall Messenger*, which stated, "The railroad is open to some miles west of Sleepy Eye."[559] That the tracks were open west of Sleepy Eye may have done more to raise the spirits of readers had that detail not been published on the day of the next storm.

Following the Storm of February 11

Even the eastern end of the region was experiencing train delays. Towns east of Janesville endured a multiday blockade, with trains stuck and passengers resorting to walking alongside the tracks to reach their destinations.[560]

A group of travelers, stranded in Sleepy Eye, brought a bit of the Wild West to the winter, causing a flurry of activity. According to the *Sleepy Eye Herald*, the group had left Deadwood, in western Dakota Territory, on January 19. They traveled by team to Pierre, expecting to board a train there. Trains not running, the group was forced to travel by team and foot, reaching Sleepy Eye nearly a month later. Still unable to procure a train within which to ride, they became angry and "flourished revolvers and threatened to shoot every railroad official on sight." In passing, the reprinted article out of Janesville added, "One of the party struck Road Master Bidwell, at Springfield, because he would not send them by train to Sleepy Eye. It was a rough experience anyway and the party are not to be blamed for a little ill humor."[561]

The costs along the Winona & St. Peter were many, whether it be the physical efforts of the shovelers, the repairs to broken equipment, or the harm done to railroad employees taking "one on the chin" for the situation. The *Mankato Review* published an article that put more of a financial spin on it, characterizing the daily cost to the railroad company as "a good many $3,000.00 piled up then and no relief in sight."[562]

Along the Dakota Central

The *Brookings County Press*, which had previously been an excellent source of information for the winter, ceased publication, presumably due to lack of supplies. The *Fort Pierre Weekly Signal*, the second extant paper along the Dakota Central, was quiet about any work being done to liberate the tracks to its distant east.

However, a telegraph dispatch from Huron, relayed to the *Pioneer Press* in St. Paul and reprinted in the *Janesville Argus*, noted, "There were fears of suffering at sidings west, but the arrival of 120 shovels in charge of a large work train with five engines from Pierre to-day, reports all O.K."[563] That puts a train in Huron, from the west, on February 28.

Along the Southern Minnesota

The activity along this line was no different than that experienced by the Hastings & Dakota, the Winona & St. Peter, or the Dakota Central. Egan's paper reported, "Nearly all of our male population has been engaged in shoveling on the railroad."[564] Indeed, reports throughout the month indicated that hundreds of men, in dozens of locations, were thrusting shovels into barely yielding snowdrifts that were miles long and tens of feet deep.

The editor in Flandreau captured the overall essence of the Southern Minnesota's valiant efforts, remarking that it displayed "a patient zeal that would seem between the pathetic and the ludicrous if it were anyone but a railroad company...." The article continued, "The persistence of the company in carrying on an apparently hopeless contest with the elements is most commendable, and ought long to be remembered to the credit of the company."[565]

Following the Storm of February 3

This is the storm that came in from the southeast, causing the snow to drift in a different pattern than had previously afflicted the cuts and tracks. Calls to connect towns to other railroad lines via extensions became more numerous.

Pipestone wanted options to solve its isolation and looked toward the Sioux City line, via a branch extension to a nearby town. Taking to the columns of their paper, Pipestone residents called upon the railroad company to link the towns together as soon as the coming tracklaying season, citing the minimal blockades experienced by the Sioux City.[566] Meanwhile, they had to deal with their situation as it stood. And that meant tired railroad workers and citizens:

> Superintendent Egan and Road Master Rafferty . . . looked weary and worn with fatigue having been from Saturday until Tuesday working their way from Fulda to here [Pipestone], a distance of about forty miles. They brought three trains through with them, however, a passenger and two freights, which gave us a mail and a fresh supply of fuel. Mr. Egan says this is the hardest winter he ever experienced railroading.[567]

The *Pipestone Star* of February 10, the "Blizzard Edition," was dedicated to news related to the storm and blockade. Appropriately printed on colored paper, due to nondelivery of regular paper, it smacked of disappointment. The previous week, it had campaigned for connection to the Sioux City road; however, that line was also hopelessly blocked, worse than any other time that winter. The Pipestone editor further shared that "the cuts on that line were well protected from the northwest storms but were all exposed from the south east."[568]

Also on February 10, the *Egan Express* published a summary of the winter thus far that filled considerable column space. It began with a flourish of headlines, stacked one upon another: "TERRIBLE TIMES. Railroads Badly, and it is Feared Effectually, Blocked. Scarcity of Food and Fuel in Many Places. Storm after Storm adds Terror to Despair."[569] It then went on to detail the innumerable unpleasantries faced thus far. Woe that it was not even mid-February!

Much like the county histories we saw in the introduction, the opening paragraph of this summary is fraught with phrases such as "one as few of our hardy settlers have ever experienced" and "storm has followed storm in such rapid succession that it might almost be called a winter of perpetual elemental fury." It then began the tallies. Only six trains since Christmas. No prospect of a train until spring, despite the "strenuous efforts" of the railroad company. Cuts forty to fifty feet deep in the snow, "packed almost as hard as ice." Barely a single mile of road that did not need clearing of snow. "The task is almost, if not altogether, hopeless."[570]

Despite the hardships incurred, there was sympathy and support for the Southern Minnesota. "In justice to the railroad company," conceded the writer, "it must be said that the fault is not theirs; either that the road is not kept open, or that famine in some places is impending. They have, at great expense, opened the road at diverse times, but each time it has been again filled up, and the task of reopening become more serious." The article noted that the number of men taking part in shoveling crews was "growing smaller day by day." While a reason was not given, it could have been any combination of fatigue, diet, frostbite, snow blindness, illness, or just plain resignation. The section about the crews ended with the thought that only warmer weather and a stronger sun would "crown their labors with success."[571]

The summary article, not done just yet, then turned to the weather of the moment: "To-day the wind is again blowing with sufficient force to undo much of the work done, and it is feared it will be worse before it is better." As if the winds outside the walls were blowing away the optimism that had sustained the residents thus far, the writer noted that it was "altogether probable that the work of opening the road will be abandoned. . . ." It continued,

> If such is the case, the present inconvenience of the people in the
> snow-bound regions of Minnesota and Dakota will become desperate.
> Wood and coal has long since been exhausted, and at present, ties, and
> in some cases, bridges, household furniture, and in fact anything that
> will burn, are being used as fuel. Should the winter continue cold, and
> last, as it often does, till the last of March, much suffering must be
> endured.[572]

It is a blessing that they were unaware that the winter would well outlast the end of March.

Several details included in the article above would have provided fodder for the rumors and fears that the railroads would eventually abandon the settlers to the elements. But perhaps the most forlorn article of the winter appeared in the *Janesville Argus* of February 22. Relaying information about a valley centered a dozen miles east of Pipestone, it noted that mile after mile of standing telegraph poles were "snowed under" and that passenger coaches parked near a water tank were "completely covered and lost sight of." Worse yet was the destitution of the people "shut off from supplies of fuel and food and unable to travel away from their snow bound homes." Additionally, the residents were consolidating their living quarters, "with three and four families [moving into] one house and using the other houses for fuel."[573]

The impacts of the blockades were felt not only within the region but farther afield as well. The editor in Pipestone wrote, "The managers of a . . . booth at a fair being held at Cleveland, Ohio, telegraphed C. H. Bennett of this village for all the Pipestone trinkets he could send them. But the railroads were all blocked and

Charlie [Cawley] was powerless to comply with the request."[574] Pipestone is the easy-to-carve red stone, found locally, for which the town of Pipestone is named.

A Train Gets Through!

Considering the deprivation and isolation expressed over the past few months, one would expect the arrival of a train in eastern Dakota Territory to bring out celebratory words. But when, on February 19, a train bringing needed provisions reached Madison, all the editor of the nearby town of Egan cared to share, blandly, was, "The snow shovelers succeeded in reaching Madison Saturday evening, and the train went through with fuel and flour for the isolated citizens."[575]

Following the Storm of February 22

The tracks were clear for one day before the next storm blew in, closing everything up again. The *Egan Express* mixed in humor to help lighten the blow, printing, "It is the opinion of those who are best posted that we will have a through train by the 4th of next July. We hope there may be no mistake about this matter as we want to go to the celebration."[576]

The *Dell Rapids Exponent* reported that despite the snow, the cuts were "not so badly filled as at first reported." The editor continued, "Small cuts about two-thirds full and large cuts have from 1 to 2 feet of snow in them—this is where they have lately been shoveled out. The company is working all the men obtainable and working hard."[577] It seems that a cut "two-thirds full" was still considered a formidable task to clear.

Indeed, the *Janesville Argus* relayed that the "little blow of the 22nd" had again blocked the Southern Minnesota, and further remarked that "fifteen minutes of snow and five of blow chokes every railroad to death now."[578]

The first consistent reports of a condition called snow blindness appeared as well, as described by the editor in Egan when he wrote, "Many who have been out shoveling snow on the railroad are suffering severely with sore eyes."[579] We'll touch on that more in the March chapter.

Along the Sioux City

Throughout the winter, blockages were less severe along the Sioux City road, which ran diagonally from Minneapolis to Omaha via Sioux City, Iowa. However, the late-January storm put even that line out of commission, depositing ten to fourteen inches of snow between Sioux City and Sioux Falls.[580] Approximately thirty people were snowbound on a train at Mountain Lake,[581] and the Flandreau paper indicated that the line was not open again until February 17.[582]

Tracks Clogged with Cars

Early in the month, "about half a million bushels of grain were stored in different elevators and warehouses along the [Southern Minnesota], awaiting shipment."[583] The situations at grain elevators, even on the eastern edge of the region, were not improving as mid-February approached, and the newspapers continued to hint that farmers should not bother trying to bring their grain into town just yet.

One article put a different spin on the situation—instead of counting cars, it counted miles of sidetrack covered in said cars: "The Mankato Review says there are twenty nine miles of side track east of Sleepy Eye occupied with loaded freight cars bound west for points now snowed in."[584] That would be a lot of parked cars.

Other Railroad Business

"Men who are willing to work and are not afraid of exposure can't complain for want of employment this winter, for the railroad company take all the men they can get for snow shovelers at a dollar and a quarter a day and board."[585]

—*Moody County Enterprise*, February 3, 1881

Expansion Work / Business as Usual

A wide variety of articles provided insight into the breadth of facilities and other accoutrements that accompanied the building of the railroad's infrastructure in newly settled areas, including continued work to survey the routes west of the Missouri River.

Despite the lack of success running trains west of Sleepy Eye, the New Ulm paper passed along news that the Chicago & North Western contemplated "running a lightning train between Chicago and Tracy." It continued, "They have been running a lightning train west of St. Peter nearly all winter, but it is not very often that the lighting has struck the stations."[586] The base information about the lightning train first appeared in the *Murray County Pioneer* out of Currie on January 6, but wasn't passed along (sarcastically) by the New Ulm paper until early February.

Food

> "Things were never livelier than the past week.
> Wheat was coming in in large quantities and wood in perfect
> avalanches. / Everybody says 'roads are bad' but farmers are
> anxious to get a little money and make their arrangements
> for the approaching spring."[587]
> —*Janesville Argus*, February 22, 1881

Food Available

As could be expected, mentions of food shortages appeared more frequently in February, despite many locations reporting plenty of provisions. In her autobiography, Wilder noted,

> The two grocery stores were small and started with only a little capital.
> Not having much money to buy with and expecting to be able to replace
> the stock as it was sold the store keepers had only a small supply on hand
> when the trains stopped running and it was to [sic] late to get more. It was
> the same with the coal sold at the lumber yard. Now with no way of
> getting more supplies of both food and fuel were running short.[588]

Nearly four months after the October storm, the food situation was becoming more tenuous, and examples were found throughout the region. Lamberton, east of Walnut Grove on the Winona & St. Peter, reported being short of flour, though local farmers had more to supply the residents.[589]

A grocery ad for the Red Front Bee Hive appeared in the *Marshall Messenger* of February 25, informing readers, "Our team arrived last week with 2,200 pounds of groceries. We were glad to see them as some of the goods we were in need of." Included in the list of newly arrived goods were fresh oysters, apples, dried apples, mincemeat, spices, and fish. The ad included that fish was "always on hand," leading one to wonder if this was fresh fish obtained locally by way of ice fishing. There were also "canned goods of all kinds," coffee, honey, nuts and candies.[590]

February food reports along the Dakota Central came from the far western end, which was not directly experiencing the debilitating snows. While they were certainly impacted by the train blockades, team roads away from the main storm-prone areas likely allowed supplies to come in from less affected areas.

Throughout February, the pages of the *Fort Pierre Weekly Signal* touted the availability of a variety of fish;[591] potatoes ("not a frozen one amongst them");[592] and bread, candies, and other groceries, all to be had at cheap market rates.[593]

Back east at the border between Minnesota and Dakota Territory, towns along the Southern Minnesota line reported that provisions remained available. In Egan, over "half a ton of flour" had been sold one week, though the purchasers were "compelled to carry it home on their backs, owing to the impassable condition of the roads." In addition to the in-town sales, the same supplier "shipped over 5 tons of flour to neighboring towns" that week alone.[594]

A resident of Tracy made his way to Pipestone with "a barrel of the sweets of this earth, that so many have so much desired. . . ."[595] The phrase "sweets of this earth" may be a poetic reference to potatoes, turnips, beets, or carrots, somehow attained after an absence.

A New Ulm resident made visits to Springfield and Sleepy Eye mid-month, and upon his return reported that provisions were "plenty in Springfield and that no cases of want or suffering had been reported up to the time of his departure."[596]

Scarcity

Reports mentioning food along the Hastings & Dakota were rare for February, but when they did appear, they spoke of destitution. A February 10 article from Milbank read, "It was learned that a certain family residing in this place were suffering for the actual necessaries of life. [Two residents] started around town and collected a fund with which groceries and provisions were purchased and supplied to the family."[597]

The newspapers along the Winona & St. Peter were more prolific in their reporting, showing a mix of scarcity, optimism, and true plenty. Springfield reported, "Merchants are nearly all out of tea and sugar."[598] The *Murray County Pioneer* announced, "As yet we have learned of no serious suffering here abouts in consequence of the storm, although many admit the inconvenience of a short supply of some articles of food and the prospect of less in the future."[599] And the *Marshall Messenger* included, "There has been some suffering among stock for want of feed this week, but it will soon be supplied now."[600]

An article from the Janesville paper shared telegraph-sourced reports from along the various railroad lines, as originally shared by the St. Paul *Pioneer Press*. The editor began his review with skepticism, saying that the reports he'd received "do not indicate any great suffering in the west. They may be true, but shivering doubts crowd upon us." He continued, "If we of this locality were to be isolated for sixty days, shut off from mills, and no timber obtainable, we fear we should not be so cheerful as these telegrams read. Still, we hope they may be true."[601]

The article then relayed that Watertown reported no suffering, being in possession of "ten to fifteen tons of flour . . . a fair supply of groceries, canned goods in abundance, though meats are scarce." Additionally, Huron was "well stocked with everything but kerosene."[602]

In a report that raises new questions, the *Lake Benton News* said, "Several cars loaded with live stock were snowed in near Burns Station [Springfield]. Fine time for moving cattle and hogs to market out that way."[603] Were the animals being shipped eastward? Were they destined westward? Were they commandeered for food while waiting for the blockades to lift? No mention of their fate was found.

In the previous section, the Red Front Bee Hive grocer was mentioned as listing items recently received. That same listing included requests—offering to pay good prices—for potatoes, eggs, butter, corn, and oats.[604]

Similar reports came in along the Southern Minnesota. In Pipestone, merchants reported running low on staple groceries.[605]

The *Egan Express* reported, "Corn in this county is very scarce at present, not because the usual amount was not raised, but because farmers were unable to harvest the crop last fall and now it is nearly all covered with snow."[606]

The *Sioux Valley News* reported, "During the last snow storm twenty hogs perished at the stock yards. . . . They piled up and those underneath were smothered."[607] Anyone with experience keeping livestock will know animals sometimes do seemingly stupid things under stressful conditions.

Antelope/Deer

A memorable chapter in *The Long Winter* is devoted to a herd of antelope that wandered near town.[608] De Smet was not the only locality visited by small herds of wild animals foraging for food. Eleven antelope were spotted near Flandreau, and local farmers and their dogs "took after them." When the hunt was complete, the hunters "most kindly remembered ye editor with a generous portion." The editor confirmed that "the antelope were in very good condition contrary to the general expectation."[609]

A second, similar article appeared the week before in the Egan paper, but described the animals and their number as "eleven deer." What is interesting about that earlier article is that the resident who saw the animals reported that he "paid no particular attention to them and thought nothing more about the matter" until one of his dogs took chase.[610] The gentleman was evidently uninterested in a herd of animals that could have provided solid protein, possibly indicating a nonscarcity of food.

Wheat

Throughout February, reports continued to appear of farmers bringing their wheat to elevators, though trains could not carry it away. In Flandreau, buyers somehow found storage space for the new deliveries.[611] Along the full stretch of the Southern Minnesota, "about half a million bushels of grain were stored in different elevators and warehouses along the road, awaiting shipment."[612]

We've seen evidence of wheat in abundance all across the region. What was the status of the elevator at De Smet? One can assume that the harvest around De Smet was similar to other towns, which were by this point reporting overflowing elevators. But we do not have evidence of the actual situation. Instead, we have *The Long Winter*, which indicates that the wheat in De Smet was limited to a few dozen bushels, hidden between the walls of the Wilder Feed Store.

The Seed Wheat Run

> " 'Almanzo,' Royal said solemnly, 'if I let you lose your fool self out on these prairies, what'll I say to Father and Mother?' "[613]
>
> —*The Long Winter*

The newspaper record confirms that some locations had individuals going out, on foot or with teams, to retrieve fuel, mail, and sometimes food throughout the winter. We've also seen that wheat was stored in large quantities across the region, but no mentions of any of the elevators handing out stored grain to hungry settlers, or even requests for such. However, there are a few surviving newspaper records from towns along the Dakota Central, including De Smet—the region that appears to have been the hardest hit.

The actual and fictional versions of De Smet were, according to Wilder, destitute of food, surviving on a dwindling supply of wheat that was being endlessly ground into flour in coffee mills all over town. As the supply became critically low, a rumor spread of a homesteader about twelve miles southeast of town who had grown wheat the previous summer and kept at least a portion for next season's seed. Loftus, a merchant, offered to front the funds to trade for the wheat, putting a plan into action assuming someone brave enough to face the blizzards would do the legwork.[614]

Based upon that rumor, the knowledge that people were facing starvation, and what is conjecture of considerable soul-searching, Almanzo Wilder and Cap Garland, two of De Smet's fine young men, took on the task of risking their lives to bring that wheat back to the hungry residents. The heroic journey seemed fool-hardy: They set out in a general direction, not entirely sure where they were heading, hoping they would stumble upon the homesteader and convince him to sell his seed wheat. They would then turn around and return to town, the wheat as cargo, before the next blizzard struck.[615]

The slough-pocked landscape sapped considerable precious energy. The snow had a habit of accumulating high in the grass, forming a crust over large air pockets. Any real weight would collapse the crust and, depending upon the terrain beneath, cause unsteady footing or capsize a sled.[616]

Men could navigate this situation well enough. So could some more-experienced horses, but not all horses. A horse falling through the crust, tethered to a sled, will either keep his wits or panic. And a panicking horse is a dangerous horse. An expert horseman with a steady hand, Almanzo was able to keep both horses calm when they encountered air pockets.[617]

The two men pushed on, encouraging, teasing, and pushing each other into action as needed. They found themselves on the crest of a knoll when they spotted a wisp of smoke that led them to the dugout dwelling of the rumored homesteader with seed wheat. Fervent negotiations took place; the homesteader was as strongly uninterested in selling his wheat as Almanzo and Cap were interested in purchasing it. We'll revisit this aspect in a bit.[618]

In what was perhaps seen as a two-against-one scenario, the homesteader sold the wheat to the young men, and they loaded it onto the sleds. The lonely home-steader wanted their company and reminded them it was dangerous to start their return trip so late in the day. The same stubbornness that got the pair to the home-steader's house led them back out into the cold; they feared a delay would leave them stranded in a blizzard.[619]

As they made their way back toward De Smet, daylight slipped away, and the men became colder and colder. Sunset found them near a familiar landmark, a lone cottonwood a few miles south of town, just as the also familiar "dark cloud in the northwest" appeared. The stars overhead were beautiful, but the cloud of blowing snow swallowed them as it pushed southward. The race to town was barely won, but barely won is still won. De Smet had wheat to keep its people going for the foreseeable future.[620]

One intriguing aspect of this episode is that Almanzo had been adamant about not selling his own wheat, which was in a quantity similar to that of the homesteader. Yet to persuade that homesteader to sell, he used many of the same arguments that Royal had used on Almanzo.

Why had he been willing to risk his life to obtain another's wheat rather than part with his own? Wilder attributed it to her husband's "kindness," along with the knowledge that the amount he had stored would not have been enough to provide for the town until spring.[621] But there may have been another factor.

Over a year before, during the summer of 1879, while on a trip that Almanzo, Royal, and Eliza Jane took to Yankton to file on their homesteads, one of Almanzo's horses died after being pushed too hard in the heat. He would continue to make loan payments on that horse for several years.[622] During the summer of 1880, he worked as a teamster on the railroad west of De Smet, then returned to Marshall to harvest his wheat. Various expenses accumulated, and he returned to De Smet in the fall of 1880 with little beyond those precious bags of seed wheat.[623] On the heels of the death of his horse, and with the disappointment of learning that Huron (not De Smet, where he had elected to invest his energies) was chosen as the division point—and would become a major town—for the railroad, it is possible Almanzo was determined not to lose his prized seed wheat as well. In a note to Lane, answering questions about era, he had written, "My life has been mostly disappointments."[624]

As for timing, the autobiography is not in reliably chronological order, and the seed wheat run's placement within the novel may have been adjusted for dramatic effect. Appendix I explores possible timing for the event.

Fuel

> "Wood and hay are beginning to be a much sought after
> article in this city and some enormous prices have been asked
> and paid for during the past week, but as the roads in the
> country are getting opened the strain upon our citizens
> will soon be relaxed."[625]
>
> —*New Ulm Weekly Review*, February 16, 1881

Along the Hastings & Dakota

The *Grant County Review* in Milbank reported that the town was well supplied with wood, though it was unseasoned, green wood. While not optimal, it "nevertheless admirably answer[ed] the purpose of fighting off that pugnacious intruder, Jack Frost."[626]

A correspondent from Milbank reassured readers, both local and of other regional papers in which the story was reprinted, that the "stormy weather had subsided," allowing farmers to venture into town, where shops were "amply supplied with provisions" and wood, brought in from the Dakota Hills, was "in sufficient quantity." Those in "sections remote from the timber" were still burning hay.[627]

The Dakota Hills lay approximately twelve miles west of Milbank and ran north–south along the ridge of the Coteau des Prairies plateau for many miles. As the land tilted westward after the crest, numerous streams provided an environment wet enough for timber.

Hay was readily available but came at a physical cost. In a letter to her daughter, Rose, Wilder explained, "To keep from freezing we could twist hay but it was a steady job for one man. We figured we must burn coal in the winter. Could not really be warm with hay."[628] This letter was written in the late 1930s, but the experience had been gleaned from the hard winter.

Along the Winona & St. Peter

The number of articles concerning fuel in this deepest part of winter was overwhelming. Watertown was so short of wood that railroad ties and at least one bridge had "already added fuel to the flame of many a settler's hearthstone."[629] In contrast, Mankato was described as "one vast wood yard," where vacant lots across the city were commandeered and turned into "immense piles" of wood.[630]

Marshall's location near a large wooded area had conveniently provided a source of fuel up to this point. However, recent heavy snows made the team roads impassable and the woods inaccessible.[631]

Reports that there was suffering beyond the blockades became more frequent, though editors tended to report it about other communities, not their own. The *New Ulm Weekly Review* noted, "Some of the farmers out west have commenced to burn wheat for fuel."[632]

A traveler who walked to New Ulm from Lamberton shared, "There is beginning to be considerable suffering in the vicinity of Lamberton and farther west for the want of fuel," and that in the vicinity of the Walnut Grove, residents had resorted to burning hitching posts, parts of stables, and even their liberty pole.[633]

Unable to provide a warm, safe learning environment without fuel, schools throughout the blockaded region to the west closed,[634] and families west of Marshall were reported as keeping to their beds to stay warm.[635] New Ulm also reported a welcome delivery of fuel and "51,000 pounds of freight for merchants."[636]

Cooperative efforts were widespread, and there continued to be reports that settlers were "moving into buildings previously occupied and burning the vacated residences."[637] Meanwhile, Tracy continued to claim "no actual suffering," noting that the town had procured soft coal by team from one nearby location and provisions likewise from Sleepy Eye.[638]

One wonders whether the phrase "no serious suffering" was used to couch or downplay instances of actual suffering. "As yet," wrote the Currie editor, "we learn of no serious suffering in consequence of the blockade, but some of the merchants are placed on half rations with certain goods, while the consumption of the stock of kerosene in this and surrounding villages has necessitated the introduction of the tallow dip, as in bygone days."[639] A tallow dip is similar to the button lamp employed by Ma earlier in the winter.

Along the Dakota Central

Again, the only information about the Dakota Central in February comes from the *Fort Pierre Weekly Signal*. While the area had plenty of food, warmth was a more difficult commodity to come by. "Coal is again exhausted," wrote the Pierre editor, "and if there is not wood enough in town, we will commence to play freeze out from now until spring."[640]

Along the Southern Minnesota

In Pipestone, February began with a dispatch of wood rationing, followed by reports of shortages all along the Southern Minnesota line. Mid-month, the railroad shipped a "large number of piles" to be sold by Station Agent Cawley to the droves of people that had been "burning sills and other heavy timbers from the lumber yards."[641]

When two carloads of wood arrived in Pipestone on February 1, it only took a few hours for the entire stock to be dispersed, despite rationing no more than a quarter cord to each buyer.[642] An additional six cars of ties were distributed among the residents of Madison, Pipestone, and Edgerton.[643] At least one location in Dakota had started using corn for fuel.[644]

While kerosene was reported to be unavailable along the Winona & St. Peter, Pipestone boasted that merchants had "fortunately laid in big fall stocks," and while the supply was running low, it was holding out.[645] Sioux Falls claimed to be "superabundantly supplied with coal and kerosene," adding that it had "seen blizzard winters before."[646]

Railroad employees had the unique opportunity to see conditions firsthand across multiple locations. One conductor, working on a track-clearing crew, reported that the people of Madison were "in a suffering condition."[647] Superintendent Egan arranged to sell ten railcars of coal "to the residents of Flandreau at . . . actual cost, transportation added . . . as soon as it can be got through."[648] The *Pipestone Star* shared that another station agent could not bear seeing his fellow citizens suffer; the agent "very kindly threw open the coal bins of the railroad company and supplied all who made application." The writer of the article warmly added, "The people thereabouts will not be apt to forget this very generous act."[649]

Out and About

"Quite a number of teams were in from the country Saturday, notwithstanding the roads were in an almost impassable condition."[650]

—*Egan Express*, February 24, 1881

Weatherwise, February was arguably the worst month thus far. But it did little to deter travel and recreation throughout the region.

Travels

Again, we see a combination of train travel in the eastern portion of the region and travel by team or on foot as one moved west. Upon returning, many shared reports of the blockades and how they maneuvered around them.

Along the Hastings & Dakota

As people were able to get out, they did, as observed by the Milbank editor when he wrote, "Every day that it is possible for a team to travel, and there are very few times that it is not possible, our streets are lined with them."[651]

Along the Winona & St. Peter

An abundance of articles detailed attempts to travel, successful or not. The eastern and central portions of the region reported deeper snow and more problems than at any previous point in the winter.

A visitor to Waseca reported that "snow on the track was from two to five feet deep," which required that he and his five companions walk ten miles west to Janesville.[652] West of Janesville, in New Ulm, "three teams started for Marshall . . .

but were compelled to turn back after proceeding only about a mile and a half. They reported the snow on the prairie to be from three to four feet deep on the level."[653]

Team travel wasn't the only activity hindered by the impassable roads. The Janesville school board canceled school for the week because it thought it impossible for children "residing in the outskirts of the city" to navigate the drifts.[654]

Articles about team roads were nowhere near as numerous throughout the winter as updates about the railroad, but they did appear. As we read earlier, a crew had been working to open a wagon road near Marshall to allow wood from a nearby stand of timber to be retrieved. That crew encountered yet another group, which was clearing a road in order to deliver a load of flour. The next day, the two crews gathered to discuss further attempts to clear the wagon roads.

During the meeting, one attendee read an official railroad telegram from New Ulm advising towns on the line west of there "to save their strength till the railroad was open near enough to make our efforts sure to be of use to them." A large crew was laboring at and to the east of New Ulm, and because "the snow worked more easily than before, confidence was expressed that the road would soon be open." The wagon roads from town were opened, and "volunteers made up some four parties to break [clear] roads" toward several nearby communities.[655]

Walking will always be the lowest-common-denominator method of travel, and residents relied upon their legs to convey them throughout the Hard Winter. Many articles shared the experiences of such pedestrians, nearly always men. One resident of New Ulm started home from Springfield on foot, "using a billiard cue for a walking cane," and described it as "the toughest game of billiards that he ever played." Fortunately, he was able to finish the trip via team.[656]

As the above resident returned to New Ulm from the west, two others were headed east, driving teams. They arrived in Mankato just prior to the storm of February 11 and were forced to "remain in place" for the duration. When the storm abated, they began their return trip to New Ulm. They reached a point about twenty miles west of Mankato, approximately halfway home, before the horses were "unable to proceed any farther" and were "left in the care of some farmers."[657]

The travelers continued their return trip on foot and made it as far as Courtland, where they hoped to catch the train. The same snows that thwarted the horses had done the same to the trains, so the pair "resumed their weary march." They encountered two others, who had walked west from St. Peter and "were also pretty well tuckered out." When the four made it to New Ulm, "weary and foot-sore," they declared their plans to take "a good, long rest before undertaking a similar tour."[658]

Walking any distance in the frigid air, the threat of a blizzard ever present, was a dangerous endeavor. Most stories ended relatively well, but not always. According to the *Winona Republican*, one family attempted to return to Pepin County, Wisconsin. Unfortunately, "they were caught in a blizzard on the open prairie near Watertown, and the whole family, consisting of five persons, were frozen to death. The team also perished."[659]

Along the Dakota Central

The limited reports from along the Dakota Central in February came from Fort Pierre, sharing the difficult conditions suffered on the western end. Despite the inherent challenges, travel attempts continued. Deep snows the first week of February limited stage travel, though at least one person made it to the Black Hills.

One of the Northwestern Stage Company drivers reported a "hard trip" upon making it to Fort Pierre on February 13, "having been out over a week."[660] The stage from Yankton reached Fort Pierre on February 19, ending a twelve-day absence.[661]

Being cooped up in their homes did not necessarily mean boredom for residents, however. A rare correspondence from Huron reassured readers when it read, "Our citizens, although shut off from communication with the outside world, are enjoying themselves with parlor dramas, theaters and literary entertainments, and are in the best of spirits."[662]

Along the Southern Minnesota

Just to the south of the Dakota Central, travel seemed a bit easier and more consistent, supporting the theory that perhaps the worst conditions were indeed along the Winona & St. Peter and the Dakota Central, the two lines that directly impacted De Smet.

The stage successfully functioned between Sioux Falls and Flandreau at the beginning of the month,[663] though by February 10, "immense drifts of snow in every direction [made] the roads almost impassable," causing "quite a number of traveling men" to wait it out in Flandreau.[664]

On February 17, the *Pipestone Star* reported that several of the town's citizens were out working to "open communications with the southern portion of the country."[665] It is not clear whether this was an attempt to open a team road or the railroad, or if the telegraph lines had come down and they were working to restring them.

Mid- to late month, the communities of Flandreau and Egan, close together on the western end of the railroad line, reported numerous teams coming into town to conduct business. While the stage drivers near the Missouri River were having difficulties, the route linking Sioux Falls, Dell Rapids, Egan, and Flandreau was operating, and the stages were able to haul a "full load of passengers armed with shovels" out of town.[666]

Community Building

Along all railroad lines, the development of the various communities was interrupted by the weather throughout February. Whether it was school, church services, literary societies, masquerade balls, dances, singing schools, or sleighing for fun, cancellations or postponements were common. As weather and travel conditions permitted, however, people from nearby towns joined the festivities of their neighbors.

Compared to the other lines, fewer events were canceled along the Southern Minnesota. The *Egan Express* of February 3 shared, "Two sleigh loads of our young people went out to the lyceum in the Cameron school district, last Saturday evening. They report a good time."[667] The school was also flourishing "despite the tempestuous weather."[668]

In Flandreau, "a few farmers succeeded in getting in to town,"[669] with spring work being on the minds of many despite the storms. The Flandreau editor reported that "snow balling was the main amusement in town" and that "five dances in one week is keeping it up pretty lively."[670] But the citizens hungered for all types of distractions beyond the ones already being offered. "The numerous dances, of late," wrote the editor, "show the natural tendency to seek recreation and amusement in such times as these. Why not vary the form of amusement by getting up some kind of a literary entertainment or a spelling school or something of that sort!"[671]

It wasn't always weather or trains that doomed an activity. In Egan, a tilting schoolhouse delayed at least one event. "It has been the intention of the ladies ... to give an oyster supper in the school house," wrote the Egan editor, "but it now transpires that the building is so out of level that the soup would unavoidably be spilled over the western horizon of the soup-plates. Hence, the project has for the present been abandoned."[672]

In an era in which sarcasm was in frequent employ, one could see an event organizer postponing an event for seven months to *hopefully* avoid the snows, as when the *Egan Express* printed, "The next sociable will be held Wednesday evening, Sept. 23rd, at the residence of J. H. Eno. A general invitation is extended,"[673] though a misprint is more likely. J. H. Eno was the editor of the *Egan Express*.

It wasn't just the human residents who were getting out and about, however. Near Egan, residents were warned that "the heavy fall of snow has made the wolves uncommonly bold and troublesome."[674]

Newspapers and Mail

"The papers come down from the west printed on brown paper in some instances. Those fellows out there won't be beaten, and we expect yet to see them shoving out cabbage leaves and elm slabs at $1.50 a year."[675]

—*Janesville Argus*, February 8, 1881

As the January blockades continued into February, postmasters began in earnest to organize delivery methods that did not depend upon trains. They began noting the amount of time between deliveries in terms of weeks rather than days.

The newspaper editors plodded on as best they could. On the western edge of the region, Fort Pierre received a shipment from Sioux Falls or Yankton—likely via team, but that is merely conjecture.[676] "We are now in receipt of a large amount of print paper," wrote the Fort Pierre editor, "enough to last us until after the blockade is raised, so you may look for the Signal regularly unless something worse happens."[677]

Like January, February saw a cacophony of articles about the mail. As one editor noted, "Marshall has a post office, but it is of little use this winter."[678] Delivery by train was still relatively common on the eastern edge of the region, though on an irregular schedule. When it did arrive, there was considerable volume. The New Ulm paper reported "the largest mail that has ever been received at the New Ulm post office at one time," including "2167 letters and postal cards and 39 sacks of papers. . . ." The mail delivery was so large, "it was as much as two horses could haul."[679]

As contracts and arrangements for team delivery were put into action, reports about the teams experiencing their own trials and tribulations began to appear. "The mail to Wells was abandoned on Monday and Wednesday of last week," wrote the Janesville editor. "Carrier went as far as Vivian on Monday and to Alma [City] on Tuesday and Wednesday also on Thursday, also Friday, ditto Saturday, likewise Monday."[680]

When trains and teams were not sufficient, foot traffic came into play. The *Moody County Enterprise* noted that its town's only mail in a week had been brought by a carrier who delivered "about 150 pounds of mail which he drew on a hand sled."[681]

As already noted, when mail did make it through, the quantities were often quite large, and the readers were told how many items or sacks were delivered and how many hours it took to sort them. It is here that the editors started sharing a new statistic: the mail included the coveted newspapers from other locations, and editors shared the dates of those publications as a way of illustrating how long the mail had been delayed on its journey.[682] By February 24, even Sioux Falls had been without mail for three weeks.[683]

At the end of February, Milbank received "a large sack of mail matter, principally newspapers," which had taken a circuitous route through central Minnesota to reach it. This "mail from the old country" was the first in a month and "was regarded as a big bonanza to the famishing soul that had been yearning for intelligence of what was going on in the world at large."[684] The reference to the east as "the old country" further reminded readers that they were in a "new" region and inconveniences should be expected.

Boosterism

"The Mankato Free Press predicts an exodus from Dakota next spring."[685]

—*Janesville Argus*, February 15, 1881

As February dawned, the ongoing blockade was only a few weeks old, and it is likely that few were imagining it would last for months. With an easy grin-and-bear-it fortitude, the individual editors continued to show the kind of towns they represented.

The February 3 edition of the *Grant County Review* noted that despite it being "the dead of winter," Milbank was showing "itself off to good advantage...." The editor further touted that the town had "a live set of merchants and business men ... who calculate to give their customers a 'square deal,'" the consequence being that all businesses were "doing a lively business."[686] A week later, the *Review* continued to laud the benefits of its portion of the territory. "Dakota in itself," wrote the editor, "is a great and mighty empire. Home is where the heart is, and the heart is ever happy when in Dakota—the future granary of the world. In Dakota you will always find health, wealth, and happiness without stint. . . ."[687]

Egan issued a challenge: it would "see more activity displayed . . . than in any town in southeastern Dakota." That activity would happen once the weather became more agreeable, allowing those anxious to build in town to do so. The editor anticipated "a big boom in Egan the coming season."[688]

Flandreau was a little less unwavering in its positivity, though it did try. Its February 10 edition shared that a group of travelers caught in a storm "inaugurated a dancing party," during which "a party of young people and all made the dining room floor blossom with quicksteps till half past eleven." The editor added, "Verilly [sic], Flandrau hotels are a good port in a snow storm."[689] One week prior, the paper had somberly noted that while it did not expect its town to stagnate due to the storms, the season's severity had a silver lining. "The only consolation that we can get out of it," wrote the editor, "is that a winter of deep snows is almost invariably followed by unusually large harvests."[690] These halfhearted cheers had the ring of the earlier article that encouraged farmers to plant fruit near rivers so they wouldn't burn in the prairie fires.

As we've seen, not much set the typesetting fingers flying like a whiff of an easterner with a negative view of life in Dakota Territory. One such retort appeared in the February 10 edition of the *Grant County Review*, reprinted from the *Sioux Falls Independent*. Humorously, it heralded the climate not for its own benefits but because it was "not too far south to be dried up by drouth and hot winds, where the inhabitants are laid up nine months in the year with malaria and yellow fever; and not too far north for the winters to be long and unpleasant; but the location in that 'golden mean' between extremes." The writer continued, describing Dakota Territory as "a country that is rapidly settling up, where you will find good society, good schools and free education for your children, good market, good government, good railroad facilities, good newspapers, and no taxes until you have proved up on your land, and that can be delayed seven years if you desire it."[691] The article went on for some length, with what feels like an attitude of "and another thing!" It is insightful and entertaining, and the full text is available at thebeautifulsnow.com.

A Good Place to Be Snowed In

Always trying to make the best of things, towns seemed to compete over which was the more hospitable location in which to be snowbound. The *Moody County Enterprise* in Flandreau made frequent mention of such reviews, as seen in the following extracts:

"Two of the pleasantest towns on the line of the Southern Minnesota for a blockaded traveller to bring up in are Jackson and Lanesboro. They are both protected from the storms and have hotels that it is a comfort to stop at."[692]

"Fairmont is said to be the best town on the line for hungry snow shovelers to bring up in. The landlord of the Occidental hotel at that place as a phenominal [*sic*] capacity for scaring up numerous meals."[693]

"Seven traveling men partook of the hospitalities of the Sioux Valley House during the late storm and there isn't one of them that wouldn't enjoy getting snowed in at Flandrau again."[694]

Conditions in De Smet

We've reached the end of February with little specific information about what was going on in De Smet. We've seen that the railroad handed out coal there after the earliest blizzards. We've seen that residents of De Smet traveled outward and people from other places visited the town. But how were things for the residents?

One extant page of the De Smet newspaper, the *Kingsbury County News*, was in the possession of Aubrey Sherwood, who included its contents in *Beginnings of DeSmet*. That extract, published on Thursday, February 24, 1881, contained little tidbits that read the same as the articles we've seen throughout other regional newspapers:

Weather:
- For a buster, how does this winter strike you?

Railroad:
- The leading question is, when shall we have a train from the east?
- Will Foster, of Volga, who has been spending a couple of weeks in town, returned home on the snow plow Sunday.
- Conductor Nash with his snowplow and nearly a hundred men pulled up for De Smet from the snow blockade.
- A dollar and a half a day for shoveling snow on the Dakota Central takes most of our business and professional men out. It's more fun to shovel snow than to go without bread or coal.

Food:
- Hen fruit [eggs] is an expensive luxury just now.
- The first wheat ground in De Smet was turned out by Dan Loftus. Dan makes a good miller.

Fuel:
- How much coal have you?
- Hay fire is all the rage now in town.
- Coal is very scarce along the D. C. line just now.

Mail:
- We are liable to get a mail from the east this week.
- At last we have a mail. It arrived the fore part of last week.

Out and About:
- Ed McCaskell is back.
- Our school goes bravely on.
- John Fairbanks, of Nordland, is in town.
- A nice little hop at the Exchange Tuesday night.
- Harthorn went down to Volga on a forage expedition trip the fore part of the week.
- Ole Quam, H. V. Hall and John Pettis, of Nordland, were over to De Smet Monday.[695]

De Smet appeared to be in similar circumstances to the rest of the region. Mail came infrequently. Coal was scarce, and hay was being used for fuel. At least one train, possibly two, pushed a snowplow through, but it is unclear whether it was eastbound or westbound. Perhaps food was delivered, but there is no indication. This marks the second known mention of a train moving on the Dakota Central during February, the other being the train from Pierre that pulled into Huron on February 28. The railroad was paying each man $1.50 per day to shovel out cuts, and people were traveling around the general region.

One of the motivations for this project was to see if there were attempts to obtain provisions from other locations, via wagon or sleigh relay teams, in the absence of trains. The item noting that Harthorn, a grocer, went to Volga "on a forage expedition" confirms the suspicion that townspeople did more for their situation than simply wait for the trains to return.

A few vague references throughout the winter appear to allude that trains were capable of running along the western section of track. However, no evidence was found in the issues of the Fort Pierre paper to indicate that food from that location, which appeared to have had plenty on hand, was carried eastward to towns between the Missouri River and Brookings.

Perhaps track conditions were not as positive as some of the local editors insisted they were. Or maybe there wasn't as much food in Fort Pierre as claimed. Or perhaps there was not enough coal or wood in that region to fuel the locomotives.

In *Pioneer Girl* and the Brandt version (quoted here) of the autobiography, Wilder noted that "the storms were so terrible and so frequent that no teaming from Brookins [sic] could be done, and in Brookins [sic] supplies were also running short, for no train could run west of Tracy."[696] Because the *Brookings County Press* did not publish for most of February and March, we have no records of food status in that location. However, Watertown, Marshall, and Fort Pierre all reported plenty of food on hand, as well as excess wheat in the elevators. Based on the efforts of other communities to obtain food via teams, we can surmise that someone from De Smet at least attempted to do so (in addition to Almanzo and Cap's seed wheat run), and the squib about Harthorn's "forage expedition" confirms that it did, indeed, happen.

The item "Our school goes bravely on" is surprising, as Wilder indicated it had stopped following the fourth blizzard in the novel.[697] It is possible that school continued, at least for some time, but Charles and Caroline kept their children at home, safe from the weather.[698]

And that hint about Loftus having the first wheat ground in De Smet? Perhaps he obtained some from one of the area's overflowing elevators. But it also coincides nicely with the time frame for the seed wheat run bravely carried out by Almanzo Wilder and Cap Garland.

MARCH 1881

Sunday	Monday	Tuesday	Wednesday	Thursday	Friday	Saturday
		1 warm clear	2 ///////////	3	4 ▬▬▬	5 /////////// sunny, mild "sugar weather"
6 sunny, mild "sugar weather" melting	7 sunny, mild "sugar weather" melting	8 sunny, mild "sugar weather" melting, thaw	9 sunny, mild "sugar weather" melting, thaw	10 mild "sap weather"	11 --------------Thundersnow-------------- mild east wind "sap weather"	12
13 clear pleasant	14 ▬▬▬ wind drifting	15 /////////// nice mild	16 wind, drifting soft snow	17 warmer	18	19 /////////// heavy wind caused drifting
20	21	22 fine weather	23 fine weather warmer, thaw melting	24 fine weather warmer, thaw snow settling	25 cooler	26
27	28	29	30 snow fast disappearing cold nights, warm days	31 ▬▬▬ windy NW wind −13F		

▬▬▬ Blizzard or significant snow event

/////////// Lighter snow or mixed precipitation

March 4: Pipestone reported "Snow piled up in some places to the height of fifteen feet."

March 17: Marshall reported "It is said that every Friday or Saturday since the October blizzard has been stormy."

March 19: Snow two feet on the level between Fort Pierre and Huron.

March 22: Marshall reported "Snow three-to-four feet on the level."

This calendar shows weather reports gleaned from the various newspaper articles.
If the weather was significantly different in one portion of the region versus another, that is noted.

Psychologically, March may have been the most difficult month. The bulk of winter was over. Spring was technically a short time away. Indeed, signs of it were appearing—small flocks of northbound waterfowl, a patch of prairie emerging beneath a thin spot in the snow cover here and there. Yet it was still winter. It was still cold. It was still most definitely stormy.

The sun began to do its work on the snow between blizzards, but the cuts themselves were encased in layers of ice, which would take significant effort to remove. Then, cruelly, the melting led to flooding of epic proportions, especially close to the Missouri, James, and Big Sioux Rivers. The weather continued to overpower the railroads.

Fuel was so difficult to come by that, in some locations, families moved in together, sharing a single house and sacrificing the other for fuel in order to survive a few more weeks.

While residents had found ingenious ways to travel in previous months, March saw much less mobility, due to mud that kept teams and wagons at bay. People were more effectively trapped now, maybe more so than at any other time during the winter. Still, travel continued.

The newspaper editors were at peak frustration, though their choices of printing materials, out of necessity, reached a peak of creativity. They also chose to express their irritation in the columns of their papers, authoring angry missives about how very wrong easterners were about life in Dakota Territory.

The Month for the Ingalls Family

"There was nothing in the world but cold and dark and work and coarse brown bread and winds blowing. The storm was always there, outside the walls, waiting sometimes, then pouncing, shaking the house, roaring, snarling, and screaming in rage."[699]

—*The Long Winter*

March was undefined in the novel; perhaps the energy of both the author and her family had been expended by the time February played out. In fact, of the 334 pages in the 2004 edition of the book, fewer than two are devoted to March.

The days were cold and dull, and lessons under Ma's direction had stopped. Monotony filled their time. Several paragraphs in the short chapter titled "It Can't Beat Us" describe the family's miserable morning procedure of leaving their warm beds and stepping into the cold air.[700] Meals were reduced to nothing but brown bread. But there was hay to twist and wheat to grind—a few things to be grateful for.

In *Pioneer Girl*, Wilder wrote, "We were getting shorter tempered. Pa did not sing in the morning about the happy sunflower." When Laura had previously heard Pa singing that song, she knew he was troubled but trying to keep a positive mindset, or at least appear that way for his family. (That he had stopped singing it altogether may have been due to sheer exhaustion or a resignation to their situation.) In the Brandt version, it was altered to include, "Everyone was pale and weak from lack of food, and tempers had worn thin." The Bye version retained the "pale and weak" statement and omitted the bad tempers.[701] Differences aside, one thing the novel and all versions of the autobiography support is that the lack of proper nutrition was taking its toll on the family—physically, emotionally, and mentally.

Fitting for the novel, Pa's optimism began to return after learning that Almanzo Wilder and Cap Garland safely returned with the wheat in February. (One might wonder whether he wrestled with guilt over not having gone himself, though he must have been greatly relieved upon their safe return.) As April, and the presumed start of spring, came ever closer, Pa reminded his family that winter "hasn't got much more time. March is nearly gone. We can last longer than it can."[702] Yet the storms continued.

The Weather

"The blockade has some consolations. Poets have been unable to forward us poems on the "beautiful snow."[703]

—*Brookings County Press*, March 24, 1881

Similar to February, March was a wild month with multiple storm events. Reports of flooding along the major rivers began to outnumber reports of snow, and the railroad tracks were being washed away instead of—or in addition to—being blocked by snow. Since the rivers generally ran north–south, once flooding began, it impacted multiple east–west rail lines at the same time. Fortunately, positive signs of the coming spring also began to appear.

Reports of flood warnings from American Indians appeared across the region. In Milbank, one such warning came from Lorenzo Lawrence (Towanetaton), a longtime resident and a native of the region. "Well known as a shrewd and close observer," he predicted a vast spring flooding event. He visited the office of the *Grant County Review* "for the express purpose of requesting [that the paper] publish his opinion that about the 20th of the present month there will be a very general thaw, and that folks may look out for a tremendous freshet."[704]

Lorenzo Lawrence (Towanetaton)

Lorenzo Lawrence, a Dakota Sioux, was born in the early 1820s in the vicinity of Milbank, near what is now the Minnesota–South Dakota border. His mother had been living among Christian missionaries, and she decided to convert; her deeply pious involvement in Christianity was a significant model for young Lorenzo as he grew up.

When the Dakota War of 1862 began, Lawrence's mother hid some white settlers to protect them, though she knew the location was not secure. She then asked Lawrence to guide them to a safer location. Lawrence and the settlers traveled for five days, but only at night, picking up additional refugees along the way. By the time the group reached Fort Ridgely (approximately eleven miles north of Sleepy Eye) the refugees comprised three women and thirteen children, all of whom were transferred to the care of the post's garrison.

Lawrence produced a beautifully handwritten forty-one-page memoir that is held in the archives of the Minnesota Historical Society. He is recorded as the first Dakota to receive US citizenship. He passed away in 1897 and is commemorated on a stone obelisk in Morton, Minnesota.[705]

The Storm of March 4

Much of March was described as mild and pleasant, though punctuated with significant storms, and the newspaper record conveys a tumultuous mix of hope and disappointment. The *Pipestone Star* described the March 4 storm as "the worst blizzard of the season. Snow piled up in some places to the height of fifteen feet."[706] The Janesville editor appreciated the lovely "sap weather" that the month started with—that is, until "the storm of Friday night and Saturday" ruined it all again. "Meanest kind of weather," the article concluded.[707]

Southeast of Sioux Falls, along the Dakota Territory–Iowa border, the *Canton Advocate* (Dakota Territory) waxed a bit more poetic. The editor began by supposing the recent mild weather would cause one to think that "spring time had come indeed, gentle Anna!" The article continued, "Old Sol having put forth all his illuminating powers, refreshing and giving new life to everything generally—fairly filling the heart of man with a feeling equal to that experienced after being rescued from a desperate struggle with the surging tide." After perhaps giving the reader a sense of lighthearted hope, he then reminded them, "This calmness may yet be followed by another old-fashioned 'nor'wester' which will cause a feeling of awe to steal over all, and if a storm cometh it will, might, could, would, or should, be the death knell of winter. The present is a most terrible storm."[708]

East of Vermillion, Dakota Territory, along the Missouri River, the *Elk Point Tribune* noted that hay was so deeply "buried in the drifts of the 'beautiful'" that it was difficult to free the grassy fuel and food for use. Some of those piles of hay were being used as landmarks, so their removal made navigating the open prairies more difficult, forcing people to adapt once again.[709]

A correspondent from Tracy wrote, "We have shared equally with others in the many storms. . . . Last month was a month of snow and wind, although the temperature, on the whole, was not so low as the forepart of the season."[710]

The Storm of March 10: Thundersnow

The days after the March 4 storm were described as springlike, and melting had begun in earnest. The *Marshall Messenger* exuded, "Indications of Spring now multiply day by day. This week has been warm and snow is fast becoming soft water."[711] However, like so much weather in the Midwest, the transition from one season to the next was not a smooth one. The thunderstorm on March 10 delivered snow instead of rain.[712]

Following the storm, some roads on the periphery of New Ulm were "almost impassable, while others were completely blocked up." Several teams riding in from Courtland "were all compelled to turn back, being unable to get through some of the huge drifts in the cuts. . . ."[713]

In Flandreau, the editor described the storm as possessing a force of wind "that has not been equaled in any storm this winter," and further added that "the air was more completely filled with snow than in any previous storm." An eating establishment in town reported that drifts covered its first-floor windows and continued growing until they reached the second story.[714]

"The great peculiarity of the storm," continued the editor, "however lay in the fact that it was a thunder-snow-storm." He mentioned that "a number of flashes of lightening" lead most to think "that the snow would turn to rain." But it did not.[715]

While the excitement of thunder and lightning was a "peculiarity," the emotional impact of the storm feels poignant. The Flandreau editor conveyed this when he wrote, "The hopes of seeing the railroad opened that had arisen during the comparatively long continued spell of good weather that preceded this storm have been necessarily deferred and a consequent air of sadness was somewhat observable when the storm was over."[716]

This particular storm was powerful enough to exhibit a phenomenon that, in modern terms, is called thundersnow. These storms are associated with intense snowfall; the *Egan Express* estimated that the March 10 storm dropped a foot of new snow.[717]

Adding insult to injury, the unpleasant weather lingered, alternating with days that teased of the coming spring. A midmonth article from the *Dell Rapids Exponent* illustrated the irregular temperament of the weather when the editor wrote, "Last week's storm lasted through all of Thursday and Friday and until Saturday noon when the wind stopped blowing and the snow stopped drifting. Sunday was clear and pleasant. Monday there was more drifting; likewise Wednesday."[718]

The Storm of March 14 and the Blizzard and Wind Event of March 19

Just days after the storm on March 10 came another that, fortunately, lasted only one day. The *Egan Express* described the March 14 storm as a "light blizzard,"[719] and the *Dell Rapids Exponent* added that "about three inches of light 'feathery' snow fell" the following day, which then drifted on the third day.[720]

Several papers included articles with descriptions similar to one out of Brookings, saying, "Such a blizzard as we had for a little while Monday! The air was full of snow and the wind howled fiercely, about midnight it blew out and Tuesday was a very nice day."[721]

The *Moody County Enterprise*, however, seemed to have had about enough of the winter storms and put plaintive howls amid a list of news items focused mostly on snow:

Dull!
Quiet!
Lonely!
Isolated!

Snow-Bound.

No more mails.

Still more snow.

The Storm king reigns.

Did you hear the thunder?

"O THE long and cruel winter!"

"EVER deeper, deeper fell the snow."

. . . .

Snow, blow and flow, all rhyme. Is that suggestive?

. . . .

The ides of March have come and gone but spring has failed to put in appearance.

. . . .

March has not been a cold month but it has not been warm enough to melt the snow much.

. . . .

Some of the Indians living near here say that the snow is deeper this winter than it has been any winter before since 1852, and that tremendous floods are occasioned by the melting snow that year.[722]

The above outburst aside, the regional editors tended to nudge the readers toward caution, as the Marshall editor seemed to do when, following the storm of March 14, he wrote, "The last day or two threatened warm weather again. Don't you bet on it though. It is said that every Friday or Saturday since the October blizzard has been stormy."[723] Looking at the calendars at the beginning of each chapter in this book thus far, it appears that most weekends were, indeed, stormy.

A Mirage

"One of the handsomest mirages" presented itself to the residents of Pipestone on March 18, and they were again able to peer at their neighbors in Lake Benton, over seventeen miles to the north. "The Lake Benton timber and the lake itself never were so plainly seen," wrote the Pipestone editor, "and it was indeed a beautiful sight. It lasted a couple of hours."[724]

Spring Asserting Itself

March held one more blizzard in its arsenal, but not before signs of spring had begun appearing in the newspapers among the storm reports. Geese started appearing from the south, and snowbanks were melting down into slush. The March 10 edition of the *Egan Express* reported a stretch of "very fine" weather, noting that a significant amount of Egan's snow had melted and that it was expected that the town's farmers could begin seeding before long. This optimism was sprinkled with humor, as well. "We have been having some good sugar weather for the past week," wrote the Egan editor. "All we lack is the trees to have a good supply of maple sugar and syrup, this spring."[725]

Farther east, the Janesville editor shared, "The crows were flying about last week hurrahing as if about to foreclose on old winter, but there appears to be a hitch in the proceedings somewhere."[726]

On the western edge of the region, the Fort Pierre paper reported, "The snow is at least two feet deep on a level between here and Huron, and all the cuts on the railroad are filled plump full."[727] Two feet on the level may not seem like a sign of spring, but with prior mentions indicating depths twice that or more, the snow was diminishing noticeably.

As the intensity of the sun and intermittent rains began to take their toll, the snow compressed, and if the residents didn't notice it on their own, the local papers were sure to make mention. The *Egan Express* of March 24 noted, "The snow has settled considerably for the past two or three days. / Winter's backbone is somewhat weaker than it was a week ago, and we hope to be able to report next week that it is broken."[728]

Back in New Ulm, where conditions had been decidedly less difficult, it seems that winter had worn out its welcome. "This has been a dreary winter for us," began the New Ulm editor. What followed was not so much a tally of incidents and boredom but a moan about the ongoing lack of mail and correspondence.[729]

The Storm of March 31

The second-to-last storm of the winter came at the end of March, and reports indicate it was one of the season's strongest. Between Watertown and Marshall, it was called the, "biggest, bluest and blizzardiest storm of the season."[730]

Pipestone was relieved that the snow already on the ground was not of the loose type, or the town "would have undoubtedly experienced the worst blizzard of the year." The temperature that morning showed –13 degrees.[731]

The *Dell Rapids Exponent* reported that the weather was very cold, but there wasn't much snow, indicating that the bulk of the storm may have stayed in the more northern portion of the region. However, the editor took the time to note, "It reached the size of a respectable (?) blizzard . . . and plugged up our railroad again, . . . and, as a result, we cannot look for trains before next week some time—if nothing prevents. Otherwise trains would probably have been running into Dell Rapids tonight."[732] (That "(?)" was in the original article.)

In Milbank, the storm's winds were so strong that "five cogs were broken out of a piece of machinery" because the windmill that powered it rotated too furiously.[733]

The month finished up with what must have been a hopeful sign. "The first wild geese of the season," wrote the New Ulm editor, "flew over the city last Thursday. Since then, almost all kinds of aquatic fowls have been daily seen flowing northward."[734]

Flooding along the Missouri and Big Sioux Rivers

Along the Missouri River, near Fort Pierre, the river had "risen about two feet" by the start of the month, and water was "running over the ice and breaking it all up."[735] The rising Missouri spurred residents of Pierre and Fort Pierre to move valuables to higher ground during the first week of the month, and by March 19, the river was reported to be five feet above normal.[736] By the end of the month, the two towns were in full flood.

Papers across the region kept their readers apprised of the situation along the river. The *Brookings County Press* resumed operations just in time to report, "The railroad tracks are four feet under water and the inhabitants have been obliged to take to the hills." The editor also shared that "about two thousand feet of the railroad track" had washed away near Pierre. The article did note one upside of the melting: "the beautiful snow is fast disappearing."[737]

The town of Elk Point, approximately sixty miles south of Sioux Falls, also reported flooding in early March. "When the wind don't blow," wrote the editor of the *Elk Point Tribune*, "the sun warms up the tops of the snow banks a little. It is thawing considerably to-day; the streets look beer-y, and water is running into cellars in some localities."[738]

The worst of the flooding, however, was centered around Yankton and Vermillion. Contrary to what one might expect, the melt began well to the north, close to Pierre. The rising waters flowing downstream ran into and broke up river ice that then flowed along with the current. This caused an ice gorge, or natural dam, that backed up the floodwaters. "At 11.30 Sunday night, Mar. 27," wrote the Dell Rapids editor, "the Missouri river broke up at Vermillion. A gorge was formed two miles below the city, and in less than an hour the town was from four to six feet under water."[739] There is more about this cataclysmic event in the next chapter.

To finish the meteorologically frustrating month of March, let's take a moment to enjoy the poetic joy expressed in the *Canton Advocate*, reflecting on the beautiful spectacle of the night sky:

> A great deal of star-gazing was indulged in by our people last Thursday evening, but the occasion was unusual—not resembling such events as transpire when the air is filled with the fragrance of new-blown roses. It was Venus in all her brilliancy walking through the heavens in an easterly direction and coming in close proximity to the moon, which presented a strange and beautiful phenomena.[740]

The Railroads

> "The Dakota Central is off time but on track.
> We hope for the best."[741]

—*Brookings County Press*, March 31, 1881

Rumors Continue

March brought additional snowfall, which further buried railroad tracks that had already been blockaded for, in most areas, approaching two months. Concern over abandonment continued to appear in print, whether explicitly stated or inferred. Boosterism sometimes slipped in, and some newspapers painted competing railroad lines serving other towns as less dedicated to their dependent residents. The opposite appeared as well—isolated towns envied what they supposed were more strenuous efforts elsewhere.

On March 2, the *New Ulm Weekly Review* printed, "This division of the R. R. [Winona & St. Peter] has been completely suspended. We [New Ulm] have not seen the iron horse for many a day."[742] Along the Southern Minnesota, the *Dell Rapids Exponent* reprinted a story from the *Volga Gazette,* saying that the Chicago & North Western had walked away from shoveling the cuts and would wait for the sun to melt the snow. Adding its own editorial, the *Exponent*'s editor wryly noted, "That is the Northwestern. Now down this way, the S. M., for instance, they keep their men shoveling constantly."[743]

Things weren't all rosy along the Southern Minnesota, however. One community, tired of waiting for a train to get through on that line, put into motion the idea of utilizing a different railroad to obtain their goods, in a manner that contradicts the assertions of the *Exponent* above:

> Elk Point merchants have abandoned the idea of ever receiving any freight over the Milwaukee road [Southern Minnesota], and now order their goods via. [*sic*] the Chicago and Northwestern road to Sioux City, and have [paper deteriorated] ... place to this city. It appears that the Chicago and Northwestern road do not wait for the snow to thaw from their road-bed, but manage in some way to bring their passengers, mail, express and freight with but little if any delay.[744]

The distinction here is likely geography. The branches of the Chicago & North Western that were derided by the *Volga Gazette* (the article was also reprinted in the *Dell Rapids Exponent*) were the Winona & St. Peter and the Dakota Central, both located well north of the Sioux City segments from which the Elk Point residents obtained their goods. And due to deterioration in the newspaper copy, the method of getting the goods northward from Sioux City cannot be verified, but it was probably a combination of train to Sioux Falls and teams north from that point.

A Brief Return to the Abandonment Issue and the Superintendent Story

At the end of the January chapter, we explored the dramatic actions of the superintendent from the East. A secondary factor in that tale was the abandonment by the railroad company of the towns on the other side of the blockade.

Abandonment along the Dakota Central: From the East

In addition to the ongoing articles about snow blockades, a few additional clues appeared supporting an actual season-long suspension of efforts to clear blockades along the Dakota Central.

The *Dell Rapids Exponent* of March 26 published that, according to a two-week-old paper from Volga, the Dakota Central "suspended a large portion of their men ... in disgust, intending to let the road thaw out in its own good time."[745] This reprint from Volga is one of the few reports available from along this railroad line in midwinter, and it reinforces the theory that things were indeed worse along the Dakota Central. Of the newspapers regularly included in this research, the *Brookings County Press* was the only one that ceased operations instead of curtailing size or resorting to alternative materials (though the *Lamberton Commercial* also stopped printing for a time). While the *Fort Pierre Weekly Signal* remained in operation, it did not tend to publish many details about railroad concerns farther east.

An Elmer & Tenney photo of cars in Kelly's Cut, along the Winona & St. Peter, just west of Sleepy Eye. Photo courtesy of the Chicago & North Western Historical Society.

The above photo was taken on March 29, 1881, in Kelly's Cut, to the immediate west of Sleepy Eye, Minnesota. This was, in reality, the cut that stopped trains from traveling west of Sleepy Eye most of the winter—that is the true culprit of the deprivations in places like De Smet. While Wilder used the Tracy Cut as the antagonist in *The Long Winter*, the reality is that trains couldn't get far enough west to be hindered by the Tracy Cut.

The blockades between Sleepy Eye and the vicinity of Tracy were significant, and until trains could get to Tracy, there was no hope of getting trains and goods moving westward on the Dakota Central. Barring any reasonable hope of reaching Tracy, an official stop of work on the Dakota Central makes perfect sense in terms of energies, expenses, and outcomes. Most of the goods needed past Tracy remained east of Sleepy Eye. However, efforts to clear the tracks continued along the Winona & St. Peter too, as it was part of the Chicago & North Western. (With that said, and despite the lack of proof via the newspaper record, it is likely that efforts did continue, at least to some extent, to minimize buildup in the Tracy Cut, as this would have expedited efforts when trains were able to reach Tracy from the east.)[746]

Abandonment along the Dakota Central: From the West

On the other hand, the town of Fort Pierre appeared to be decently supplied with food, possibly via stage or wagon teams or from well-stocked warehouses prior to the blockades. A number of articles earlier in the winter claimed that the railroads were not blockaded in Dakota Territory. If true, why did trains not appear to be running between Fort Pierre and Huron, De Smet, or Brookings?

It could have been a combination of distance between population centers, a shortage of fuel to run the locomotives, or the landscape that required trains to consume more fuel between Huron and Brookings than from Huron westward. While running trains may have looked good on the books, there was little local passenger or freight traffic and no through traffic, so the cost of operation would not have come close to paying for itself. Or perhaps conditions were worse than claimed by the various editors in Dakota Territory.

There is evidence of attempts to clear the rails west of Huron. Somewhere around March 1, a work crew of one hundred men headed toward Pierre from Huron "for the purpose of shoveling out the filled up cuts which had defied the efforts of snow plows, and had blockaded the road for weeks."[747] Despite being "thoroughly equipped including explosives," they were only successful in getting about halfway to Pierre before additional storms and colder temperatures hindered progress.[748]

Because the area was sparsely populated, provisions ran out, and "the entire gang was reduced to one biscuit a day to each man." The citizens of Huron sent out a rescue party, who "found the men in a perilous situation," with hands and feet frozen "to such an extent that amputation became necessary" in some instances.[749] The crew estimated that, at the time, "there was over two feet of snow covering the prairies of Dakota, all packed and solidified by occasional thaws followed by freezing."[750]

An article from the March 26 *Fort Pierre Weekly Signal* noted, "The whistle of the locomotive will be heard here before long if this weather holds out,"[751] indicating a lack of running trains in that location. At least one locomotive was wintering in Huron, so it could have run between that point and Brookings, to the east, if fuel was available and if provisions were on hand to distribute.

At least two work trains ran on the Dakota Central during February: One reported in De Smet.[752] The other reported in Huron, having arrived from Pierre.[753] But they were only mentioned as having a plow (De Smet) or carrying shovelers (Huron) and bringing news that there was no suffering along the route.

The old teasing adage "uphill both ways" applies to the stretch of track from Huron to Brookings. Looking at it in person, the landscape appears relatively flat, or gently sloping at best. But according to H. A. Stimson, son of a turn-of-the-century De Smet station agent, the terrain was anything but, especially coming into De Smet from the east. He described the stretch as "a long slowly rising knoll that trapped many an engineer with tonnage and caused him to double-in especially if a strong head wind got in the picture. Or a wet or snowy rail."[754]

The need for additional fuel to travel the tracks west of Brookings, when fuel was hard to find, was likely a strong deterrent to running trains. That all assumes, of course, that the tracks were as clear as the editors reported.

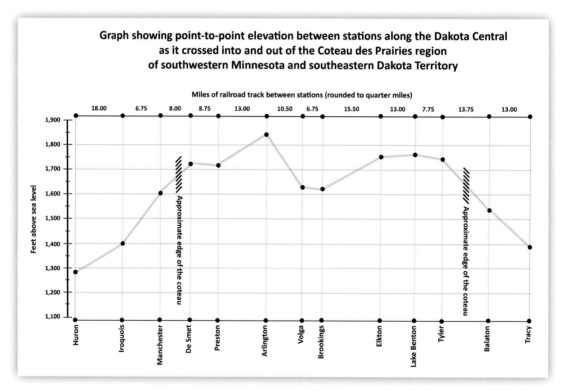

Note: Elevations are exaggerated in scale compared to the miles

Railroad Blockades

"A gang of about 30 men under charge of Section Boss McKende are shoveling out from this point. It will probably be very near spring before they reach the State Line."[755]

—*Moody County Enterprise*, March 3, 1881

Along the Hastings & Dakota

There were successful transits. On March 14, an express train (the first since January 25) reached Bird Island,[756] approximately one hundred miles east of Milbank, and by the end of the month, things were looking positive for this line along the northern edge of the region explored in this book.

Energized by news of that midmonth train and by reports that other towns had sent citizens "to assist the company's force in clearing the track," the Milbank paper reported that some of the town's "public spirited citizens and business men . . . shouldered their shovels last Friday and started out."[757] A week later, the paper reviewed the prospects for the arrival of a train, saying they had been "highly favorable." The weather was moderating, and hopes were up. Then, of course, the skies opened and "a heavy blizzard blew up, accompanied by considerable snow, . . ." changing prospects to "quite dismal."[758]

Upon second look, however, it noted that the snowfall had been light, and, rallying readers, said, "The probability is that no very great amount of trouble will be experienced in shoveling out the cuts again."[759] The editor must have paused a moment to contemplate the past few months, however, as he added a final caution to the article: "If, however, travel is seriously impeded for a week, we give notice to the readers of the *Review* that next week they may look for a paper about the size of a postage stamp."[760]

Along the Winona & St. Peter

The Chicago & North Western kept up its efforts. "Superintendent Sanborn boards the women and children who get caught in the blockades," wrote the editor in Mashall, "but when the men apply he points to a big pile of shovels and tells them he will give them board and good wages if they will take hold and help open the road; but nary board as long as they lie still."[761]

Humor continued to appear among the articles, as illustrated by this quip from Sleepy Eye: "The people in the towns west of us will probably remain isolated from the rest of the world until the opening of navigation. When the snow melts a steamboat will probably be sent to their relief."[762]

Via the *Egan Express*, a traveler from the area reported, "The people [along the Chicago & North Western] don't look for a train on that road till some time next month. In many places the snow is so deep that it had to be shoveled off the telegraph wires."[763]

Following the Storm of March 4

A passenger train spent three days trapped between New Ulm and Sleepy Eye during and after the storm. When a plow was finally able to reach New Ulm, its efforts were hindered some by another plow that had been working westward from St. Peter. It had ditched twice in two days, "causing considerable delay in the operations from that end."[764]

The editor in Janesville reported the trapped passenger train to his readers by writing, "The train ventured into the jaws of death again last Thursday by going to Sleepy Eye. Of course a storm came up, a half an inch of snow fell and blocked it in."[765]

The storm of March 4 blockaded even the eastern portion of the region. Janesville, which had served more as narrator than active party in the blockades, indignantly threw the blame even farther east, to Wisconsin. "Trains suspended last Friday," wrote the editor of the *Janesville Argus*. "Thats [sic] twice this thing has occurred this winter and we forbid the banns [sic]. We understand the difficulty was in Wisconsin. No trains came through from Chicago."[766]

Throughout the winter, the New Ulm paper received infrequent correspondence from Tracy, the division point of the Winona & St. Peter and the Dakota Central lines. The March 16 edition of the *New Ulm Weekly Review* carried one such letter. In it, the Tracy correspondent noted that no trains had reached the town since January 19, nearly two months prior. While residents had helped to shovel multiple times, "no good came of it." Many trains had been through town on January 12, but there were complaints that Tracy "received nothing of which to speak." Interestingly, the writer claimed, "Towns west of us were the fortunate ones," implying that the volumes of cargo that passed through on January 12 were distributed among the towns beyond Tracy.[767]

The town's "hopes of receiving fuel were dashed [and those] who thought they had a sufficient supply found themselves getting short." Earlier in the blockades, the railroad company had been selling coal to the residents, "but stopped some time ago as they were getting short for their own use."[768] Locomotives pushing plows or bucking snow needed more coal and wood than under normal operations.

After the litany of grumbles at the beginning of his letter, the writer then waxed a bit more philosophical, adding, "Doubtless there were times when the [railroad] company could have done more than it did for us; and possibly we might have done more for ourselves. We all have failed in our calculations of the weather. . . . It is an easy, natural thing to blame others for our misfortunes."[769] Then, as if not wanting to completely exonerate the railroad, the writer finished the letter with the recommendation that the railroad company "furnish a better rolling stock for this western region." He further added, "The engines have not been fit to cope with such a winter. There have not been snow ploughs enough to work efficiently the blockaded lines."[770]

Following the Storm of March 14

Frustration and hope intermingled in the wake of this midmonth storm, with predictions of incoming trains west of the blockade sites measuring in weeks rather than days, after months of waiting already.[771]

New Ulm, not often a victim of long blockades, took advantage of a short opening the evening of March 14 (Monday): "The railroad was opened so that a passenger train from the east [could come] through . . . , trains having been suspended since Friday morning." There was another blockade mere hours later.[772]

The *Salem Register* of March 18 and the *Janesville Argus* of March 22 both listed a tally of nonarrivals, noting that Springfield had been without a train since January 19, that it had been seven weeks since Pierre had heard the whistle of a locomotive, and that Marshall had not seen a train since January 9.[773]

As we've seen, despite the ongoing frustrations of the settlers, support remained strong for the superintendents and their continued efforts, as when the *Fort Pierre Weekly Signal* published, "It is reported that superintendant Sanborn of the Winona and St. Peter R. R. is out with the boys shovelling snow west of Sleepy Eye. Sanborn is a rustler and if this report be true we may look for a train through sometime."[774]

Another weekend brought more inclement weather. According to the *New Ulm Weekly Review* of March 23, Saturday's offering was more of a "heavy wind storm," which "sifted enough snow into the cuts between New Ulm and Sleepy Eye to detain the west bound passenger train for several hours." They managed to open the road on Sunday, "but the cuts were again filled up during the night and it took all day Monday and part of Tuesday to clear the track." While trains were having difficulty west of New Ulm, the article further indicated, "No trouble has been experienced in operating the trains east of here."[775] The March 22, 1881, photo by Elmer & Tenney on page 218 shows the tracks about twenty-five miles east of New Ulm. They may not have had any trouble running trains there, but the tracks were by no means clear.

Optimism rebounded toward the end of March, as reflected in the papers along the western lines of the Chicago & North Western. The *Marshall Messenger* shared its hopes that a train would appear by the first week of April.[776] The New Ulm editor couched the Marshall article in caution, saying, "We very much fear that the *Messenger* man is doomed to disappointment."[777]

True to their role as boosters, the editors kept the papers sprinkled with humor, even after yet another month of heavy winter weather. One correspondent to Marshall quipped that they "recom[m]end the use of oak posts instead of cedar for railroad fence. It makes better firewood."[778]

Meanwhile, New Ulm was bursting with travelers waiting for the road to open, eager to continue their travels west. "Some live in hopes of getting out of here by the 4th of July," wrote the New Ulm editor, "but they are being well cared for and are calmly putting up with the inevitable."[779]

At month's end, with another storm brewing, the *Brookings County Press* lamented, "Oh! My kingdom for a train!"[780] The railroad company had "a large force between Sleepy Eye and Tracy" working to clear the tracks. "A general movement all along the line is expected soon. If the present weather continues a few days we will be all right, 'Hold the fort.'"[781]

Photo taken at Kelly's Cut, along the Winona & St. Peter, just west of Sleepy Eye, dated 1880. This photo illustrates how narrow the cuts were. The snowbank clearly shows grooves where the train cars brushed against the side of the cut. Collection photo from the Minnesota Historical Society.

Along the Dakota Central

The aforementioned March 26 article out of Fort Pierre—"The whistle of the locomotive will be heard here before long if this weather holds out"[782]—rang with optimism, even after residents had endured months of disappointment. Again, that article provides evidence that trains were not running, or were at least running infrequently, on the western end of the Dakota Central.

Along the Southern Minnesota

As along the other lines, optimism and disappointment mixed as the warming sun raised hopes and lingering blizzards dashed them.

Following the Storm of March 4

The first storm of March was followed by the usual optimism that a train would get through as soon as the recent snows were removed. Articles became more peppered with the added confidence that the warming sun would help the shovelers.

Praise for the efforts of the railroad companies and the gangs of workers continued. On March 10, the *Pipestone Star* predicted the arrival of a train within ten days.[783] The *Egan Express* made a similar hopeful prediction, printing, "Since last Saturday morning the weather has been very fine, and under the influence of the sun considerable of our snow has disappeared. . . . The railroad company has a full force and if we have no more blizzards the road will be open and trains running in ten days or two weeks."[784]

Following the Storms of March 11 and 14

Among the monotony of shoveling reports—or reports of the monotony of shoveling—appeared stories bordering on the incredible. Near Pipestone, a family found themselves "entirely closed in by the storm of last Friday." A group of railroad shovelers learned of their situation and, on Tuesday morning, liberated the family from their abode. The *Pipestone Star* reassured its readers that "the family did not suffer any" as a result of their confinement.[785] While the family was freed, the tracks still needed attention.

In the wake of these two storms, the papers published articles that looked similar to those printed all winter. The railroad was working with "unabated vigor"[786] and making "good headway—when it does not snow."[787] They were doing "the same work that was done last week, that was also done the week before; in fact, that has been done nearly weekly since the beginning of last January, and no nearer trains than then,"[788] wrote the Dell Rapids editor.

Despite it being late March, and with signs of spring teasing here and there, trains continued to be snowed in place along the tracks. Such was the case west of Fulda, where a train was "almost buried in snow" without hopes of being freed until a rescue train and crew could reach it from the east.[789]

Following each storm, stubborn hope held tight that *this* would be the last, that the end of the blockades was truly in sight. With confidence, the *Egan Express* relayed information from the local station agent, that large crews were working out of every station along the line and that trains would arrive soon. Of course, tucked in at the end of the proclamation was the omnipresent phrase, "providing the present good weather continues."[790]

In another bit of optimistic foreboding, the *Pipestone Star* printed, as the March 31 storm approached from the northwest, "The boys are making rapid progress clearing the track and the sun is helping them."[791]

The Expense Continues to Add Up

The cost of these efforts was becoming astronomical. As reported in the *Winona Republican* and reprinted in the *Janesville Argus* of March 15, the January blockade cost the Winona & St. Peter $70,000. Furthermore, "not a dollar was taken in west of Sleepy Eye and very little west of St. Peter. The beautiful snow hits things where they live."[792]

The above update covered cleanup expenses for a single month. For the collective winter, amounts were much higher. According to a reprinted St. Paul *Pioneer Press* article, the Chicago, Milwaukee & St. Paul (parent company of the Hastings & Dakota and the Southern Minnesota) and the Chicago & North Western (parent company of the Winona & St. Peter and the Dakota Central) had spent "at least $300,000 in cash." The article also estimated that the Chicago, Milwaukee & St. Paul had spent $200 per mile fighting a blockade on the Hastings & Dakota. It also noted, "For a number of miles at the western end the railway has been used for the ordinary travel, and the snow has been packed down so hard that it is made necessary to loosen it with picks."[793] The packed snow compounded existing difficulties.

Converting 1881 Dollars to 2019 Dollars

To provide context for the newspapers' reports about money spent by the railroad companies, let's do some conversions. According to the Bureau of Labor Statistics Consumer Price Index, $1 in 1881 has the purchasing power of $25.15 in 2019.[794] Using that number to convert the expenditures in the above paragraph, we get these numbers:

Expense	1881	2019
January blockade of the Winona & St. Peter	$70,000	$1,760,500
Work on the Hastings & Dakota and the Southern Minnesota	$300,000	$7,545,000
Blockade fight along the Hastings & Dakota	$200/mile	$5,030/mile

This was not inconsequential spending, and in the end, the results didn't give the railroads any real immediate advantage. However, it did likely provide the shovelers across the region with a windfall of unexpected income.

Threats of Flooding

Throughout March, the melting snow and threat of flooding added to the superintendents' worries. And flooded tracks and washed-out bridges were not the only water-related hindrances for the trains, either. At least one article reported, "The water is so deep over the track in many places between Sioux City and Yankton that it runs into the fire boxes of the locomotives."[795] However, according to railroad historian John C. Luecke, that report may have been more drama than fact, as the firebox of a locomotive at the time was approximately five feet above the rails, and "no engine crew that was not drunk or stark raving mad would ever attempt to pass through water that had even the most remote possibility of being that deep."[796]

In Egan and Dell Rapids, bridges were fortified to protect them from anticipated floods.[797] While the task appears to have been accomplished efficiently in Egan, the *Dell Rapids Exponent* noted that some were suspicious of the quality of work nearby, mentioning, "Several have asked if the bracing wasn't put on the wrong side? Impertinence personified! Later. – as we go to press a number of workmen are busy raising the bridge."[798]

Snow Blindness

March brought an avalanche of articles reporting snow blindness. With the spring equinox approaching and the days getting longer, increased sun exposure may have been a factor in the proliferation of cases at this point in the winter.

In medical terms, pain in the eyes resulting from their exposure to ultraviolet rays, such as those from the sun, is called photokeratitis. When the sun's rays are reflected off snow or ice, the condition is sometimes called snow blindness, though that name can also refer to a freezing or severe drying—both possible during the winter—of the surface of the cornea, "the clear front window of the eye." As experienced, it is essentially a painful sunburn of the eye, and much like a sunburn on skin, damage to the eyes may not be noticed until it is too late. Fortunately, a few days out of the sun usually resolves any pain or temporary vision loss.[799]

In *The Long Winter*, Pa experienced similar symptoms after returning from shoveling snow for the railroad just before the Christmas storm: "His eyes were red and puffed. He answered cheerfully, 'Shoveling snow in the sunshine is hard on eyes. Some of the men are snow-blind. Fix me up a little weak salt-water, will you, Caroline? And I'll bathe them after I do the chores.' "[800]

Tracks Clogged with Cars

As March dawned, reports of car backups were more frequent in the papers, allowing a glimpse of the conundrum faced by the yardmasters in charge of sorting cars as the snow melted. Waseca, on the Winona & St. Peter, reportedly had "130 loaded freight cars waiting to go west"[801] while five hundred cars, loaded with goods, were stranded at various locations along the Hastings & Dakota.[802]

Other Railroad Business

"The Chicago, Milwaukee & St. Paul railway company has purchased the Sioux City & Dakota railroad."[803]

—*Egan Express*, March 10, 1881

Expansion Work / Business as Usual

The Janesville editor's sense of humor could always be counted on to lighten a situation. The Chicago & North Western had a spur line that went into Mankato, and evidently, their depot there was a bit on the decrepit side: "The *Mankato Review* says the North Western company will erect a new depot at that place. We should hope so. The chicken coop in use there for the last fifteen years is a disgrace not only to Mankato but to every man, woman and temperance lecturer that unloads there."[804]

Wrecks and Accidents

As far as the record shows, February had been fairly accident-free, aside from minor mishaps experienced by snowplows and the locomotives pushing them. March similarly brought in only a few gory reports, mostly involving people caught in the cuts and unable to escape approaching trains.

Outside of St. Peter, one unfortunate young woman was walking through a cut when she noticed an approaching train. She was unable to scramble up the ten-foot banks on either side of the cut, and the snow being hurled by the plow obscured the engineer's view. Her death was inevitable. Even if the engineer had seen her, he likely would not have been able to stop in time.[805]

This uncredited 1917 photo shows how people used the cuts as a thoroughfare. Unable to climb the snow walls, these unfortunate pedestrians could be run down by oncoming trains. Photo courtesy of the Chicago & North Western Historical Society.

But even those able to climb certain sections of the cut walls were not ensured survival. As reported in the New Ulm paper,

> A sixty-four year old man . . . was caught in a cut, and when he heard the train coming he clambered out onto the snow bank. When the train came up, and after the engine had passed him, he made an attempt to get farther back, but the snow gave way under him and he rolled down on the rails and under the passing train. His injuries proved fatal in a few hours after the incident.[806]

A crew of men on a handcar had their own encounter. The article describing the incident seems to indicate that the group was out in the open, not trapped in a cut, but found themselves being chased down the tracks by a train that was "six minutes ahead of time." While most of the men jumped clear and crawled away from the tracks, one crewman "seemed paralized [sic] with fear and made no effort to save himself."[807]

Food

"[The town of Tyler is] out of all luxuries over there, such as fuel, light and provision."[808]

—*Marshall Messenger*, March 4, 1881

Wheat Piled Up across the Region

The relentless grinding of wheat into flour, which could be turned into bread, anchored much of *The Long Winter*'s story line. The precious grain was hard to convert into a usable substance, and even harder to come by for the Ingalls family. Yet it appears that it was available in mountainous excess throughout the larger region.

An elevator operator in Elk Point let farmers know that he would furnish wheat storage if they could get their grain to him before the spring thaw made roads impassable, even offering to insure their product against fire.[809]

Farther east, in New Ulm, the roads were already in "very poor condition," but despite that, farmers were bringing "quite a large amount of wheat" into town.[810] Twenty-two thousand bushels of wheat were stored in two elevators at St. Peter.[811] In Egan, one thousand bushels of seed wheat were offered for sale.[812] To the north, in Ortonville, east of Milbank, an additional ten thousand bushels of wheat were available for purchase.[813] Even Brookings reported the arrival of "considerable wheat."[814]

Excess wheat lay in giant piles in some areas while the Ingalls family (and presumably others) were rationing their food. The unfortunate ingredient here is distance. De Smet is forty-one miles from Brookings, fifty-two miles from Egan, and eighty-three miles from Ortonville. It would have been simple enough to set up a relay system for food, similar to the system for mail, between De Smet and Brookings, though riskier between De Smet and Egan or Ortonville. One might wonder whether this happened without young Laura being aware.

In the extant correspondence records, it appears Wilder believed the town to be completely isolated and that only her father and the Wilder brothers were brave enough to venture out.[815] None of the articles researched indicated that wheat was obtained for hungry towns from overflowing elevators, but it is entirely possible that this occurred and went unreported.

Along the Winona & St. Peter and the Dakota Central

The March newspapers showed the full breadth of the food situation, from surplus to deprivation, depending on location. Some merchants and residents ran teams to towns where supplies were available, bringing back fuel, mail, and food.

New Ulm, in the eastern portion of the region, reported having "plenty of provisions."[816] On the western edge, Fort Pierre shared, "There are plenty of provisions here to last until the river breaks up and boats begin to run. Only a few staple articles of goods are getting low." Further, a hotel operator reported having "provisions to last his hotel until the blockade is over, if it should last two months longer." He had "plenty of meat and vegetables" and had yet to run out of butter, having the means to make his own.[817]

In the central portion of the region, teams were venturing to nearby towns in search of provisions and returning successful. The March 4 issue of the *Marshall Messenger* included a note from the Red Front Bee Hive grocer that said, "We have sent three teams to Sleepy Eye for groceries which will be back this week. We have a lot of them there, and will be glad to see them here. We have sent for five barrels of oil. We mean to have groceries if horses can get them."[818]

Later in the month, reports of additional expeditions came in. The March 18 *Marshall Messenger* reported, "Two teams with goods . . . came in from St. Peter this week. Tuesday night we received mail by one of [the grocer's] teams. It brought us dailies [other towns' newspapers published in the interim] up to March 8."[819]

The March 21 edition of the *Dakota News* out of Watertown included typeset ads for two different grocers that boasted of having meats, canned goods, fruits, and other groceries.[820]

To the southwest of Marshall, the Brookings editor was irritated to read that, according to a visitor from Lake Benton, the town of Brookings was low on certain groceries. In reply, he wrote, "The *Lake Benton News* says some one from that town came to Brookings for sugar and found the town on the last barrel. . . . We don't know what store he struck, but we know there are several barrels of sugar here."[821]

Also in Brookings, it was reported that potatoes were "scarce as hen's teeth."[822] Meanwhile, Fort Pierre touted a local merchant who planned to "open up the finest stock of groceries ever brought to Pierre, as soon as the railroad blockade is over, and he can get his stock of goods through."[823]

Fort Pierre, perched on the western banks of the Missouri River so very many miles west of the blockade-prone spots, was not just sitting around waiting patiently for a resolution to the snow along the Dakota Central and points east. Instead, the merchants there were "seriously contemplating ordering their spring goods shipped via Sioux City and the steamboats."[824]

Along the Southern Minnesota

Even in the towns along the border between Dakota Territory and Minnesota, food had not run out, though feasts were certainly a rarity. In Flandreau, one leading citizen "set out a fine turkey dinner . . . and kindly invited in a number of friends to partake thereof." Some wheat was also brought into town.[825]

The town of Dell Rapids reported having plenty of flour on hand.[826] And as if these abundances weren't enough, in nearby Flandreau, "a large crop of ice" was harvested.[827] In Pipestone, upon determining that the amount of flour available was running low, one resident organized two teams and traveled west to Flandreau, bringing back a supply of the milled grain for the town.[828]

And in a show of amusing ingenuity (and in one of this author's favorite articles from the entire winter), the *Pipestone Star* editor painted a fascinating scene when he wrote, "Our butchers being out of wrapping paper they have conceived the novel idea of using sharpened sticks, and it is nothing uncommon to see people going through the streets with parasols made of a hunk of roast beef or a round steak."[829] Once the meat was conveyed home, the sticks were then likely used for fuel. (In case you didn't notice, one of those "meat parasols" is portrayed in the illustration at the beginning of this chapter, on page 177.)

While Flandreau reported plenty of flour, potatoes—a more substantial food—were needed by merchants. The Red Front Bee Hive grocery store placed an ad asking to purchase five hundred bushels of potatoes.[830] The town had also run out of sugar by early March.[831]

Flour may have been available in Flandreau in quantities enough to sell to the men from Pipestone, but things were not bountiful. "Flour is getting to be a very scarce article," wrote the Egan editor. "The Flandrau mill is doing no grinding, and the water is so low that the Roscoe mill can grind but a few hours a day. . . . [The mill operator] will sell only fifty pounds to any one man. . . . Matters may possibly be worse before they are better."[832]

The food in Dell Rapids was also beginning to run low, though their editor remained optimistic, writing, "The stores begin to look somewhat bare, but they will improve—when the cars arrive. When that time comes it will make business lively for everybody."[833]

On the far western end of the Southern Minnesota line, one article provided a rare mention of an actual name in connection with suffering. A man named Zelensky, along with his son, were reported to be destitute.[834] Local residents collected "flour, meat, tea, coffee, etc." and headed towards the farm on "their errand of mercy and charity." Along the way, they had to contend with a storm "for some hours." Upon arriving, to their surprise, they found not "father and son there, but a wife and three small children and a grand-mother, in destitute circumstances." Apparently, they had been eating "nothing but potatoes, and even these without salt." The article did not indicate the fate of the father and son, but the story took a circuitous route, reaching the *Lake County Leader* of Madison, Dakota Territory, via "Forrestburg [sic] from Alexandria via Mitchell."[835]

Along the Lines South and East of Sioux Falls

In that corner of Dakota Territory wedged between Iowa and the James River, south of the Southern Minnesota railroad, things were not as dire as along the lines to the north. Food was scarce, but not dangerously so. Fuel remained of higher concern.

Travelers who had ventured out specifically to procure food reported the conditions they observed, keeping newspaper readers informed. One traveler along the Southern Minnesota in eastern Dakota Territory reported that the towns along that line were "well provided with groceries and provisions," and that "trade was unusually brisk, . . . farmers from different parts of the county came to town to replenish their larder."[836]

The small towns of Parker and Swan Lake, southwest of Sioux Falls, registered a long list of items recently received, some of them via mule train. Among them were "Choice Navy Beans, Fresh Cranberries, New lot Coffee, Flour, Corn meal and Graham. . . . Oats, corn and cracked feed . . . and a fresh load of flour."[837]

While food conditions didn't appear to be as critical in this area, those living there were not out of danger. Travelers reported suffering due to "the long protracted cold weather and succession of snows which have occurred." Some localities were also running low on provisions, "with a poor prospect of replenishing the supply." A relief committee was organized to help address the people's needs during this challenging time.[838]

Across the entire region, coffee grinders—ubiquitous and indispensable tools—were being used to grind more than just coffee, and the people in and around Parker and Swan Lake were no exception. According to a March 5 article in the local paper, the *New Era*, many families were using their grinders to process breadstuff such as wheat and buckwheat, and they knew they would "continue to do so until travel with a team becomes practicable again." The editor further added, "Some of our neighbors are living on unground wheat. One family, about nine miles northwest, had not even that for three days during the late storm." On a more nourishing note, the editor shared that over the past two weeks, seventeen antelope had been harvested and shared among the residents.[839]

Cattle/Livestock

Charles Ingalls was forced out into the elements multiple times a day, either to care for the family's livestock or to venture to their homestead, south of town, to retrieve hay to feed the animals and fuel the stove. The same was true for his fictional counterpart, Pa, in the novel.

A raging blizzard did not mean a hiatus in his responsibilities, which was true for most others across the region as well. "The farmers don't have much leisure time to fool away this winter," wrote the Flandreau editor, "not if they have any stock to take care of. It takes about half the time every day to shovel an entrance into their barns and stables."[840]

Cattle and stock losses continued. The *Pipestone Star* of March 17 noted that the last two storms had caused more stock suffering and loss "than at any time during this winter."[841] Near Fort Pierre, the *Weekly Signal* reported, "Large numbers of cattle are dying all about us. Nearly every cattle owner looses [sic]."[842]

Some reports went into more detail. During the storm of March 14, one farmer near Brookings lost eight cattle, and a second lost two. In one of the cases, snow had drifted over the stable, and despite the farmer having shoveled the roof, the overnight snowfall caused the structure to collapse and kill the "two yoke of oxen" that had been designated for next season's breaking team.[843]

On the outskirts of Pipestone, a farmer "lost fifteen head of fine stock . . . owing to the scarcity of feed."[844] It must have been an extra difficult blow to have kept the animals alive through most of the winter only to lose them with spring in sight.

The toll was significant for the stage company owned by the Chicago & North Western as well. The Brookings paper reported, "The nort[h]western Stage and Transportation Company, who do the freighting business between Pierre and Deadwood, have lost nearly 600 head of work cattle by starvation."[845]

Fuel

> "*Elk Point Courier*: The prairie towns in this section are experiencing terrible times this winter on account of the scarcity of fuel. What little coal and wood there is is sold considerable above 'grange prices.'"[846]
>
> —*Madison Sentinel*, March 4, 1881

Along the Winona & St. Peter and the Dakota Central

Settlers continued to combine households to make efficient use of resources. Northwest of New Ulm, along the Minnesota River, "three families . . . moved into one house, using the other buildings for fuel."[847]

Throughout most of the winter, New Ulm had benefited from being on the "good side" of the blockades. But by March 2, the *Weekly Review* was reporting that fuel shortages and reduced food supplies had brought even that town to a level of quiet. There was very little coal left, and wood prices were climbing out of reach. Even then, it was mostly green wood.[848]

A week later, the same paper noted, "The public schools were closed on Thursday for want of fuel," despite "a few car loads of wood" having been received; they were earmarked for two mills. As for overall impact, the paper said, "Almost every business in town is now at a stand-still, and we are killing time in different ways. Some get up dances, some play cards, some post books, and still others drink beer, etc. As for the ladies, they must stay at home, simply because they cannot get out."[849]

Isolation

The comment that the ladies "must stay at home" could explain some of Wilder's perception that the entire town was isolated. She and the rest of the females within her household, along with her female friends from school, were likely confined to their respective homes. Whether due to inadequate clothing, societal convention, or fear of venturing out into the cold, most of their outings were presumably limited to their own yards.

On the other hand, plenty of community-building activities throughout the winter have shown that—for those living in more active communities—when the weather was not blizzarding, even the ladies got out and about. We don't have enough information to know whether De Smet had a similar level of activity as some of its neighbors, though the one extant newspaper page did indicate that a "nice little hop," presumably a dance, took place in February.[850]

In correspondence with Lane, there are multiple instances of Wilder writing some variation of, "People were afraid to leave their houses that winter. Pa and the Wilders [Almanzo and his brother Royal] were about the only ones who would do so except the mail carrier."[851] It was likely what she truly believed. When Wilder wanted to stray from the historical narrative for literary purposes, she tended to explain why. However, she did not do that in any of the instances of touching on this topic.

Back in Dakota Territory, the *Brookings County Press* had resumed operation by late March, having somehow obtained paper. But the editor's mood seemed to be a bit ill-tempered, scoffing, "We would suggest that the name 'hay-twisters' be applied to residents of Minnesota."[852]

On the western edge of the region, the March 12 edition of the *Fort Pierre Weekly Signal* reported, "Coal oil is becomming [sic] very scarce and what there is is offered for sale at the low price of one dollar per gallon."[853] Two weeks later, it was further noted, "Wood is very scarce, so scarce that we are immediately threatened with a fuel famine. The building boom is starting off rather slow this spring, owing to a lack of lumber."[854]

Two of the few reports out of Walnut Grove appeared in mid-March: A correspondence dated March 1 stated, "There is a scarcity of fuel as to justify great alarm." Moving deeper into dramatic prose, the writer continued, "Men of good judgment and firm minds . . . are in this place each and every day that they can get out from home, wondering, with tears in their eyes, if their families will be left to freeze to death. Corn is used for fuel, . . . and nineteen-twentieths of the people are now suffering more than it would be to die twice over, could it be done."[855]

The St. Paul *Pioneer Press* published a dispatch from Walnut Grove, shared by the *Janesville Argus,* further confirming the fuel shortage. "All out houses, pig pens, railroad fences, etc., have been burned and nothing remains but hay and straw. Walnut Grove is within easy distance of Sleepy Eye too."[856] It is unclear whether they actually burned all of the outhouses (outdoor toilets) or if *outbuildings*, such as stables or woodsheds, might have been a more accurate word.

The correspondent from Tracy was generous with information, though their reports were often disrupted due to delayed mails. In a midmonth article, they shared that the town had been short of fuel since January, and that there was "no wood to be had." Rumor placed a stock of wood less than five miles to the south, in Shetek, and after "several days' effort a road was opened and [the wood] was brought in." But this task was expensive both in physical effort and financial outlay. A team road was also "opened to Sleepy Eye" in response to word that coal was available in Burns (Springfield). With that supply line established, the merchants in Tracy, who "were out of all necessary articles," could obtain groceries and kerosene via wagon.[857]

The correspondent then returned to the concerns over fuel, sharing, "No family is able to have more than one fire and that is kept with moderation. We feel that our worst time for fuel is yet to come when the season breaks up and an embargo is put upon all teaming." Whether that "one fire" was an imposed ration or an incidental limitation due to dwindling fuel supply is unknown.[858] The correspondence concluded by saying that, despite the tribulations detailed in the article, things were not yet desperate: "Doubtless there has been suffering both here and in the country; but we have not known much of it. It will be strange, however, if we do not hear when spring comes, of considerable suffering."[859]

Along the Southern Minnesota

Reports along the Southern Minnesota for March were few in number, though similar to those along other lines. A merchant in Dell Rapids "received a barrel of kerosene oil . . . also a case of dry goods—the first of the season."[860] One enterprising resident of Madison was experimenting with an alternative to kerosene: "water-elm wood with a tallow fire. Has used up three barrels of grease on one cord of wood, and with some cursing has just got the water started."[861]

Hay for fuel and animal feed remained in demand and difficult to find in some locations. Flandreau noted, "Hay is still very scarce."[862]

"Being miles from timber," the *Canton Advocate* reminded readers, "scarcity of fuel in some of the towns is a heavy burden, and one which the people cannot overcome."[863] In an 1893 reflection about the winter, the intrepid station agent C. J. Cawley wrote, "We had orders to sell our rail ties to the people for fuel, a limit of ten ties per family. Sugar and kerosene ran out around March 1, and there were very few groceries obtainable."[864]

Along the Lines South and East of Sioux Falls

By the first week of March, people around Sioux Falls were contemplating pulling apart the railroad infrastructure for fuel. The residents of Dell Rapids were reported as already having done so. "The fuel question in Sioux Falls is assuming serious proportions," wrote the Canton editor. "Scarcely a vestige of coal or wood can be had. The impression prevails that if fuel is not received there within a few days, ties [and a] water tank belonging to the railroad company, will have to be used...." The citizens in Dell Rapids were similarly strapped for burnables, "being obliged to raze the water tank for fuel, with the timbers that supported it." They also "[tore] up the side-track to secure the ties for wood."[865]

Southwest of Sioux Falls, "Parkerites" (citizens of Parker) paid railroad representatives "fifty cents each for ties" to burn as fuel. "Nothing like pinching hard when one has a good grip," wrote the local newspaper editor.[866]

In Elk Point, the paper reported, "Large quantities of green wood are being brought to town and find a ready sale. Dry wood of a good sound quality is not easily to be had, and those that have that quality of wood for sale want fancy prices for it." Despite this influx of green wood, the town reportedly dismissed school early due to lack of fuel.[867]

According to a telegraphed message that was shared by the Currie newspaper, most people in the breaks northwest of Yankton were keeping warm by staying in bed. The article ended with, "The country is literally buried in snow."[868] It would seem that folks were coping, in part, by burying themselves in blankets.

Out and About

"The streets were quite well filled with teams from the country Monday and Tuesday."[869]

—*Moody County Enterprise*, March 3, 1881

Along the Hastings & Dakota

The melting snow permitted a noticeable increase in the distances people were traveling, with several businessmen heading to Chicago to make arrangements for the coming season, and other residents heading to Minnesota, Wisconsin, or Iowa to visit family.

The melt meant the beginning of mud season. While a messy sign of hope, it was also used as ammunition to encourage incorporation so that inconveniences could be taken care of. "The melting snow is making bad mud puddles along the streets," wrote the Milbank editor, "sadly to the inconvenience of pedestrians. If our town had been incorporated such nuisances could have been corrected, but now—well, now all hands are obliged to get around or through the water the best way they can."[870]

In preparation for anticipated spring flooding, some citizens worked to move endangered infrastructure out of harm's way. "The people of Odessa," continued the Milbank editor, "have taken the bridge which spans the river at that place from its piers and landed it high and dry in anticipation of the high water which spring is sure to give us." The people "living on the low lands near the streams" made similar preparations.[871]

Along the Winona & St. Peter

In previous sections, we've read how the repeated snows impacted the merchants' ability to conduct business. This excerpt from an article from Marshall is the one sample found pertaining to local doctors: "Our physicians, who have to make long trips over the prairie night and day, storm or sunshine, to treat patients who will pay after harvest, are talking about Oregon a good deal of late, and if a Summer doesn't intervene between this and September some of them will leave us."[872]

On March 11, the cooped-up residents of Marshall were likely relieved to read, "Roads are now open to most of the settlements around us. Many of them haven't been in here for a month before this week. Business begins to revive, and in a month or two we will have forgotten that this Winter was worse than usual."[873] The inclusion of the last sentence in that quote—in *this* book—is not without irony.

Even as the snow was melting, travelers were not always able to find easy shelter. One group found themselves turned out by local residents and punished for their resourceful solution, as related in the March 30 edition of the *New Elm Weekly Review*:

A party of travelers . . . who had been refused shelter from the severe storm . . . put up for the night in a school house near Courtland Station, taking their horses in with them, and the next morning they were fined ten dollars and costs. We are informed that the party had applied for shelter to four or five well-to-do farmers, and although they offered to pay liberally, they were refused and were finally compelled to seek shelter in the school house. While we depricate [*sic*] the use of educational buildings to such purposes, we think that under the circumstances the party was justified in their course, as the night was stormy and cold and to them it was a matter of life and death."[874]

People used all available methods of travel throughout the winter, but one trio claimed to have used a less common method of conveyance to move across the snow-covered prairies. As was relayed to the New Ulm editor, the three men "traveled a distance of thirty-two miles in three hours on a snow boat." They were able to travel in a straight line toward a station, as fences and other similar obstacles were below the snow's surface. "The boat was constructed similarly to an ice boat, had a rudder, and was easily managed." (A photo of a "snow boat" is included below.)[875]

A Chas A. Tenney photo of a "snow boat," 1880. From the Minnesota Historical Society.

Enterprising citizens found ways to capitalize on the lack of trains. For example, the operator of a livery stable in Redwood Falls, Minnesota, set up a stage line to Sleepy Eye. He oversaw routes between "division headquarters at Lone Tree Lake" and the two towns on either end of the route, coordinating the delivery of supplies and passengers. The paper reporting this mentioned that the stages ran "on time and without regard to blockades."[876]

Along the Dakota Central

The resumed publication of the *Brookings County Press* provided more insight into what was happening along the Dakota Central, such as a masquerade ball in Fort Pierre and a lecture in Brookings. Also in Brookings, a merchant vacated his store to move to a town along the Southern Minnesota. The townspeople then used his empty building to hold a "pleasant dance."[877]

Articles across the region shared stories of people taking advantage of the improving conditions by visiting neighboring communities. A resident of De Smet visited friends in Brookings at the end of March, and articles across the region reflect many such visits to and from various communities.[878] Travelers frequently reported back to their hometown newspapers about what they had encountered during their journeys, and the editors gladly shared the news. Those reports often included reassurances that there were crews of men shoveling along the railroad tracks.

The *Brookings County Press* printed, "Shoveling snow has been the popular amusement lately,"[879] but there is not enough context to decipher whether that might mean amusement for the spectators or the participants—or just how amusing it may have been for either.

It wasn't only the trains that residents looked forward to. In Fort Pierre, the ice-out of the Missouri River would signal spring as much as the sound of a train whistle. In that town, the sound of the ferryboat *Joe Leighton* preparing for spring work was excitedly noted in the March 19 edition of the *Fort Pierre Weekly Signal*.[880]

Along the Southern Minnesota

In prior months, the towns along this line appeared to have been more successful at holding events as scheduled. March, however, slowed things down considerably.

Numerous sociables were canceled due to storms, as was a school exhibition, a concert, and a lyceum. Planners in Egan gave up altogether and said they'd give it another try when spring arrived. Dell Rapids, however, appears to have success-fully held at least one midmonth event. "The concert . . . last Sunday evening," wrote its editor, "was a fine success, as usual, and largely attended, considering the blockaded condition of the walks and roads."[881]

Travel by foot, at least for a portion of the route, was the most successful method, though fraught with danger. Precarious though it may have been, sometimes the incentive was worth the risk. One visitor to Madison "complained somewhat of the walking but, being one of those who cannot get along without his regular weekly reading matter, he [needed] to come to town for his mail anyhow." Those attempting to travel out of town by team were turned back by deep snow after only a few miles.[882]

This bit of news from Egan could also be considered more of an advertisement: "J. H. Eno returned from Yankton one week ago to-day, where he had been to assist (?) Fred Pettigrew on the Flandrau Court House bill."[883] Eno, the lawyer assisting Mr. Pettigrew, was none other than the editor of the *Egan Express*, and it was likely he who put the "(?)" into the article, slightly objecting to, or winking at, the verb "assist."

Despite the still-considerable piles of snow hindering travel, the calendar indicated that spring planting time was approaching, and farmers began visiting their local towns, making preparations. Knowing what the feared spring flooding was capable of, some folks in Egan were planning ahead. "A crew of men spent considerable time working on the bridge," wrote the town's editor, "and it is now in shape so that teams can cross and . . . so that the high water will not take it out."[884] The bridge was a crucial piece of infrastructure—the only way in and out of town.

Along the Lines South and East of Sioux Falls

This portion of the region was less impacted by travel restrictions, as easily seen in voluminous newspaper reports. Merchants reported booming business, and while drifts still vexed travelers on the team roads, travel was on the rise. Naturally, the transitional phase between sleigh and wagon use caused some issues.

Elk Point reported that the roads were "in the best tipping-over condition ever known," further adding, "The moment a sleigh attempts to turn out of the beaten road, the outside runner sinks toward terra firma and over she goes, and then the divil is to pay. Five such cases were noticed within a mile of town, one day this week."[885]

Newspapers and Mail

"The Brookings papers all suspended publication some time ago, on account of the blockade."[886]

—*Moody County Enterprise*, March 3, 1881

The note about the Brookings papers being suspended, found in several regional papers, led to an interesting discovery. The records available on microfilm have a gap, after which the subsequent individual issues have two dates. A little conjecture assumes that they used the out-of-date, preprinted pages (patents) when they arrived, causing the exterior page to have an earlier date, with the "local news" pages reflecting the actual publication date.

The *Brookings County Press* printed consistently through January 20. The front page dated January 27 opened to reveal internal pages dated March 24; the next few issues reflected the same discrepancy in dates: February 3/March 31, February 10/April 7. April 14 was a singular issue, but the next edition has an April 21 exterior and May 5 interior—that is the edition that celebrated the return of the trains.

By early March, with mail having been highly irregular and print-worthy news dwindling even further, the editors of the region's papers prodigiously sprinkled pithy little sayings and phrases into the "Local News" sections, presumably to fill space. In one issue of the *Marshall Messenger*, the editor seemed to have been having a frustrating week. "Three or four feet of snow on our prairies is, of course, considered a big thing," he wrote, "and is liable to give to our usual balmy climate a reputation for severity that does not belong to it." Next, he quoted another paper to the west, printing, "'The beautiful snow' – this winter is a gol darned fraud you know – *Lake Benton News*." And finally, "If you think we are talking about the weather too much, tell us something else to talk about."[887]

Providing insight into the editors' attempts to obtain paper from various sources, the editor in Milbank shared that while he had tried to outsmart the blockades by ordering a large quantity of paper from the north, where blockades had not been a problem, he, too, was running low on paper. After much soul-searching, he declared that it was better to continue in reduced size, as neighboring publications had done, rather than be forced to suspend operations altogether.[888]

The *Madison Sentinel* mused, "If this style of weather should remain in vogue much longer many of our territorial papers will be compelled to issue on pineshavings. For the *Sentinel*, if paper does not arrive in the meantime, we propose to 'come out' on chips next week."[889]

That same edition included this sentimental piece about the importance of publishing:

A newspaper is a window through which men look out upon the world. Without a newspaper a man is shut up in a small room and knows little or nothing of what is happening outside of himself. In our day the newspaper will keep a sensible man in sympathy with the world's current history. It is an untold encyclopedia, an unbound book forever issuing and and [sic] never finishing.[890]

As March wore on, more and more papers resorted to printing smaller editions. "The *Leader* this week," wrote the editor of the *Lake County Leader* (Madison), "is printed on seven different colors of tissue paper, on linen pocket handkerchiefs, cotton cloth, silk neckties, shingles, and antelope skins." It is possible that not *all* of the options listed here were employed, but the paper offered, "These forms will be held on press until Saturday evening, and parties desiring an impression on any kind of material will bring the same in at once."[891] The *Dakota Pantagraph and Sioux Falls Independent* was printed on colored linen on occasion, as was the *Canton News*.[892]

While newspaper editors dealt with their own inconveniences, others fought to get the mail moving. Pipestone's own Station Agent Cawley came through again, organizing an effort to retrieve mail from Flandreau. "On Thursday morning last," wrote the local editor, "[Cawley] was informed that two or three sacks of mail were at Flandrau, for Pipestone, having been carried to Sioux Falls and thence by stage to that place." Three young men headed to Flandreau and returned two days later having "had a stormy ride but they brought the mail which was quite a treat to our people, although there were no papers later than the 17th of February."[893]

The editor of the *New Ulm Weekly Review* humorously noted that when the large volumes of delayed mail arrived, people enjoyed seeing "the post master skip around to distribute it."[894] Lest we worry that he was poking fun at the expense of another, it should be pointed out that the editor was also the postmaster.

In Fort Pierre, two small pouches of mail were delivered by a team that traveled over the railroad tracks.[895] Meanwhile, Elk Point bemoaned the lack of its own mail, the editor writing, "Another week without mail. 'How long Lord, oh, how long' will this winter last?"[896]

Elk Point was not alone. "Minneapolis was without an eastern mail for five days. All owing to snow banks down Chicago way."[897] New Ulm, despite being in the region with some train service, noted, "This has been a dreary winter for us, especially so as our mail facilities for the past two and a half months have been rather limited."[898]

Boosterism

"The fuel question about which they talk so much has never caused the least apprehension. It has not been because we could get no fuel but because we could not get just what we wanted that has brought that question into prominence."[899]

—*Brookings County Press*, March 31, 1881

As we've seen in previous articles, editors got their feathers ruffled by whiffs of fear or disrespect from the east. The article below isn't so much boosterism as an angry retort. On the last day of March, the *Brookings County Press* went on a bit of a tirade, to the point of claiming that there was no shortage of fuel upon the treeless prairie and that, of course, the trouble was really Minnesota and not Dakota Territory at all, and that, besides—those Easterners were every bit as bad off as Dakota Territory was. So there.[900]

This piece was likely written during the more pleasant days leading up to the storm that hit on publication day, but it is amusing to contemplate—after several months of blockades, fuel deprivation, and storm after storm—what inspired the editor to print some of these stretched truths, these twisted pieces of reality, these little white lies. It is almost its own version of "the beautiful" in its audacity. Because it wonderfully represents a particular strain of boosterism, it is included here in full:

> The opinion seems to have got abroad in some manner that there is much suffering in Dakota in consequence of the hard winter. To read eastern papers one would think that between being buried and suffocated in the snow, frozen to death for want of fuel, and starvation there must be but few persons left alive in the territory. We have been right here all winter and have yet to hear of the first case of suffering. The fuel question about which they talk so much has never caused the least apprehension. It has not been because we could get no fuel but because we could not get just what we wanted that has brought that question into prominence. It is true that we have been unable to get coal for some time, owing to the bad doings in Minnesota, but Dakota is not nearly so badly supplied with timber as some people suppose. Hay has been used in many cases for fuel, and all report it a good substitute for wood.

As to the question of provisions it is utterly absurd to suppose that we are in want. The people of Dakota have plenty to eat burn and wear, and were it not for the inconvenience to business occasioned by the blockade, there would be nothing left to wish for.

While the winter all over the United States is universally admitted to be the longest and hardest ever known, and while the roads have been blocked by snow from Hudson's Bay to St. Louis, there has not been any time here when three days work with an ordinary force of men would have failed to clear the Northwestern R. R. from the Minnesota line to Pierre.

The principal cause of the blockade has been that all our great lines of railroads run from east to west and consequently pass through Minnesota, where blizzard has succeeded blizzard with a rapidity that startles the oldest inhabitant. As soon as some of the many projected lines from the south are built it will be impossible to block us in.

From all we can learn from the most trustworthy sources we find that the winter here has not been near as severe as in Wisconsin and Iowa while it has been almost summer in comparison with Minnesota. The weather now gives every appearance of being ready to 'let up' and in the boom of business and emigration which will soon be upon us we shall forget the trials of the ever to be remembered winter of '80 and '81, while we are convinced that the crops of next season will prove that it was just what we wanted.[901]

Despite the editor's beseeching words portraying the winter as being no big deal, the reality was that the railroad tracks were concealed by monstrous piles of snow, which were further encased in ice in an increasing number of places.

How *Was* All That Snow Removed?

Before we leave the month of March, let's look at what the shoveling crews dealt with, and examine photos taken around the region during March and April of 1881.

The photos are simply amazing, and we are fortunate to have the work of the intrepid photographers who took their equipment out into the frigid conditions to capture the scenes. Most of the photos below were taken between March 22 and April 15, 1881, within the last month or so of the blockades.

Blowing or drifting snow stops moving or settles when the wind speed decreases, as when it encounters features such as tree lines, hills, snow fences, or railroad cuts. Cuts in windblown areas acted as effective "snow catchers." The narrower the cut, the more effective it was in capturing snow. Toward the end of winter, as melting on the open prairie exposed the soil, the wind also picked up dirt and dust, which mixed with the snow and ice in the cuts, making an even more difficult, concrete-like compound.

Snow fences were placed near the tracks to block and divert the snow away from troublesome areas. However, as we've seen, many of these were disassembled and burned by settlers who were low on fuel. The remaining fences were not always sufficient to deal with the abundance of snow and force of wind that this winter presented.

Easiest Snow Removal: Run a Train along the Tracks

In the best of circumstances, a train simply ran along the tracks, pushing the snow aside as it went. The thought was that if they did this often enough, the snow could not accumulate. In expansive regions that saw relatively few trains, this was an unrealistic process, and snow was bound to accumulate in deep drifts on top of the tracks.

When That Wasn't Enough . . .

Gangs of hundreds of men worked throughout the winter to shovel, chop, and fling the snow and ice away from the cuts, often in conjunction with a snowplow, but not always. As the winter went on, the sides of the cuts became deeper and deeper, and tiers—terraces, really—were chiseled into the banks to allow the men to get the snow out of the cuts.

In a later reminiscence, Station Agent C. J. Cawley, stationed in Pipestone, described the process of chopping the snow out of the cuts. "The equipment of the snow fighters of those days was a pick and shovel, . . ." wrote Cawley. "The snow in the cuts had to be taken out in tiers, with men on each level throwing the snow up and out . . . finally cutting a block of snow about as large as a box car, slipping a cable around it, and pulling it out with an engine."[902] The following photos illustrate the process.

This crew is using shovels and picks to remove the snow and ice. Note how little room is on either side of the locomotive. Elmer & Tenney photo, taken March 22, 1881, one and a half miles west of Oshawa Township (between St. Peter and Nicollet, just east of New Ulm) on the Winona & St. Peter. Photo courtesy of the Chicago & North Western Historical Society.

This photo captured the tiers that developed as shovelers worked to move snow up and over the ever-expanding banks. Elmer & Tenney photo, taken March 22, 1881, at a cut in Oshawa Township. Photo courtesy of the Chicago & North Western Historical Society.

Note that the snow is in solid clumps as it is chopped from the cut.
This is also a good example of the trench-like structures that formed along the cuts.
The close-up (*right*) shows the photographer's shadow. Elmer & Tenney photo, taken
March 29, 1881, along the Southern Minnesota. Photo courtesy of the Chicago & North
Western Historical Society.

This photo shows the process of carving out some of the volume to reduce the weight of the larger blocks so that the locomotive could pull them out of the cut. Elmer & Tenney photo, taken April 15, 1881, near Lamberton, along the Winona & St. Peter. Photo courtesy of the Chicago & North Western Historical Society.

This photo illustrates how cables were wrapped around the blocks of snow so they could be attached to the locomotive, which then pulled them out of the cut. The blocks were then unceremoniously dumped onto the open prairie. Elmer & Tenney photo, taken April 15, 1881, near Sleepy Eye, along the Winona & St. Peter. Photo courtesy of the Chicago & North Western Historical Society.

This Chas A. Tenney photo, taken along the Southern Minnesota, shows a block of snow after removal from a cut, backed out by a locomotive. Notice how the surrounding prairie has relatively little snow cover, illustrating how thick and compacted the cut snow was compared to the snow "on the level." From the Minnesota Historical Society.

Elmer & Tenney photo, taken March 22, 1881, at Kelly's Cut on the Winona & St. Peter, just west of Sleepy Eye. Photo courtesy of the Chicago & North Western Historical Society.

This captivating photo shows gloveless shovelers taking a break, their pants caked with snow. Elmer & Tenney photo, taken March 22, 1881, along the Winona & St. Peter, near Sleepy Eye. Photo courtesy of the Chicago & North Western Historical Society.

In *The Long Winter*, when Pa was working as a shoveler, the girls watched him dress for the job. Wilder described the process: "He was putting on an extra pair of woolen socks while he talked. He wound the wide muffler around his neck, crossed it on his chest, and buttoned his overcoat snugly over it. He fastened his ear muffs, put on his warmest mittens, and then with his shovel on his shoulder he went to the depot."[903] That may seem like a lot, but he needed every layer—at least at first.

Many photographs from that winter show men shoveling sans gloves, scarves, etc., working not far from piles of unidentifiable objects, which could very well have been articles of clothing, discarded as the shovelers warmed up. Anyone who has shoveled their driveway on a nice winter day has likely done the same. But that is entirely conjecture. (The Elmer & Tenney photo that was featured a few pages back, taken on March 29 along the Southern Minnesota, is a good example; look near the top of the image.)

We will leave March with one last image, an impressive photo of a railroad cut. Its location is noted as southern Minnesota (the region, not the Southern Minnesota Railroad), 1881.

Another view of a deep cut; likely also an Elmer & Tenney photo.
From the Minnesota Historical Society.

APRIL
(AND A LITTLE OF MAY) 1881

Sunday	Monday	Tuesday	Wednesday	Thursday	Friday	Saturday
					1	2
3	4	5	6 melting	7 12"–14" snow	8	9
10 storm (west) 4" snow cold rain (east)	11 storm (west) heavy snow cold rain (east)	12 storm (west)	13	14	15 six-month anniversary of first snow	16
17 robins reported in Sioux Falls	18 rain melting and muddy	19 rain melting and muddy	20 melting and muddy	21 slush and water "very muddy mud"	22	23 mirage reported in eastern D.T.
24 rain	25	26 snow gone in Marshall	27 prairie fires in southeasern D.T.	28 prairie fires in southeasern D.T.	29 prairie fires in southeasern D.T.	30 prairie fires thunder/hail (east)

▬▬▬▬▬ Blizzard or significant snow event

//////////// Lighter snow or mixed precipitation

Early April: "sudden rise of Missouri River." Serious flooding along the Missouri River all month.

April 5: Gary (near Watertown) had reports of snow five to seven feet on the level.

April 6: New Ulm reported Minnesota River still has thirty-six inches of ice.

April 7: Pipestone reported "Had there been a little loose snow on the ground [the storm of March 31] would have undoubtedly expressed the worst blizzard of the year."

April 12: Janesville reported unsafe lake ice.

April 12: Sioux Falls reported ice gorge sixteen miles long between Yankton and Sioux Falls (Big Sioux River).

April 14: Pipestone reported six feet of ice on lakes north of town.

April 17: New Ulm reported ice out on Minnesota River.

This calendar shows weather reports gleaned from the various newspaper articles.
If the weather was significantly different in one portion of the region versus another, that is noted.

Even as signs of spring began to hearten the settlers, one last blizzard slapped down their hopes in April. It was the last, however, and the situation began to improve in fits and starts. Ironically, despite the onslaught of flooding, prairie fires were also on the upswing.

Trains began to reach communities that had been isolated since January, and reactions in the papers ranged from what equated to a near-ear-shattering celebration to what read as almost haughty disinterest. Trains remained somewhat irregular for a time, though, owing to the floodwaters. Rivers, streams, and even tiny creeks all carried away the meltwater with exuberance, but the undulating prairies held onto it like so many soup bowls. Whether the railroad infrastructure was washed away amidst a violent current or slowly undermined by standing water, the washouts caused significant damage across the entire region and prevented the beleaguered railroad workers from taking a break to recover from their winter efforts. Their heroism got it all put back together, and within a relatively short time, life returned to normal.

The editors were not quite done venting their frustrations, however, and had a few last quips to share with their readers.

The Month for the Ingalls Family

Laura said nothing; she was too happy.
She could hardly believe that the winter was gone,
that spring had come. When Pa asked her why she was so silent,
she answered soberly, "I said it all in the night."

"I should say you did! Waking us all from a sound sleep to tell
us the wind was blowing!" Pa teased her. "As if the wind hadn't
blown for months!"

"I said the Chinook," Laura reminded him.
"That makes all the difference."[904]

—*The Long Winter*

In the novel, April featured more storms, lacking detail, and while they were further apart in time, they remained furious and bitterly cold.[905] Winter held on until the bitter end.

Both fictionally and factually, a long winter of snow, ice, and dirt mixing together in the cuts meant the blockades could only be cleared by chipping away at them with picks, progressing inch by inch—a slow and laborious task.[906] This snow-ice-dirt composite that vexed the shovel crews was not the only antagonist. The melting snows had washed out tracks and bridges, further complicating the situation. All the while, the family continued relentlessly grinding seed wheat. The remaining commentary in this section pertains to the novel unless otherwise noted.

In a bit of humor amid the darkness, Pa teased Laura for waking the family to tell them that the wind was blowing. But "the Chinook," a warm, dry wind, promised the end of winter and was worth shouting about.[907] With the improving weather, crews were reported to be at work in the Tracy Cut, bolstering hope that a train would soon get through.[908]

On the brink of trains returning, food was truly running out. Ma wondered if food could be hauled in, but Pa answered that flooding prevented teams from going anywhere for fear of becoming mired in the mud.[909]

One memorable day a whistle was heard—"The train stopped. It was really here, a train at last."[910] The first train through was a work train carrying a crew and supplies for repairing the tracks after a winter of disuse and hard conditions. The next train left behind three freight cars that had been snowed in all winter. Much to the dismay of the townspeople, it brought not a bulk of food but farm equipment, telegraph poles, and an emigrant car, the last of which contained some staple food items.

As noted in the autobiographies as well as the novel, Station Agent Woodworth broke into the emigrant car, and the men distributed the edible contents to hungry families. In the novel, Ma was disturbed by the theft, but Pa was defiant, making no apologies for procuring a few meals' worth of potatoes, flour, and fat salt pork for his hungry family.[911] " 'I'm past caring what we ought to do!' Pa said savagely. 'Let the railroad stand some damages! This isn't the only family in town that's got nothing to eat.' "[912]

The second train brought groceries, kerosene, and the longed-for Christmas barrel, with its still-frozen turkey. The novel ended with the awakening of the floral smells of the prairie, a Christmas-in-May celebration, a veritable feast, and the sweet refrains of Pa's fiddle. "And as they sang," wrote Wilder, "the fear and the suffering of the long winter seemed to rise like a dark cloud and float away on the music. Spring had come. The sun was shining warm, the winds were soft, and the green grass growing."[913]

> **Emigrant Cars**
>
> In the transition between isolation and abundance, an emigrant car was broken into, and the food within distributed among the hungry townspeople. But what, exactly, was an emigrant car?
>
> In today's parlance, it would be akin to a rented moving truck. A settler "purchased" a boxcar and put their worldly goods within it to move to a new location. It could contain household items, farming tools and implements, and/or staple food items to last for some number of months. Railroad companies often offered discounted or free transport of these cars as an enticement for settlement along their lines, especially if the settler had used the same railroad to inspect offered lands on an earlier excursion trip.
>
> In a letter to Lane, Almanzo detailed how he "got an Emigrant car to De Smet." In it, he packed some oats as well as building supplies: "some lumber to build a shanty on my homestead that would do to live in and a small barn for my team you see the first shanty was just enough to make believe we staid there + one could have if he realy had to."[914]

The Weather

"Even at this time, the beginning of April, the air is still too cool to cause a rapid disappearance of the snow, which must, ere long, succumb to the melting rays of the sun and cause a rapid resumption of the business that has been suspended for so many months in consequence of the fierceness of the winds and the amount of snow deposited within our borders."[915]

—*Murray County Pioneer*, April 7, 1881

Lingering Winter

The unending optimism about trains getting through did not always translate into optimism toward the weather. Marshall reported that while the "snow has rapidly settled," a cold wind blew that "furnished a freeze up every night."[916]

In New Ulm, the Minnesota River reportedly retained "thirty-six inches thickness of ice." Despite the wagon roads being "next thing to impassable,"[917] farmers were working in their fields in preparation for seeding.

As if to reaffirm the extraordinary nature of the winter thus far, one article informed readers that "according to the records kept at Ft. Snelling [in Minnesota], the snow fall this winter has been four times as great as for the previous nine years, and nine times the average of nineteen years."[918]

French explorers had left behind their own records, which were "dug up at Huron." Written in French, the documents recounted the "severe winter of 1830 and '31 and the disastrous floods which ensued in the month of April, by which whole villages were swept away by the sudden going off of the snow."[919]

The *Dell Rapids Exponent* took a different tack. Instead of sharing impressive statistics or historical documents, it wearily sighed, via typesetting, that "six months of sleighing is quite enough for one winter."[920]

In its April 14 edition, the *Pipestone Star* thought to observe the six-month anniversary of the October blizzard, including the notation, "There is much of that same snow upon the ground now."[921]

The Storm of April 7—the Last!

The final storm of the winter struck between April 7 and 10, depending upon location. Reports from Sioux City noted the earliest snowfall as occurring on April 7, and the Pipestone paper described the worst of it happening on April 10. Compared to reports of the flooding that had begun, however, little column space was devoted to the snow's last hurrah.

Along the Winona & St. Peter

As the final storm blew, the correspondent from Tracy noted, "Storm after storm has arisen, and to this day the snow has not failed to make regular visits.... The wind persists in the north; and while it continues there we do not look for a very rapid departure of snow."[922] The New Ulm paper reminded its readers that while this final storm's snowfall was light, it was still winter.[923]

Along the Southern Minnesota and the Sioux City

Reports indicated that "two feet of snow" had fallen in the most southern portion of Dakota Territory, and as a result the Sioux City road was blockaded and had been forced to suspend operations for a day. Despite the minimal disruptions on this line throughout the winter, the Janesville editor quipped, "Perhaps by July they may be able to run regularly."[924] The storm extended south to Omaha and east into Illinois.[925]

The *Sioux Falls Times* of April 12, printed on linen, described the snowfall as quiet at first, then heavier, then "in force" during the second day, with three more to go. "Nearly twelve inches of the beautiful fell," though it compressed quickly because of its high moisture content. While the editor in Dell Rapids, to the north, had had enough of sleighing for the winter, the editor of the *Sioux Falls Times* wasn't ready to give up just yet, writing, "People cannot afford to lay inside their sleighs only two-thirds worn out."[926]

While Sioux Falls reported twelve inches of new snow, the *Pipestone Star* described the storm as "a stunner," and added, "How many feet of snow fell we shall not attempt to say, but there was enough to make the drifts look like mountains again and to deprive us of any hopes of a train for at least ten days to come."[927]

A Mirage

Atmospheric conditions were unusual on April 16, producing a mirage reported by at least two parties in the vicinity of Milbank:

Last Saturday morning a remarkably distinct mirage was observed about six o'clock. Residents of Twin Brooks, eight miles west of Milbank, say that for about ten minutes this town appeared to be within half a mile, and that the buildings seemed to be greatly elongated and to extend high up in the air. The scene then changed and the town rapidly retreated until it appeared in the far distance. [Two men from Ortonville] reported that in the morning the Dakota Hills (12 miles west of Milbank and 24 miles west of Ortonville) appeared to be within a very short distance of their town, and that the trees and branches were clearly discernible.[928]

Melting and Flooding

Flooding held the attention of the newspapers throughout much of the region, especially along the major rivers—the Big Sioux, the James, the Missouri, and the Minnesota.

Along the Hastings & Dakota

The Milbank paper told its readers, "The Missouri has been on the rampage badly.... The great amount of snow yet remaining is sufficient to make the streams boom at a lively rate when it melts."[929]

A week later, the floodwaters of the Whetstone River began to impact Milbank. "The 'break-up' has arrived," wrote the town's editor, "and travel by team has been suspended. The snow commenced to melt and run about the middle of last week, and Saturday was the last day that teams could travel. Every low spot on the prairie is a small lake, and the [streams] are gradually swelling."[930]

Along the Winona & St. Peter

On April 20, New Ulm reported that the ice on the Minnesota River had broken up, but along with that bit of progress came a six-foot rise in water, flooding the bottomlands. Teams were no longer able to cross the bridge, and people traveling on foot had to be "transferred with skiffs."[931]

South of Tracy, Currie experienced excitement when "the immense amount of snow deposited during the winter" began to melt under the "warming influence of the sun, . . . entirely inundating the flat land just north of the village."[932]

Along the Dakota Central

The two towns at the western terminus of the Dakota Central were experiencing the might of the Missouri River, which forced residents up into the safety of the bluffs, where they watched the towns being swallowed by the waters. Five feet of water washed through the main street of Pierre, and while the property damage was immense, no lives were lost.[933]

Among the property and valuables set adrift in the frothy brown waters of the Missouri were the office, presses, and other equipment of the *Fort Pierre Weekly Signal*. Its March 26 issue was its last until May 14. The postflood inaugural edition explained the gap by printing, "The water rose to such a height as to slightly demoralize us and compelled us to go east and get new material."[934]

Along the Southern Minnesota

Flandreau was upstream of Egan by about five miles if you traveled straight and approximately eight miles if you traveled the winding river. In early April, a resident of Flandreau reported that the river, at its highest height known to the settlers, was experiencing an ice dam, and he feared "serious damage below" when the ice broke free.[935] A week later, the residents of Egan found the Big Sioux "bank full and still rising."[936] By the end of the month, "thirteen hundred feet of railroad track" east of Egan were "displaced by the high waters," and the Flandreau editor forecasted, "No trains will venture to cross this place until the flood has subsided."[937]

The *Egan Express* did a thorough summary of the flooding at the end of April. The melting had begun in earnest on a Sunday. By Monday the banks were full, and Tuesday saw the lowlands flooded. The flooding grew until Saturday, at which point, "it looked more like the mighty Mississippi than the placid Sioux. . . ." In some places, the flow of water was "over a mile wide, whereas originally it [was] only a couple of hundred feet." The impacts of the floodwaters were significant, especially for railroad bridges that spanned the rivers. Just east of Egan, the railroad bridge over the Big Sioux was "completely swept away." While the land close to the river was inundated, the town itself was reported as being "perfectly safe so far as water is concerned."[938]

In Egan, ice gorged above a railroad bridge, causing the water to back up. When the jam broke free, half a mile of track was washed out, along with the bridge. The bridge itself floated a short distance downstream, but was wrangled, rescued, and returned to its piles, which had remained in place. It was expected that it would "take but a few days to put it in shape. . . ."[939]

In addition to the railroad bridge and length of track, the highway bridge also took a float down the river but became entangled in trees not far downstream. Once the water receded, "the remnants were collected together and a ferry boat constructed of them, large enough to carry a team and loaded wagon." A boat was launched, allowing those wishing to cross the river to safely do so.[940]

At the end of the month, the *Egan Express* noted how quickly the snow had melted and the streets had dried up. Over only "a few days," snow measuring up to "ten feet in depth" in some places melted away. "Now the snow is all gone," wrote the town's editor, "and strange as it may seem to those not acquainted, a person can walk anywhere in the village with slippers on and not wet their feet. Truly Egan is not . . . a mud hole."[941]

Along the Lines South and East of Sioux Falls

Articles about lives lost along the Missouri River between Yankton and Vermillion appeared throughout April, along with enduring concerns. At midmonth, "an ice gorge sixteen miles in length" was "reported between Yankton and Sioux City." The *Sioux Falls Times* described the predicament, printing, "The ice is piled up in every conceivable manner, and is preserved by quantities of sand well mixed in. When the ice fairly starts, mountains will scarcely be a barrier."[942]

The End of an Era: Steamboats Give Way to the Railroad

Steamboats first reached Yankton in 1859 and served the area for twenty-two years. Steamboats had been crucial in establishing and building the river communities of Yankton and Vermillion. They also played a significant role in conveying hopeful miners toward the gold-rush towns west of the Missouri River.

The Black Hills gold rush had peaked by 1878, and as the cascade of hopeful miners dried to a trickle, so did that aspect of the passenger business. By the early 1880s, railroads had established main lines, branches, and spurs throughout much of the lands leading up the Mississippi and Missouri Rivers east and south of Minnesota, and they were making speedy inroads into Dakota Territory. While more expensive, trains could move more goods, at faster speeds, over greater distances, along more efficient routes. As the booming railroads expanded into markets previously dominated by river travel, the long-established riverboat industry was already beginning to die away.

On March 27, 1881, as the ice and snow of an unprecedented winter were finally retreating, an ice dam upriver from Vermillion gave way. The torrent of water, debris, and blocks of river ice caused significant damage to the town and its steamboat industry, destroying boats and facilities. The number of boats actually destroyed is contested, noted as anywhere between two and "hundreds," but the exact number is not pertinent. Many boats were able to be repaired and continued being used, but the impact of the March 27 flooding on the steamboat business was significant—the flourishing growth of the railroads only accelerated the older industry's decline.

Yankton, located upstream of the mouth of the James River, was spared from the raging debris-filled floodwaters that decimated Vermillion, another twenty-five miles downstream. As originally platted, Vermillion was in the river bottoms. By the time the flood receded, most of the town had been washed away, and a new channel of the Missouri River had been formed. Surviving residents wisely rebuilt above the bluffs.

Prairie Fires and Other Signs of Spring

Signs of spring began to appear in earnest, interspersed with decidedly wintry weather. In addition to the challenges presented by melting snow, muddy roads, and thunderstorms, settlers also had to contend with prairie fires.

By mid-April, Sioux Falls reported that its titular falls were "booming" thanks to the recent melting and that hundreds of spectators were "witnessing the grand sights."[943] Meanwhile, Sleepy Eye's paper reported that all that its citizens were seeing was lots and lots of mud.[944]

As the open prairie became visible from beneath the deep blankets of snow, the *Sioux Falls Times* commented on the return of local fauna, printing, "The first robins were heard . . . and right welcome was their whistle. Birds of many kinds begin to put in an appearance, which we have reason to believe is a sure harbinger of spring. So mote it be." The editor even speculated that the "prairie chickens are happy again."[945] But their blooming habitat was not without danger.

In its April 28 issue, the *Grant County Review* out of Milbank warned its readers, "Prairie fires can now be seen in every direction. No time should be lost in making fire-breaks."[946] Milbank is approximately seventy-four miles to the northeast of De Smet. About forty-six miles to the south of De Smet, Salem also reported "prairie fires raging."[947] Into early May, the *Egan Express* continued to caution residents to "look out for" the pervasive and erratic fires.[948]

And in what must have been a highly satisfactory moment, Milbank was able to share, "The rain on Sunday [April 24] had the effect of washing away nearly the last vestige of snow from in and around town."[949]

A correspondent to the Flandreau paper took the opportunity to write a poetic ode, sharing, "Lo, the winter is past, the rain is over and gone, the flowers appear on the earth, the time of the singing birds is come, and the voice of the turtle is heard in our land."[950]

The *New Ulm Weekly Review* also noted the town's "first thunder and hail storm of the season" had passed over at "about eleven o'clock a.m." on April 30, moving "from south-east to north-west." The hailstones "came down thick and fast" for "a few minutes." The editor further added, "Soon after, the floodgates were opened and during the remainder of the day heavy showers fell at intervals. At one time during the afternoon it became so dark that it was necessary to light the lamps."[951]

As spring began to assert itself, the Janesville paper bade winter a not-so-fond farewell. "It is generally conceded on all sides," wrote the editor, "that no more old fashioned Minnesota winters are wanted. Let the dead past bury its dead, winters and all, and the big drifts too. A foot of snow in some of the western counties yet, and threshing and corn husking is not done either."[952]

The Railroads

"No sooner is the snow blockade over than the water embargo sets in. All this make it very bad for the people who have wintered down this way and are anxious to get back to their farms to do spring seeding."[953]

—*Janesville Argus*, May 3, 1881

There was a great deal of railroad activity during April. The battles against "the beautiful" continued, though the substance that remained in the cuts was less snow and more a stubborn snow-ice-dirt mixture that was significantly more difficult to attack, and decidedly less beautiful.

H. A. Stimson experienced similar conditions while working for the railroad in the early 1900s under the watch of his father, the station agent at De Smet. "Each flurry of snow and daily thaw laminated the drifts and cuts became marbleized, veneered and reinforced," wrote Stimson in his autobiography.[954] That description was of conditions over twenty years after the Hard Winter, yet the problem was the same. Adding that to the flooding and washed-out tracks and bridges, one might wonder whether the railroad employees were as excited about the coming spring as the average citizen.

Along the Hastings & Dakota

The northernmost line in the region was the first to see trains, though making progress there wasn't necessarily any easier than along the lines to the south.

Trains Approach

Milbank reported a train in Ortonville, a little over ten miles to the east, on April 6.[955] While the paper predicted the train would push westward to Milbank within the next few days, some weren't willing to wait. Instead, several merchants, along with Milbank's station agent, went to Ortonville with teams to bring badly needed goods back to the town.[956]

Train Through—Milbank, April 19

While hopes were high that trains would make the final miles from Ortonville by April 9, it took an additional ten days to bust the blockade. As the first train triumphantly pulled into Milbank, it was heralded with poetic joy:

THE BLOCKADE RAISED.

Railroad Travel Again Resumed.

Freight Pouring In by the Train Load.

Business Booming and all Hands Rejoicing.

The blockade at Milbank is raised. On Tuesday afternoon at half-past two o'clock engine No. 176 . . . sped into town, having bucked through the last drift about a quarter of a mile east of town. As the engine dashed into town she serenaded us with a long, shrill, hearty, whistle that was welcomed with shouts of joy by all hands. It was exactly twelve weeks to a day since a locomotive had been seen in Milbank. The comparative quiet and dullness that had reigned for three months in our town was changed in the twinkling of an eye to a scene of buzz and activity.[957]

The article went on to describe the abrupt increase in activity experienced by the town, no longer isolated by the blockades. If the editor had his dates correct, the last train would have arrived on January 25. He further added,

In about an hour the first freight train arrived, and later on another freight with a caboose containing passengers. Towards midnight the regular passenger train arrived. On Wednesday morning, lumber dealers, merchants and all hands generally had a busy time getting in new stocks, and business took a boom indicative of a still bigger boom that is destined to bring Milbank to the front as one of the most prosperous cities in Dakota.[958]

The Hastings & Dakota Back on Track

One last report came in summarizing work to repair damages to the tracks from the snow-and-ice blockades and spring washouts and to remove the tempo-rary tracks, called shooflies, that had been built to steer trains around some of the damage and obstacles. The editor of Milbank's *Grant County Review* spoke with the civil engineer in charge. The engineer informed him that repairs had been made and that trains were now running to Ortonville. However, the work was far from over. "A vast amount of work will be required to make good the devastation and destruction caused by the floods," wrote the editor, "and it will probably be at least ten days yet before trains can get through to this point." Part of the problem was a washed-out bridge over the Whetstone River, though plans were in place to construct a temporary bridge to allow freight to be delivered using teams and wagons. The editor was satisfied with the efforts, adding, "This action upon the part of the railroad company is certainly very commendable, and shows clearly the desire of the company to assist our business men and farmers in every possible manner."[959]

Along the Winona & St. Peter and the Dakota Central

The blockades along the Winona & St. Peter hindered the opening of this line and of the Dakota Central, to the west of Tracy. The cuts seemed to be holding on to the snow and ice.

Progress on the Blockades

For the first week or so of April, it was evident that the shovelers were close to breaking through the last of the snow and that trains would finally get through. But as happened so many other times throughout the winter, there was one more disappointment ahead.

An April 1 article out of Marshall reported that Superintendent Sanborn was in town and described some of the work being done:

> [He] proceeded to tear up things to heat the engine that has been stored here for several weeks, and began work on the road between here and Tracy. As the company is now at work at both ends of the blockade and some in the middle, we can hope to connect with the civilized world in a few weeks. Later.—This item was a little too previous. A slight change of weather has delayed things some."[960]

That "slight change of weather" was some lighter precipitation that occurred the day the paper was published.

The papers in both Janesville and New Ulm reported that the tracks had been cleared to a point about four miles west of Sleepy Eye. Work beyond that, however, was progressing slowly. "Slow work opening those cuts now," wrote a correspondent from Sleepy Eye, "as since the thaw solid ice has formed in the bottoms."[961] The ice was a formidable adversary. In the April 6 edition of the *New Ulm Weekly Review*, the editor included that the ice had to be "loosened with picks," and predicted, "It will be two weeks yet before the main line will be open for traffic as far west as Marshall."[962]

The next town west of Sleepy Eye, Springfield, confirmed that the shovelers had not quite reached them, but that work was advancing, and hopes were high. "The day is not far distant," wrote the New Ulm editor, "when the welcome locomotive whistle will again be heard announcing the approach of the passenger train." Fuel was "getting mighty low," but the snow was "slowly but surely melting away," and the town's warehouses were full.[963]

A correspondent from just southeast of Brookings announced, "We still live, which we think is saying a good deal." Despite that opening line, they then proclaimed that the severe winter had not discouraged them, though they conceded that conditions had been such that they thought they had "had a taste of prison life."[964]

On April 8, two days before the final blizzard of the season hit Marshall, the editor of the *Marshall Messenger* had felt encouraged by the "air of Spring" that had permeated the previous week. During the favorable weather, the railroad company had "been hiring all the men they could get to shovel snow" and they were getting the upper hand. As mentioned in the previous edition, crews were using whatever fuel was available to operate the locomotive that had wintered in Marshall, in anticipation of the cuts being opened. The April 8 edition added,

> The coal shed and other things that could be spared were chopped up for
> fuel to feed the engine that has been Wintered here, and as long as that
> holds out fair progress will be made. The cuts are everywhere filled full,
> and the snow is almost as hard as ice in some places. As there is no snow
> plow here, every foot of the cuts has to be shoveled out by hand. The
> work will therefore be slow, and Tracy will not be reached before next
> week probably.

To temper any unrealistic hopes of a train getting through, the article finished by reminding readers, "At the Sleepy Eye end of the trouble the drifts are much worse than here, and although as large a force as they can get is at work their progress west is not rapid. If the road is open by the last of next week, our largest expectations will be realized."[965]

Those "largest expectations" were, indeed, unrealistic. On April 10, the familiar nemesis swept down upon them yet again.

Following the Final Storm of the Winter

This final storm must have tried the will and resilience of the hundreds of men who continued to chip away at the snow and ice that encased the tracks. Clearer skies meant the sun could help weaken the thick ice, but it also contributed to more cases of snow blindness, hindering progress further. And as if the pressure of the hungry towns beyond the blockades wasn't enough, towns on the eastern side of the blockades were filling up with travelers anxious to head west.

The editors knew that with April half-gone, it was only a matter of time before spring weather would put an end to the tiresome business of the blockades. Articles monitoring the progress at the trouble spots became more infused with a bated-breath tone, raising the drama.

Two days after the storm, the *Janesville Argus* editor shared that a veritable army of "eight hundred men" was chipping away at the ice covering the tracks of the Winona & St. Peter west of Sleepy Eye. "At latest accounts," continued the editor, "only a few miles had been cleared. Ice two feet in thickness on top of the rails is found in places. No snow plow could 'buck' such a drift. . . . Warm weather alone is likely to take out such ice banks."[966]

Closer to the action, Currie's *Murray County Pioneer* noted, "The railroads were blocked by the late storms as bad as at any time this winter. How long shall this be thus."[967]

On April 15, five days after the storm hit Marshall, the *Messenger* reassured its readers, "Supt. Sanborn passed through here today, bound westward which means business along the line."[968] Another five days later, the *New Ulm Weekly Review* published a correspondence from Tracy that may have shaken the confidence of its readers. "From this look-out it does not appear that the railroad company is doing all it can to open the road," accused the writer. "One day we hear that a large force is to be put on and men even start out to work. The next day, however, we learn that all the men are off work the wages having been reduced. And thus it goes on. Well, having stood the blockade so long we can endure it awhile longer."[969]

Whatever was actually happening to the shovelers out of Tracy, things were progressing elsewhere. Crews had reached Walnut Grove by midmonth, with hopes that the entire road—through Tracy and Marshall and on to Watertown—would be open within a week.[970] A snowplow had done considerable work west of Marshall until it reached "an extensive wash-out" at a landmark known as the "Lone Tree" near Canby, Minnesota.[971] Taking a moment to reflect, Superintendent Sanborn expressed "himself much pleased with the very material aid and encouragement rendered by Marshall in opening the road" and said he would remember the townspeople for it.[972]

Trains through to Tracy and Marshall, April 18 and 19

Reminiscent of Mary Ingalls's admonition that waiting to read the family's copy of the *Youth's Companion* would "help [them] to learn self-denial"—that is, it would be good for them[973]—the April 22 edition of the *Marshall Messenger* waxed philosophical, expounding on the benefits of *want*. The editor declared,

We have met the beautiful beyond once more and are more or less happy. An open railroad to eastern supplies is the way we long have sought and mourned, froze, starved, and gone without beer and white bread because we found it not. But all these privations were intended to put us en rapport with a better state of existence, to fit us for the sensations of the coming perihelion and to teach us the inherent value of the common things of life. There are a good many other lessons that this Winter has taught us. We have not quite as much faith in the beautiful Autumn that we used to preach as an immigration inducement, but we still brag on being able to furnish a Winter free from mud, and have learned that the great universal want of this region is fuel.

The editor also threw forth some playful chiding about the residents of Tracy, where, as we just read, a crew had quit work after their wages were reduced.[974] Considering the number of articles throughout the winter mentioning that people were shoveling voluntarily, this seemed a bit odd, especially when the result could have been the resumption of trains.

In those final days of effort, the crew who came down from Marshall to bust the blockade seemed to have also found things a little more "relaxed" in Tracy, at least according to the Marshall editor. In what likely amounted to a good-natured ribbing between two rival communities, the editor wrote,

> Last Monday about 100 men went down from [Marshall] bound to reach the other train. Tracy was found and dug out just after dinner, and as our men dug out the depot at that enterprising village they timidly asked what all the able-bodied men of Tracy had been about of late.... The Tracy-ites came out and snowballed them while they were uncovering the town. That pastime worked like a boomerang, however, and flew back on them rather severely. As the train left Tracy going east, six or eight of Tracy's sons caught the spirit of enterprise and went out to shovel. They all returned however on the first train in about two hours. Tracy has plenty of water and plenty of beer, but she is rather short on live men.

With a train approaching Marshall from the east, things were going so well that the workers were sent home around eight o'clock that evening. However, with a familiar ring of frustration, the editor announced that the train did not make it through: "In bucking a snow drift . . . the fire was put out, and the road was not really opened till Tuesday, April 19."[975]

Trains Blockaded Again

Two days after the liberation of the western end of the Winona & St. Peter, several bridges washed out between a point east of New Ulm and the Cottonwood River near Lamberton, bringing train travel to a halt once again.[976]

The *Marshall Messenger* of April 29 noted that the town's last train had arrived on the twentieth and that the melt had washed out or carried away a considerable amount of track, six or eight bridges between Sleepy Eye and Marshall, and a trestle near New Ulm. No train was expected for several more days despite crews of men hard at work. "Supt. Sanborn is between Lamberton and Walnut Grove with a large force of men," wrote the Marshall editor, "and the track is being put in repair as rapidly as possible. . . . A force of snow shovelers returned from the west on Wednesday, and have gone below to assist in the work of repairing the track."[977]

That crew had been working on the western end of the Winona & St. Peter, going as far as Goodwin, Dakota Territory, about thirteen miles east of Watertown. They reported that the sun had cleared the tracks west of that point. It wasn't all good news, however, as a 180-foot bridge went missing just east of Canby.[978] The article did not indicate whether said bridge had been washed away or hauled off for fuel.

The growing intensity of the sun that had cleared the western tracks was aiding crews in removing the stubborn remains of snow and ice all along the line, and doing even more work on the open fields. " 'Old Sol' made short work of our three feet of snow when he got down to biz,"[979] wrote the Marshall editor.

According to the *Janesville Argus*, the town's older residents were chagrined over losing some of their bragging rights. "They feel humiliated," wrote the Janesville editor, "that they who have lived there thirty years have seen no more than those who have lived there but a year. The present rise was said to have been two feet higher than the oldest settler ever before saw."[980]

Blockades Open—Again

By early May, trains were running to a point west of Marshall on the Winona & St. Peter and just to the east of Brookings on the Dakota Central, bridge repairs having been completed.[981]

New Ulm and Sleepy Eye reported the arrival of numerous emigrant cars along with shipments of fuel and merchandise. One day alone saw eighteen trains.[982] Some of these cars had been sidetracked for "several days" the previous week,[983] meaning they had arrived more recently and were able to continue their journey much more quickly than cars that had been sidetracked for longer, perhaps since early January.

With trains once again moving regularly, the *Lake Benton Times* shared its joy with other papers, and the *New Ulm Weekly Review* celebrated with it: "The *Lake Benton News* [*Times*] expresses its joy at the opening of the railroad as follows: The suspense is over—'RAH!' The blockade has been raised—TIGER!! Through trains and daily mails—WOOP!!!"[984] However, a week later New Ulm also shared Lake Benton's frustration, similar to that experienced in De Smet. "*Lake Benton Times*— It was generally supposed that the first freight shipments would be provisions. Yesterday we saw a railroader uncarring a lot of forks, rakes, etc. and remarking to himself, 'This is a dashed blanked pretty looking lot of stuff to eat!'"[985] The phrase "dashed blanked pretty looking lot" was a polite way to put into print what was likely a much more colorful exclamation.

Trains Push Past Brookings and through De Smet, May 4 or 5

There is an excitement in reading the list of items below, which was printed in the *Brookings County Press* on May 1. The long blockade along the Dakota Central was over, not just to Brookings, but all the way to Huron. Once the train hit Huron, it was likely also able to reach Pierre unimpeded.

That railroad employees walked to Brookings from Volga on Wednesday, May 4, may mean that the train pushed west out of Brookings, through De Smet, on Thursday, May 5. As indicated, emigrant cars were numerous. The giddiness is clear:

- The
- Blockade
- Is badly busted.
- Everybody is busy.
- Delightful weather!
- How is your garden?
- Lumber is in demand.
- Plant your tree claims!
- The hotels are crowded.
- Get out your linen duster.
- We have got coal in town again.
- The season for fleas has opened.
- Farm machinery is now plenty.

- All our merchants are happy again.
- Ham and eggs are on the turf now.
- The grass is starting on the prairie.
- School commenced Tuesday morning.
- The Southern Minnesota R. R. is open.
- A car load of flour came in, Wednesday.
- Prairie fires still light up the horizon nightly.
- Trade off your buffalo coat for a refrigerator now.
- The first freight train ran into Huron this morning.
- The pay car was at this place on Wednesday. It gladdened the hearts of the railroad boys exceedingly, as it was its first appearance since last November.
- By the aid of providence and other volunteers from Brookings we are again permitted to hear the whistle of locomotive.
- The number of freight cars being rolled over the road now looks like business. Emigrant cars are prominent among them.
- Several of the railroad boys walked over from Volga to meet the pay car on Wednesday.[986]

The arrival of the train in De Smet, as remembered by Wilder, evolved between the autobiographies and the novel. In the autobiographies, wording changed slightly across the versions but maintained that everyone was excited about the train's arrival, that the men ran to the depot to welcome it, and that to Wilder, "no sound in the world could have been as wonderful to us then as the sound of that whistle."[987] Interestingly, the specific reaction at the depot changed more across the autobiographies than anything else.

In *Pioneer Girl*, Wilder wrote, "The train came rolling in while everyone cheered and then it was found that it was a whole train of farm machinery." The Brandt version is similar, changing "everyone cheered" to "a mighty cheer went up." In the Bye version, the account appeared as, "The train came rolling in, while a weak cheer went up. And then it was found that this was a whole train of farm machinery." The novel bypassed the cheer altogether, though townsmen were described as meeting the train.[988]

First Train into Watertown, May 5

While some editors had predicted an exodus from Dakota Territory come spring, what happened instead was a mass infusion of new people. Some post-blockade trains were made up entirely of emigrants and their possessions. The

Chicago & North Western even published a circular to let everyone know that travel was now possible across all of its lines, all the way to the Black Hills (via stage).[989] Meanwhile, some employees did the work of multiple men, handling the flood of goods coming in. The *New Ulm Weekly Review* of May 11 printed,

> The westward emigration has already assumed such proportions that the Winona & St. Peter railroad has found it necessary on several occasions of late to run double-header passenger trains; in fact they have found their rolling stock almost insufficient to accommodate the vast number of emigrants now pouring into this State and Dakota. Freight trains made up wholly of cars containing emigrants and their stock and household effects pass this station daily.[990]

Along the Southern Minnesota

While crews continued pecking at the cuts between Dell Rapids and Flandreau, some inventive citizens got around the blockade. "The first train since the middle of February," wrote the local editor, "came into Dell Rapids Wednesday afternoon from Flandrau—it was a 'dump' car drawn by two horses. . . . Next morning the car returned with nails and flour."[991] It is possible, even likely, that those "nails" were "mails," though on the brink of the spring construction season, it may have actually been nails.

The weather continued to be a problem. On March 31, Egan experienced "one of the severest blizzards" it had seen the entire winter. "Had it not been for the storm," wrote the editor of the *Egan Express*, "trains would have been running by Saturday [April 2] night. On Saturday we had another two-horse blizzard, which partially filled the cuts and it is not probable the road will be open until the first of next week."[992]

Following the Storm of April 10

Roads in the vicinity of Pipestone again became impassable, but that was not the worst of the problems. Just when the Southern Minnesota was close to clearing recent snow and the remaining vestiges of ice, the shovelers "tired of the work" and abandoned it to head home and tend to their farms, causing "the railroad managers considerable vexation." Compounding the problems, tracks were "washing out in many places."[993]

The *Mankato Review* reported that just before the final storm, approximately 800 men had been working under Superintendent Egan's command, costing the Southern Minnesota around $1,200 per day. Just when the track between the

Mississippi River and Flandreau had been cleared, "in one single night the expensive job was undone, and the road was blocked tighter than ever before."[994] By extrapolating the cost, we can estimate those ten days of work alone cost the railroad $12,000. Then it snowed again.

One Step Forward, Two Steps Back

Snow-removal efforts opened the road to Fulda,[995] and the toll of that work on railroad employees was evident when the *Moody County Enterprise* welcomed the local road master home "after a continuous absence of over three months among the snow drifts."[996]

Flooding picked up where the snow left off, and Flandreau reported that "about half a mile of the track" between there and Egan was washed out, though the planking on a river bridge near Egan had been taken up and protected in advance of the waters. The partial dismantling of bridges wasn't inexpensive. "Minnehaha county expended $400.26 in raising the Dell Rapids bridge and $1,204.00 in raising the two bridges at Sioux Falls," wrote the Flandreau editor.[997]

Despite the arrival of trains here and there, deliveries were still not dependable. The *Moody County Enterprise* in Flandreau held off normal publication. "We delayed our time of issue this week in hopes that a train would arrive and bring us a bundle of paper," wrote the editor, "but the washouts east of here have dashed our hopes in that respect and we are again obliged to come out on a small sheet of wrapping paper."[998]

With their own farms and businesses needing attention, some of those who had been at work with shovels preferred to return home, much to the chagrin of the railroads, which still needed the man power. The Janesville paper sided with the workers. "The Southern Minnesota railroad company served their snow shovelers very mean lately," wrote the Janesville editor. "Most of the men are farmers along the line and they wanted to quit shoveling when seeding time arrived. But the company would not pay them or transport them home. Wouldn't even allow the men to ride home on the trains. Such injustice should receive its reward."[999]

A Train Reaches Pipestone, April 26

Residents of Pipestone welcomed the first train like a returning hero, which their local railroad employees certainly were. "The first train that has reached here since the first of February pulled up at our station," wrote the editor of the *Pipestone Star*. "Of course the people were glad to see it and many of them went to the depot to welcome the boys who have fought nobly for months. . . . The snow blockade is raised for this season."[1000]

Work Continues to Shore Up the Rails

Superintendent Egan was busy in the wake of the flooding, checking out the condition of the tracks along the line and making repairs. "The railroad company is making good progress in repairing its wash-outs and destroyed bridges," wrote the editor in Flandreau, "and Superintendent Egan thinks that we can pretty certainly count on seeing the road open to this point by Friday [April 29] night."[1001]

Bridge builders arrived in Egan to begin repairs, raising hopes that a train would soon follow. Having spoken with officials, the Egan editor wrote,

> The railroad company has been busy since the flood, and have it in running order to Pipestone Creek, four miles this side of Pipestone, and it is expected the train will reach Flandrau this evening or to-morrow morning [April 29]. . . . The company's bridge builder says it will take about four days to repair [one particular] bridge, after they get at it. The prospects now are that trains will be running regularly to this place by the last of next week.[1002]

The two photos below are not identified by date or location but do a nice job of showing some of the issues caused by flooding.

In these photos, you can see that the railbed has been compromised, allowing the tracks (the structure comprised of ties and rails) to flex and float free. It took considerable effort to reinforce the rail bed and make it safe for trains to pass over again. Courtesy of the Chicago & North Western Historical Society.

Trains Reach Flandreau and Egan, May 4

After a winter full of deprivations and waiting, one would expect that a long-anticipated train rolling into town would occasion celebratory words from all newspapers across the region. Yet the neighboring towns of Flandreau and Egan appeared more nonchalant than elated. "A railroad town once more,"[1003] wrote the Flandreau editor, hazarding no more than a simple fact. The Egan editor kept his tone equally straightforward, printing, "The first train for nearly four months arrived in Egan yesterday, and our people are accordingly happy."[1004] Perhaps these editors wanted the arrival of a train to appear normal, in accordance with their roles as boosters.

Nearing mid-May, a few towns were still awaiting their first train. Dell Rapids was one of them, still inaccessible by rail owing to flooding along the Big Sioux. "The road from here to Dell Rapids is nearly fixed up," wrote the Egan editor in the May 12 edition, "and regular trains will run to that point on Saturday [May 14], and possibly to-morrow. As soon as this is done the bridge across the Sioux will probably be fixed so it will be safe for passenger trains to run to Egan."[1005]

The optimism that people had shown so frequently throughout the winter was finally rewarded. "The long and severe winter is a thing of the past," wrote a correspondent to the Flandreau editor. "The prairies are already beginning to look green, and in a short time the fields will look green also. Farmers are sowing their grain with the hope that they will reap an abundant crop this season."[1006] The signs of spring were likewise visible in Egan. Its paper printed, "The prairies have donned their suit of green, and cattle can now get a good living. Grass is from ten days to two weeks earlier this season than it was last."[1007] It's fascinating that at least one location reported the prairies greening ahead of expected schedule. What a welcome sight it must have been!

Along the Sioux City and Other Lines

Prior to the storm of April 10, conditions were rapidly improving in the southern portion of the region. Following the storm, the *Sioux Falls Times* of April 13 provided an update about which areas were accessible and via which forms of transportation. "The passenger train reached Canton Friday, April 8," wrote the editor, "but the storm within the next few days filled the roads again and delayed trains a week or more. The S. F. & S. C. train is yet at Elk Point, shut in by means of high water, bridges gone, and grades washed out." The editor went on to predict the town's outlook, saying, "It is quite certain that nearly a month will elapse before the road, entire, will be in good order and trains running."[1008]

Six days later, the *Sioux Falls Times* noted, "The disappearance of the snow reveals quite a number of loose railroad ties, which were supposed not to be."[1009] The flooding caused more damage along this railroad line than the snows had. The editor shared that "men capable of judging" were "of the opinion that the current roadbed" had been poorly placed, and that it would "necessarily have to be abandoned, and an entirely new [site] surveyed."[1010]

The April 14 edition of the *Dakota Pantagraph and Sioux Falls Independent*, printed on linen instead of paper, provided a more detailed report, tinged with a bit of whimsy, following the storm: "The railroads had just the previous evening succeeded in making this community believe that may be perhaps possibly we should directly after while in the near future get a train, when all the work . . . has been done." The new snowfall trapped several trains along the tracks, and the editor used the occasion to get creative, describing the landscape those trains had ventured into before being detained:

> The lines run in narrow canyons gulled through the vast expanse of
> snow, whose walls are perpendicular, almost as solid as ice, and in some
> places over forty feet high. These canyons are now drifted chuck full of
> snow, and . . . the snow is in some places piled up in ridges several feet
> high for miles right along above the track, the edges of these ridges
> having been trimmed up so nicely by the wind that they look as if they
> had been cast in gigantic moulds and then laid over the railroads as an
> elongated tombstone. No amount of bucking can squeeze this snow off
> the track into the walls of the canyons, nor can a snow plow throw it high
> enough to get it up to the level of the surrounding country.[1011]

While trains were lost in the evocative canyons near Sioux Falls, three locomotives at Yankton, along the Missouri River to the south, were destined to "remain there for some time painfully idle, in consequence of the track being entirely washed away for some miles between that point and Sioux City."[1012]

Tracks Clogged with Cars

The backlog of freight cars, parked on sidetracks along each of the railroad lines across the region, was significant. One can sympathize with the railroad workers responsible for liberating each car and sending it along to its destination.

Following a last-in-first-out process for efficiency, the cars easiest to reach were likely the first ones sent along their way, leading to the frustration expressed in both Lake Benton and De Smet, where the first trains to arrive were full of farm equipment instead of food or fuel. One wonders whether these particular trains were met with similar hostility at each and every town in which they arrived.

According to its annual report for the 1879 fiscal year, the Winona & St. Peter owned 27 locomotives, 893 box freight cars, and 133 platform freight cars. The Chicago, Milwaukee & St. Paul did not publish rolling stock counts for each subsidiary railroad line, but the company as a whole owned 9,111 box freight cars; 1,419 stock cars; and 2,785 flat and coal cars as of the end of 1880.[1013] One article from the beginning of April noted that the Chicago, Milwaukee & St. Paul had 15,000 cars of freight waiting to move.[1014] Because that number accounts for nearly all of the company's rolling stock, we can assume that those cars were not all packed up and ready to move; rather, they had that much freight backed up and awaiting cars. As of 1880, the Chicago & North Western stopped including rolling stock counts in its published annual reports.

In mid-April, the New Ulm paper shared, "The *Waseca Herald* states that there are still seventy-five car loads of freight at that place designed for points west of Sleepy Eye, waiting for the snow blockade to be raised."[1015] A month later, the paper provided an update, printing, "Every available portion of the side-tracks and Y at this place has been crowded with loaded freight cars. Nearly 300 cars were in the yard at one time last week."[1016] The scale of efforts to untangle the cars from their various storage spots along sidings and sidetracks, not to mention get them to their intended destinations, is nothing short of mind-boggling.

How long did it take to untangle the backlog following the winter? While *The Long Winter* has the Ingalls family celebrating the arrival of their Christmas barrel with the second train, in early May, in reality things may have been different. Wilder provides a clue in a letter to Rose, writing, "The Christmas barrel came the first of June. Train got through the middle of May but freight was so congested all along the line that it was not straightened out until June."[1017]

First Train Arrival Dates

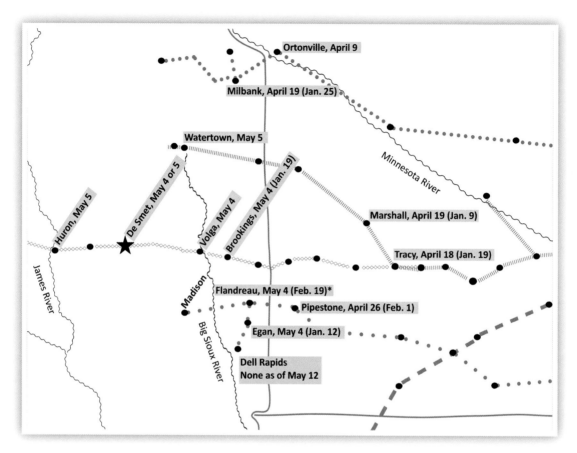

All dates are based upon the newspaper record.
Those in parentheses indicate the last known train into town.
(*The town of Madison, west of Flandreau, reported a train through on February 19;
therefore, a train is assumed to have been in Flandreau on that date as well.)

Financial Impact

We've seen articles about the cost to the various railroad lines of trying to keep the lines open throughout the winter. But the cost of business that could not be conducted also added up, as conveyed in the April 7 edition of the *Murray County Pioneer*:

The immense loss of capital sacrificed in endeavoring to keep the roads open is unprecedented in the annals of the State, and, then, without availing any benefits there from. Heretofore the railroads of this State have suffered but lightly from the snow blockades, then resulting from imperfect snow fences, but this winter nothing could be devised to afford any protection to the tracks. Trains on the prairie were imbedded in the snow the same as if in cuts of twenty foot depth."[1018]

When it was all over, the railroads had expended a great deal of money with very little to show for it. In addition, damaged rails and equipment needed to be repaired. In its annual report for the year ending May 31, 1881, the Chicago & North Western offered,

The considerable increase in operating expenses arises, in part, from the greater cost of material and supplies, and the higher rates of wages; and, in part, from the extraordinary requirements of the early, severe and protracted winter, and the late and backward spring that followed it. The interruption of traffic from the deep snows and intense cold of last winter, and from floods and freshets during the spring, not only diminished the earnings, but greatly augmented the operating expenses; and it is a matter of congratulation that the earnings were unstintedly applied to restoring the property to its usual good condition at the close of the fiscal year, and were sufficient to leave a fair margin of profit to the stock holders.[1019]

The charts below, from the published *Annual Report of the Chicago and North Western Railway Company for the Twenty-Second Fiscal Year, Ending May 31st, 1881*, quantify the impact.[1020]

Monthly Earnings for the Year ending May 31st, 1881.

Months.		From Passengers.	From Freight.	From Express.	From Mails.	From Miscellaneous.	Total.
June,	1880,................	$385,066 97	$1,229,837 20	$24,311 88	$24,696 16	$7,264 87	$1,671,177 08
July,	"	376,590 00	1,264,687 46	24,756 14	24,694 81	8,957 27	1,699,685 68
August,	"	408,179 50	1,293,823 01	24,605 04	24,694 81	16,636 19	1,767,938 55
September,	"	438,408 86	1,522,855 44	25,647 08	24,694 81	8,638 39	2,020,244 58
October,	"	386,073 04	1,659,123 36	25,993 25	24,877 83	9,149 25	2,105,216 73
November,	"	335,823 21	1,453,126 30	25,710 62	25,387 36	15,574 25	1,855,621 74
December,	"	297,036 10	1,112 936 91	29,282 77	24,804 14	13,842 24	1,477,902 16
January,	1881,................	271,409 49	910,459 27	24,804 17	24,804 14	9,190 28	1,240,667 35
February,	"	197,224 76	711,803 61	23,112 75	24,804 14	6,259 37	963,204 63
March,	"	290,765 80	831,057 13	26,313 79	24,804 12	5,854 71	1,178,795 55
April,	"	360,629 79	1,057,536 82	25,656 82	24,804 14	5,984 13	1,474,611 70
May,	"	410,922 29	1,366,904 58	30,038 93	24,313 56	46,826 94	1,879,006 30
Total,................		$4,158,129 81	$14,414,151 09	$310,233 24	$297,380 02	$154,177 89	$19,334,072 05

CHICAGO AND NORTH WESTERN RAILWAY AND PROPRIETARY ROADS.
Operations per Mile for Six Years ending May 31, 1881.

Year ending May 31st.	Miles Operated.	Earnings per Mile.	Expenses and Taxes per Mile.	Net Earnings per Mile.	Increase in Miles Operated.
1876,....................	1,992.08	$7,034 72	$4,153 59	$2,881 13	....
1877,....................	1,993.28	6,538 52	3,775 74	2,762 78	1.20
1878,....................	2,036.98	7,241 63	3,741 30	3,500 33	43.70
1879,....................	2,129.37	6,847 53	3,619 69	3,227 84	92.39
1880,....................	2,215.83	7,829 73	3,805 17	4,024 56	86.46
1881,....................	2,644.16	7,311 99	3,942 96	3,369 03	428.33
Average for six years,.............		$7,134 02	$3,839 74	$3,294 28	108.68

Wrecks and Accidents

As the sun melted the stubborn ice and the last of the snow was being shoveled off the tracks, locomotives and cars began emerging from winter quarters. What followed was a series of accidents that made good copy for the local editors.

A few miles west of Windom, in southwestern Minnesota, "the engine propelling [a] snow plow was ordered into a cut before the [shoveling crew] could be removed, whereby one man was killed and four others wounded." It was estimated that two of those four would probably not recover.[1021]

The *Marshall Messenger* shared that there was "considerable discussion of the right and wrong of Sunday work." By the end of the debate, "it was concluded that the conditions of the blockade offered sufficient reason for calling it right and proper to turn out and help open the road." The men of town then prepared for their morning departure to work on the Sabbath, but the morning dawned amid a snowfall, and the crew of seventy men did not get underway until noon. The article continued,

> It was thought best to take the baggage car. . . . It is a little wider than the caboose, and . . . a little wider than the snow cuts. . . . In one of [the cuts] at Lake Marshall [a baggage car] was thrown off the track and after running a few rods swung down the bank and nearly tipped over. As it was loaded with men, the excitement for a few moments was rather engrossing.[1022]

The report of a simple broken axle derailing a passenger coach east of Janesville[1023] seemed somewhat mundane among the more dramatic cut disasters and washouts, and definitely mundane compared to the excruciating experience of a man who had been shoveling snow west of Milbank: He and his crew were distributed among four handcars, which were returning to town at high speed. The unfortunate man had been on the first car when he "fell between the rails in front of the car. . . . When picked up he was found to be badly bruised about the head, and complained of pain in his back." He was delivered to the town doctor, and "several ugly cuts and bruises were found on the head, but no bones appeared to be broken." All of the handcars had passed over him, and "the bruises were made by the pumping gear."[1024]

The flooding of late April had receded but left the tracks "in a very bad condition." A train traveling along a stretch near New Ulm "was ditched . . . by the spreading of the rails. No one was hurt by the accident, however."[1025]

Farmers and Merchants

> "The building enterprises are completely stagnated,
> as both lime kilns are on opposite sides of the two rivers.
> The Empire City mills will also be compelled to shut down early
> next week on account of the scarcity of wheat."[1026]
>
> —*Murray County Pioneer*, May 5, 1881

The Farmers

Despite snow remaining on the ground, farmers needed to prepare for spring planting or resume threshing last fall's harvest. Sadly, prairie fires destroyed some of that harvest, which also eliminated the need to do some of the aforementioned work.

Along the Hastings & Dakota

By the end of April, farmers near Milbank and Wilmot were threshing.[1027] Early May found farmers seeding, and "a good many farmers" were also backsetting.[1028] *Backsetting* is an additional plowing of the dirt, further breaking up the sod to allow the grass roots to rot and enrich the soil.

In the vicinity of Milbank, one farmer "had seven tons of hay destroyed by prairie fire. A stable, belonging to a farmer whose name we did not learn, was also burned."[1029]

Along the Winona & St. Peter and the Dakota Central

Farther east, weather remained uncooperative and the Janesville editor joked, in mid-April, that planting may not take place until fall . . . and if not this fall, then next fall.[1030] A week later, he noted that despite "exceedingly unfavorable weather the past week, a number of farmers started their seeders in this vicinity."[1031]

Things were improving near New Ulm, where seeding had "become quite general, and a number of farmers living on the bluffs opposite the city [were] pretty well advanced with the work."[1032]

By the first week of May, things had improved for Sleepy Eye. An account from the town read, "Our streets are now dry and on Sunday our livery men had their hands full. . . . Farmers are now in the midst of their spring seeding and about another week will see the work completed."[1033]

Crop work may have been moving along nicely, but according to the *New Ulm Weekly Review*, farm animals along the Dakota Central were "dying off with great rapidity." The editor further shared, "The cattle are so weak from hunger that they cannot range far enough away to get good grazing. The prairie is covered with water and melting snow, and the cattle, which are almost dead from hunger, fall down from exhaustion, are unable to rise, and die where they fall."[1034]

The Merchants

The fits and starts of breaking the blockade meant frequent backups of cars on sidetracks, causing the merchants' freight to arrive irregularly. Each early delivery was heralded—or anticipated, if the trains hadn't actually arrived yet.

Along the Hastings & Dakota

The April 28 edition of the *Grant County Review* included two items that seem contradictory, setting the merchants' anticipation to build against the uncertain availability of the means to do so: An advertisement noted that everything needed for building could be found at the "Pioneer Lumber Yard." Yet elsewhere, it was announced that the construction of the new school building was delayed due to the "unavoidable delay in procuring the lumber necessary."[1035]

Along the Winona & St. Peter and the Dakota Central

As the returning trains brought in goods, the merchants of New Ulm reported replenished stocks. It was also noted that the spring trade was expected to be vigorous thanks to the surplus of wheat from the 1880 growing season that had not yet been marketed.[1036]

At least one merchant from Brookings had made his way to Chicago early in April, "making arrangements for a large stock of goods to be shipped through by fast freight."[1037]

The arrival of farm equipment and clothing was celebrated, and inventory of both commodities was quickly reduced through brisk purchasing. In Marshall, "a carload of Buckeye seeders was received and quickly distributed among the farmers." A large ad in the same issue declared, "AT LAST," clothing had arrived for spring.[1038] Just to the south in Currie, "two barrels of kerosene" allowed the editor to boast, "Our light shines as formerly."[1039]

One Mankato merchant was dealt an unfortunate and ironic blow, losing "2,000 tons of ice by the flood." The writer of the story was not without a sense of humor, adding, "However . . . the butter man, will have plenty to spare, so Mankato wont [sic] 'liquidate' entirely."[1040]

The flooding also damaged or cut off access to the kilns and mills needed by farmers to dry and grind the wheat from last fall's crop. As reported in Currie, "the head of the flume near the mill broke loose and for a few hours the united exertions of a number of willing hands was all that saved the utter demolition of the grist mill."[1041]

Along the Southern Minnesota

As with the other lines, merchants along the Southern Minnesota were working to reinvigorate their businesses. The proprietor of the meat market in Dell Rapids put the word out that he would "pay the highest cash price . . . for hides and pelts."[1042]

The Egan paper teased its readers by enticing them to shop at one particular merchant, once the trains brought his stock.[1043] While Egan was still anticipating its deliveries, the village of Pipestone was already reporting an abundance of provisions, including sugar, kerosene, and the ever-longed-for mail.[1044]

At times during the winter, the editors filled column space with short, snappy squibs as a way of conveying dejection or excitement. The arrival of goods on the trains brought a similar reaction from the *Moody County Enterprise* in Flandreau:

> Butter is out of the market.
> Seeding is progressing rapidly.
> The merchants are happy now.
> Flandrau's winter supply of wood is now arriving.
> The wheat that has accumulated here all winter is now rapidly going eastward.
> Business locals are pretty numerously interspersed in our local columns this week.[1045]

Jointly, the neighboring towns of Flandreau and Egan celebrated the sudden abundance the trains brought forth. Flandreau told of "an immense amount of goods . . . and still there are more coming," [1046] and Egan boasted, "Our farmers can find everything here that they want."[1047] Interestingly, these were the two towns that had so flatly announced the busting of the blockades and the return of the trains.

Food

> "All goods in the line of groceries and provisions . . .
> delivered free of charge."[1048]
>
> —*Sioux Falls Times*, April 19, 1881

Along the Hastings & Dakota

As already noted, the arrival of trains in Ortonville prompted merchants in Milbank to head there with teams, returning with flour and other "goods that were badly needed."[1049] In nearby Twin Brooks, Dakota Territory, a correspondent mentioned that even in early May, people were still relying on fish harvested from the Whetstone River.[1050]

Along the Winona & St. Peter and the Dakota Central

One of the purposes of this research was to determine whether there was evidence of residents organizing to obtain goods where they were available and get them distributed to towns with less access. There is certainly evidence of goods moving around the region, though the items themselves were not always what one would expect.

Providing a chuckle in early April, the *Sleepy Eye Herald* reassured its readers that "the people of Tracy [would] be able to stand a blockade a little longer" because some of the townsmen had taken a team to Sleepy Eye, a distance of nearly fifty miles to the east, and "returned with a load of ten kegs of beer and four barrels of whisky."[1051] Similarly, residents of Lake Benton made a forty-mile round trip to retrieve "whisky and cigars" from Pipestone.[1052]

In mid-April, the *Marshall Messenger* shared a note from the little town of Amerit, Minnesota, located between Tracy and Marshall. The correspondent proudly noted that the stores in their tiny town had somehow managed to keep "a very good supply of groceries during the weather, and when Marshall and Tracy were out of some articles most needful," the merchants in Amerit were able to help them out. The article concluded with a request to remember how helpful Amerit had been to its neighbors, and to continue frequenting their shops after the trains resumed running.[1053]

According to the St. Paul *Pioneer Press*, as reprinted by the *Janesville Argus*, the residents of Gary, Dakota Territory (east of Watertown), were using a tool somewhat larger than a coffee mill to grind their wheat. "Groceries, flour and meats were long since exhausted," wrote the editor. "A feed mill driven by horse power cracks the wheat which is eaten unbolted. Graham flour and molasses has been the diet for weeks. The only means of getting about there is by snow shoes."[1054]

A grocery ad from Volga noted that "flour, corn, oats, seed corn, potatoes, corn meal, graham flour, [and] garden seeds" were available.[1055] With food that close to De Smet weeks ahead of the first train, and taking into account the February note that the grocer Harthorn had gone on a "foraging expedition," we can presume that a relay team was established to move some of that nourishment to the west.

Toward the end of the month, the Red Front Bee Hive grocer in Marshall reported, in an excited large font, that a carload of groceries was received and ready for distribution.[1056] A week later, the *Marshall Messenger* shared that one of its editors and a merchant had "made a successful trip to Sleepy Eye in a skiff, by way of Lake Marshall and the Cottonwood River."[1057] In fact, six people made that adventurous boat journey over the prairies, and the story was shared the following week in a lengthy article, titled "Boating on the Prairie" with the subheading, "The 'rime of an ancient mariner' sung to modern music. From Marshall to Sleepy Eye by water overland."[1058]

As weather improved, Brookings happily announced that eggs were becoming more plentiful and that the town further hoped "to see a large emigration of hens to this country soon."[1059] Early May brought a carload of flour to town as well.[1060]

As we've seen, a significant amount of wheat had piled up in storage around the region, and farmers continued to thresh the fall's harvest. The editor of the *Marshall Messenger* speculated about potential bounty, writing, "We will soon know what the wheat left in stack over Winter amounts to. There is a good deal of it and, if it is not too badly damaged to market, our people will be put on their feet again for Summer business."[1061]

There remained "considerable grain" that needed threshing near New Ulm, though it had to wait until spring seeding was complete. Representatives from the elevator in New Ulm warned farmers to watch out for damaged product.[1062]

Moisture in the Wheat

The warning from the elevator in New Ulm to take care and ensure that grain was properly dried led to a question. Today, grain can be dried using large fans and then stored in metal bins. But in 1880, bins and elevators were both made of wood, which itself contained moisture. Knowing that, how was the grain kept dry? Wilder answered that question herself in a letter to Lane:

> Wheat was left in the stack six to eight weeks to go through the sweat before threshing. After that when threshed the wheat could be kept in bins on the farm or in elevators for years and stay sweet and good. If it were threshed before going through the sweat in the stack, the grain would get musty in the bins and spoil so even stock wouldn't eat it. It could be saved by shoveling it over into other bins every few days. But sometimes when a man threshed to [sic] early he lost the grain entirely. Couldn't sell it if it was musty. . . . The price was better for wheat that had gone through the sweat and was properly threshed than for wheat that was threshed to [sic] early."[1063]

Good sources of protein were difficult to procure during the winter, so the loss of livestock was particularly tragic. The New Ulm paper reported that one entity "lost 400 sheep and 500 head of cattle on their Jim River ranch in Dakota. The snow prevented the stock from reaching the hay and feed stored for them."[1064] The time frame for these losses was not specified, so we do not know whether that was a winter-long tally or if there was a large die-off just as spring began to replenish the rangelands.

A Rare Glimpse of Superintendent Nicholl

A correspondent from Huron wrote to the *New Ulm Weekly Review* in mid-April "to disprove and contradict some of the false and groundless rumors" that he had seen printed "in the St. Paul papers concerning the suffering and destitution prevailing along this line of railroad." He even included a rare glimpse into the winter activities of Superintendent Nicholl. The correspondent wrote,

We have had an abundance of everything necessary for the comforts of life. The R. R. Co. had 1200 tons of coal here, and they have been selling it to the people. . . . There are about two hundred tons left yet. Flour and provisions are selling at the same prices that they were last summer. . . . Superintendent Nichols [sic] has done everything in his power to render assistance to the less fortunate in towns along the line of road, and also in getting in mail on snow shoes and hand sleds. . . . I have had a family of 25 persons to feed all winter, and I have had no difficulty in procuring plenty of everything for them, and still have enough on hand to last till the first of May."[1065]

Since there are no extant newspaper records from Huron during this period, it is not possible to compare the above account to a wider record, but it could represent a mix of reality and protective boosterism. Or perhaps the people of Huron truly did have "an abundance of everything necessary for the comforts of life." At least, a frontier life in Dakota Territory in 1881.

Along the Southern Minnesota

At midmonth, approximately "40,000 bushels of wheat and barley" were waiting to ship out of Flandreau while its residents anxiously awaited a shipment in of groceries, which were expected to "go off like hot cakes when once a supply of them reaches here." The Flandreau editor added, "Those merchants will be in luck whose stocks get in first."[1066]

In the relatively large community of Sioux Falls, the availability of food seemed to be less consistent, as reports ran the gamut from depletion to abundance. This was, in all likelihood, simply the result of residents visiting stores before or after supplies arrived, then telling their favorite editor about their experiences—not necessarily a widespread condition. For instance, the *Moody County Enterprise* of April 14 shared a traveler's opinion: "Sioux Falls is not much better off in the grocery line than Flandrau. No sugar, kerosene, candles, corn meal, oat meal, syrup and very little coffee and the people there are generally in quite a suffering state of mind."[1067] However, within a week of the *Enterprise* piece, the *Sioux Falls Times* provided a list of merchants with plenty on hand: one offering "canned goods, in endless variety"; another boasting a "fresh and carefully selected stock of goods always on hand"; and a third who delivered their "groceries and provisions" free of charge.[1068]

In another odd juxtaposition, a settler near Egan offered "several bushels of butternuts" for sale to "those desiring to plant them this spring."[1069] Meanwhile, the local editor attempted to collect on bartered payment for the paper, writing, "Several of our subscribers have promised to bring us potatoes on subscription this spring. To all such we will say, that if there ever was a time when we wanted potatoes, and in fact anything eatable, it is NOW."[1070] If butternut squashes were available, one wonders why they were not eaten and the seeds saved for planting. One possible answer is that the butternuts were seedling trees, not squash.

Fuel

"Wood has been selling at $24 per cord in Pipestone county all winter, and hard to get at last. Don't you want to go to Dakota?—*Spring Valley Vidette.*—We will merely state that Pipestone county is in Minnesota; but then we think, [the Spring Valley editor] has got the figures pretty high, even for Minnesota."[1071]

—*Dell Rapids Exponent*, April 2, 1881

If it is not immediately apparent in the above quote, the editor of the *Spring Valley Vidette*, a Minnesota paper, had sarcastically dismissed the idea of moving to Dakota Territory because the price of wood was so high. The editor in Dell Rapids, Dakota Territory, took issue, as the county in question—Pipestone—was, in fact, in Minnesota, not Dakota Territory. Confusion about geography aside, the price quoted was indeed high; using the conversion rate presented earlier, $24 in 1881 had the buying power of $603.60 in 2019.[1072]

The end of winter was in sight, but fuel to keep the settlers warm and fed was still of utmost priority. Territorial Governor Ordway received a dispatch midmonth asking whether anything could be done to get fuel to those along the Missouri River, which was still overflowing. "The governor replied advising them to gather in the churches and larger buildings and burn the smallest and poorest houses for fuel," relayed the *Marshall Messenger*. "It is estimated that between five and six thousand people have been made homeless wanderers by the flood, and must depend upon charity for the necessities of life for some time to come."[1073]

Along the Hastings & Dakota

An earlier article in the *Marshall Messenger* announced that the railroad company was looking to purchase "extensive coal fields in the west." As we've seen, the railroad companies were experienced in purchasing fuel sources to minimize operating expense for the trains. But in this instance, it was further noted,

The condition of the colonists at the western end of the Hastings & Dakota, Southern Minnesota [and other] divisions during the present Winter has received the serious consideration of the company's officials, and it has been decided that something must be done to provide alleviation for the sufferings of the colonists if another severe Winter should come upon them."[1074]

Along the Winona & St. Peter and the Dakota Central

Messages were mixed along the Winona & St. Peter in April. When Marshall ran out of kerosene, a resident traveled by mule team to Mankato and returned five days later with four barrels. He was heartily welcomed by his fellow townsmen: "His approach was heralded, and a procession of citizens and a brass band turned out and escorted him into town. The drum bore the inscription 'Struck Oil.' There was great enthusiasm as the procession marched through town."[1075]

The town of Amerit affirmed it had ridden out the winter with plenty of food on hand for its citizens as well as those of neighboring towns. A correspondent admitted, however, that perhaps "some" were "getting very short" on fuel but had not yet run out. The writer added, "We have more snow fence near us than any other station along the line as near as we can learn, which speaks well of our townsmen at least."[1076]

Throughout the winter, most articles retained a tone of dignity or at least an understanding of the broader fuel situation. But when Superintendent Sanborn was quoted in the *Winona Republican* as having said, six months after the first blizzard, that there had been "no real suffering" among the settlers affected by the blockades, the editor of the *Lamberton Commercial* had a bit of a meltdown. As reprinted in the *New Ulm Weekly Review*, the Lamberton editor wrote,

> The question is often asked, 'has there been any real suffering?' We answer, if you mean to ask whether or not any one has starved or frozen to death, no; no one starved, but if you wish to know whether or not any one had to burn many things which he could ill afford to burn or pay exorbitant prices for the necessaries of life, yes. If freezing and starving are the only things to be called suffering, then we have not suffered. But that we have been just as well off as if the trains had run is far from true. We have been without kerosene ten days at a time. . . . We have been out of flour several times. All our supplies have been hauled by team from Sleepy Eye or New Ulm, costing us from 50 to 100 per cent more than the regular prices. Those of our merchants who had goods on the road have had to pay the freight clear to Lamberton and then pay for hauling them by team from Sleepy Eye.[1077]

With the tracks opening up, carloads of wood were headed westward, but that did not mean the fuel was inexpensive. In Marshall, "one car of wood was received [April 19] . . . and was divided up among those out of fuel in a short time." The Marshall editor added, "Wood will be plenty and back to old prices in a day or two."[1078] Injecting a bit of sarcasm into his comments about the impact of the high prices for even green wood, the editor of the *Sleepy Eye Herald* wrote, "Of course there would be no suffering among poor people with such fair weather prices." That item was reprinted in the *Janesville Argus*, and that paper's editor included, "The American Express Co. is carrying donations to the Dakota sufferers free of charge."[1079] Such a charitable service surely helped said sufferers offset the burden of the high price of wood somewhat.

Along the Southern Minnesota

Kerosene was reported as nearly or entirely exhausted in multiple communities. Pipestone and Flandreau noted, "Even candles have become an almost unattainable luxury," though with a fortunate circumstance: "These are moonlight nights."[1080] Items that could be burned for heat remained of high interest in the newspaper columns.

According to the Flandreau paper, wood remained scarce and expensive, and railroad ties were "getting uncomfortably scarce."[1081] Resourceful settlers near Egan found a "good supply of firewood" by harvesting the wood that was floating down the flooded Big Sioux.[1082]

Flandreau also reported that hay, of all things, had become "an unattainable luxury . . . at the present time."[1083] The incongruity of wood floating into the hands of the prairie settlers while hay became scarce is one of the fascinating scenarios that hid within the larger stories of the winter.

A blacksmith from Flandreau went on an expedition to Sioux Falls, a distance of about thirty-four miles, to get coal, but he returned without having obtained any. He then learned that the town of Luverne had a supply. He then left and headed to Luverne, also about thirty-four miles from Flandreau, but in a slightly different direction.[1084]

Throughout the winter, two draymen (a *dray* is a cart or wagon without sides) had supplied Flandreau with railroad ties, though not in the official manner of payment to the railroads. In mid-April, the paper took a moment to thank them and acknowledge their efforts. "It has been a very difficult task to get the ties out of the snow," praised the Flandreau editor, "and yet they have not raised their prices in proportion to the difficulty of the work, but have satisfied themselves with less than half the ordinary wages received for the work of a man and team."[1085]

Relief Efforts

Overall, it does not appear that the winter had been considered harsh enough to elicit a large-scale relief response. On the local level, there were relief efforts to tend to single families, and shovelers felt motivated to head out and clear the tracks to help nearby towns. But it was not until the spring flooding that an official effort was put into place.[1086]

The flooding that had killed so many and washed away much of Vermillion in late March had spurred the formation of an aid society. The society spent the first half of April trying to help the estimated eight thousand people who had been "rendered destitute on the Dakota bottoms."[1087] Articles across the region spent considerable column space recounting the flooding, sharing stories of families washed away, and touting the brave survivors who had moved to the bluff tops to rebuild a newer, safer Vermillion, not as centered upon the river as it once was.

One entry in *History of Dakota Territory* provides larger insight into relief efforts. Territorial Governor Ordway was on the east coast when news of the flooding reached him and he set about to fundraise. The New York Produce Exchange and the Chicago Board of Trade both became engaged in soliciting funds. An Episcopal diocese in Nebraska also raised "$1,000 in cash in less than one hour" along with "large contributions of provisions and clothing." Once trains could run, the railroads agreed to transport "all relief supplies free of charge."[1088]

When the residents of Watertown reported that they were out of fuel and provisions, the information was passed on to the relief committee, who then telegraphed the Chicago & North Western headquarters in Chicago. The relief committee representative suggested that if the railroad company was unable to get a train through, they should "relieve the people by wagon trains." In response, the railroad company "admitted that the line was so solidly blocked with huge drifts of snow and ice that the opening of it would not be practical until warmer weather." Around April 1, the US Government "began issuing rations of flour and bacon to the destitute, through military channels."[1089]

Out and About

"New Ulm, April 30th: – On account of high water business was almost at a standstill in this city during the past week, as we are alike penned in by the Minnesota on one side and the Cottonwood on the other, and only skiff communications are established with the people on either side."[1090]

—*Murray County Pioneer*, May 4, 1881

Along the Hastings & Dakota

Inbound travelers were undeterred by reports of the winter just past and were crowding into Milbank. According to the town's editor, existing boarding houses were "already far over-crowded," and there were concerns about where to put all of the newcomers. The editor further offered, "No better opportunity is afforded anywhere in the west for an experienced man to build and open a first-class hotel. . . . The truth of the matter is that Milbank has not ample accommodations for all that are coming."[1091]

The April 21 edition of the *Grant County Review* featured an intriguing piece of correspondence from a Dakota Territory settlement called Yellow Bank: "Among the half-dozen young men of this settlement who have returned of late is F. Richardson who was reported in the Appleton paper last winter as being dead. C. Fredrickson has also returned bringing a young bride with him."[1092] That the writer casually mentioned these somewhat-disparate stories together only emphasizes how joyous the return of the young men was for their community.

Along the Winona & St. Peter

Despite the circulation of frightening reports in the eastern parts of the country—about the horrors of a Dakota Territory winter—towns throughout the region noted that a considerable number of travelers were headed westward, crowding the hotels and boarding houses along the way.

Walking continued to be a reliable form of travel during April, no matter the stretch: "A distance of 133 miles was walked last week by . . . one of the engineers on the Winona & St. Peter railroad. [He] was at Huron and was telegraphed that his wife, who was at Tracy, was very sick with diphtheria. He at once started out over the snow. – *Winona Republican*."[1093]

High water caused some excitement for two gentlemen near Currie, who

permitted their bravery to supersede their discretion and attempted to cross the body of water north of the mill, varying in depth from two to ten feet, in a wagon at about 9 o'clock at night, [one] narrowly escaping drowning in consequence, the wagon having upset a few minutes after leaving the shore.

Fellow citizens rallied to help the hapless lads who had endangered themselves.[1094]

The Minnesota River caused more havoc in New Ulm and its vicinity than the snows had. While trains had been able to get into New Ulm throughout much of the winter, the flooded river and its tributaries brought business to a near standstill.[1095]

Along the Dakota Central

News was not as abundant along the Dakota Central in April, but we do have these glimpses: In its April 7 issue, the *Brookings County Press* reported that the roads were "somewhat bad" and that the "bare ground [was] appearing in many places." It also mentioned that one Brookings resident visited De Smet. Perhaps most welcoming was the news that efforts to clear the tracks had been "progressing rapidly."[1096]

Along the Southern Minnesota

In the wake of the April 10 storm, the *Sioux Falls Times* reported, "Three or four teams were in late last week . . . from the adjoining towns for flour, feed and other supplies. Their orders could not be filled, entire."[1097] Flandreau's *Moody County Press* of April 14 also reported that residents went to Sioux Falls for supplies.[1098]

The flooding affected more than just the railroads and team roads. Its impact was widespread and general. "Any well located quarter section has either a lake or a water tower on it this week," wrote the Flandreau editor.[1099]

Despite the flooded, muddy roads and trains that were not yet operating, regional travel picked up, particularly for business or people returning west after the winter. Travel between eastern Dakota Territory and Iowa, Wisconsin, and especially Minnesota was mentioned in most papers as their residents returned home from visits of varying lengths.

Newspapers and Mail

"Dakota publishers have been put to their wits end this winter to get something on which to print their papers.
Wrapping paper of all kinds, cloth, wall paper and foolscrap, but the *Dell Rapids Exponent* is entitled to the belt for utility. Two or three weeks ago we sent the *Express* out printed only on one side, and on Tuesday we received the one sent to [them] with the *Exponent* printed on the blank side."[1100]

—*Egan Express*, April 7, 1881

By early April, things appear to have improved, as the *Brookings County Press* reported, "Most of the newspapers of the territory are printing on white paper again."[1101] The content, however, still relied upon the arrival of the mail.

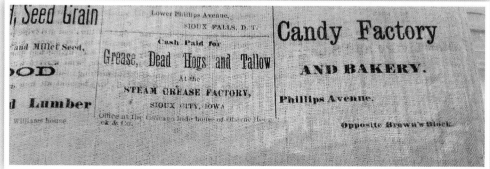

Photos of the April 13, 1881, edition of the *Dakota Pantagraph and Sioux Falls Independent*, printed on linen. Courtesy of the Siouxland Heritage Museums, Sioux Falls, South Dakota.

Flooding was as much a factor in April as snow had been previously. Mail began to arrive more frequently, often in large volumes all at once, and sometimes wet. Dell Rapids reported the delivery of thirty-six sacks of mail over the course of three days, the first they'd received since February 22 with the exception of "a very little March 2d and 5th."[1102] Included was a bonanza of area newspapers going back nearly two months.

The editor of the *Dell Rapids Exponent* published a front-page chronological report of flooding across the area, describing the weeklong rise of water, the grinding sound of ice breaking apart on the Big Sioux, and the (failed) efforts to protect the railroad bridge. At one point, the water was within forty feet of the *Exponent's* back door, leading the editor to observe that another foot of water rise would have filled the cellar. Updating readers, he wrote, "Saturday evening still finds us at our post, but we have not issued The *Exponent*, from the simple fact that there has been too much going on—or, rather, too much excitement and anxiety, as it were. Now this is not often the case in an editor's life, but it was in this."[1103]

While much of the focus had shifted to flooding, snow remained a problem. The editor of the *Dell Rapids Exponent* let his readers know that while he had had every expectation that paper would arrive in time to print, it turned out that a "Windysota blizzard again filled up the track," and he predicted that the next issue might have to be printed on shingles.[1104]

The April 5 issue of the *Janesville Argus* shared, "A *Pioneer Press* letter from Geary [sic], Dakota, says the snow is five to seven feet deep on the level, and not thawed since October 15th. Only four mails have arrived since Christmas."[1105] The writer from Gary (misspelled in the article), east of Watertown, may have been leaning a bit toward the dramatic by claiming that there had been no thaw since the October storm, as we know there were many weeks of pleasant weather that followed. But it is plausible that only four mails had graced their town over the three months following the Christmas storm.

A milestone for the winter was recorded in the *Marshall Messenger* when it reported that the mail brought *yesterday's* newspaper from another town[1106]—the incoming news from Marshall's neighboring town was nearly current.

The *New Ulm Weekly Review* of April 13 published a correspondence from Huron, written March 27. The writer reported the receipt of a large stack of issues of the *New Ulm Weekly Review*, adding, "Our mail sometimes comes by way of Sioux City and from Yankton by stage. . . . For the last three weeks we have had a weekly mail from Tracy and the East, horses taking the place of a locomotive. Sometimes a train of three or four sleds comes loaded with mail." And it seems the telegraph had been operating along the Dakota Central, because the correspondent also included, "We have had daily telegraphic news from the *Chicago Times* office, keeping us posted on the most noted current events."[1107]

Conditions were such that even the reliable stage driver Mr. Wells, who had been heroically transporting the mail over the previous months, regardless of conditions, failed to complete a trip between Luverne and Pipestone. It was not the snow that stopped him, however, but a slough just three miles from Pipestone that was "so full of water that he could not cross and was obliged to return."[1108] By the end of the month, things had dried up and Mr. Wells was back in the swing of things.[1109]

Mr. Wells wasn't the only carrier who experienced trouble. A mail carrier out of Watertown attempted several trips but was forced to return each time. On the final attempt, "the water was so deep his horse narrowly escaped drowning." He stayed in Watertown until the roads were passable. When the mail was finally delivered and opened, "letters and papers were quite badly water-soaked."[1110] Late in the month, mail was successfully procured, via boat, from Dell Rapids for the residents of Egan.[1111]

In late May, an interesting piece, originally from the *Mitchell Capital*, was reprinted in the *Salem Register*. It noted that over the course of the winter, the printing of Mitchell's publication had "used up all the paper and every handkerchief," and the editor added, "Consequently no bustles are now worn by the ladies, and napkins and shirt . . . sleeves now perform the duty of a handkerchief."[1112]

Another favorite find among the winter's articles was this gem: "Mrs. Sparber, of Oporto, is a plucky woman. She swam a horse across the Yellow Bank during the flood, carrying a mail pouch in one hand and a sack containing two cats under the other arm."[1113] Nice work, Mrs. Sparber.

Boosterism

"Never speak anything to the disparagement of your town.
Do everything you can for your laborers, mechanics, merchants,
doctors, ministers and printers. . . . Encourage every movement
that will bring a dollar to your town by honest means,
and discouraging everything that tends to [drive] away labor
and capital. Stand by your town at all times and under all
circumstances. This is the way to make things lively
and prosperous."[1114]

—*Sioux Falls Times*, April 12, 1881 (printed on linen)

At the end of March, the editor of the *Brookings County Press* had published an intemperate missive about how wonderful it had been in that vicinity all winter, refuting reports of suffering in Dakota Territory. He was not finished. In early April, he continued his tirade, mocking the claims of suffering by characterizing the people of Brookings as having "starved-to-death on turkey and oysters all winter" and wondering "whether the people who set [the rumors of suffering] going are as big liars as the people are fools who believe them or not."[1115] Digging out his fighting words, he challenged the easterners to visit Brookings and experience it for themselves: "Come out here, you great, long, lean, lank, half-starved corn-crackers you." He promised that upon their arrival, "We will show you how we starve to death up here by putting more meat on you than you ever had before."[1116]

Also in early April, the editor of the *Dell Rapids Exponent* discovered an article in the *Spring Valley Vidette* (Spring Valley is south of Rochester, Minnesota) that claimed a man in the vicinity of Dell Rapids lost his entire flock of eighty sheep when a blizzard blew them into a creek, where they drowned, "every one of them." At first noting that the incident sounded plausible, the Dell Rapids editor wrote, "And why shouldn't we believe it when people in Dakota this winter, have actually burned up houses, railroad ties, lumber, furniture, hay and even clothing to keep from freezing to death. . . . It is enough to damn that country [Dakota Territory] in the estimation of any sensitive being, for all time to come."[1117] Then, as if feeling guilty for having put it into print, he continued, "It is not 'the suffering in Dakota this winter' that is going to 'damn this . . . country,' but it is the constant publishing of such stuff." The article concluded with a factual dismissal of the story's very premise: "The idea of eighty sheep drowning in a stream covered with two feet of solid ice."[1118]

Later in April, the editor of the *Grant County Review* in Milbank announced the results of an investigation. Someone had forwarded him a copy of a newspaper published in Wisconsin. The issue included a letter from a resident—who claimed to be from Milbank—describing how people had supposedly "frozen and starved to death, while others" barely managed to survive "on the scantiest subsistence."[1119] The Milbank editor made it his mission to find the letter writer and "made diligent inquiry," seeking anyone in the vicinity matching the name given in the offensive article. While he conceded, "There may be such a person by that name in the remote part of the county or in Dakota somewhere," he declared that no such person existed in Milbank and made sure to end with,

We deem it a duty to publicly denounce the slander and falsehood. Milbank has been well stocked with all kinds of provisions and fuel all winter, until the past week when the supply of flour gave out, and folks had to eat graham and oatmeal, of which there was plenty.[1120]

In many respects, the *Egan Express*, edited by a lawyer, was less emotional than other regional newspapers. While some of the other editors fought back against negative reports, the Egan editor tended to take a more direct and positive approach. This final example of boosterism shines with understatement, yet may be every bit as effective as the long, emotional tirades of other editors:

Letters are being received almost daily from business men in the east inquiring about Egan, her future prospects, the surrounding country, &c. To all such we candidly say that we know of no better point in southeastern Dakota for business men to locate. The town is surrounded by one of the best farming countries in the world and is bound to grow and prosper. Those who contemplate making a change should look the town over before locating.[1121]

End of the Hard Winter of 1880–81

And finally, we conclude the winter months with a fitting bit of legacy—a short-lived newspaper named after the phenomenon that granted residents the right to say that they, indeed, had experienced the winter of 1880–81 firsthand:

Well, we should smile! As the oddest of all the odd names a weekly newspaper could adopt, the *Blizzard*, the name of a new paper just started at Bird Island, takes the cake. Blizzards are sometimes very destructive, but whether the *Bird Island Blizzard* can get up force enough to blow away the *Post*, which seems to be its objective aim, will only be decided by time. The *Blizzard* makes a very creditable appearance, however, and shows considerable 'blowing' ability on the part of its managers.[1122]

(The *Bird Island Blizzard* was published weekly from April 21, 1881, until April 13, 1882.[1123])

EPILOGUE

"The beautiful snow is all gone and none are found
who mourn thereat."[1124]

—*Egan Express*, April 28, 1881

The winter lived on in many ways over the coming decades. Depending upon the specific experience, it led to investigation, productive and permanent adjustments, and even, perhaps, a hint of bitterness.

Disaster Averted

During the process of surveying the Dakota Central, Charles Wood Irish noted that his various camps received multiple visits from Chicago & North Western officers Marvin Hughitt and John Blunt, who jointly had ultimate decision-making power over the final route selection.

In a diary entry from mid-July 1879, Irish noted that after one such visit there had been a "change of programme"[1125] in the vicinity of Lake Preston (just east of De Smet). It appears that Irish disagreed with Hughitt and Blunt about the specific location of the final route. The officers likely wanted a more direct route through a dry lake, and Irish advocated for a more cautious, but expensive, detour. Irish prevailed, but the event and outcome evidently weighed on him.

The postwinter melt in March 1881 caused a relatively permanent alteration in the landscape of the Prairie Pothole region of Dakota Territory. In 1884, three years after the Hard Winter, Irish wrote a letter to legendary explorer John C. Frémont, inquiring about lakes throughout east-central Dakota Territory. It read,

> When I constructed the Dakota Central Railway in 1879–80, all these
> lakes excepting Thompson, Poinsett, and Kampeska, were dry; and it

took me a long time and no small research to ascertain when they last held water. They had been known to be dry for the twenty-five years preceding 1879, or at least persons who had lived there or in the vicinity for twenty-five years said that the lakes were dry when they came into the locality, and had, with numerous smaller ones, been dry ever since; and all who knew about them had a theory that they had dried up long since, and that they never would fill again; but I found old Frenchmen who had seen these lakes full of water in 1843–46, and I, in studying over the matter, found that you had seen and named them in 1836–38, and I would thank you very much if you will take the time and trouble to describe them to me as you saw them.

I came very near locating the railroad line through Lake Preston, for the head men of the railroad company believed that it had dried up for all time; but on my presenting the testimony of certain reliable voyagers, they allowed me to go around it. It was well that they did, for the winter of 1880–81 gave a snow-fall such as had not been seen since the years 1843–44, and in the spring of 1881 all these lakes filled up, bank full, and have continued so ever since.[1126]

Ongoing Problems for the Railroads

Despite lessons learned over the winter of 1880–81, there was only so much that could be done against the weather. In an autobiography written approximately ninety years after that winter, about his childhood experience with the railroad in and around De Smet, H. A. Stimson wrote, "A small cut filled to the brim with snow can stop a train as easily as a broken bridge. The Dakota division was full of four foot cuts. Skimmer plows stave off the inevitable for a few days or weeks but all know that each spurt of snow thrown back merely makes the drift deeper."[1127]

During the fall of 1883, the Winona & St. Peter invested in widening the cuts between New Ulm and Tracy. Additionally, twenty miles of snow fence were constructed along the route, with nearly fourteen miles of fence added in 1889.[1128] The railroads also started employing rotary plows to fight the impressive snows of the region. Yet mother nature continued to test the companies' capabilities, as shown in the photo below from 1909.

SNOW CUT NEAR STORDEN MINN
THIS CUT 24 FT. DEEP   FEB, 23, 09,

While lessons were learned during each subsequent winter, snow continued to vex the
railroads for decades. This uncredited photo from the winter of 1909 shows a
twenty-four-foot-deep cut along the Currie branch of the Omaha line (built sometime after
the winter of 1880–81), between the Winona & St. Peter and the Southern Minnesota,
south of Tracy. Note that the area of cleared snow along the tracks is wider than that seen
in other images that appear in this book. From the Minnesota Historical Society.

Throughout the winter, we saw that the railroad companies put up lengthy
expanses of wooden snow fence to help divert snow away from the cuts. We also
saw that much of that was harvested for fuel, leaving the cuts exposed and vulnerable. Even apart from the poaching, wooden snow fences were an ongoing
maintenance issue for the railroads. So they eventually adopted a more long-term
solution to the problem: living snow fences (windbreaks), made up of vegetation of
some type, began to replace the less permanent installations.

The drone photograph below, taken above the Tracy Cut and looking eastward,
clearly shows a tapering line of trees within an otherwise relatively flat and open
field on the north and south sides of the tracks. These wedges of vegetation are
living snow fences, protecting a notoriously difficult stretch of track.

The Tracy Cut in 2018, with living snow fences on the north and south sides of track.
Drone photography by Steve Devore.

An aerial photo from 1938 showing that the living snow fence along the Tracy Cut was well
on its way to maturity at that time. Photo courtesy of GeoMOOSE Interactive Mapping,
Geographic Information System, GIS Department, Lyon County, Minnesota.

It's Just a Bad Cut

Saturday, July 20, 2019. I'd left my house, east of Mankato, at half past eight in the morning, during a severe thunderstorm warning. About an hour later, the weather forced me to pull off the road in Springfield. Those storms turned out to be part of the double-derecho system that raced from western South Dakota to eastern Michigan that day. Why was I out in this weather? I had an appointment in Tracy at half past ten to interview retired railroad safety engineer Jim Wichmann, whose territory had stretched from Tracy to Huron. He had stories about the Tracy Cut, and I wanted to talk to him.

Weather system, July 20, 2019, near Springfield, Minnesota. Photo by author.

Despite the weather, I pushed on, sending Jim texts to let him know I was delayed but still coming. The radio was abuzz with weather warnings, and being a trained spotter for the National Weather Service, I knew enough to know I shouldn't have been out on the roads. I also knew, from looking at the sky and checking the radar, that once the front moved past me, taking the vehicle-rocking winds with it, I'd only have to contend with the rain—it would be safe to continue my journey. I had to veer around downed trees in several of the towns between Springfield and Tracy but eventually pulled into the parking lot at the Wheels Across the Prairie Museum on the west end of Tracy.

Jim arrived with a box full of memories, including photos and newspapers, and settled in to go through them with me. He had begun working for the railroad in the 1960s and served in the same location under three different railroad companies: the Chicago & North Western Railway Company; the Dakota, Minnesota & Eastern Railroad (DM&E); and the Canadian Pacific Railway (CP).

As Jim shared his memories, Wilder's story of the superintendent from the East did not seem so far back in history. In March of 1965, a train headed by a plow and two locomotives went west out of Tracy and got stuck in the Cut. Jim went out to the site and, using binoculars, could see the crew crawling out of the locomotive's window on hands and knees, indicating how deep the snow was. The officer out of Huron told Jim, "It's your duty to get them trains through them cuts, we got a payroll to do. I want you to get that unstuck whatever you gotta do."[1129]

A March 1965 photo of the Tracy Cut, along what used to be called the Dakota Central. Photo courtesy of Jim Wichmann.

Under Jim's direction, the railroad sent out three locomotives and hooked onto the rear of the two that were stuck. The attempt to back them out together failed, so they separated the two stuck engines and pulled them out one at a time. The rear engine dislodged without much trouble, but the lead locomotive was more difficult; it was attached to the plow, and the plow had buried its nose four to five feet deep into the dirt beneath the tracks.[1130] Extensive work was required to return the tracks to working order.

Among the other stories Jim shared was this traumatic one: A train had gotten stuck in a drift during a storm, and Jim brought the crew back into Tracy via snowmobile. The storm cleared, and the sun was shining when orders came through: "Get that track open! I know you've got three more, five more engines sitting down by the depot. You get a crew out there and you hook on and you pull out and get 'em cleaned out and you hit it at thirty miles an hour."[1131]

The operation began, and Jim had his binoculars, headset, and radio for communications. He could hear the crews talking to each other over the radio, and he heard the *whomp* as the snowplow hit the drift and stuck tight. The engines behind the plow kept moving, however, and the lodged plow "ripped the first engine completely apart like a sardine can." Jim was about half a mile away from the scene and, through his binoculars, could see a chair from inside the locomotive swiveling in the open air. Grabbing the radio, he asked for a status. After a beat, he finally heard, "Who the hell told us to hit this at thirty?" The man was getting up off the floor, where the engineers try to lie "in situations like this." He had to report that the other man in the compartment did not survive the attempt to clear the drift, having suffered severe trauma in the collision.[1132] A locomotive with a plow on the front hits with a lot of force, no matter how fast it's going. This was a trying story for Jim to relate. As the emotions subsided and he came back into focus, he paused a moment, then said, "It's just a bad cut."

The regional terrain is the problem. Pocked with marshes and small lakes, this rolling landscape requires more cuts, fills, and bridges than other regions. Adding further complication, the winds that blow over the Buffalo Ridge, a prominent feature of the landscape in southwestern Minnesota and eastern South Dakota, leads to more erratic drifting than in other locations. Jim noted that when the Canadian Pacific purchased the stretch of track that includes the Tracy Cut, the company only held it for six years. There were many factors involved in its release of the segment, but one reason was that maintenance costs were simply too high in relation to the revenue coming in from the western end of the tracks.[1133] The wind blowing over the Buffalo Ridge may cause problems for the railroads, but it's no surprise that the area is now home to hundreds of wind turbines.[1134]

Badges of Honor & Supporting Photos

A short little blurb in the *Marshall Messenger* of April 22, 1881, mentioned a documentary activity that has aided historians and the curious for nearly a century and a half since: "A Winona photograph firm has been taking stereoscopic views of the snow cuts in southwestern Minnesota. They found some terrible piles of snow to take."[1135] The example below was meant to be viewed in a two-lens stereoscope, a common item seen in history museums today.

A stereoscopic Elmer & Tenney image showing shovelers posing with an impressive pile of snow. Photo courtesy of the Chicago & North Western Historical Society.

Photographs taken by Elmer & Tenney, stereoscopic or otherwise, are sprinkled throughout this book and provide visuals to match the descriptions of seemingly incomprehensible snow. Their work was very popular, as conveyed when the editor of the Janesville Argus wrote,

> Have you seen the stereoscopic views made by Elmer & Tenney of
> Winona, of the snow banks west? If not you should scratch round and get
> a squint.... The pictures are very fine, showing excellent artistic skill,
> and exceedingly true to nature – especially snow bank nature. If you
> have a stereoscope you need these pictures, as no Minnesota collection is
> complete without them....[1136]

Many of their photos from that winter, as well as similar images from other photographers, were turned into novelty postcards, which were either retained as keepsakes (badges of honor for having survived the unprecedented winter) or shared with family and friends who lived to the east. Many such postcards are now in the hands of state, county, and local historical societies across the region—they are now considered treasures.

As mentioned above, Elmer & Tenney were not the only photographers capturing these scenes. The photograph of the St. James train yard following the October blizzard was taken by J. W. Palmer, and the *Janesville Argus* often mentioned a photographer named Manderfeld (other spellings were also used), who they touted could "fit you out with snow drifts mountain high, and other scenery fully as interesting."[1137]

Not all photographs were taken for amusement. The *Canton Advocate* of March 3 reprinted a piece from the *Sioux City Journal*, which noted that photographers were documenting—"by order of [the Sioux City] company"—the "cuts, station houses and cars on side track[s] nearly drifted under, and that sort of thing" to show the general public why the blockades were happening.[1138] The concept of a public image was not lost on the railroad companies, and they worked to craft their message.

Should you ever find yourself in De Smet, stop by the Depot Museum, which houses a wonderful collection of artifacts from the area. Among the displays is an unassuming frame containing ribbons dated from 1903 to 1960, commemorating Old Settlers Reunion and Hard Winter Pioneer participants. Standing before these humble strips of silken fabric (even on a hot, humid summer day) can bring goosebumps worthy of the cold and brutal winds of a midwestern winter.

Noticing References Everywhere

Once research was complete and analysis done, I saw the region differently. Now when I cross railroad tracks, my mind makes note of which railroad line they belong(ed) to or if that route was established after the winter of 1880–81. As I drive through towns mentioned in this book, I think about the experiences of the people living there during the Hard Winter, as told through the newspaper articles I've spent so much time with. I think of Agent Cawley out of Pipestone. I think of the stage driver Wells, who determinedly kept things moving in the southwest corner of Minnesota. Living near Janesville, I frequently think—and wryly smile—about the delightful editor Clarence E. Graham. The region simply looks different now.

While I was reading the children's book *May B.* by Caroline Starr Rose, a portion of a poem caught my attention, so I contacted Caroline for more details. While rummaging through the book section at an antique store, she'd found a copy of *The American Educational Readers. Fifth Reader.* (periods appear in title), published in 1873 as part of a series of early American textbooks. It included a poem called "Voices of the Wind" that read, in part,

> *I* am the wind, and I blow, blow, blow,
> Driving the rain and the beautiful snow;
> Making confusion wherever I go;
> > Roaring and moaning,
> > Wailing and groaning.[1139]

A quick internet search found several such poems within the various *Readers*, such as Lesson CXXI, "The Lost One's Lament," in *Sanders' Union Fourth Reader*, published in 1867:

> Oh! the snow, the beautiful snow,
> Filling the sky and earth below;
> Over the housetops, over the street,
> Over the heads of the people you meet,
>
> . . . .
>
> Gone mad in the joy of the snow coming down;
> To lie and so die, in my terrible woe,
> With a bed and a shroud of the beautiful snow![1140]

Comparing the publication date to my research, I wondered, were these poetic textbook references so well known that the newspaper editors used them as common speech? It's fascinating to think about and yet another example of the exciting, fun correlations that continue to rise up. As Caroline Starr Rose wrote in her email back to me, "I love the layers—intentional, discovered, and dreamed—that exist in the creative world."[1141]

Aftereffects for Wilder

A major theme throughout the novel was that of settlers deserted by the railroad companies and left to endure the blizzards. The impact of that sense of abandonment seems to have lasted the rest of Wilder's life. She wrote to Lane with animosity about the railroads while the two women worked on the De Smet novels.[1142] Decades after the winter had melted into the fog of history, Wilder included in her autobiography, "Unreasonable as it was I think no one who was there at that time could ever again feel kindly toward a R. R. Co."[1143]

One wonders whether the Ingalls girls experienced symptoms similar to what today is called post-traumatic stress disorder. When Laura lived in the stressful, hostile Brewster household during her first teaching job, as shared in *These Happy Golden Years*, she "dreamed again that she was lost in a blizzard. She knew the dream; she had dreamed it sometimes, ever since she really had been lost with Carrie in a blizzard. But this blizzard was worse than before."[1144]

The winter may have had other impacts, too. A letter to Lane dated August 19, 1937, noted, "Our winter coal is in the basement. We think enough to last through."[1145] When first reading the note, I wondered whether the experience of the winter of 1880–81 had taught the Wilders to ensure that a quantity of coal sufficient to last the winter was on hand as early as August, or whether it was merely an economic decision based upon cheapest prices during summer months. Unknowable, but interesting to contemplate nonetheless.

An interpretive sign at the Laura Ingalls Wilder Historic Home & Museum in Mansfield, Missouri, mentions that Wilder's family Bible had been a planned birthday gift from her parents in 1888. However, it arrived late "due to a snow blockade," and her mother, Caroline Ingalls, needed to backdate the inscription to reflect Wilder's birthday, February 7. The Bible had likely been stuck on a train somewhere east of De Smet, as it was ordered via Montgomery Ward & Company and was printed in Chicago.

Prior to researching the Hard Winter, I most associated that time period with endless storms and near starvation. After reading the newspaper accounts, however, things shifted significantly. The weather was certainly challenging, and while it was not the nearly six-month blizzard William Stennett, of the Chicago & North Western, claimed it to be, it came close to living up to the mythology that has risen around it. And in truth, starvation was not as big of a threat as many historical sources have made it out to be. As noted earlier, there were pockets of deep deprivations, and it does appear as if the region around De Smet bore the worst of the food shortages.

Instead, the most difficult shortages were of fuel and mail. One was necessary for physical survival, and the other perhaps critical for emotional health. The incoming mail was critical for the newspaper editors, of course, and the laments published are mostly from their perspectives. But for settlers who had recently come to live on the prairies, leaving friends and families behind, the lack of communication must have had an isolating impact beyond the physical isolation of snow-blocked tracks. Despite the quantity of extant newspapers, it is indeed a pity that so many others have been lost to fire or water, or simply discarded. Beyond that treasured fragment carefully preserved by Aubrey Sherwood, what additional information might have been in even one more edition from De Smet?

After reading the newspaper accounts about mail deliveries being more heralded than the arrival of provisions, a new perspective shone upon this note from Wilder's autobiography:

> We had begun to wonder in December how we would get through the winter, and there was a great feeling of relief when on January 4th we had heard a train whistle. Everyone ran to the depot, but it was only a train carrying passengers and mail. We thought surely there must be another train behind it with food and fuel, but none came, and that night there was the worst storm yet.[1146]

Being in her early teens, Wilder likely related to the events of that winter in a different way than her parents and the other adults in her community. She may have been less concerned about the emotional effects of the lack of connection and intellectual stimulation that others wrote about, and more focused on the deprivations of her immediate family. And we must remember that she was human. There are discrepancies between her memory and the historical record. While somewhat prone to boosting some of her characters to heroic status, Wilder did not tend to lie (though Lane was known to stretch the facts to their breaking point). The differences between Wilder's memory and the historical record could be attributed to a combination of youth, malnourishment, the psychological impact of isolation, and the all-too-human reality that our memories are prone to narrow perspectives.

As the two women wrestled with plotlines, Lane wanted to bring in additional characters, but Wilder pushed back. The winter, she said, must boil down to the immediate family and their battle against the raging blizzards. In explaining her vision for the plot, Wilder explained to Lane,

[Pa] does the chores and starts the fire in the morning and helps grind wheat at night and twist hay. Ma and I twist hay and keep up the fire. We grind wheat and get the meals and with Carrie's help do the rest of the work and take care of Mary and Grace.[1147]

Perhaps the most poignant piece found among Wilder's correspondence with Lane had to do with the impact of the ongoing storms on her parents. Throughout the series, Pa is characterized as physically strong, calm, brave, whimsical, and a bit mischievous. Likewise, Ma is portrayed as emotionally strong, patient, unflappable, and continuously on guard so her children would see her as a stoic, resilient caretaker.

After Lane typed Wilder's manuscript, the older woman set about making corrections and notes. In the appropriately named chapter "Cold and Dark," she noticed the song lyrics she had included were missing, with lyrics from another song in their place. She made notes to her daughter, in two separate locations, not to cut the hymn as originally used. The original lyrics read,

I will sing you a song of that beautiful land,
The far away home of the soul
Where no storms ever beat on that glittering strand
While the years of eternity roll.

Between the two separate notes, she told Lane,

Don't cut the hymn Ma sang to Grace while a blizzard raged. . . . Shows she was almost hopeless of this world. . . . A land where storms never beat would have been thought of with longing. It was a wailing tune too. The kind Ma sang when she did sing. We must show the effect the winter was having. It nearly broke Ma down when she sang of the land where there were no storms. And Pa when he shook his fist at the wind. Don't leave that out. We have shown that they both were brave let's show what the winter nearly did to them. No one could live through that winter however brave and not come that near to breaking down and as Pa did when he shook his fist at the wind.[1148]

The toll the winter took on her parents likely influenced her life perspective going forward, and the novels' portrayal of her family as independent may have been one outlet.

As Wilder wrote to her daughter, after finding an old record book kept by her father, she lamented, "What a pity he didn't write about the Hard Winter."[1149] Indeed. If he had, many of the questions I still have would possibly be answered.

What Was Found: Enlightenment

This project started as a simple attempt to locate the infamous "big cut west of Tracy." As the work evolved, an incredibly rich and rewarding story was discovered, and a wide range of emotions experienced.

Early in the research stage, in an official history of the Chicago & North Western Railway Company, I found this statement: "Though many had to live on wheat or corn ground in coffee mills or pounded in a mortar, none was allowed to starve."[1150] My initial response was indignation—I had become accustomed to the perspective established in *The Long Winter* and in county and regional histories that painted a picture of "endless snows from the sky and abandonment from the East." How could a railroad representative say that none were *allowed* to starve when it was the railroads that encouraged settlers to emigrate to the area in the first place, that incidentally placed those settlers in harm's way, and that were unable to keep their roads clear to allow the transportation of much-needed provisions? They didn't *allow* struggling families and communities to band together and make the best of a bad situation—those communities had no choice.

As railroad historian John C. Luecke points out, the railroad companies "were overwhelmed, almost before they could mount a good defense. They did what they could, but at the same time they lured people onto their lands with a considerable amount of false advertising and fluff, ranging from false claims about the climate to the productivity of the land. The railroad companies paused only briefly after the revelations of 1880–81 before reverting to their standard operating procedures to exploit every opportunity to show a profit."[1151]

As my research progressed and deepened, I encountered things I had expected. I read about terrible blizzards with howling winds and cataclysmic snow. About bitter cold, isolation, hunger, and deep frustration. What I hadn't expected to encounter were the delightful humor, the community activities, the extent of travel, the lack of true hunger in most locations, and the steadfast optimism that remained throughout the winter. And certainly unexpected were the relentless and valiant efforts on the part of the railroad companies to clear the roads; my view of their efforts had previously been based solely upon the story of the superintendent from the East. Far from abandoning the lines under their care, the railroad superintendents and those in their employ worked tirelessly, in abhorrent conditions, to clear the tracks in hope of getting trains through.

Some had predicted that Dakota Territory would empty out when spring arrived. Quite the opposite occurred. The winter did little to dim the optimism that had shone so brightly before the flakes began to fall and accumulate en masse.

Delving into the construction of the Winona & St. Peter and Dakota Central Railroads was similarly exhilarating, and I explored deeper into their history with excitement. While I withheld much of that research for inclusion in a follow-up book, it was fascinating to discover that the earliest attempts at establishing railroads included at least one instance of a train being pulled down the tracks by draft animals. Locomotives were so expensive that the financiers of one particular venture had only enough money to pay for the establishment of the tracks and some cars, or a single locomotive . . . but not both.

The diary of surveyor Charles Wood Irish was another delightful find. It was full of information, ranging from the mundane daily weather reports that helped contextualize the hard work performed by so many to the more fascinating encounters, such as when Irish and his men all became ill and Irish experimented with different doses of whiskey, quinine, and muriatic acid until he found a successful concoction to treat the ailing, himself included. Treasured stories such as these will also be expanded on in my follow-up book about the railroads.

Along the way, I developed an affinity for some of the newspaper editors. I even visited a few of their graves to thank them for the work they did and to contemplate their accomplishments. Through their writing, we are able to look back upon this era and see it through their eyes, laughing anew at some of their offerings.

As the weather warmed in the early days of that long-awaited spring, people were quick to return to their normal lives, buoyant for not being cold, hungry, or cut off from the rest of the world. They'd earned valuable bragging rights that lasted their whole lives, and a certain young woman carried memories with her that eventually blossomed into a wonderful novel with what Pamela Smith Hill, the annotator of *Pioneer Girl*, called "a perfect plot." *The Long Winter* remains my favorite of the Little House books. Like the other novels, it diverted from the historical facts, but stuck to the larger truths.

Appendix I:
Timing of the Seed Wheat Run

Weaving together clues from the autobiographies, correspondence, manuscript, novel, and newspaper record, we can make an educated guess as to an approximate date for the seed wheat run. We can presume that details about the day itself came from Almanzo and that the autobiographies and correspondence are closer to the actual event's details than what was published in the novel. The following addresses specific differences:

- **The autobiographies**, as previously stated, are not in reliably chronological order, but they describe that morning as cold and clear, with the earliest version including that it was "still."[1152] The initial version did not include a temperature, but subsequent ones indicated it was thirty-five below zero. Each version mentions a predawn blizzard as they returned, but none mention a storm prior to the trip.[1153] The final version of the autobiography noted, "There was never more than one day between blizzards," but the prior versions simply said the run had to take place "between storms."[1154]

- **The newspaper record** describes February 11 through 16 as cold, moonlit, and well below zero. Snow events occurred on Friday (11), Saturday (12), Monday (14), and Thursday (17). Most of the week prior was described as moderate. The week following February 16 was also noted as relatively mild. There were blizzard events on February 22 and again the February 24–26. If we use the cold temperatures mentioned in the autobiographies and novel as our baseline, the mild temperatures of that week may eliminate February 23 as a candidate.[1155]

- **The novel** noted that the "temperature was ten below zero, the wind blew steadily. The day promised to be fair."[1156] The morning star visible at dawn indicated a clear sky, and "the rising sun poured down sunshine that seemed colder than the wind. There was no cloud in the sky, but the cold steadily grew more intense."[1157] Later in the day,

  > darkness slowly settled down. . . . The snow was palely luminous. The wind had died, not a breath of air moved in the darkening stillness. Stars shown in the sky overhead and to the south and the east, but low in the north and the west the sky was black. And the blackness rose, blotting out the stars above it one by one.[1158]

- **The sun and the moon:** The full moon occurred on February 14, providing plenty of light for early departure. In the novel, Almanzo woke at "nearly three o'clock,"[1159] so the full moon would have been a great help, especially if he started out that early the first few days of the week. Furthermore, the sun rose around 7:40 a.m. and set around 6:10 p.m. on February 14, 15, and 16.; each day had approximately ten and a half hours of sunlight.[1160]

In a typewritten note to Lane in the manuscript, while the women were jointly editing, Wilder told her daughter to place the seed wheat run "as early as possible, but not so early that the wheat that Almanzo gets can not last until the train comes. Or so late that his seed wheat would not last until spring might reasonably be expected."[1161] In a handwritten note during corrections to the manuscript, Wilder further commented that the wheat needed "to last through 2 weeks of Feb. and all of March and April, into May."[1162] The first note was clearly in regard to plot building and storytelling, but the phrasing of the second note could suggest that Wilder was relying more on her memory. Assuming the event took place in February, as related in the correspondence, and further using clues from the newspaper record and details from the autobiographies, an educated guess would make both February 15 and 16 strong candidates for the date of the seed wheat run.[1163]

Following Almanzo's death, the *Mansfield Mirror* added even more daring to the action by giving him credit for "driving 40 miles through a blizzard" to provide food for De Smet's residents.[1164]

Appendix II:
A Glimpse at a Few
of the Editors

Across the region, individual editors and typesetters each had their own style and concept of what they wanted their community's newspapers to be. Those whose words painted the history of these exciting and difficult months are worthy of examination in their own right. Most were among the founders of—and postmasters for—their respective towns. Four of them are briefly profiled here.[1165]

C. F. Case and the Marshall Messenger of Marshall, Minnesota

Photo courtesy of the Waseca County Historical Society.

The *Marshall Messenger* began with the 1874 sale of the *Prairie Schooner*, whose proprietor had tired of frontier living. The paper was purchased and renamed by C. F. Case, but the timing was less than optimal; as Case was setting up his business inside the print shop, a cloud of grasshoppers began devouring the vegetation for miles around the building. Mr. Case was determined, however, and published the paper at his own expense, rather than relying upon income from subscriptions. This was noticed and appreciated by residents, and they supported the paper once the regional economy improved. A 1916 county history noted that Case was "one of the pioneer residents of Lyon county and a highly respected citizen of Marshall."[1166]

Joseph Bobleter and the New Ulm Weekly Review of New Ulm, Minnesota

From the Collection of the Brown County Historical Society, New Ulm, Minnesota.

In April 1881, as the sun melted the monumental piles of snow and the Minnesota River reached out to explore the landscapes well beyond its banks, the Austrian-born founder and editor of the *New Ulm Weekly Review,* Joseph Bobleter, turned thirty-five. Similar to many editors, he also served as the town's postmaster, from 1873–1886. A Union veteran of the Civil War, he continued to perform in a military capacity for many years, becoming known as the "father of the Minnesota National Guard." It was not uncommon for well-liked leading citizens to serve in public office, and Bobleter was no exception: he served as mayor of New Ulm, was elected to the Minnesota House of Representatives, and performed a rotation as Minnesota state treasurer. He was also a Mason, a husband, and a father. He died in July 1909 at age 63.[1167]

Clarence E. Graham and the Janesville Argus of Janesville, Minnesota

Photo courtesy of the Waseca County Historical Society.

Each editor had their own personality, of course, but Mr. Clarence Eugene Graham stood out for his wit, sarcasm, and sometimes pointed prickliness. Grounded and solid, he had a creative and expansive vocabulary and was not afraid to take on his critics. Some of my favorite articles from the winter of 1880–1881 are his, and many are referenced in this book.

Born in New York in 1841, he moved to Missouri, back to New York, then on to southeastern Minnesota by the early 1860s. He served in Company D, Second Wisconsin Cavalry in the Civil War, and at war's end, moved to Waseca County, Minnesota, to farm. In 1873, he relocated to nearby Janesville, established the *Argus,* and served as editor and postmaster. He turned thirty-nine just before Christmas 1880. Mr. Graham produced the *Janesville Argus* until August 1881, when he moved a few miles east to Waseca, purchased the *Waseca Radical,* and ran it until 1902. The *Waseca Herald* announced his death at age 62 in 1904, sadly noting, "Though not unprepared for the announcement, our citizens were pained to hear of the death of Clarence E. Graham. . . . The cause of his death was dropsy from which he has suffered for some time." Today, dropsy is more commonly known as edema, but the term was previously "used to describe generalized swelling and was synonymous with heart failure."[1168]

An official county biography written during his life noted, "As a writer Mr. Graham has an easy, graceful style, and conducts his paper in an able and business-like manner."[1169] One can imagine that his sense of humor was appreciated among his readers, and I sincerely hope that new readers will feel an appreciation for his work after reading this book.

Alfred H. Lewis/Henry S. Volkmar and the Grant County Review of Milbank, Dakota Territory

Photo courtesy of the Grant County Review.

While each of the editors featured in this book had his own story to tell, Alfred H. Lewis, who turned twenty-eight in March 1881, steals the show by a landslide. Or, more accurately, Henry Singer Volkmar does.

As Alfred H. Lewis, he ran the *Grant County Review,* which he founded in August 1880, until his political leaning ran him afoul of the opposing faction and its associated newspaper. Competition can be good for business, but Lewis made enemies, and they were not content to simply have their say. Instead, they dug for dirt, and with Mr. Lewis, they found some miry, murky mud.

Possibly working off suspicion elicited by his mother and unmarried sister having a different last name, Mr. Lewis's foes were able to discover his real name and uncover an 1876 Philadelphia arson charge against him. Henry

Volkmar was accused of setting fire to a printing business. Working off of what he later called "bad, very bad, advice," he jumped bail, fled, invented a new identity, and established a new life. As Alfred Lewis, he moved west, teaching school in Iowa, then subsequently serving in various positions at two newspapers in Owatonna, Minnesota, where he married. In spring of 1880, he and his bride planted themselves as founding citizens of Milbank, Dakota Territory. President Arthur even appointed him postmaster under his assumed name. Despite all this, the dark cloud of Volkmar's past haunted him.

The charade worked for over a decade, until Mr. Lewis's enemies discovered his true identity. Having received a requisition from the governor of Pennsylvania, he knew he was caught. Lewis/Volkmar calmly returned to Philadelphia to face his past. According to an article in the *Baltimore Sun*, he entered a Pennsylvania county prison in September 1887, only to be liberated in late November thanks to the volume of letters that landed upon the desk of the district attorney. Those letters were written by "prominent citizens of Minnesota and Dakota Territory, interceding for the prisoner and representing that for the last eleven years he has been leading a most exemplary life, had married and was universally respected." The judge released Volkmar to return to his life as an upstanding citizen under his real name. In his absence, his wife, Katie, a "plucky little woman," helped keep the paper operating.[1170] Volkmar died on November 13, 1935.

APPENDIX III:
TOWN AND COUNTY POPULATIONS

(DT = Dakota Territory; * = Data not available)

Towns along the Hastings & Dakota			
	1870	**1880**	**1890**
Bird Island, MN	*	289	441
Montevideo, MN	*	862	1,437
Ortonville, MN	*	*	768
Milbank, DT	*	*	1,207
Wilmot, DT	*	*	*
Bristol, DT	*	*	199
Totals	**Unknown**	**1,151**	**4,052**

Towns along the Winona & St. Peter			
	1870	**1880**	**1890**
Janesville, MN	*	1,021	921
St. Peter, MN	2,124	3,436	3,671
Nicollet, MN	*	99	263
Courtland, MN	*	*	*
New Ulm, MN	1,310	2,471	3,741
Sleepy Eye, MN	*	997	1,513
Springfield, MN	*	167	716
Lamberton, MN	*	149	202
Walnut Grove, MN	*	153	127
Currie, MN	*	78	*
Tracy, MN	*	322	1,400
Marshall, MN	*	961	1,203
Canby, MN	*	331	470
Watertown, DT	*	746	2,672
Totals	**3,434**	**10,931**	**16,899**

Towns along the Dakota Central			
	1870	**1880**	**1890**
Balaton, MN	*	*	*
Tyler, MN	*	81	137
Lake Benton, MN	*	184	513
Elkton, DT	*	*	331
Aurora, DT	*	*	*
Brookings, DT	*	*	1,518
Volga, DT	*	287	298
Arlington, DT	*	*	270
Lake Preston, DT	*	*	337
De Smet, DT	*	116	541
Huron, DT	*	164	3,038
Ft. Pierre, DT	*	287	360
Totals	**Unknown**	**1,119**	**7,343**

Towns along the Southern Minnesota			
	1870	**1880**	**1890**
Fairmont, MN	*	541	1205
Jackson, MN	*	501	720
Heron Lake, MN	*	163	496
Fulda, MN	*	150	348
Edgerton, MN	*	86	178
Pipestone, MN	*	222	1,232
Flandreau, DT	*	471	569
Egan, DT	*	23	399
Dell Rapids, DT	*	260	993
Madison, DT	*	96	1,736
Totals	**Unknown**	**2,513**	**7,876**

Towns along other lines			
	1870	**1880**	**1890**
Sioux Falls, DT	*	2,164	10,177
Salem, DT	*	*	429
Forestburg, DT	*	*	*
Cameron, DT	*	*	*
Canton, DT	*	675	1,101
Elk Point, DT	*	719	*
Totals	**Unknown**	**3,558**	**11,707**

County Populations: Minnesota

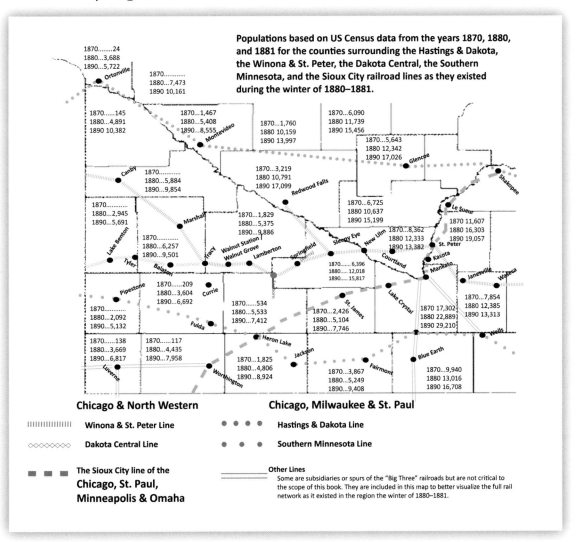

Populations based on US Census data from the years 1870, 1880, and 1881 for the counties surrounding the Hastings & Dakota, the Winona & St. Peter, the Dakota Central, the Southern Minnesota, and the Sioux City railroad lines as they existed during the winter of 1880–1881.

Chicago & North Western

||||||| Winona & St. Peter Line

◇◇◇◇◇◇◇◇ Dakota Central Line

▬ ▬ ▬ The Sioux City line of the **Chicago, St. Paul, Minneapolis & Omaha**

Chicago, Milwaukee & St. Paul

● ● ● ● Hastings & Dakota Line

● ● ● Southern Minnesota Line

Other Lines
Some are subsidiaries or spurs of the "Big Three" railroads but are not critical to the scope of this book. They are included in this map to better visualize the full rail network as it existed in the region the winter of 1880–1881.

Some of these were subsidiaries or spurs of the "Big Three" railroads but were not critical to the scope of this book. They are included in this map to better visualize the full rail network as it existed in the region the winter of 1880–1881.

County Populations: Dakota Territory

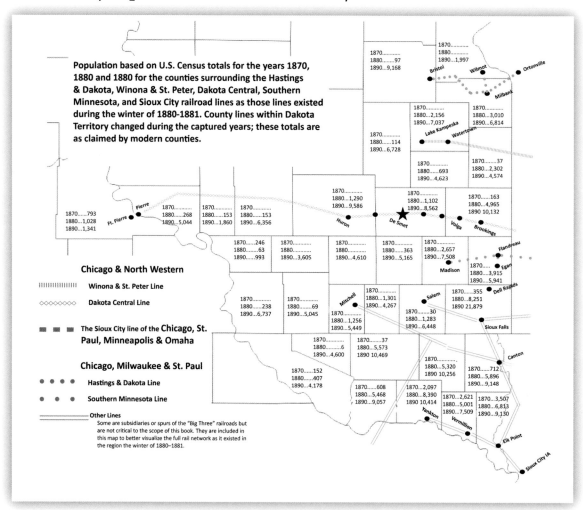

Some of these were subsidiaries or spurs of the "Big Three" railroads but were not critical to the scope of this book. They are included in this map to better visualize the full rail network as it existed in the region the winter of 1880–1881.

Appendix IV:
Autobiographies and Novel

There are multiple versions of Wilder's autobiography, *Pioneer Girl*, and both a manuscript and final version of the novel *The Long Winter*. The following is a short breakdown of how the versions used in this book are delineated, based on how they are described in *Pioneer Girl: The Annotated Autobiography*, edited by Pamela Smith Hill:[1171]

Pioneer Girl

Original Handwritten Version

This is believed to be the earliest version, completed in spring 1930. It covers Wilder's childhood in general order of home locations, but the format is more free flowing than chronological. An annotated version of this was published in 2014 as *Pioneer Girl: The Annotated Autobiography*. After the original first draft, additional versions were typed and edited by Wilder's daughter, Rose Wilder Lane, in an attempt to craft the work into a marketable product after the initial manuscript was rejected by Lane's literary agent.[1172] Two of those additional versions were referenced in this book.

Brandt Version (Cited throughout as "Brandt")

Lane took her mother's original handwritten manuscript, typed it, and made relatively minor edits. According to Hill, this version "closely resembles Wilder's original text." It was sent to Lane's literary agent, Brandt, in May 1930, ten days after Wilder gave her the original manuscript.[1173] It was rejected by Brandt and returned to Lane, who did more heavy editing to create a revised version (below). Those edits end partway through the manuscript with a note to "Pick up other ms."

That "ms" is believed to be the Brandt revised version, which I will be referencing in my follow-up book.

Bye Version (Cited throughout as "Bye")

Lane did heavier revisions of the autobiography and submitted it in September 1930 to George T. Bye, who would become her literary agent the following spring.[1174]

The Long Winter

Manuscript Draft Typescript with Corrections by Wilder
(Cited throughout as "Manuscript")

Wilder's draft of *The Long Winter*. The version used for the book you are now reading is a typescript in the Laura Ingalls Wilder files of the Rose Wilder Lane Papers, a manuscript collection in the Herbert Hoover Presidential Library and Museum. The original is housed at the Detroit Public Library. Based on the hand-written notes that Wilder left on the typescript, there do appear to be differences between it and the original manuscript. In my opinion, some of the phrases that were cut from the final novel were among the more lyrically beautiful and descriptive in the manuscript. The pagination of the manuscript is nonlinear; there are multiple pages with the same page number, and some sections have a *p* after the page numbers. In the book you are reading, each endnote that references the manuscript of *The Long Winter* includes the page number indicated at the top of the given page in the manuscript; such entries may refer to one of several pages with that number in the typescript.[1175]

Published Novel

The final version of the novel closely resembles the typescript manuscript in episodes and flow, though specific language was changed and some scenes were expanded.[1176]

APPENDIX V:
RAILROAD GLOSSARY

Word or Term	Definition
Ballast	A medium spread out beneath the tracks to hold them in place and assists in drainage to help prevent washouts. It could initially be composed of compressed dirt during construction then upgraded to rock at a later time, once the route was more established and regularly used. Cinders, a byproduct of burning wood for steam, were also sometimes used as ballast.
Cut	A trench dug through a hill to provide a more level path for the roadbed.
Emigrant car	A train car rented by someone moving from one location to another, to transport their belongings.
Express company/ Express messenger	A company specializing in shipping small packages.
Extension	Any additional length of track or a new branch off of a main line of track.
Fastenings	A system of iron or steel members used to attach rails to ties and other rails.
Fill	Arguably the opposite of a cut; the process of adding material/ dirt to a depression to create a solid and relatively flat path upon which the roadbed is built.
Freight bill	Part of the paperwork necessary to move freight from its point of origin to its destination.
Freight train	A train that carries freight cars only.
Grade	The vertical slope of the roadbed.

Word or Term	Definition
Grader	A railroad employee who works to shape the roadbed upon which the tracks are laid.
Grading	The process of preparing the roadbed.
Grain elevator	An agrarian structure that stores grain brought in by farmers until it can be loaded onto grain cars.
Iron rails	Rails made of iron. These were softer, more fragile, and prone to breakage. This was the standard material used in the early years of railroad construction in the United States. Eventually, iron was replaced by steel, which was stronger, heavier, and more reliable.
Journal boxes	Enclosures on a truck assembly that house the ends of the axles and keep the bearings lubricated. Without the proper amount of lubrication, bearings fall victim to friction—they heat up and melt, destroying the integrity of the trucks, which could lead to derailment. Early versions contained plain bearings and oil-soaked rags. Modern versions are sealed, filled with lubricant, and contain sets of roller bearings. There are now also "hot box detectors" located along the tracks to detect problems before they become emergencies. Also called axle boxes.[1177]
Junction point	Where two or more railroad lines intersect.
Lightning train	An "express" in modern terms, it would leave a city, then travel a long distance without stopping at smaller towns, until its destination.
Main line	Generally, a main line is a primary set of tracks, such as the Winona & St. Peter or the Dakota Central. At the local level, the term could be used to describe the primary track through a town or yard.
Mixed train	A train with both freight and passenger cars.
Rail yard	The area that contains the major infrastructure of the railroad in a given town. It can include additional sidetracks, spurs, warehouses, water tanks, coal houses, and all other equipment and structures needed to operate the railroad in that location.

Word or Term	Definition
Rails	The pieces of iron or steel upon which the wheels of a train are run.
Roadbed/railbed	The prepared earthen foundation that supports the ballast, ties, and track.
Rolling stock	A collective term that refers to locomotives, tenders, cattle cars, flat cars, passenger cars, cabooses, work cars, wrecking cars, etc.
Rotary plow	A plow incorporating a circular set of blades, similar to modern snowblowers.
Roundhouse	A semicircular facility used for the servicing and storage of locomotives, usually surrounding or adjacent to a turntable.
Section house	A house built for the person(s) responsible for maintaining a particular stretch of track.
Sidetrack	A short length of auxiliary track (up to a mile long) used to store and rearrange cars.
Siding	A length of auxiliary track parallel to a main track that allows one train to pull over to allow another train to pass.
Snow bucking	The process of driving a locomotive and plow into an accumulation of snow to clear the track.
Steel rails	Rails made of steel. Railroads replaced iron rails with steel, as they were able.
Stockyard	An area near a town's rail yard where animals under transport would be let out for exercise, food, and water before continuing their journey, if they had not yet reached their destination.
Surveying	The process of determining the features of a land area in order to construct a map, define a route, or other such purposes.
Surveyor	A skilled worker who determines the path along the ground to place the railbed, using specialized techniques and tools.
Switch	The mechanism that allows trains to pass from one set of tracks to another.

Word or Term	Definition
Tender	The car that carried a locomotive's fuel (either wood or coal) and water, always located directly behind the locomotive.
Terminus/Terminal	The "end of the rails" or the end point for a particular railroad line. It could be a temporary status until additional construction extended the line further.
Ties	The wooden crossbeams that support and hold the rails. Ties are supported by the ballast.
Timetable	A chart that details the times a train arrives at and departs from stops along the railroad line (also sometimes referred to as "time cards" in the newspaper articles).
Track	The combination of rails, fasteners, and ties.
Trucks	The assemblies that hold the wheel sets of a car.
Turntable	A large rotating mechanism that allows individual locomotives or cars to "turn around." Usually located at the ends of railroad lines and also often found near roundhouses, where they could be used to direct cars to specific bays for maintenance.
Water tank	Large, generally elevated reservoir for the storage of water, which was the critical element in the operation of steam engines.
Way car	Another name for a caboose.
Wedge plow	A V-shaped piece of metal used in snowplowing. The point of the V heads into the snow to throw it to either side of the track. This was the style of plow available during the winter of 1880–81.
Wye	A Y-shaped track configuration that facilitates three-point turns; an alternative to a turntable. The locomotive would go up one arm, back into the other arm, then pull forward, back onto the main rail. (Also sometimes spelled *whye* or just *Y*.)
Work Train	Used by the railroad for work purposes, not shipping freight or passengers.

Appendix VI:
Conversion of Degrees Fahrenheit to Degrees Celsius and Miles to Kilometers

°F	°C	Miles	Kilometers	Miles	Kilometers
−50	−45.6	1	1.6	110	177.0
−45	−42.8	2	3.2	120	193.1
−40	−40.0	3	4.8	130	209.2
−35	−37.2	4	6.4	140	225.3
−30	−34.4	5	8.0	150	241.4
−25	−31.7	6	9.7	160	257.5
−20	−28.9	7	11.3	170	273.6
−15	−26.1	8	12.9	180	289.7
−10	−23.3	9	14.5	190	305.8
−5	−20.6	10	16.1	200	321.9
0	−17.8	11	17.7	210	338.0
5	−15.0	12	19.3	220	354.1
10	−12.2	13	20.9	230	370.1
15	−9.4	14	22.5	240	386.2
20	−6.7	15	24.1	250	402.3
25	−3.9	16	25.7	260	418.4
30	−1.1	17	27.4	270	434.5
35	1.7	18	29.0	280	450.6
40	4.4	19	30.6	290	466.7
45	7.2	20	32.2	300	482.8
50	10.0			310	498.9
55	12.8	25	40.2	320	515.0
60	15.6	30	48.3	330	531.1
65	18.3	35	56.3	340	547.2

°F	°C	Miles	Kilometers	Miles	Kilometers
70	21.1	40	64.4	350	563.3
75	23.9	45	72.4	360	579.4
80	26.7	50	80.5	370	595.5
85	29.4	55	88.5	380	611.6
90	32.2	60	96.6	390	627.6
		65	104.6	400	643.7
		70	112.7		
		75	120.7		
		80	128.7		
		85	136.8		
		90	144.8		
		95	152.9		
		100	160.9		

APPENDIX VII:
GRAPHIC DESCRIPTION OF A BATTLE WITH SNOWDRIFTS

The Egan Express, February 24, 1881

This article closely resembles the story about the superintendent from the East from *The Long Winter*.

Graphic Description of a Battle With snow Drifts.

Below will be found an exciting account of a battle with snow on on the Kansas Pacific railroad, taken from the Denver Tribune, which will be read with interest by our readers:

"During Sunday night Sup't Odell made arrangements to clear the track of snow, and realizing how great a task it was, perfected plans on the most thorough and extensive sca'e. Four of the largest and strongest engines on the road had been sent on from the Smoky Hill division, together with construction cars and a commissary outfit, the latter containing provisions and general supplies sufficient to sustain five hundred men five days. A gang of 100 shovelers was got together and boarded the construction cars, and Sup't Odell and his two most efficient road bosses stepped into the Superintendent's car. In selecting the men for the great engines Mr. Odell exercised unusual care. Summoning an engineer or fireman, he asked, "Are you afraid to go where I tell you?" Each man selected for duty on the engines was asked this question. Only one engineer expressed hesitation, and he was quickly and kindly relieved. When the train was made up it consisted of

AN IMMENSE SNOW PLOW, four engines, three construction cars, the commissary car, and the superintendent's car, in the order named. When all was in readiness Mr. Odell said. "I've got the best crew for such work I ever had. You will see some fun." As so early Monday morning saw the expedition move out of Wallace.

From Wallace to Cheyenne Wells there are twenty deep cuts from 400 to 700 feet in length, and it had been reported, and such was found to be the case, that snow had drifted and packed in each one of these from 7 to 12 feet deep, the drifts for a few feet in some instances being still deeper. These drifts were plowed through successfully. In one or two instances a second trial was necessary, but in most cases the engineers, by crowding on a full head of steam and going at the cut with increased force, carried the train through the drifts and out beyond, leaving a clear path as they progressed. In one cut eleven head of cattle were killed, and in another, the last one before Cheyenne Wells was reached, an east bound freight train, headed by two engines, was found unable to move. The snow fighters added the strength of their four big engines, and the freight was backed up to Cheyenne Wells. When the head locomotive of the snow train would sound the signal that a drift was to be attacked, and the increased motion of the train would denote the approach to the cut, all hands would make ready for the shock. Those who have been in a railroad collision can appreciate the sensation produced upon the occupants of the cars when the immense iron snow plow was sent with tremendous force against the solid mass of snow twelve feet high, wedged in for a distance several hundred feet between two perpendicular walls of rock and earth.

Cheyenne Wells was at last reached, and here it was learned that the worst cuts were yet to be met with. The train, after a slight halt was ordered forward and several b'g banks were met and overcome and finally the largest and deepest cut on the division was reached. The Sup't knew that the most difficult place on the road had yet to be surmounted. This cut is a very deep one, its west end terminating at First View. It is 1,700 feet long, the walls rising high, and both openings being at points where the strong winds from the rolling prairie, which

305

sweeps out for hundreds of miles, sweep with full force and drive the snow into the semi-tunnel until the space is filled and packed in as if driven with immense sledge hammers. This point was reached about 7 o'clock in the evening, just as a large full moon was lighting up the night. It was clear, the air cold and chilly, but the wind had entirely subsided. The train was brought up to the east end of the cut and a survey of the task to be accomplished was taken. All hands were ordered out, and the locomotives pushed the cars back for about two miles, where they were left upon the main track. The shovelers were ordered to go upon the bank and as rapidly as possible, in gangs of four men each, cut trenches across the track, as deep as could be without too much loss of time, and about five feet apart. This work was for the purpose of disturbing the solidity of the mountain of snow, and of breaking up the mass as much as possible. The shovelers went at the work with a will, and in a short time this labor had been accomplished. Then everything was made ready for the charge on the snow with the ponderous plow. All hands secured as eligable a position as possible to witness the grand sortie. The engines went back for the distance of a mile and a half to gain a greater degree of velocity. The engineers and firemen stood at their posts firm and fast. Full head of steam had been attained, and the powerful engines fairly trembled to exhaust their strength. The word was given and the engines were thrown wide open and came rush-

ing along the track at a rate of speed which sent the sparks flying from the flanges and shot clouds of flame from the smoke stacks. As the gigantic plow was driven with frightful and resistless force into the the wall of snow, the effect upon the spectator was such as can be experienced under no other circumstances. Balls of snow weighing 1,000 pounds were sent from the chute of the great iron plow, as the monstrous machine pushed for a distance of 600 feet into the cut. Then the wonderful force was spent, and it was known that another and perhaps several trials would be necessary before the entire 1,700 feet could be got through. The plow and locomotives were completely buried in snow and several men walked over the smoke stacks and cabs on the snow piled upon them. The shovelers were ordered to cut out the engines and the hundred men went to work with a with a will to remove the snow from around them. It consumed about one hour to accomplish the task, and then another charge was made with the same terrible excitement and danger. It required four charges to cut thro' the snow, and then the plow was pushed through into the open plain beyond, and then the station of First View was reached at about 11 o'clock. From First View to Hugo the snow encountered was overcome with comparative ease, and Hugo was reached early Tuesday morning. At this point the snow brigade from Denver was met, and the road was declared "open for travel."

ACKNOWLEDGMENTS

The staffs at these locations: the Minnesota Historical Society, St. Paul, MN; the South Dakota State Historical Society, Pierre, SD; the Lyon County Historical Society, Marshall, MN, especially Jennifer Andries; the Waseca County Historical Society, Waseca, MN, especially Joan Mooney and Linda Taylor; the Sleepy Eye Historical Society, Sleepy Eye, MN; the Nicollet County Historical Society, St. Peter, MN; the Brown County Historical Society, New Ulm, MN, especially Darla Gebhard; the Herbert Hoover Presidential Library and Museum, West Branch, IA, especially Matt Schaefer and Craig Wright; Debbie Hemmer of the *Grant County Review*, Milbank, SD; and Aaron VanMoer, PE, Lyon County, Minnesota.

Mac Gill, a graduate student at the University of Iowa, Iowa City. She patiently and expertly waded through diary pages and the Charles Wood Irish Papers, unfurled giant maps of railroad segments, and sent me photographs of every relevant piece she had access to, returning to the university's archives multiple times when some clue within one of the documents led to more questions.

Craig Pfannkuche of the Chicago & North Western Historical Society gifted me a most extraordinary experience. A box containing land records from the Winona & St. Peter had recently been discovered, and I asked Craig if he could dig into the box and look for the records for De Smet. He and his daughter located and photographed the De Smet pages, which he said had sat unnoticed for over seventy years. Before making the records public, he emailed photos of the original plat map, the handwritten notes by the Western Town Lot Company agent, and the handwritten entry pages from the land sales. The pages of lot sales read like a who's who of characters from the novels. There were many moments during the research for this book that gave me goose bumps, but opening that email and looking at those photos was the most exciting.

Steve Devore for the drone photography; T. J. Malaskee for his expertise on Grange history; Brad Sabin, Iowa Northern Railroad, for patiently answering questions about railroad operations and the physical structure of railroads (both modern and historical) and for helping me muse about how things may have functioned in the early 1880s; Ivan Flitter, retired engineer and neighbor, who worked the route from Waseca to Tracy and Watertown; Jim Wichmann, retired railroad safety engineer for the stretch of track that ran through the Tracy Cut and into Dakota Territory; and Marcy Schramm, for going on the hunt with me to locate the Tracy Cut.

Early readers (J. H., P. C., T. L., L. W., R. W., T. L.): Your mix of knowledge about Laura Ingalls Wilder, general history, and railroad history helped fine-tune the content of this book.

John C. Luecke, railroad historian and author, for befriending an overly curious railroad neophyte and making sure that the railroad history and terminology used in this book are accurate.

Ray, for patiently driving up and down county roads looking for specific landmarks, for digging deep and figuring out some of the peskier details I required, and for writing a program to help identify inconsistencies in word usage.

My daughter, Laura, for asking questions and excitedly supporting me despite being interested in just about every era of history *except* this one.

The Laura Ingalls Wilder Legacy and Research Association: The formation of this organization gave me a community that shared my passion for the literary and historical details surrounding the Ingalls family. The goal of this book is to add to the knowledge base of Wilder scholarship and to give a few hours' joy to readers interested in the story surrounding *The Long Winter*.

Lily Coyle, James Monroe, Margarita Sikorskaia, and the entire team at Beaver's Pond Press for all they did to help make this project happen.

"Team *Snow*" (my editors): Angela Wiechmann, Kris Kobe, and Ruthie Nelson. You are the best. Thank you for your support, your personalities, your talents, and your skills. Simply the best!

And finally, my muses. One knows who they are. Thank you. The other is the "hunter and trapper, musician and poet"[1178] who inspired his daughter to write down his stories and gift us all the Little House series of books.

ENDNOTES

Author's Note and Introductions

1. Laura Ingalls Wilder to Rose Wilder Lane, 19 February 1938, box 13, folder 194, Rose Wilder Lane Papers, Laura Ingalls Wilder Files, Herbert Hoover Presidential Library, West Branch, IA.

2. Dr. Barbara Mayes Boustead (meteorologist, National Weather Service), email message to author, October 14, 2019.

3. "Inflation Calculator: 1881 Dollars in 2019," Official Data Foundation, Alioth LLC, https://www.officialdata.org/us/inflation/1881. The Official Data Foundation is a public benefit arm of Alioth LLC, which has worked with organizations such as NASA, SETI, and UCSF to create websites and visualizations that bring complex data to the fingertips of internet users. The ODF's public data sources include the US Bureau of Labor Statistics, EPA, and NHTSA.

4. Diaries of Charles Wood Irish, series 3, box 5, Charles Wood Irish Papers, Special Collections, University of Iowa Libraries, Iowa City, IA.

5. Lyon County, MN, Township Grid, *State of Minnesota Plat Book - 1916*, John R. Borchert Map Library, University of Minnesota Libraries, accessed February 2, 2019, http://geo.lib.umn.edu/plat_books/stateofmn1916/counties/lyon.htm.

6. Barbara M. Walker, *The Little House Cookbook* (New York: HarperCollins, 1979), 14.

7. Laura Ingalls Wilder, *The Long Winter* (1940; repr., New York: HarperTrophy, 2004), 177–178 (citations refer to the HarperTrophy edition); Wilder, *The Long Winter* manuscript draft typescript with corrections by Laura, n.d., box 15, folders 234–237, Rose Wilder Lane Papers, Laura Ingalls Wilder Files, Herbert Hoover Presidential Library (hereafter cited as Manuscript), 51p–52. In the original version of her autobiography, Wilder wrote, "The two grocery stores were small and had been started with little capital. Not having much money with which to buy, and expecting to be able to replace their stocks as they were sold, the store keepers had only a small supply of groceries on hand when the trains stopped running and it was too late to get more. It was the same with the coal sold at the lumber yard." Each version of the autobiography had a similar paragraph. Wilder, *Pioneer Girl: The Annotated Autobiography*, ed. Pamela Hill Smith (Pierre: South Dakota Historical Society Press, 2014), 210, 212; Wilder, Brandt copy of autobiography, 1930, box 14, folders 205–206, Rose Wilder Lane Papers, Laura Ingalls Wilder Files, Herbert Hoover Presidential Library (hereafter cited as Brandt), 98; and Wilder, Bye copy of autobiography, 1930, box 14, folders 209–210, Rose Wilder Lane Papers, Laura Ingalls Wilder Files, Herbert Hoover Presidential Library (hereafter cited as Bye), p. 123.

8. Arthur P. Rose, *An Illustrated History of Lyon County, Minnesota* (Marshall, MN: Northern History, 1912), 80.

9. John C. Luecke, *More Chicago & North Western in Minnesota* (St. Paul: Grenadier, 2012), 97–100.

10. Alan R. Woolworth, *The Genesis & Construction of the Winona & St. Peter Railroad, 1858-1873*, Rural and Regional Essay Series (Marshall, MN: Society for the Study of Local and Regional History and the History Center at Southwest Minnesota State University, 2000), 34.

11. *Lyon County News* (Marshall, MN), June 4, 1879.

12. *Cameron Pioneer* (Cameron, Dakota Territory), August 15, 1879.

A New Look at the Hard Winter

13. See population charts in appendix III.

14. Laura Ingalls Wilder, *Pioneer Girl: The Annotated Autobiography*, ed. Pamela Hill Smith (Pierre: South Dakota Historical Society Press, 2014), 217; Wilder, Brandt, 102; and Wilder, Bye, 127.

15. Arthur P. Rose, *An Illustrated History of Lyon County, Minnesota* (Marshall, MN: Northern History, 1912), 92.

16. George Washington Kingsbury, *History of Dakota Territory*, ed. George Martin Smith (Chicago: S.J. Clarke, 1915), 2:1158.

17. *History of Southeastern Dakota: Its Settlement and Growth, Geological and Physical Features—Counties, Cities, Towns and Villages—Incidents of Pioneer Life—Biographical Sketches of the Pioneers and Business Men, with a Brief Outline History of the Territory in General* (Sioux City, IA: Western, 1881), 61–62.

18. Arthur P. Rose, *An Illustrated History of the Counties of Rock and Pipestone, Minnesota* (Luverne, MN: Northern History, 1911), 282–284, 415.

19. Thomas Hughes, *History of Blue Earth County and Biographies of Its Leading Citizens* (Chicago: Middle West, 1901), 190.

20. Charles A. Smith, *A Comprehensive History of Minnehaha County, South Dakota: Its Background, Her Pioneers, Their Record of Achievement and Development* (Mitchell, SD: Educator Supply, 1949), 48–49.

21. William G. Gresham, *History of Nicollet and LeSueur Counties, Minnesota: Their People, Industries and Institutions; With Biographical Sketches of Representative Citizens and Genealogical Records of Many of the Old Families*, vol. 1 (Indianapolis: B.F. Bowen, 1916). See pages 342–343 and 366 for references to the April 1881 flooding.

22. William H. Stennett, *Yesterday and To-day: A History* (Chicago: Rand, McNally, 1905), 65–66.

October 1880

23. Laura Ingalls Wilder, Manuscript, 23. Some of the more lyrically beautiful phrasings of the sun playing upon the prairie landscape are found in the autobiography or manuscript versus the finished novel. This particular description first appeared in the manuscript, and also appears in the finished novel without the word "cautiously." Wilder, *The Long Winter* (1940; repr., New York: HarperTrophy, 2004), 28.

24. Laura Ingalls Wilder, *Pioneer Girl: The Annotated Autobiography*, ed. Pamela Smith Hill (Pierre: South Dakota Historical Society Press, 2014), 198; Wilder, Brandt, 91–92; Wilder, Bye, 115; Wilder, Manuscript, 8; and Wilder, *The Long Winter*, 10. In the manuscript and novel, instead of working to earn money for the winter, Pa harvested slough hay to sell to newcomers in the spring.

25. Wilder, *The Long Winter*, 28–30; Wilder, Manuscript, 24–26; Wilder, *Pioneer Girl*, 198; Wilder, Brandt, 91; and Wilder, Bye, 115. In the autobiographies, Wilder mentions only turnips being seeded. In the manuscript and novel, the harvest is sizable compared to the simple turnips, though still meager for winter preparations. Also in the autobiographies, it is noted that the "country so newly settled that no crops had been raised except a few sod potatoes."

Wilder, *Pioneer Girl*, 210; Wilder, Brandt, 95; and Wilder, Bye, 123. This may have been a 14-year-old's understanding of the situation, as elevators around the region were overflowing, unless De Smet was an anomaly.

26. Wilder, *Pioneer Girl*, 198; Wilder, Brandt, 92; and Wilder, Bye, 115. This factor was not included in the manuscript or in the novel. Instead, the family is shown as enjoying satisfying meals from their own garden.

27. Wilder, *Pioneer Girl*, 201; Wilder, Brandt, 92; and Wilder, Bye, 115. The prestorm plan to move to town was excluded from the manuscript and novel.

28. Wilder, *The Long Winter*, 40; and Wilder, Manuscript, 36

29. Wilder, Bye, 117; Wilder, *Pioneer Girl*, 202; and Wilder, Brandt, 93.

30. Wilder, *The Long Winter*, 47; and Wilder, Manuscript, 40.

31. Wilder, *The Long Winter*, 59–62; Wilder, Manuscript, 51; Wilder, *Pioneer Girl*, 203; Wilder, Brandt, 94; and Wilder, Bye, 117–118. All versions mention the warning by the elderly Native American.

32. Wilder, Manuscript, 53; and Wilder, *The Long Winter,* 64.

33. Wilder, *The Long Winter*, 73; and Wilder, Manuscript, 60–61. This wonderful bit of foreshadowing first appeared in the manuscript.

34. *Murray County Pioneer* (Currie, MN), October 21, 1880.

35. *Marshall Messenger* (Marshall, MN), October 22, 1880.

36. *New Ulm Weekly Review* (New Ulm, MN), October 20, 1880.

37. *New Ulm Weekly Review*, October 20, 1880.

38. *New Ulm Weekly Review*, October 27, 1880.

39. *Fort Pierre Weekly Signal* (Fort Pierre, Dakota Territory), October 27, 1880.

40. Diaries of Charles Wood Irish, series 3, box 5, Charles Wood Irish Papers, Special Collections, University of Iowa Libraries, Iowa City, IA.

41. *Brookings County Press* (Brookings, Dakota Territory), June 12, 1879

42. Diaries of Charles Wood Irish, Charles Wood Irish Papers.

43. Diaries of Charles Wood Irish, Charles Wood Irish Papers.

44. *Brookings County Press*, October 21, 1880.

45. *Brookings County Press*, October 21, 1880.

46. *Brookings County Press*, October 21, 1880.

47. *Brookings County Press*, October 28, 1880.

48. *Egan Express* (Egan, Dakota Territory), October 21, 1880.

49. *Pipestone Star* (Pipestone, MN), October 21, 1880.

50. *Pipestone Star*, October 21, 1880.

51. Thomas Curtis Clarke, *The American Railway: Its Construction, Development, Management and Trains* (1889; repr., New York: Skyhorse, 2015), 154–155 (citations refer to the Skyhorse edition).

52. *New Ulm Weekly Review*, October 27, 1880.

53. *Tyler Tribune* (Tyler, MN), quoted in the *New Ulm Weekly Review*, November 3, 1880.

54. Arthur P. Rose, *An Illustrated History of Lyon County, Minnesota* (Marshall, MN: Northern History, 1912), 93.

55. *Brookings County Press*, October 28, 1880.

56. *Murray County Pioneer*, October 21, 1880.

57. *Murray County Pioneer*, October 21, 1880.

58. *Forestburg Miner County Mercury* (Forestburg, Dakota Territory), October 22, 1880.

59. *Brookings County Press*, October 21, 1880.

60. *Janesville Argus* (Janesville, MN), November 2, 1880; and *New Ulm Weekly Review*, November 3, 1880.

61. *Elkader Register* (Elkader, IA), reprinted in the *Brookings County Press*, November 11, 1880.

62. *History of Southeastern Dakota: Its Settlement and Growth, Geological and Physical Features—Counties, Cities, Towns and Villages—Incidents of Pioneer Life— Biographical Sketches of the Pioneers and Business Men, with a Brief Outline History of the Territory in General* (Sioux City, IA: Western, 1881), 151, 355, 360; Realto E. Price, ed., *History of Clayton County, Iowa: From the Earliest Historical Times Down to the Present; Including a Genealogical and Biographical Record of Many Representative Families, Prepared from Data Obtained from Original Sources of Information*, 2 vols. (Chicago: Robert O. Law Company, 1916),

230; United States, *Register of Officers and Agents, Civil, Military, and Naval, in the Service of the United States on the Thirtieth of September, 1877* (Washington: Government Printing Office, 1878), 579; and D. H. Talmadge, "The Press of Fayette County," chap. 10 in *Past and Present of Fayette County, Iowa* (Indianapolis: B.F. Bowen, 1910).

63. *Pacific Rural Press* (San Francisco, CA), August 28, 1880.

64. *New Ulm Weekly Review*, October 27, 1880.

65. *Pipestone Star*, October 21, 1880.

66. *New Ulm Weekly Review*, October 27, 1880.

67. *Pipestone Star*, October 28, 1880.

68. *New Ulm Weekly Review*, October 20, 1880.

69. *Murray County Pioneer*, October 21, 1880.

70. *Brookings County Press*, October 21, 1880.

71. *Dakota News* (Watertown, Dakota Territory), October 25, 1880.

72. *Pipestone Star*, October 28, 1880.

73. *Dakota News*, October 25, 1880.

74. William Stennett, *Yesterday and Today: A History of the Chicago and North Western Railway System*, 3rd ed. (Chicago: Winship, 1910), 22.

75. Wilder, *Pioneer Girl*, 202; Wilder, Brandt, 93–94; Wilder, Bye, 117; Wilder, Manuscript, 41–42; and Wilder, *The Long Winter*, 46–50.

76. *Murray County Pioneer*, October 21, 1880.

77. *Murray County Pioneer*, October 21, 1880.

78. *Pipestone Star*, October 21, 1880.

79. *Janesville Argus*, November 2, 1880.

80. *Forestburg Miner County Mercury*, October 22, 1880.

81. *New Ulm Weekly Review*, October 20, 1880.

82. *Egan Express*, October 21, 1880.

83. *Brookings County Press*, October 28, 1880.

84. *Fort Pierre Weekly Signal*, October 27, 1880.

85. *Grant County Review* (Milbank, Dakota Territory), October 28, 1880.

86. *Forestburg Miner County Mercury*, October 22, 1880.

87. *The Dakota News*, November 1, 1880.

88. *Pipestone Star*, October 21, 1880; *Brookings County Press*, October 21, 1880; *Dakota News*, November 1, 1880; and *Fort Pierre Weekly Signal*, October 20, 1880.

89. *Brookings County Press*, October 28, 1880.

90. *Pipestone Star*, October 28, 1880.

91. *Brookings County Press*, October 28, 1880.

92. *Brookings County Press*, October 28, 1880.

93. *New Ulm Weekly Review*, October 27, 1880.

94. *Fort Pierre Weekly Signal*, October 20, 1880.

95. *Fort Pierre Weekly Signal*, October 27, 1880.

96. *Fort Pierre Weekly Signal*, October 20, 1880.

97. *Fort Pierre Weekly Signal*, October 27, 1880.

November 1880

98. Laura Ingalls Wilder, *The Long Winter* (1940; repr., New York: HarperTrophy, 2004), 96; and Wilder, Manuscript, 80.

99. Laura Ingalls Wilder, *Pioneer Girl: The Annotated Autobiography*, ed. Pamela Smith Hill (Pierre: South Dakota Historical Society Press, 2014), 203; Wilder, Brandt, 95; and Wilder, Bye, 118. Wilder noted that the school building was brand new. Her father had helped organize the school district and had done carpentry work in town after the haying was complete. It is likely that Charles helped construct the school building.

100. Wilder, *Pioneer Girl*, 203, 207; Wilder, Brandt, 95–96; Wilder, Bye, 118–120; Wilder, Manuscript, 68–70; and Wilder, *The Long Winter*, 84–91.

101. Wilder, *Pioneer Girl*, 207–208; Wilder, Brandt, 96–97; Wilder, Bye, 120; Wilder, Manuscript, 89; and *The Long Winter*, 105.

102. Wilder, *The Long Winter*, 105; and Wilder, Manuscript, 89. At this point in the autobiography narratives, the cuts are described in general, and the text transitions into a short version of the superintendent story. Wilder, *Pioneer Girl*, 2017, 209; Wilder, Brandt, 96–97; and Wilder, Bye, 120–123.

103. Wilder, *The Long Winter*, 106; and Wilder, Manuscript, 89. This incident is not in the autobiographies. However, on Manuscript page 93, Wilder wrote, "Actually, it is

Wednesday morning—Laura and Carrie go to school—it is early next morning when Pa leaves and they see him on their way to school, or from the school." It is unclear whether this means she is remembering the actual incident or putting Laura and Carrie into the proper perspective to watch Pa head eastward on the handcar.

104. Wilder, *The Long Winter*, 120; and Wilder, chap. 13 in Manuscript, 4.

105. Wilder, *The Long Winter*, 118; and Wilder, "Alone," in Manuscript, n.p.

106. Wilder, *The Long Winter*, 142–143; and Wilder, Manuscript, 22p–23p.

107. Wilder, *The Long Winter*, 102-104; and Wilder, Manuscript, 84–85.

108. Wilder, *The Long Winter*, 97; and Wilder, Manuscript, 81.

109. *Dakota News* (Watertown, Dakota Territory), November 1, 1880.

110. *Fort Pierre Weekly Signal* (Fort Pierre, Dakota Territory), November 3, 1880.

111. Wilder, *Pioneer Girl*, 203, 207; Wilder, Brandt, 95; Wilder, Bye, 118; Wilder, Manuscript, 68; and Wilder, *The Long Winter*, 84. Each description of the moment the storm hit the school building varies in subtle ways. However, the original version, from *Pioneer Girl*, is my favorite due to the phrasing of "whirling chaos of snow."

112. Wilder, *The Long Winter*, 84–92; Wilder, Manuscript, 68–76; Wilder, *Pioneer Girl*, 203, 207; Wilder, Brandt, 95–96; and Wilder, Bye, 118–120. In the autobiography, it was Mr. Holmes who bumped into the hotel.

113. Wilder, *The Long Winter*, 68; Wilder, Manuscript, 62; Wilder, *Pioneer Girl*, 203; Wilder, Brandt, 95; and Wilder, Bye, 118. In the manuscript, Wilder notes that school began on a Monday. In the novel, the family is setting up their household in the store building on a school day, as they see the students returning home after their day of learning. Ma tells Laura and Carrie that they, too, will be going to school the next day. In the autobiography, Wilder notes school starting "the first of November," which could mean Monday, November 1, or could simply mean early November. Within the Hard Winter portion of the autobiographies, Wilder wrote more about

this episode (from starting school through the schoolhouse blizzard) than any other.

114. Laura Ingalls Wilder to Rose Wilder Lane, 7 March 1938, box 13, folder 194, Rose Wilder Lane Papers, Laura Ingalls Wilder Files, Herbert Hoover Presidential Library, West Branch, IA.

115. *Egan Express* (Egan, Dakota Territory), November 11, 1880.

116. *Egan Express*, November 11, 1880.

117. *Egan Express*, November 11, 1880.

118. *New Ulm Weekly Review* (New Ulm, MN), November 17, 1880.

119. *New Ulm Weekly Review*, November 24, 1880.

120. *Egan Express*, November 25, 1880.

121. *Dakota News*, November 1, 1880.

122. *Grant County Review* (Milbank, Dakota Territory), November 4, 1880.

123. Warren Upham, *Minnesota Geographic Names: Their Origin and Historic Significance* (1920; repr., St. Paul: Minnesota Historical Society, 1969), 509.

124. *Brookings County Press* (Brookings, Dakota Territory), November 18, 1880.

125. *History of Southeastern Dakota: Its Settlement and Growth, Geological and Physical Features—Counties, Cities, Towns and Villages—Incidents of Pioneer Life— Biographical Sketches of the Pioneers and Business Men, with a Brief Outline History of the Territory in General* (Sioux City, IA: Western, 1881), 149, 151, 153.

126. *History of Southeastern Dakota*, 334.

127. *Egan Express*, November 11, 1880.

128. T. Addison Busbey, *The Biographical Directory of the Railway Officials of America* (Chicago: Railway Age and Northwestern Railroader, 1893), 110.

129. *Janesville Argus* (Janesville, MN), November 16, 1880.

130. *Brookings County Press*, November 4, 1880.

131. *Grant County Review*, November 11, 1880.

132. *Dakota News*, October 25, 1880.

133. *Brookings County Press*, November 18, 1880.

134. *Janesville Argus*, November 16, 1880.

135. *Dakota News*, November 15, 1880.

136. *Brookings County Press,* November 18, 1881.

137. *Janesville Argus*, November 16, 1880.

138. *Dakota News*, November 22, 1880.

139. Wilder, *Pioneer Girl*, 209; Wilder, Brandt, 96; and Wilder, Bye, 120. This arrival was not brought into the manuscript or the novel.

140. Robert J. Casey and W. A. S. Douglas, *Pioneer Railroad: The Story of the Chicago and North Western System* (New York: Whittlesey House, 1948), 203.

141. *Pipestone Star* (Pipestone, MN), November 25, 1880.

142. *Janesville Argus*, November 30, 1880.

143. *Grant County Review*, November 25, 1880.

144. *Volga Gazette* (Volga, Dakota Territory), reprinted in the *Fort Pierre Weekly Signal*, November 17, 1880.

145. *Grant County Review*, November 25, 1880.

146. To further elaborate, per John C. Luecke, the 1880s were a transitional period when both iron and steel were used. Iron was not necessarily an inferior rail but was generally used to build a line quickly and cheaply and would then be replaced by steel as the line became established. Also, iron would be used for extensions that would see lighter traffic, with steel replacing iron on lines that carried heavier traffic. Email message to author, September 24, 2019.

147. *New Ulm Weekly Review*, November 17, 1880.

148. *Dakota News*, November 29, 1880.

149. *Volga Gazette*, reprinted in the *Fort Pierre Weekly Signal*, November 17, 1880.

150. This is an oversimplification of complex situational differences. The Winona & St. Peter was a new venture, growing out of unsuccessful predecessors and difficult financial conditions. The Dakota Central was an extension of an existing line built under better economic parameters. This history will be explored in the follow-up book.

151. *Brookings County Press*, November 11, 1880.

152. *Fort Pierre Weekly Signal*, November 10 1880.

153. *Fort Pierre Weekly Signal*, November 3, 1880.

154. *Murray County Pioneer* (Currie, MN), November 25, 1880.

155. *Brookings County Press*, November 18, 1880.

156. *Egan Express*, November 11, 1880, and November 18, 1880.

157. *New Era* (Parker, Dakota Territory, and Swan Lake, Dakota Territory), reprinted in *Dakota News*, November 15, 1880.

158. James H. Lees and S. W. Beyer, "History of Coal Mining In Iowa & Coal Statistics," *Iowa Geological Survey* 19 (1908): 521–597, https://doi.org/10.17077/2160-5270.1149.

159. Chicago and North Western Railway Company, *Annual Report of the Chicago and North Western Railway Company for the Twenty-Second Fiscal Year, Ending May 31st, 1881* (New York: Chicago and North Western Railway Company, 1881), 19.

160. Laura Ingalls Wilder, *By the Shores of Silver Lake* (1939; repr., New York: HarperTrophy, 2004), 19. Citations refer to the HarperTrophy edition.

161. *Janesville Argus*, March 15, 1881.

162. *Brookings County Press*, November 4, 1880.

163. *Egan Express*, November 11, 1880.

164. *Grant County Review*, November 18, 1880.

165. *Marshall Messenger* (Marshall, MN), November 19, 1880.

166. *Dakota News*, November 29, 1880.

167. *Dakota News*, November 8, 1880.

168. *Dakota News*, November 22, 1880.

169. *Dakota News*, November 29, 1880.

170. Arthur P. Rose, *An Illustrated History of Lyon County, Minnesota.* (Marshall, MN: Northern History, 1912), 91.

171. Rose Wilder Lane and Almanzo Wilder, Rose's Questionnaire for Almanzo Wilder on Dakota Territory, n.d., box 33, folder 421, Rose Wilder Lane Papers, Manuscripts.

172. *Brookings County Press*, November 18, 1880.

173. *Egan Express*, November 25, 1880.

174. *Egan Express*, November 25, 1880.

175. *Janesville Argus*, November 30, 1880.

176. Wilder, *The Long Winter*, 73; and Wilder, Manuscript, 61.

177. *Minneapolis Tribune*, reprinted in the *Janesville Argus*, November 30, 1880.

178. *New Ulm Weekly Review*, November 17, 1880.

179. *Grant County Review*, November 11, 1880.

180. *Dakota News*, November 29, 1880.

181. *New Ulm Weekly Review*, November 17, 1880.

182. *Brookings County Press*, November 4, 1880.

183. *Egan Express*, November 18, 1880.

184. *Brookings County Press*, November 18, 1880.

185. *Dakota News*, November 15, 1880.

186. *Brookings County Press*, November 18, 1880.

187. Eliza Jane Wilder, *A Wilder in the West: The Story of Eliza Jane Wilder*, ed. William Anderson (De Smet, SD: Laura Ingalls Wilder Memorial Society, 1971), 14–15.

188. *Grant County Review*, November 4, 1880.

189. *Brookings County Press*, November 4, 1880.

190. *Dakota News*, November 8, 1880.

191. *Dakota News*, November 15, 1880.

192. *Egan Express*, November 25, 1880.

193. *Dakota News*, November 15, 1880.

194. *Egan Express*, November 25, 1880.

195. Ken Woody (chief of interpretation, Little Bighorn Battlefield National Monument),

email message to author, July 18, 2019. The title of general was awarded posthumously.

196. Joseph Mills Hanson, *The Conquest of the Missouri; Being the Story of the Life and Exploits of Captain Grant Marsh* (Chicago: A.C. McClurg, 1909), 237–239.

197. *Fort Pierre Weekly Signal*, November 17, 1880.

198. *Egan Express*, November 25, 1880.

199. *Egan Express*, November 11, 1880.

200. *Dakota News*, November 29, 1880.

201. *Dakota News*, November 29, 1880.

202. *Dakota News*, November 29, 1880.

203. *Dakota News*, November 29, 1880.

204. *Dakota News*, November 29, 1880.

205. *Dakota News*, November 29, 1880.

206. *Dakota News*, November 29, 1880.

207. *Dakota News*, November 29, 1880.

208. *Dakota News*, November 29, 1880.

December 1880

209. Laura Ingalls Wilder, *The Long Winter* (1940; repr., New York: HarperTrophy, 2004), 192; and Wilder, Manuscript, 63p.

210. Wilder, *The Long Winter*, 158; and Wilder, Manuscript, 36p–37p.

211. Wilder, *The Long Winter*, 164–167; and Wilder, Manuscript, 42p–45p.

212. Laura Ingalls Wilder, *Pioneer Girl: The Annotated Autobiography*, ed. Pamela Smith Hill (Pierre: South Dakota Historical Society Press, 2014), 220; Wilder, Brandt, 104; and Wilder, Bye, 130.

213. Wilder, *The Long Winter*, 169; and Wilder, Manuscript, 45p–46p. In the autobiographies, the letter promising the Christmas barrel is recorded as having arrived with last train through town in January. Wilder, *Pioneer Girl*, 212; Wilder, Brandt, 99; and Wilder, Bye, 123.

214. Wilder, *The Long Winter*, 170; and Wilder, Manuscript, 46p.

215. Wilder, *The Long Winter*, 173; and Wilder, Manuscript, 49p.

216. Wilder, *The Long Winter*, 174; and Wilder, Manuscript, 49p.

217. Wilder, *The Long Winter*, 173; and Wilder, Manuscript, 48p.

218. Wilder, *The Long Winter*, 193; and Wilder, Manuscript, 63p.

219. Wilder, *The Long Winter*, 177–178; and Wilder, Manuscript, 51–52.

220. Wilder, *The Long Winter*, 174–175; and Wilder, Manuscript, 49 1/2p–50p.

221. Wilder, *The Long Winter*, 184–185; Wilder, Manuscript, 57–58p; Wilder, *Pioneer Girl*, 213; Wilder, Brandt, 100; and Wilder, Bye, 125. In a letter to Rose dated March 23, 1937, Wilder wrote (about a late-1880s winter), "To keep from freezing we could twist hay but it was a steady job for one man. We figured we must burn coal in the winter. Could not really be warm with hay." Laura Ingalls Wilder to Rose Wilder Lane, box 13, folder 193, Rose Wilder Lane Papers, Laura Ingalls Wilder Files, Herbert Hoover Presidential Library, West Branch, IA.

222. Wilder, *The Long Winter*, 196–197; Wilder, Manuscript, 66p; Wilder, *Pioneer Girl*, 213; Wilder, Brandt, 100; and Wilder, Bye, 124. The button lamp was included in all

versions. A few newspaper articles mention tallow-dip candles, a similar concept.

223. *Grant County Review* (Milbank, Dakota Territory), December 23, 1880.

224. *Grant County Review*, December 9, 1880; *Pipestone Star* (Pipestone, MN), December 9, 1880; and *Marshall Messenger* (Marshall, MN), December 10, 1880.

225. *Marshall Messenger*, December 10, 1880.

226. *Dakota News* (Watertown, Dakota Territory), December 6, 1880.

227. *Egan Express* (Egan, Dakota Territory), December 9, 1880.

228. *Janesville Argus* (Janesville, MN), December 14, 1880.

229. *Egan Express*, December 16, 1880.

230. *Pipestone Star*, December 16, 1880.

231. *Egan Express*, December 23, 1880.

232. *Brookings County Press* (Brookings, Dakota Territory), December 23, 1880.

233. *Grant County Review*, December 23, 1880.

234. *Grant County Review*, December 30, 1880.

235. *Janesville Argus*, January 4, 1881.

236. *Brookings County Press*, December 30, 1880.

237. *Egan Express*, December 30, 1880.

238. *Marshall Messenger*, December 31, 1880.

239. *Murray County Pioneer* (Currie MN), December 30, 1880.

240. *Marshall Messenger*, December 31, 1880.

241. *Janesville Argus*, December 21, 1880.

242. *Marshall Messenger*, January 14, 1881.

243. *Grant County Review*, December 9, 1880.

244. Chicago and North Western Railway Company, *Annual Report of the Chicago and North Western Railway Company for the Twenty-Second Fiscal Year, Ending May 31st, 1881* (New York: Chicago and North Western Railway Company, 1881), 12.

245. *New Ulm Weekly Review* (New Ulm, MN), December 1, 1880.

246. *Tracy Gazette* (Tracy, MN), quoted in the *Sleepy Eye Herald* (Sleepy Eye, MN), reprinted in the *Janesville Argus*, December 14, 1880. The same article from the *Tracy Gazette* was paraphrased in the *Marshall Messenger* of December 3.

247. *Dakota News*, December 6, 1880.

248. *Murray County Pioneer,* December 30, 1880.

249. *New Ulm Weekly Review*, December 8, 1880.

250. *Brookings County Press*, December 9, 1880.

251. *Dakota News*, December 13, 1880.

252. *Dakota News*, December 13, 1880.

253. T. Addison Busbey, *The Biographical Directory of the Railway Officials of America* (Chicago: Railway Age and Northwestern Railroader, 1893), 327.

254. *Janesville Argus*, December 14, 1880.

255. *Brookings County Press*, December 16, 1880.

256. *Janesville Argus*, December 21, 1880.

257. *Egan Express*, December 2, 1880.

258. *Egan Express*, December 23, 1880.

259. *New Ulm Weekly Review*, December 29, 1880.

260. *Marshall Messenger*, December 30, 1880.

261. *Dakota News*, December 27, 1880.

262. *Egan Express*, December 30, 1880.

263. *Brookings County Press*, December 30, 1880.

264. *Egan Express*, December 16, 1880.

265. *Murray County Pioneer*, December 9, 1880.

266. *Janesville Argus*, December 21, 1880.

267. *Grant County Review*, December 30, 1880.

268. *New Ulm Weekly Review*, December 29, 1880.

269. H. Price, *Annual Report of the Commissioner of Indian Affairs to the Secretary of the Interior for the Year 1882* (Washington: Government Printing Office, 1881), 25–26

270. *Egan Express*, December 2, 1880.

271. *Egan Express*, December 16, 1880.

272. *Egan Express*, December 30, 1880.

273. *Janesville Argus*, December 14, 1880.

274. *Egan Express*, January 20, 1881, and March 24, 1881.

275. John C. Luecke, *Dreams, Disasters and Demise: The Milwaukee Road in Minnesota* (Eagan, MN: Grenadier, 1988), iii.

276. According to John C. Luecke, trains could, indeed, move across the prairie stealthily and go unnoticed. When drifting (cruising along with no need to be working, such as on downgrades), they can be amazingly quiet. Other factors, such as weather, wind direction, temperature, and the attentiveness of a potential victim, all play a part. Email message to author, September 23, 2019.

277. *Egan Express*, December 9, 1880.

278. *New Ulm Weekly Review*, December 15, 1880.

279. *Marshall Messenger,* December 17, 1880.

280. *Marshall Messenger*, December 17, 1880.

281. *New Ulm Weekly Review*, December 15, 1880.

282. *New Ulm Weekly Review*, December 15, 1880.

283. *Janesville Argus*, December 28, 1880.

284. John C. Luecke, email message to author, January 21, 2019.

285. *Marshall Messenger*, December 17, 1880.

286. *New Ulm Weekly Review*, December 1, 1880; and *Marshall Messenger*, December 17, 1880.

287. *New Ulm Weekly Review*, December 29, 1880.

288. *Dakota News*, December 27, 1880.

289. *Grant County Review*, December 23, 1880.

290. *New Ulm Weekly Review*, December 15, 1880.

291. *Dakota News*, Watertown, December 27, 1880.

292. *Janesville Argus*, December 7, 1880.

293. *Grant County Review*, December 9, 1880.

294. *Grant County Review*, December 23, 1880.

295. *Grant County Review*, December 30, 1880.

296. *Janesville Argus*, December 28. 1880.

297. *Janesville Argus*, December 28, 1880.

298. *Dakota News*, December 13, 1880.

299. *Brookings County Press*, December 9, 1880.

300. *Grant County Review*, December 2, 1880.

301. *Egan Express*, December 2, 1880.

302. *Grant County Review*, December 30, 1880.

303. *Grant County Review*, December 9, 1880.

304. *Ortonville Herald* (Ortonville, MN), reprinted in the *Grant County Review*, December 9, 1880.

305. *Grant County Review*, December 2, 1880.

306. *Grant County Review*, December 9, 1880.

307. Springfield Items, *New Ulm Weekly Review*, December 8, 1880.

308. *Dakota News*, December 13, 1880.

309. *Dakota News*, December 20, 1880.

310. *Janesville Argus*, December 14, 1880.

311. *Janesville Argus*, December 21, 1880.

312. Springfield Items, *New Ulm Weekly Review*, December 29, 1880.

313. *Fort Pierre Weekly Signal* (Fort Pierre, Dakota Territory), December 4, 1880.

314. *Fort Pierre Weekly Signal*, December 4, 1880.

315. *Fort Pierre Weekly Signal*, December 4, 1880.

316. *Brookings County Press*, December 16, 1880.

317. *Brookings County Press*, December 23, 1880.

318. *Dakota News*, December 27, 1880.

319. *Brookings County Press*, December 30, 1880.

320. *Brookings County Press*, December 30, 1880.

321. *Brookings County Press*, December 30, 1880.

322. *Brookings County Press*, December 30, 1880.

323. *Egan Express*, December 30, 1880.

324. *Grant County Review*, December 16, 1880.

325. *Brookings County Press*, December 9, 1880.

326. *Grant County Review*, December 9, 1880.

327. *Grant County Review*, December 16, 1880.

328. *Dakota News*, December 27, 1880.

329. *Marshall Messenger*, December 31, 1880.

January 1881

330. Laura Ingalls Wilder, *The Long Winter* (1940; repr., New York: HarperTrophy, 2004), 223; and Wilder, Manuscript, 86p.

331. Laura Ingalls Wilder, *Pioneer Girl: The Annotated Autobiography*, ed. Pamela Smith Hill (Pierre: South Dakota Historical Society Press, 2014), 223; Wilder, Brandt, 106; Wilder, Bye, 133; Wilder, *The Long Winter*, 199–204; and Wilder, Manuscript, 68p–71p.

332. Wilder, *Pioneer Girl*, 223; Wilder, Brandt, 106; and Wilder, Bye, 133.

333. Wilder, *Pioneer Girl*, 221; Wilder, Brandt, 105; Wilder, Bye, 131–132. In all versions of the autobiography, it was a man named French who butchered his oxen. In the manuscript and novel, the butchered oxen came from Foster, an already-introduced character. Wilder, *The Long Winter*, 213; and Wilder, Manuscript, 78p.

334. Wilder, *The Long Winter*, 213–223; Wilder, Manuscript, 79p–86p; Wilder, *Pioneer Girl*, 209; Wilder, Brandt, 97–98; and Wilder, Bye, 121–123.

335. Wilder, *The Long Winter*, 214; and Wilder, Manuscript, 80p. The autobiography tells the story in a matter-of-fact telling without the family interaction.

336. Wilder, *The Long Winter*, 214; and Wilder, Manuscript, p. 80p. In the novel, Pa reassures the family by saying, "There's only this month, then February is a short month, and March will be spring." In a letter to Lane dated January 6, 1938, Wilder wrote, "I am glad Christmas is over and we are started on the way toward spring. It won't be long now, just two months and one of them short." Laura Ingalls Wilder to Rose Wilder Lane, box 13, folder 194, Rose Wilder Lane Papers, Laura Ingalls Wilder Files, Herbert Hoover Presidential Library, West Branch, IA.

337. Wilder, *Pioneer Girl*, 210; Wilder, Brandt, 99; Wilder, Bye, 124–125; Wilder, *The Long Winter*, 232; and Wilder, Manuscript, 94p.

338. Wilder, *Pioneer Girl*, 210; Wilder, Brandt, 99; Wilder, Bye, 124; Wilder, *The Long Winter*, 233, 236; and Wilder, Manuscript, 94p–95p, 97p.

339. Wilder, *The Long Winter*, 238–240; and Wilder, Manuscript, 98p–99p. On page 129 of the Bye revision of the autobiography, Wilder noted, "All this did not especially dishearten us or make us gloomy. Living went on about as usual, except that each family kept more to itself, staying by its fire and being very busy. There was almost no visiting from house to house. Pa brought us news of anything that happened. We talked and joked and sang about our work as we had always done, and the greatest difference was that Pa did not play his fiddle in the evenings, but went to bed early to save fuel."

340. *Janesville Argus* (Janesville, MN), January 4, 1881.

341. *Janesville Argus*, January 25, 1881.

342. *Dakota News* (Watertown, Dakota Territory), January 17, 1881.

343. Laura Ingalls Wilder, *On the Banks of Plum Creek* (New York: HarperTrophy,

1937, 2004), 199. Citations refer to the HarperTrophy edition.

344. *Pipestone Star* (Pipestone, MN), January 20, 1881.

345. *Dakota News*, January 17, 1881.

346. *Brookings County Press* (Brookings, Dakota Territory), January 13 and January 20, 1881.

347. *Brookings County Press*, January 20, 1881.

348. *New Ulm Weekly Review* (New Ulm, MN), January 19, 1881.

349. *Egan Express* (Egan, Dakota Territory), January 20, 1881.

350. *Grant County Review* (Milbank, Dakota Territory), January 20, 1881.

351. *Murray County Pioneer* (Currie, MN), January 20, 1881.

352. *Pipestone Star*, January 20, 1881.

353. *Encycolpaedia Britannica Online*, s.v. "Mirage (Optical Illusion)" accessed August 12, 2019, https://www.britannica.com/topic/mirage-optical-illusion

354. *Pipestone Star*, January 27, 1881.

355. *Pipestone Star*, February 3, 1881.

356. *Minneapolis Tribune*, February 1, 1881.

357. *Minneapolis Tribune*, February 1, 1881.

358. *Dakota News*, January 31, 1881.

359. *Murray County Pioneer*, March 10, 1881.

360. *Janesville Argus*, January 4, 1881.

361. *Grant County Review*, January 13, 1881.

362. *Janesville Argus*, January 11, 1881.

363. *Janesville Argus*, January 11, 1881.

364. *Marshall Messenger* (Marshall, MN), January 28, 1881.

365. *New Ulm Weekly Review*, January 19, 1881.

366. Wilder, *The Long Winter*, 213; Wilder, Manuscript, 79p; Wilder, *Pioneer Girl*, 212; Wilder, Brandt, 99; and Wilder, Bye, 123.

367. *Marshall Messenger*, January 21, 1881.

368. *Fort Pierre Weekly Signal* (Fort Pierre, Dakota Territory), January 29, 1881.

369. *Murray County Pioneer*, January 20, 1881.

370. *Grant County Review*, January 20, 1881.

371. *Janesville Argus*, January 11, 1881.

372. *Grant County Review*, January 6, 1881.

373. *Grant County Review*, January 20, 1881.

374. *Grant County Review*, January 20, 1881.

375. *Grant County Review*, February 3, 1881.

376. *Janesville Argus*, January 4, 1881.

377. *New Ulm Weekly Review*, January 5, 1881.

378. *Dakota News*, January 17, 1881.

379. *Janesville Argus*, January 18, 1881.

380. *New Ulm Weekly Review*, January 26, 1881.

381. *New Ulm Weekly Review*, January 26, 1881.

382. *New Ulm Weekly Review*, January 26, 1881.

383. *New Ulm Weekly Review*, January 26, 1881.

384. *Murray County Pioneer*, January 27, 1881.

385. *Marshall Messenger*, January 28, 1881.

386. *Dakota News*, January 31, 1881.

387. *Fort Pierre Weekly Signal*, January 8, 1881.

388. *Fort Pierre Weekly Signal,* January 29 and February 5, 1881.

389. *Pipestone Star*, January 6, 1881.

390. *Egan Express*, January 6, 1881.

391. *New Ulm Weekly Review*, February 9, 1881.

392. *Pipestone Star*, January 27, 1881.

393. *Egan Express*, January 27, 1881.

394. *Egan Express*, January 27, 1881.

395. *Egan Express*, January 27, 1881.

396. *Pipestone Star*, January 20, 1881.

397. *Moody County Enterprise* (Flandreau, Dakota Territory), January 27, 1881.

398. *Brookings County Press*, January 6, 1881.

399. *Egan Express*, January 20, 1881.

400. *Brookings County Press*, January 13, 1881.

401. *Egan Express*, January 13, 1881.

402. *Janesville Argus*, January 25, 1881.

403. *Moody County Enterprise*, January 27, 1881.

404. *Pipestone Star*, January 13, 1881.

405. *Egan Express*, January 27, 1881.

406. *Pipestone Star*, January 20, 1881.

407. *Grant County Review*, January 27, 1881.

408. *Murray County Pioneer*, January 6, 1881.

409. *Murray County Pioneer*, January 6, 1881.

410. *Dakota News*, January 17, 1881.

411. *Murray County Pioneer*, January 13, 1881.

412. *Marshall Messenger*, January 28, 1881.

413. *Egan Express*, January 13, 1881.

414. *Moody County Enterprise*, January 27, 1881.

415. *Marshall Messenger*, January 14, 1881; and *New Ulm Weekly Review*, January 12, 1881. The quoted article was taken from the *Marshall Messenger*, and additional details were taken from both the *Marshall Messenger* and the *New Ulm Weekly Review*.

416. *New Ulm Weekly Review*, January 19, 1881.

417. *New Ulm Weekly Review*, January 5, 1881.

418. *Marshall Messenger*, January 28, 1881.

419. *Egan Express*, January 6, 1881.

420. *Fort Pierre Weekly Signal*, January 22, 1881.

421. *Dakota News*, January 17, 1881 and January 31, 1881.

422. *Murray County Pioneer*, January 20, 1881.

423. *Egan Express*, January 20, 1881.

424. *Janesville Argus*, January 4, 1881.

425. *Brookings County Press*, January 6, 1881.

426. *Egan Express*, January 6, 1881.

427. *Egan Express*, January 6, 1881.

428. *Grant County Review*, January 13, 1881.

429. *Janesville Argus*, January 11, 1881.

430. *St. Paul Globe*, reprinted in the *Grant Count Review*, January 13, 1881.

431. *St. Paul Globe*, reprinted in the *Grant Count Review*, January 13, 1881.

432. *St. Paul Globe*, reprinted in the *Grant Count Review*, January 13, 1881.

433. *Pipestone Star,* January 27, 1881.

434. *Moody County Enterprise*, January 27, 1881.

435. *Marshall Messenger*, January 28, 1881.

436. Calculations by Jim Hicks (retired physics instructor), using coalpail.com to calculate volume, density, and weight values. One ton represents forty cubic feet of volume, with air spaces. Variations, such as type of coal (hard, anthracite, or soft), must be taken into account. The density of coal varies greatly by type, but the coal available to the prairie towns at this time was most likely soft. The estimates used for these calculations are approximate values for bulk purchases. Email message to author, October 9, 2019.

437. *Fort Pierre Weekly Signal*, January 29, 1881.

438. *Dakota News*, January 31, 1881.

439. *Janesville Argus*, January 4, 1881.

440. *Janesville Argus*, January 4, 1881.

441. *Grant County Review*, January 13, 1881.

442. *Brookings County Press*, January 6, 1881.

443. Wilder, *Pioneer Girl*, 216n37.

444. *Janesville Argus*, January 11, 1881.

445. *New Ulm Weekly Review*, January 19 and 26, 1881.

446. Almanzo Wilder to Rose Wilder Lane, 12 March 1937, box 13, folder 193, Rose Wilder Lane Papers, Laura Ingalls Wilder Files; Wilder, *Pioneer Girl*, 221; Wilder, Brandt, 105; and Wilder, Bye, 132.

447. *Grant County Review*, January 6, 1881.

448. *Grant County Review*, January 20, 1881.

449. *Grant County Review*, January 20, 1881.

450. *Brookings County Press*, January 6, 1881.

451. *Brookings County Press*, January 20, 1881.

452. *Grant County Review*, January 27, 1881.

453. *Dakota News*, January 31, 1881.

454. *Pipestone Star*, January 27, 1881.

455. *Egan Express*, January 20, 1881.

456. *Murray County Pioneer*, January 13, 1881.

457. *Murray County Pioneer*, January 13, 1881.

458. *Moody County Enterprise*, January 20, 1881.

459. *Egan Express*, January 20, 1881.

460. *Brookings County Press*, January 20, 1881.

461. *Grant County Review*, January 20, 1881; and *Pipestone Star*, January 27, 1881.

462. *Pipestone Star*, January 13, 1881.

463. *Moody County Enterprise*, January 27, 1881.

464. *Pipestone Star*, January 27, 1881.

465. *Marshall Messenger*, January 28, 1881.

466. *Pipestone Star*, January 27, 1881.

467. *Grant County Review*, January 13, 1881.

468. *Dakota News*, January 17, 1881.

469. *Dakota News*, January 24, 1881.

470. *Dakota News*, January 24, 1881.

471. *Dakota News*, January 24, 1881.

472. *Dakota News*, January 24, 1881.

473. *Dakota News*, January 24, 1881.

474. *Dakota News*, January 24, 1881.

475. *Dakota News*, January 24, 1881.

476. *Dakota News*, January 31, 1881.

477. *Dakota News*, January 31, 1881.

478. Wilder, *The Long Winter*, 220.

479. Wilder, *Pioneer Girl*, 209; Wilder, Brandt, 97–98; Wilder, Bye, 121-123; Wilder, *The Long Winter* typed manuscript fragments with corrections by Rose, n.d., box 15, folder 240, Rose Wilder Lane Papers, Laura Ingalls Wilder Files; and Wilder, *The Long Winter*, 213–223.

480. Pamela Smith Hill, "'Will It Come to Anything?': The Story of *Pioneer Girl*," introduction to Wilder, *Pioneer Girl*, xvi. "Pioneer Girl was nonfiction, the truth as only Wilder remembered it."

481. John C. Luecke, email message to author, August 19, 2019. Wilder perhaps melded plows and locomotives in her mind, but in reality the engineers would have linked multiple locomotives, with a plow on the front engine. They would not have chained multiple plows.

482. Wilder, *Pioneer Girl*, 209; Wilder, Brandt, 97; Wilder, Bye, 122; Wilder, Manuscript, 83p; and Wilder, *The Long Winter*, 218.

483. Wilder, *Pioneer Girl*, 209; Wilder, Brandt, 97–98; Wilder, Bye, 121–123; Wilder, *The Long Winter* typed manuscript with corrections by Rose; and Wilder, *The Long Winter*, 213–223.

484. Wilder, *The Long Winter*, 220.

485. Per John C. Luecke, the efforts put forth by the railroad companies to keep the tracks clear were fruitful, even if trains remained unable to travel. The efforts were in part an attempt to triumph over nature. In the end, the companies did triumph, but it was only with the assistance of nature itself, in the form of changes in the weather including an end of the snow, ice, and cold and a return to warm weather. By pounding away at the drifts and ice throughout the winter, the railroads were knocking down barriers, and this paid dividends when spring came. A section of track may have been operational a day or two (or more) earlier than it would have been had efforts not continued throughout the winter. In addition, clearing part of the right of way of snow and especially ice would tend to limit the wear and tear "the beautiful" caused to rails, ties, bridges, and other structures. Email message to author, September 23, 2019.

486. *Minneapolis Tribune*, February 1, 1881.

487. *Janesville Argus*, February 8, 1881.

488. *Moody County Enterprise*, February 24, 1881.

489. I admit, I exaggerate the tedium of the research here for effect. Truly, I enjoyed all of the research phase, the thrill of the hunt for information. Scrolling, scrolling, scrolling did become tiresome sometimes,

and my eyes did, on occasion, gloss over so that I had to rescroll, rescroll, rescroll to make sure I didn't miss anything. But just as I started to think that I wasn't going to find the article I was looking for, there it—or at least an excellent candidate—was.

490. In memoriam: As I was excitedly reading the article through the microfilm glass, my phone rang. It was my ex-husband, with news that his father, John Miles Lundahl, one of the most kind and gentle humans I have ever known, had passed away. The emotions of the moment, of excitement and loss, mixed together, and I think of Miles when I remember the discovery.

491. *Egan Express*, February 24, 1881.

492. Angus Sinclair, "Locomotive Engine Running: A Treatise on the Economical Management of the Locomotive Engine on the Road and in the Round House," *Railway Age Monthly and Railway Service Magazine* 3, no. 1 (January 1882): 403.

493. Sinclair, "Locomotive Engine Running."

494. Sinclair, "Locomotive Engine Running."

495. Sinclair, "Locomotive Engine Running."

496. Sinclair, "Locomotive Engine Running."

497. Sinclair, "Locomotive Engine Running."

498. Sinclair, "Locomotive Engine Running."

499. Sinclair, "Locomotive Engine Running."

500. Sinclair, "Locomotive Engine Running."

February 1881

501. Laura Ingalls Wilder, *The Long Winter* (1940; repr., New York: HarperTrophy, 2004), 252.

502. Wilder, *The Long Winter*, 244; and Wilder, Manuscript, 104p. In the autobiographies, it was not presented as a rumor but rather stated as fact. Laura Ingalls Wilder, *Pioneer Girl: The Annotated Autobiography*, ed. Pamela Smith Hill (Pierre: South Dakota Historical Society Press, 2014), 220; Wilder, Brandt, 104; and Wilder, Bye, 130.

503. Wilder, *The Long Winter*, 244–245; Wilder, Manuscript, 104p–105p. In the autobiographies, Wilder said that no one was willing to undertake the dangerous trek until Almanzo and Cap stepped forward. Wilder, *Pioneer Girl*, 220; Wilder, Brandt, 104; and Wilder, Bye, 131.

504. Wilder, *Pioneer Girl*, 220; Wilder, Brandt, 104; Wilder, Bye, 130; Wilder, *The Long Winter*, 247; and Wilder, Manuscript, 106p–108p. In a letter to Lane dated March 7, 1938, Wilder, speaking of human nature, noted, "We were shorter on food than anyone later and they gave Pa breakfast and let him have wheat. If anyone had been without food they would have divided but if the town had known the wheat was there there would have been a rush for it and even those who didn't need it badly would have taken as much as anyone." Laura Ingalls Wilder to Rose Wilder Lane, box 13, folder 194, Rose Wilder Lane Papers,

Laura Ingalls Wilder Files, Herbert Hoover Presidential Library, West Branch, IA.

505. Wilder, *The Long Winter*, 252.

506. Wilder, *The Long Winter*, 255–259, 262; and Wilder, Manuscript, 114p–117p. In the autobiographies, there is only a mention that volunteers for the dangerous attempt were hard to find until "the young Wilder boy" and Cap stepped forward. In *Pioneer Girl* and the Brandt version, Almanzo is listed first, but in the Bye version, Cap is first. Wilder, *Pioneer Girl*, 220; Wilder, Brandt, 104; and Wilder, Bye, 130–131.

507. Wilder, *The Long Winter*, 257; and Wilder, Manuscript, 102p. On page 102p of the manuscript, a note in Wilder's handwriting notes, "Almanzo had 30 bu. of seed wheat . . . he does not think the train will bring in wheat in time for sowing, knowing blizzards will likely come in March, and wheat must be sown in April. If he has no seed he loses the whole year. Reason enough to take a chance to get wheat to eat. He and Cap got 30 bu. each. Sixty bu. to last through 2 weeks of February and all of March and April into May." Almanzo, in corresponding with Lane, noted that he had brought 50 bushels to Dakota from his harvest in Marshall, Minnesota. Almanzo Wilder to Rose Wilder Lane, 23 March 1937, box 13, folder 193, Rose Wilder Lane Papers, Laura Ingalls Wilder Files.

508. Wilder, *The Long Winter,* 264; Wilder, *Pioneer Girl,* 220; Wilder, Brandt, 104–105; Wilder, Bye, 131; and Wilder, *The Long Winter,* Typed final manuscript (carbon) with corrections by Laura and Rose, Parts of Chapter 27 and 29, n.d., box 15, folder 240, page 231, Rose Wilder Lane Papers, Laura Ingalls Wilder Files. The earliest autobiography indicates a "clear, still, cold day"; Brandt changes this to a "clear, cold morning," and Bye changes it to a "clear, cold dawn."

509. Wilder, *The Long Winter,* 287. I've often wondered whether one of the intentions of this outburst, within the story arc, was to convey that Pa felt a little guilty for not having gone after the seed wheat himself, instead of "the young Wilder boy and Cap Garland" being the ones in harm's way.

510. Wilder, *The Long Winter,* 297. In a letter to Lane dated March 7, 1939, Wilder noted that, "Manly did go after the wheat to feed the town so they might keep their own for seed. Risking his life for his seed wheat. He got it before anyone went hungry." Laura Ingalls Wilder to Rose Wilder Lane, box 13, folder 194, Rose Wilder Lane Papers, Laura Ingalls Wilder Files.

511. Wilder, *The Long Winter,* 306.

512. *Grant County Review* (Milbank, Dakota Territory), February 17, 1881.

513. *Janesville Argus* (Janesville, MN), February 15, 1881.

514. *New Ulm Weekly Review* (New Ulm, MN), February 9, 1881.

515. Marshall Messenger (Marshall, MN), February 11, 1881.

516. Wilder, *The Long Winter,* 225, 230; and Wilder, Manuscript, 88p.

517. *Marshall Messenger,* February 11, 1881.

518. Wilder, *Pioneer Girl,* 217, 219; Wilder, Brandt, 102–103; Wilder, Bye, 128; Wilder, *The Long Winter,* 155; Wilder, Manuscript, 34p.

519. *Pipestone Star* (Pipestone, MN), February 3, 1881.

520. *Pipestone Star,* February 10, 1881.

521. *Murray County Pioneer* (Currie, MN), February 10, 1881.

522. *Egan Express* (Egan, Dakota Territory), February 10, 1881.

523. *Grant County Review,* February 10, 1881.

524. *Grant County Review,* February 10, 1881.

525. *Janesville Argus,* February 8, 1881.

526. *Pipestone Star,* February 17, 1881.

527. Wilder, *The Long Winter,* 232–233; and Wilder, *Pioneer Girl,* 210.

528. *Egan Express,* February 17, 1881.

529. *Egan Express,* February 17, 1881.

530. *New Ulm Weekly Review,* February 16, 1881.

531. Wilder, *Pioneer Girl,* 210; Wilder, Brandt, 99; Wilder, Bye, 124–125; Wilder, *The Long Winter,* 232; and Wilder, Manuscript, 94p.

532. *Moody County Enterprise* (Flandreau, Dakota Territory), February 24, 1881.

533. *Pipestone Star,* February 24, 1881.

534. *New Ulm Weekly Review,* February 23, 1881.

535. *Egan Express,* February 24, 1881.

536. *Egan Express,* February 24, 1881.

537. *Marshall Messenger,* February 25, 1881.

538. *Murray County Pioneer,* March 10, 1881.

539. *New Ulm Weekly Review,* March 2, 1881.

540. *Moody County Enterprise,* February 24, 1881.

541. *New Ulm Weekly Review,* February 16, 1881.

542. *New Ulm Weekly Review,* February 16, 1881.

543. *New Ulm Weekly Review,* February 16, 1881.

544. *New Ulm Weekly Review,* February 16, 1881.

545. *New Ulm Weekly Review,* February 16, 1881.

546. *Grant County News,* February 3, 1881.

547. *Pipestone Star,* February 17, 1881.

548. *Moody County Enterprise,* February 3, 1881.

549. *Grant County Review,* February 17, 1881.

550. *Janesville Argus,* February 1, 1881.

551. *Janesville Argus,* February 1, 1881.

552. *New Ulm Weekly Review,* February 2, 1881.

553. *Janesville Argus,* February 8, 1881.

554. *Janesville Argus,* February 8, 1881.

555. *New Ulm Weekly Review,* February 9, 1881.

556. *New Ulm Weekly Review,* February 9, 1881.

557. *New Ulm Weekly Review,* February 9, 1881.

558. Springfield Items, *New Ulm Weekly Review,* February 9, 1881.

559. *Marshall Messenger,* February 11, 1881.

560. *Janesville Argus,* February 15, 1881.

561. *Janesville Argus,* February 22, 1881.

562. *Janesville Argus,* February 22, 1881.

563. *Pioneer Press* (St. Paul, MN), reprinted in the *Janesville Argus*, March 8, 1881.

564. *Egan Express*, February 10, 1881.

565. *Moody County Enterprise*, February 24, 1881.

566. *Pipestone Star*, February 3, 1881.

567. *Pipestone Star*, February 3, 1881.

568. *Pipestone Star*, February 10, 1881.

569. *Egan Express*, February 10, 1881.

570. *Egan Express*, February 10, 1881.

571. *Egan Express*, February 10, 1881.

572. *Egan Express*, February 10, 1881.

573. *Janesville Argus*, February 22, 1881.

574. *Pipestone Star*, February 17, 1881.

575. *Egan Express*, February 24, 1881.

576. *Egan Express*, February 24, 1881.

577. *Dell Rapids Exponent* (Dell Rapids, Dakota Territory), February 26, 1881.

578. *Janesville Argus*, March 1, 1881.

579. *Egan Express*, February 24, 1881.

580. *Minneapolis Tribune*, February 1, 1881.

581. *New Ulm Weekly Review*, February 16, 1881.

582. *Moody County Enterprise*, February 24, 1881.

583. *New Ulm Weekly Review*, February 9, 1881.

584. *Janesville Argus*, February 22, 1881.

585. *Moody County Enterprise*, February 3, 1881.

586. *Redwood Gazette* (Redwood Falls, MN), reprinted in the *New Ulm Weekly Review*, February 2, 1881.

587. *Janesville Argus*, February 22, 1881.

588. Wilder, *Pioneer Girl*, 210, 212; Wilder, Brandt, 98; and Wilder, Bye, 123.

589. *New Ulm Weekly Review*, February 23, 1881.

590. *Marshall Messenger*, February 25, 1881.

591. *Fort Pierre Weekly Signal* (Fort Pierre, Dakota Territory), February 12, 1881.

592. *Fort Pierre Weekly Signal*, February 19, 1881.

593. *Fort Pierre Weekly Signal*, February 26, 1881.

594. *Egan Express*, February 17, 1881.

595. *Murray County Pioneer*, February 17, 1881.

596. *New Ulm Weekly Review*, February 16, 1881.

597. *Grant County Review*, February 10, 1881.

598. *New Ulm Weekly Review*, February 9, 1881 (misprinted in original header as February 6).

599. *Murray County Pioneer*, February 10, 1881.

600. *Marshall Messenger*, February 11, 1881.

601. *Janesville Argus*, March 8, 1881.

602. *Janesville Argus*, March 8, 1881.

603. *Janesville Argus*, March 8, 1881.

604. *Marshall Messenger*, February 25, 1881.

605. *Pipestone Star*, February 17, 1881.

606. *Egan Express*, February 24, 1881.

607. *Sioux Valley News* (Canton, Dakota Territory), February 25, 1881.

608. Wilder, *Pioneer Girl*, 223; Wilder, Brandt, 106; Wilder, Bye, 133; Wilder, *The Long Winter,* 199; and Wilder, Manuscript, 68p.

609. *Moody County Enterprise*, February 24, 1881.

610. *Egan Express*, February 17, 1881.

611. *Moody County Enterprise*, February 3, 1881.

612. *New Ulm Weekly Review*, February 9, 1881.

613. Wilder, *The Long Winter,* 258.

614. Wilder, *Pioneer Girl*, 220–221; Wilder, Brandt, 104–105; Wilder, Bye, 130–131; Wilder, Manuscript, 104p–149p; Wilder, "For Daily Bread," in *The Long Winter,* 264–284; and Wilder, "The Last Mile," in *The Long Winter,* 294–307.

615. Wilder, *Pioneer Girl*, 220–221, Wilder, Brandt, 104–105; Wilder, Bye, 130–131; Wilder, Manuscript, 104p–149p; Wilder, "For Daily Bread"; and Wilder, "The Last Mile."

616. Wilder, *Pioneer Girl*, 220–221, Wilder, Brandt, 104–105; Wilder, Bye, 130–131; Wilder, Manuscript, 104p–149p; Wilder, "For Daily Bread"; and Wilder, "The Last Mile."

617. Wilder, *Pioneer Girl*, 220–221, Wilder, Brandt, 104–105; Wilder, Bye, 130–131; Wilder, Manuscript, 104p–149p; Wilder, "For Daily Bread"; and Wilder, "The Last Mile."

618. Wilder, *Pioneer Girl*, 220–221, Wilder, Brandt, 104–105; Wilder, Bye, 130–131; Wilder, Manuscript, 104p–149p; Wilder, "For Daily Bread"; and Wilder, "The Last Mile."

619. Wilder, *Pioneer Girl*, 220–221, Wilder, Brandt, 104–105; Wilder, Bye, 130–131; Wilder, Manuscript, 104p–149p; Wilder, "For Daily Bread"; and Wilder, "The Last Mile."

620. Wilder, *Pioneer Girl*, 220–221, Wilder, Brandt, 104–105; Wilder, Bye, 130–131; Wilder, Manuscript, 104p–149p; Wilder,

"For Daily Bread"; and Wilder, "The Last Mile."

621. Laura Ingalls Wilder to Rose Wilder Lane, 7 March 1938, box 13, folder 194, Rose Wilder Lane Papers, Laura Ingalls Wilder Files; and Laura Ingalls Wilder, notation with page 102 in Laura's list of corrections to the manuscript of *The Long Winter*, n.d., box 15, folder 238, Rose Wilder Lane Papers, Laura Ingalls Wilder Files.

622. Laura Ingalls Wilder to Rose Wilder Lane, 20 March 1937 (Monday addition), box 13, folder 193, Rose Wilder Lane Papers, Laura Ingalls Wilder Files.

623. Almanzo Wilder to Rose Wilder Lane, 23 March 1937, box 13, folder 193, Rose Wilder Lane Papers, Laura Ingalls Wilder Files.

624. Rose Wilder Lane and Almanzo Wilder, Rose's Questionnaire for Almanzo Wilder on Dakota Territory, n.d., box 33, folder 421, Rose Wilder Lane Papers, Manuscripts.

625. *New Ulm Weekly Review*, February 16, 1881.

626. *Grant County Review*, February 3, 1881.

627. *Janesville Argus*, March 8, 1881.

628. Laura Ingalls Wilder to Rose Wilder Lane, 23 March 1937, box 13, folder 193, Rose Wilder Lane Papers, Laura Ingalls Wilder Files.

629. *Egan Express*, February 10, 1881.

630. *New Ulm Weekly Review*, February 9, 1881.

631. *Marshall Messenger,* February 25, 1881.

632. *New Ulm Weekly Review*, February 16, 1881.

633. *New Ulm Weekly Review*, February 16, 1881.

634. *Janesville Argus*, February 22, 1881.

635. *Pioneer Press*, reprinted in the *New Ulm Weekly Review*, February 23, 1881.

636. *New Ulm Weekly Review*, February 23, 1881.

637. *Murray County Pioneer*, February 10, 1881.

638. *Janesville Argus*, March 8, 1881.

639. *Murray County Pioneer*, February 3, 1881.

640. *Fort Pierre Weekly Signal*, February 5, 1881.

641. *Pipestone Star*, February 17, 1881.

642. *Pipestone Star*, February 3, 1881.

643. *Moody County Enterprise*, February 10, 1881.

644. *Sioux Valley News*, February 25, 1881.

645. *Pipestone Star*, February 10, 1881.

646. *Moody County Enterprise*, February 10, 1881.

647. *Moody County Enterprise*, February 10, 1881.

648. *Moody County Enterprise*, February 10, 1881.

649. *Pipestone Star*, February 24, 1881; and *Egan Express*, February 24, 1881.

650. *Egan Express*, February 24, 1881.

651. *Grant County Review*, February 3, 1881.

652. *Janesville Argus*, February 8, 1881.

653. *New Ulm Weekly Review,* February 9, 1881.

654. *New Ulm Weekly Review,* February 9, 1881.

655. *Marshall Messenger*, February 11, 1881.

656. *New Ulm Weekly Review*, February 16, 1881.

657. *New Ulm Weekly Review*, February 16, 1881.

658. *New Ulm Weekly Review*, February 16, 1881.

659. *Winona Republican*, reprinted in the *Janesville Argus*, February 15, 1881.

660. *Fort Pierre Weekly Signal*, February 19, 1881.

661. *Fort Pierre Weekly Signal*, February 19, 1881.

662. *Janesville Argus*, March 8, 1881.

663. *Moody County Enterprise*, February 3, 1881.

664. *Moody County Enterprise*, February 10, 1881.

665. *Pipestone Star*, February 17, 1881.

666. *Moody County Enterprise*, February 10, 1881.

667. *Egan Express*, February 3, 1881.

668. *Egan Express*, February 10, 1881.

669. *Moody County Enterprise*, February 10, 1881.

670. *Moody County Enterprise*, February 10, 1881.

671. *Moody County Enterprise*, February 10, 1881.

672. *Egan Express,* February 10, 1881.

673. *Egan Express*, February 17, 1881.

674. *Egan Express*, February 24, 1881.

675. *Janesville Argus*, February 8, 1881.

676. One possibility was always the river; however, an article from the *Fort Pierre Weekly Signal* of March 19, 1881, mentioned having to wait "until the river breaks up and boats begin to run," reducing the probability that goods could reach the community via the waterway.

677. *Fort Pierre Weekly Signal*, February 12, 1881.

678. *Marshall Messenger*, Marshall MN, February 11, 1881.

679. *New Ulm Weekly Review*, February 16, 1881.

680. *Janesville Argus*, February 8, 1881.

681. *Moody County Enterprise*, February 10, 1881.

682. *Dell Rapids Exponent*, February 26, 1881.

683. *Moody County Enterprise*, February 24, 1881.

684. *Grant County Review*, March 3, 1881.

685. *Janesville Argus*, February 15, 1881.

686. *Grant County Review*, February 3, 1881.

687. *Grant County Review*, February 10, 1881.

688. *Egan Express*, February 24, 1881.

689. *Moody County Enterprise*, February 10, 1881.

690. *Moody County Enterprise*, February 3, 1881.

691. *Grant County Review*, February 10, 1881.

692. *Moody County Enterprise*, February 3, 1881.

693. *Moody County Enterprise*, February 3, 1881.

694. *Moody County Enterprise*, February 10, 1881.

695. Aubrey Sherwood, *Beginnings of DeSmet: "Little Town on The Prairie" Locale of Six Books of Laura Ingalls Wilder* (De Smet, SD: printed by the author, 1979), 8, 39–40.

696. Wilder, *Pioneer Girl*, 212; and Wilder, Brandt, 98.

697. Wilder, *Pioneer Girl*, 219; Wilder, Brandt, 103; Wilder, Bye, 129; Wilder, *The Long Winter,* 143; and Wilder, Manuscript, 25p.

698. Wilder, *Pioneer Girl*, 219; Wilder, Brandt, 103; Wilder, Bye, 129; Wilder, *The Long Winter,* 143; and Wilder, Manuscript, 25p. According to an annotation in *Pioneer Girl*, "When Wilder and her husband visited Florence [the teacher] in De Smet in 1931, they 'talked of the old days of the hard winter when she taught the school before it was closed for lack of fuel and because it was too dangerous to go to the schoolhouse.' " 206n14.

March 1881

699. Laura Ingalls Wilder, *The Long Winter* (1940; repr., New York: HarperTrophy, 2004), 309.

700. Wilder, *The Long Winter*, 308–309.

701. Laura Ingalls Wilder, *Pioneer Girl: The Annotated Autobiography*, ed. Pamela Smith Hill (Pierre: South Dakota Historical Society Press, 2014), 221–223; Wilder, Brandt, 106; and Wilder, Bye, 132.

702. Wilder, *The Long Winter*, 309.

703. *Brookings County Press* (Brookings, Dakota Territory), March 24, 1881.

704. *Grant County Review* (Milbank, Dakota Territory), March 10, 1881.

705. Elden Lawrence, "Lorenzo Lawrence (Towanetaton)," interview by Deborah Locke, U.S.-Dakota War of 1862, Minnesota Historical Society, April 12, 2011, accessed August 18, 2018, http://www.usdakotawar.org/node/1297.

706. *Pipestone Star* (Pipestone, MN), March 10, 1881.

707. *Janesville Argus* (Janesville, MN), March 15, 1881.

708. *Canton Advocate* (Canton, Dakota Territory), March 10, 1881.

709. *Elk Point Tribune* (Elk Point, Dakota Territory), March 8, 1881.

710. Tracy Correspondence, *New Ulm Weekly Review* (New Ulm, MN), March 16, 1881.

711. *Marshall Messenger* (Marshall, MN), March 11, 1881.

712. *Moody County Enterprise* (Flandreau, Dakota Territory), March 17, 1881; and *Brookings County Press* (Brookings, Dakota Territory), March 31, 1881.

713. *New Ulm Weekly Review*, March 16, 1881.

714. *Moody County Enterprise*, March 17, 1881.

715. *Moody County Enterprise*, March 17, 1881.

716. *Moody County Enterprise*, March 17, 1881.

717. *Egan Express* (Egan, Dakota Territory), March 17, 1881.

718. *Dell Rapids Exponent* (Dell Rapids, Dakota Territory), March 19, 1881.

719. *Egan Express*, March 17, 1881.

720. *Dell Rapids Exponent*, March 19, 1881

721. *Sioux Valley Journal* (Brookings, Dakota Territory), March 18, 1881.

722. *Moody County Enterprise*, March 17, 1881.

723. *Marshall Messenger*, March 18, 1881.

724. *Pipestone Star*, March 24, 1881.

725. *Egan Express*, March 10, 1881.

726. *Janesville Argus*, March 15, 1881.

727. *Fort Pierre Weekly Signal* (Fort Pierre, Dakota Territory), March 19, 1881.

728. *Egan Express*, March 24, 1881.

729. *New Ulm Weekly Review*, March 23, 1881.

730. *Janesville Argus*, April 5, 1881.

731. *Pipestone Star*, April 7, 1881.

732. *Dell Rapids Exponent*, April 2, 1881.

733. *Grant County Review*, April 7, 1881.

734. *New Ulm Weekly Review*, March 30, 1881.

735. *Fort Pierre Weekly Signal*, February 26, 1881.

736. *Fort Pierre Weekly Signal*, March 19, 1881.

737. *Brookings County Press*, March 31, 1881.

738. *Elk Point Tribune*, March 8, 1881.

739. *Dell Rapids Exponent*, April 2, 1881.

740. *Canton Advocate*, March 10, 1881.

741. *Brookings County Press*, March 31, 1881.

742. *New Ulm Weekly Review*, March 2, 1881.

743. *Dell Rapids Exponent*, March 26, 1881.

744. *Elk Point Tribune*, March 8, 1881.

745. *Dell Rapids Exponent*, March 26, 1881.

746. John C. Luecke, email message to author, October 29, 2019.

747. George Washington Kingsbury, *History of Dakota Territory*, ed. George Martin Smith (Chicago: S.J. Clarke, 1915), 2:1157–1158.

748. Kingsbury, *History of Dakota Territory*, 2:1157–1158.

749. Kingsbury, *History of Dakota Territory*, 2:1157–1158.

750. Kingsbury, *History of Dakota Territory*, 2:1157–1158.

751. *Fort Pierre Weekly Signal,* March 26, 1881.

752. Aubrey Sherwood, *Beginnings of DeSmet: "Little Town on The Prairie" Locale of Six Books of Laura Ingalls Wilder* (De Smet, SD: printed by the author, 1979), 8, 39–40.

753. *Janesville Argus*, March 8, 1881.

754. H. A. (Al) Stimson, *Depot Days* (Boynton Beach, FL: Star, 1972), 41.

755. *Moody County Enterprise*, March 3, 1881.

756. *New Ulm Weekly Review*, March 23, 1881.

757. *Grant County Review*, March 24, 1881.

758. *Grant County Review*, March 31, 1881.

759. *Grant County Review*, March 31, 1881.

760. *Grant County Review*, March 31, 1881.

761. *Marshall Messenger*, March 4, 1881.

762. *Marshall Messenger*, March 4, 1881.

763. *Egan Express*, March 10, 1881.

764. *New Ulm Weekly Review*, March 9, 1881.

765. *Janesville Argus*, March 15, 1881.

766. *Janesville Argus*, March 8, 1881.

767. *New Ulm Weekly Review*, March 16, 1881.

768. *New Ulm Weekly Review*, March 16, 1881.

769. *New Ulm Weekly Review*, March 16, 1881.

770. *New Ulm Weekly Review*, March 16, 1881.

771. *Marshall Messenger*, March 18, 1881.

772. *New Ulm Weekly Review*, March 16, 1881.

773. *Salem Register* (Salem, Dakota Territory), March 18, 1881; and *Janesville Argus*, March 22, 1881.

774. *Fort Pierre Weekly Signal*, March 19, 1881.

775. *New Ulm Weekly Review*, March 23, 1881.

776. *Marshall Messenger*, March 25, 1881.

777. *New Ulm Weekly Review*, March 30, 1881.

778. *Marshall Messenger*, March 25, 1881.

779. *New Ulm Weekly Review*, March 30, 1881.

780. *Brookings County Press*, March 31, 1881.

781. *Brookings County Press*, March 24, 1881.

782. *Fort Pierre Weekly Signal*, March 26, 1881.

783. *Pipestone Star*, March 10, 1881.

784. *Egan Express*, March 10, 1881.

785. *Pipestone Star*, March 17, 1881.

786. *Moody County Enterprise*, March 17, 1881.

787. *Dell Rapids Exponent*, March 19, 1881.

788. *Dell Rapids Exponent*, March 19, 1881.

789. *Pipestone Star*, March 24, 1881.

790. *Egan Express*, March 24, 1881.

791. *Pipestone Star*, March 31, 1881.

792. *Janesville Argus*, March 15, 1881.

793. *Grant County Review*, March 31, 1881.

794. "Inflation Calculator: 1881 Dollars in 2019," Official Data Foundation, Alioth LLC, https://www.officialdata.org/us/inflation/1881. For further details on this source, see note 2.

795. *Moody County Enterprise*, March 31, 1881.

796. John C. Luecke, email message to author, October 29, 2019.

797. *Egan Express*, March 24, 1881.

798. *Dell Rapids Exponent*, March 26, 1881.

799. Daniel Porter, "What Is Photokeratitis—Including Snow Blindness?," reviewed by J. Kevin McKinney, EyeSmart Eye Health A–Z, American Academy of Ophthalmology, accessed September 28, 2019, https://www.aao.org/eye-health/diseases/photokeratitis-snow-blindness.

800. Wilder, *The Long Winter*, 174; and Wilder, Manuscript, 49p.

801. *Janesville Argus*, March 8, 1881.

802. *Grant County Review*, March 31, 1881.

803. *Egan Express*, March 10, 1881.

804. *Janesville Argus*, March 22, 1881.

805. *New Ulm Weekly Review*, March 16, 1881.

806. *New Ulm Weekly Review*, March 30, 1881.

807. *New Ulm Weekly Review*, March 23, 1881.

808. *Marshall Messenger*, March 4, 1881.

809. *Elk Point Tribune*, March 8, 1881.

810. *New Ulm Weekly Review*, March 9, 1881.

811. *New Ulm Weekly Review*, March 9, 1881.

812. *Egan Express*, March 10 and 17, 1881.

813. *Grant County Review*, March 24, 1881.

814. *Brookings County Press*, March 24, 1881.

815. Wilder expressed such beliefs multiple times in correspondence with Rose Wilder Lane. One such mention can be found in a letter dated March 7, 1938. Laura Ingalls Wilder to Rose Wilder Lane, box 13, folder 194, Rose Wilder Lane Papers, Laura Ingalls Wilder Files, Herbert Hoover Presidential Library, West Branch, IA.

816. *New Ulm Weekly Review*, March 2, 1881.

817. *Fort Pierre Weekly Signal*, March 19, 1881.

818. *Marshall Messenger*, March 4, 1881.

819. *Marshall Messenger*, March 18, 1881.

820. *Dakota News* (Watertown, Dakota Territory), March 21, 1881.

821. *Sioux Valley Journal*, March 18, 1881.

822. *Sioux Valley Journal*, March 18, 1881.

823. *Fort Pierre Weekly Signal*, March 5, 1881.

824. *Fort Pierre Weekly Signal*, March 19, 1881.

825. *Moody County Enterprise*, March 3, 1881.

826. *Dell Rapids Exponent*, March 19, 1881.

827. *Moody County Enterprise*, March 3, 1881.

828. *Pipestone Star*, March 3, 1881.

829. *Pipestone Star,* March 24, 1881.

830. *Moody County Enterprise*, March 17, 1881.

831. *Moody County Enterprise*, March 3, 1881.

832. *Egan Express*, March 17, 1881.

833. *Dell Rapids Exponent*, March 19, 1881.

834. *Lake County Leader* (Madison, Dakota Territory), March 19, 1881

835. *Lake County Leader*, March 19, 1881.

836. *Canton Advocate*, March 3, 1881.

837. *New Era* (Parker, Dakota Territory, and Swan Lake, Dakota Territory), March 5, 1881.

838. *Murray County Pioneer* (Currie, MN), March 3, 1881.

839. *New Era*, March 5, 1881.

840. *Moody County Enterprise*, March 17, 1881.

841. *Pipestone Star*, March 17, 1881.

842. *Fort Pierre Weekly Signal*, March 19, 1881.

843. *Sioux Valley Journal*, March 18, 1881.

844. *Pipestone Star*, March 24, 1881.

845. *Brookings County Press*, March 31, 1881.

846. *Madison Sentinel* (Madison, Dakota Territory), March 4, 1881.

847. *New Ulm Weekly Review*, March 2, 1881.

848. *New Ulm Weekly Review*, March 2, 1881.

849. *New Ulm Weekly Review*, March 9, 1881.

850. Sherwood, *Beginnings of DeSmet*, 8, 39–40.

851. Laura Ingalls Wilder to Rose Wilder Lane, 7 March 1938, box 13, folder 194, Rose Wilder Lane Papers, Laura Ingalls Wilder Files.

852. *Brookings County Press*, March 31, 1881.

853. *Fort Pierre Weekly Signal*, March 12, 1881.

854. *Fort Pierre Weekly Signal*, March 26, 1881.

855. *New Ulm Weekly Review*, March 9, 1881.

856. *Janesville Argus*, March 15, 1881.

857. *New Ulm Weekly Review*, March 16, 1881.

858. *New Ulm Weekly Review*, March 16, 1881.

859. *New Ulm Weekly Review*, March 16, 1881.

860. *Dell Rapids Exponent*, March 19, 1881.

861. *Lake County Leader*, March 19, 1881.

862. *Moody County Enterprise*, March 31, 1881.

863. *Canton Advocate*, March 3, 1881.

864. August Derleth, *The Milwaukee Road: Its First Hundred Years* (New York: Creative Age Press, 1948), 244.

865. *Canton Advocate*, March 3, 1881.

866. *New Era*, March 5, 1881.

867. *Elk Point Tribune*, March 8, 1881.

868. *Murray County Pioneer*, March 3, 1881.

869. *Moody County Enterprise*, March 3, 1881.

870. *Grant County Review*, March 24, 1881.

871. *Grant County Review*, March 31, 1881.

872. *Marshall Messenger*, March 4, 1881.

873. *Marshall Messenger*, March 11, 1881.

874. *New Ulm Weekly Review*, March 30, 1881.

875. *New Ulm Weekly Review*, March 30, 1881.

876. *New Ulm Weekly Review*, March 30, 1881.

877. *Brookings County Press*, March 31, 1881.

878. *Brookings County Press*, March 31, 1881.

879. *Brookings County Press*, March 31, 1881.

880. *Fort Pierre Weekly Signal*, March 19, 1881.

881. *Dell Rapids Exponent*, March 19, 1881.

882. *Madison Sentinel*, March 11, 1881.

883. *Egan Express*, March 10, 1881.

884. *Egan Express*, March 31, 1881.

885. *Elk Point Tribune*, March 8, 1881.

886. *Moody County Enterprise*, March 3, 1881.

887. *Marshall Messenger,* March 4, 1881.

888. *Grant County Review*, March 3, 1881.

889. *Madison Sentinel*, March 4, 1881.

890. *Madison Sentinel*, March 4, 1881.

891. *Lake County Leader*, March 19, 1881.

892. *Egan Express*, March 24, 1881.

893. *Pipestone Star*, March 3, 1881.

894. *New Ulm Weekly Review*, March 2, 1881.

895. *Fort Pierre Weekly Signal*, March 5, 1881.

896. *Elk Point Tribune*, March 8, 1881.

897. *Janesville Argus*, March 15, 1881.

898. *New Ulm Weekly Review*, March 23, 1881.

899. *Brookings County Press*, March 31, 1881.

900. *Brookings County Press*, March 31, 1881.

901. *Brookings County Press*, March 31, 1881.

902. Derleth, *The Milwaukee Road*, 244.

903. Wilder, *The Long Winter*, 106.

April/May 1881

904. Laura Ingalls Wilder, *The Long Winter* (1940; repr., New York: Harper Trophy, 2004), 312.

905. Wilder, *The Long Winter*, 309–310.

906. Wilder, *The Long Winter*, 315

907. Wilder, *The Long Winter*, 311; and Wilder, Manuscript, 274.

908. Wilder, *The Long Winter*, 316; Wilder, *Pioneer Girl: The Annotated Autobiography*, ed. Pamela Smith Hill (Pierre: South Dakota Historical Society Press, 2014), 225; Wilder, Brandt, 107; and Wilder, Bye, 133–134. In the Bye version of the autobiography, it was noted that men were working east of Tracy.

909. Wilder, *The Long Winter*, 315–316.

910. Wilder, *The Long Winter*, 320.

911. Wilder, *The Long Winter*, 321.

912. Wilder, *The Long Winter*, 321.

913. Wilder, *The Long Winter* typed final manuscript (carbon) with corrections by Laura and Rose, Parts of Chapter 27 and 29, n.d., box 15, folder 240, Rose Wilder Lane Papers, Laura Ingalls Wilder Files, Herbert Hoover Presidential Library, West Branch, IA.

914. Almanzo Wilder to Rose Wilder Lane, 23 March 1937, box 13, folder 193, Rose Wilder Lane Papers, Laura Ingalls Wilder Files.

915. *Murray County Pioneer* (Currie, MN), April 7, 1881.

916. *Marshall Messenger* (Marshall, MN), April 1, 1881.

917. *New Ulm Weekly* (New Ulm, MN), April 6, 1881.

918. *New Ulm Weekly Review*, April 13, 1881.

919. *Brookings County Press* (Brookings, Dakota Territory), April 7, 1881.

920. *Dell Rapids Exponent* (Dell Rapids, Dakota Territory), April 23, 1881.

921. *Pipestone Star* (Pipestone, MN), April 14, 1881.

922. *New Ulm Weekly Review*, April 20, 1881.

923. *New Ulm Weekly Review*, April 13, 1881.

924. *Janesville Argus* (Janesville, MN), April 19, 1881.

925. *Dakota Pantagraph and Sioux Falls Independent* (Sioux Falls, Dakota Territory), April 13, 1881.

926. *Sioux Falls Times* (Sioux Falls, Dakota Territory), April 12, 1881.

927. *Pipestone Star*, April 14, 1881.

928. *Grant County Review* (Milbank Dakota Territory), April 21, 1881.

929. *Grant County Review*, April 14, 1881.

930. *Grant County Review*, April 21, 1881.

931. *New Ulm Weekly Review*, April 20, 1881.

932. *Murray County Pioneer*, April 28, 1881.

933. *Egan Express* (Egan, Dakota Territory), April 7, 1881.

934. Joel Ebert, "The Great Flood: Recalling the Missouri River Flood and Ice Gorges of 1881," *Capital Journal* (Pierre, SD), January 31, 2014, https://www.capjournal.com/news/the-great-flood-

recalling-the-missouri-river-flood-and-ice/ article_74bb4c08-8a3e-11e3-9ea6- 0019bb2963f4.html.

935. *Canton Advocate* (Canton, Dakota Territory), April 7, 1881, reprinted in the *Egan Express*, April 14, 1881.

936. *Egan Express*, April 21, 1881.

937. *Moody County Enterprise* (Flandreau, Dakota Territory), May 5, 1881.

938. *Egan Express*, April 28, 1881.

939. *Egan Express*, April 28, 1881.

940. *Egan Express*, April 28, 1881.

941. *Egan Express*, April 28, 1881.

942. *Sioux Falls Times*, April 19, 1881.

943. *Sioux Falls Times*, April 19, 1881.

944. Sleepy Eye Items, *New Ulm Weekly Review*, April 20, 1881.

945. *Sioux Falls Times*, April 19, 1881.

946. *Grant County Review*, April 28, 1881.

947. *Salem Register* (Salem, Dakota Territory), April 29, 1881.

948. *Egan Express*, May 5, 1881.

949. *Grant County Review*, April 28, 1881.

950. *Moody County Enterprise*, April 14, 1881.

951. *New Ulm Weekly Review*, May 4, 1881.

952. *Janesville Argus*, April 26, 1881.

953. *Janesville Argus*, May 3, 1881.

954. H. A. (Al) Stimson, *Depot Days* (Boynton Beach, FL: Star, 1972), 84.

955. *Grant County Review*, April 7, 1881.

956. *Grant County Review*, April 14, 1881.

957. *Grant County Review*, April 21, 1881.

958. *Grant County Review*, April 21, 1881.

959. *Grant County Review*, May 5, 1881.

960. *Marshall Messenger*, April 1, 1881.

961. *Janesville Argus*, April 5, 1881.

962. *New Ulm Weekly Review*, April 6, 1881.

963. *New Ulm Weekly Review*, April 6, 1881.

964. *Brookings County Press*, April 7, 1881. The correspondence came from Town 109, Range 49, Dakota Territory.

965. *Marshall Messenger*, April 8, 1881.

966. *Janesville Argus*, April 12, 1881.

967. *Murray County Pioneer*, April 14, 1881.

968. *Marshall Messenger,* April 15, 1881.

969. *New Ulm Weekly Review*, April 20, 1881.

970. *New Ulm Weekly Review*, April 20, 1881.

971. *Marshall Messenger*, April 22, 1881.

972. *Marshall Messenger*, April 22, 1881.

973. Wilder, *The Long Winter*, 174–175.

974. *Marshall Messenger*, April 22, 1881.

975. *Marshall Messenger*, April 22, 1881.

976. *Janesville Argus*, April 26, 1881.

977. *Marshall Messenger*, April 29, 1881.

978. *Marshall Messenger*, April 29, 1881.

979. *Marshall Messenger*, April 29, 1881.

980. *Janesville Argus*, May 3, 1881.

981. *New Ulm Weekly Review*, May 4, 1881.

982. *New Ulm Weekly Review*, May 4, 1881.

983. *New Ulm Weekly Review*, May 4, 1881.

984. *New Ulm Weekly Review*, May 11, 1881.

985. *New Ulm Weekly Review*, May 18, 1881.

986. *Brookings County Press*, May 5, 1881.

987. Wilder, Brandt, 107; Wilder, *Pioneer Girl*, 225; and Wilder, Bye, 134. The quote here is from the Brandt version of the autobiography.

988. Wilder, *Pioneer Girl*, 225; Wilder, Brandt, 107; Wilder, Bye 134; and Wilder, *The Long Winter*, 320.

989. *New Ulm Weekly Review*, May 11, 1881.

990. *New Ulm Weekly Review*, May 11, 1881.

991. *Dell Rapids Exponent*, April 2, 1881.

992. *Egan Express*, April 7, 1881.

993. *Pipestone Star*, April 21, 1881.

994. *Mankato Review* (Mankato, MN), summarized in the *Pipestone Star*, April 21, 1881.

995. *Murray County Pioneer*, April 21, 1881.

996. *Moody County Enterprise*, April 21, 1881.

997. *Moody County Enterprise*, April 21, 1881.

998. *Moody County Enterprise*, April 21, 1881.

999. *Janesville Argus,* April 26, 1881.

1000. *Pipestone Star,* April 28, 1881.

1001. *Moody County Enterprise*, April 28, 1881.

1002. *Egan Express*, April 28, 1881.

1003. *Moody County Enterprise*, May 5, 1881.

1004. *Egan Express*, May 5, 1881.

1005. *Egan Express*, May 12, 1881.

1006. Twin Brooks Items, *Moody County Enterprise*, May 5, 1881.

1007. *Egan Express*, May 12, 1881.

1008. *Sioux Falls Times*, April 12, 1881.

1009. *Sioux Falls Times*, April 19, 1881.

1010. *Sioux Falls Times*, April 12, 1881.

1011. *Dakota Pantagraph and Sioux Falls Independent*, April 13, 1881.

1012. *Sioux Falls Times*, April 19, 1881.

1013. Chicago, Milwaukee, and St. Paul Railway Company, *Seventeenth Annual Report of the Chicago, Milwaukee and St. Paul Railway Company* (Milwaukee: Chicago, Milwaukee and St. Paul Railway Company, 1881), 23.

1014. *Egan Express*, March 31, 1881; and *Dell Rapids Exponent*, April 2, 1881.

1015. *New Ulm Weekly Review*, April 13, 1881.

1016. *Egan Express,* May 12, 1881.

1017. Laura Ingalls Wilder to Rose Wilder Lane, 7 March, 1938, box 13, folder 194, Rose Wilder Lane Papers, Laura Ingalls Wilder Files.

1018. *Murray County Pioneer*, April 7, 1881.

1019. Chicago and North Western Railway Company, *Annual Report of the Chicago and North Western Railway Company for the Twenty-Second Fiscal Year, Ending May 31st, 1881* (New York: Chicago and North Western Railway Company, 1881), 20–21.

1020. Chicago and North Western Railway Company, *Annual Report of the Chicago and North Western Railway Company for the Twenty-Second Fiscal Year*, 33 (monthly earnings) and 43 (earnings per mile).

1021. *New Ulm Weekly Review*, April 13, 1881.

1022. *Marshall Messenger*, April 15, 1881.

1023. *Winona Republican* (Winona, MN), April 16, 1881.

1024. *Grant County Review*, April 28, 1881.

1025. *New Ulm Weekly Review*, May 4, 1881.

1026. *Murray County Pioneer*, May 5, 1881.

1027. *Grant County Review*, April 28, 1881.

1028. *Grant County Review*, May 5, 1881.

1029. *Grant County Review*, May 5, 1881.

1030. *Janesville Argus*, April 12, 1881.

1031. *Janesville Argus*, April 19, 1881.

1032. *New Ulm Weekly Review*, April 20, 1881.

1033. Sleepy Eye Items, New Ulm Weekly Review, May 4, 1881.

1034. *New Ulm Weekly Review*, April 27, 1881.

1035. *Grant County Review*, April 28, 1881.

1036. *New Ulm Weekly Review*, April 6, 1881.

1037. *Brookings County Press*, April 7, 1881.

1038. *Marshall Messenger*, April 29, 1881.

1039. *Murray County Pioneer*, April 28, 1881.

1040. *Janesville Argus*, May 3, 1881.

1041. *Murray County Pioneer*, April 28, 1881.

1042. *Dell Rapids Exponent*, April 2, 1881.

1043. *Egan Express*, April 28, 1881.

1044. *Pipestone Star*, April 28, 1881.

1045. *Moody County Enterprise*, May 5, 1881.

1046. *Moody County Enterprise*, May 5, 1881.

1047. *Egan Express*, May 5, 1881.

1048. *Sioux Falls Times*, April 19, 1881.

1049. *Grant County Review*, April 14, 1881.

1050. *Grant County Review*, May 5, 1881.

1051. *Janesville Argus*, April 5, 1881.

1052. *Pipestone Star*, April 7, 1881.

1053. *Marshall Messenger*, April 15, 1881.

1054. *Janesville Argus*, April 5, 1881.

1055. *Volga Gazette* (Volga, Dakota Territory), April 8, 1881.

1056. *Marshall Messenger*, April 22, 1881.

1057. *Marshall Messenger*, April 29, 1881.

1058. *Marshall Messenger*, May 6, 1881.

1059. *Brookings County Press*, April 7, 1881.

1060. *Brookings County Press*, May 5, 1881.

1061. *Marshall Messenger*, April 22, 1881.

1062. *New Ulm Weekly Review*, May 4, 1881.

1063. Laura Ingalls Wilder to Rose Wilder Lane, 15 February 1938, box 13, folder 194, Rose Wilder Lane Papers, Laura Ingalls Wilder Files.

1064. *New Ulm Weekly Review*, May 4, 1881.

1065. *New Ulm Weekly Review*, April 13, 1881.

1066. *Moody County Enterprise*, April 14, 1881.

1067. *Moody County Enterprise*, April 14, 1881.

1068. *Sioux Falls Times*, April 19, 1881.

1069. *Egan Express*, April 21, 1881.

1070. *Egan Express*, April 28, 1881.

1071. *Dell Rapids Exponent*, April 2, 1881.

1072. "Inflation Calculator: 1881 Dollars in 2019," Official Data Foundation, Alioth LLC, https://www.officialdata.org/us/inflation/1881. For further details on this source, see note 2.

1073. *Marshall Messenger*, April 22, 1881.

1074. *Marshall Messenger*, April 8, 1881.

1075. *New Ulm Weekly Review*, April 6, 1881.

1076. *Marshall Messenger*, April 15, 1881.

1077. *New Ulm Weekly Review*, April 20, 1881.

1078. *Marshall Messenger*, April 22, 1881.

1079. *Sleepy Eye Herald* (Sleepy Eye, MN), reprinted in the *Janesville Argus*, May 3, 1881.

1080. *Pipestone Star*, April 14, 1881; and *Moody County Enterprise*, April 14, 1881.

1081. *Moody County Enterprise*, April 14, 1881.

1082. *Egan Express*, April 28, 1881.

1083. *Moody County Enterprise*, April 21, 1881.

1084. *Moody County Enterprise*, April 14, 1881.

1085. *Moody County Enterprise*, April 14, 1881.

1086. *Marshall Messenger*, April 22, 1881.

1087. *New Ulm Weekly Review*, April 20, 1881.

1088. George Washington Kingsbury, *History of Dakota Territory*, ed. George Martin Smith (Chicago: S.J. Clarke, 1915), 2:1161–1162.

1089. Kingsbury, *History of Dakota Territory*, 2:1161–1162.

1090. *Murray County Pioneer*, May 4, 1881.

1091. *Grant County Review*, April 14, 1881.

1092. *Grant County Review*, April 21, 1881.

1093. *Janesville Argus*, April 12, 1881.

1094. *Murray County Pioneer*, April 28, 1881.

1095. *Murray County Pioneer*, May 5, 1881.

1096. *Brookings County Press*, April 7, 1881.

1097. *Sioux Falls Times*, April 12, 1881.

1098. *Moody County Enterprise*, April 14, 1881.

1099. *Moody County Enterprise*, April 21, 1881.

1100. *Egan Express*, April 7, 1881.

1101. *Brookings County Press*, April 7, 1881.

1102. *Dell Rapids Exponent*, April 2, 1881.

1103. *Dell Rapids Exponent*, April 23, 1881.

1104. *Dell Rapids Exponent*, April 2, 1881.

1105. *Janesville Argus*, April 5, 1881.

1106. *Marshall Messenger*, April 22, 1881.

1107. *New Ulm Weekly Review*, April 13, 1881.

1108. *Pipestone Star*, April 21, 1881.

1109. *Pipestone Star*, April 28, 1881.

1110. *Watertown Courier* (Watertown, Dakota Territory), April 20, 1881, reprinted in the *Grant County Review*, April 28, 1881.

1111. *Egan Express*, April 28, 1881.

1112. *Salem Register* (Salem, Dakota Territory), May 20, 1881.

1113. *Grant County Review*, April 28, 1881.

1114. *Sioux Falls Times*, April 12, 1881.

1115. *Brookings County Press*, April 7, 1881.

1116. *Brookings County Press*, April 7, 1881.

1117. *Dell Rapids Exponent*, April 2, 1881.

1118. *Dell Rapids Exponent*, April 2, 1881.

1119. *Grant County Review*, April 21, 1881.

1120. *Grant County Review*, April 21, 1881.

1121. *Egan Express*, May 5, 1881.

1122. *New Ulm Weekly Review*, April 27, 1881.

1123. "About Bird Island Blizzard," US Newspaper Directory, 1690–Present, Chronicling America: Historic American Newspapers, Library of Congress, https://chroniclingamerica.loc.gov/lccn/sn89064727/.

Epilogue

1124. *Egan Express* (Egan, Dakota Territory), April 28, 1881

1125. Diaries of Charles Wood Irish, 10 July 1879, series 3, box 5, Charles Wood Irish Papers, Special Collections, University of Iowa Libraries, Iowa City, IA.

1126. John Charles Frémont, *Memoirs of My Life: Including In the Narrative Five Journeys of Western Exploration* [. . .] (Chicago: Belford, Clarke, 1887), 45–46.

1127. H. A. (Al) Stimson, *Depot Days* (Boynton Beach, FL: Star, 1972), 81.

1128. John C. Luecke, *More Chicago & North Western in Minnesota* (St. Paul: Grenadier, 2012), 67.

1129. Author conversation with Jim Wichmann, July 20, 2019.

1130. Author conversation with Jim Wichmann, July 20, 2019.

1131. Author conversation with Jim Wichmann, July 20, 2019.

1132. Author conversation with Jim Wichmann, July 20, 2019.

1133. Author conversation with Jim Wichmann, July 20, 2019.

1134. Lake Benton, MN (website), "Wind Power on the Buffalo Ridge," accessed October 28, 2019, https://www.lakebentonminnesota.com/?SEC=B62CE668-CE41-4427-BBCF-D3D873A5A3C9.

1135. *Marshall Messenger* (Marshall, MN), April 22, 1881.

1136. *Janesville Argus* (Janesville, MN), April 12, 1881.

1137. *Janesville Argus*, May 3, 1881.

1138. *Sioux City Journal* (Sioux City, IA), reprinted in the *Canton Advocate* (Canton, Dakota Territory), March 3, 1881.

1139. Ivison, Blakeman, Taylor & Co., "The Voice of the Wind," lesson LXXIV in *The American Educational Readers. Fifth Reader.* (New York: Ivison, Blakeman, Taylor, 1873), 200–201.

1140. Charles W. Sanders, "The Lost One's Lament," lesson CXXI in *Sanders' Union Fourth Reader: Embracing a Full Exposition of the Principles of Rhetorical Reading; With Numerous Exercises for Practice* [...] (New York: Ivison, Phinney, Blakeman, 1867), 407–408.

1141. Caroline Starr Rose, email message to author, September 20, 2019.

1142. Laura Ingalls Wilder, *Pioneer Girl: The Annotated Autobiography*, ed. Pamela Smith Hill (Pierre: South Dakota Historical Society Press, 2014), 225; Wilder, Brandt, 107–108; and Wilder, Bye, 133–13[5] (page 135 mistyped as a second page 134 in the Bye manuscript). On a scrap of paper, after recounting the first trains through in early May, Wilder had noted, "There was a good deal of feeling against the railroad because of these and other things among them being that the RR Co had let it be known that De Smet would be the end of the division, then had changed their plans and made Huron the end of the division instead.

People thought the railroad Co took unfair advantage in their freight charges...." Wilder, Laura's "Ideas for Work," 1903 and undated, box 14, folder 202, Rose Wilder Lane Papers, Laura Ingalls Wilder Files, Herbert Hoover Presidential Library, West Branch, IA.

1143. Wilder, *Pioneer Girl*, 225; Wilder, Brandt, 107–108; and Wilder, Bye, 134.

1144. Laura Ingalls Wilder, *These Happy Golden Years* (1941; repr., New York: HarperTrophy, 2004), 24. Citations refer to the HarperTrophy edition.

1145. Laura Ingalls Wilder to Rose Wilder Lane, 19 August 1937, box 13, folder 193, Rose Wilder Lane Papers, Laura Ingalls Wilder Files.

1146. Wilder, Brandt, 98–99; Wilder, Bye, 123; and Wilder, *Pioneer Girl*, 212. In the Brandt version of the autobiography, quoted here, the text indicates that the family began to wonder how they would get through the winter "in December." In the Bye version, this is changed to "in November," and in *Pioneer Girl*, no specific month is mentioned.

1147. Laura Ingalls Wilder to Rose Wilder Lane, 7 March 1938, box 13, folder 194, Rose Wilder Lane Papers, Laura Ingalls Wilder Files.

1148. Wilder, Manuscript, 90p (backside); and Wilder, Laura's list of corrections to *The Long Winter* with map of De Smet, n.d., box 15, folder 238, Rose Wilder Lane Papers, Laura Ingalls Wilder Files. The note from Laura's list of corrections is under page 86.

1149. Laura Ingalls Wilder to Rose Wilder Lane, 5 February 1937, box 13, folder 193, Rose Wilder Lane Papers, Laura Ingalls Wilder Files.

1150. William Stennett, *Yesterday and To-day: A History* (Chicago: Rand, McNally, 1905), 65.

1151. John C. Luecke, email message to author, November 15, 2019.

Appendixes

1152. Laura Ingalls Wilder, *Pioneer Girl: The Annotated Autobiography*, ed. Pamela Smith Hill (Pierre: South Dakota Historical Society Press, 2014), 220; Wilder, Brandt, 104; and Wilder, Bye, 131.

1153. Wilder, *Pioneer Girl*, 221; Wilder, Brandt, 105; and Wilder, Bye, 131. At this point in the Brandt version, the timing of the storm is suggested as being "only a few minutes after they were in shelter."

1154. Wilder, *Pioneer Girl*, 220; Wilder, Brandt, 104; and Wilder, Bye, 130.

1155. *New Ulm Weekly Review* (New Ulm, MN), February 16, 1881, and February 23, 1881; *Egan Express* (Egan, Dakota Territory), February 17, 1881, and February 24, 1881; *Murray County Pioneer* (Currie, MN), February 17, 1881; *Grant County Review* (Milbank, Dakota Territory), February 17, 1881; *Sioux Valley News* (Canton, Dakota Territory), February 25, 1881; and *Pipestone Star* (Pipestone, MN), February 24, 1881.

1156. Laura Ingalls Wilder, *The Long Winter* (1940; repr., New York: HarperTrophy, 2004), 265.

1157. Wilder, *The Long Winter*, 269.

1158. Wilder, *The Long Winter*, 284

1159. Wilder, *The Long Winter*, 264.

1160. The following times were returned by Google's sunrise/sunset search function with De Smet, South Dakota, input as the location and February 14, 15, and 16, 1881, input as the dates (for instance, the first entry in the list below was determined by performing a Google search of "Sunrise and Sunset in De Smet, South Dakota, on February 14, 1881"):

Sunrise / Sunset

Feb. 14: 7:40 a.m. / 6:08 p.m.

Feb. 15: 7:39 a.m. / 6:09 p.m.

Feb. 16: 7:37 a.m. / 6:10 p.m.

It is unknown whether Google's sunrise/sunset search function takes into account the fact that standard time was not introduced until 1883. These times may be inexact, but the 10.5 hours of sunlight should be accurate enough for our purposes.

1161. Laura Ingalls Wilder, Manuscript, 102p.

1162. Wilder, Manuscript, 102p.

1163. That the seed wheat run likely took place the week of February 14 is further supported by research conducted by meteorologist Barbara Mayes Boustead. Barbara E. Mayes Boustead, "Laura's Long Winter: Putting the Hard Winter of 1880-81 Into Perspective," (paper presented in "Climate Communications and Perspectives" at the American Meteorological Society's 19th Conference on Applied Climatology, July 18, 2011),

4–5, accessed April 3, 2018, https://ams.confex.com/ams/19Applied/webprogram/Paper190298.html.

1164. *Mansfield Mirror* (Mansfield, Missouri), October 27, 1949.

1165. It is understood that each newspaper may have had—and likely did have—multiple employees doing the composing and typesetting, and several papers were coproprietorships between two main editors. For simplicity, I have not delved into the specifics of who may have composed each article or squib, because for the most part it cannot be known.

1166. Arthur P. Rose, *An Illustrated History of Lyon County Minnesota* (Marshall, MN: Northern History, 1912), 303–304.

1167. "About New Ulm Weekly Review," US Newspaper Directory, 1690–Present, Chronicling America: Historic American Newspapers, Library of Congress; and L. A. Fritsche, ed., *History of Brown County, Minnesota: Its People, Industries and Institutions* (Indianapolis: B.F. Bowen, 1916), 1:458.

1168. Hector O. Ventura and Mandeep R. Mehra, "Bloodletting as a Cure for Dropsy: Heart Failure Down the Ages," abstract, *Journal of Cardiac Failure* 11, no. 2 (May 2005): 247–252, accessed November 12, 2019, https://doi.org/10.1016/j.cardfail.2004.10.003.

1169. *History of Steele and Waseca Counties, Minnesota: An Album of History and Biography, Embracing Sketches of the Villages, Cities and Townships; Educational, Civil, Military and Political History; Portraits of Prominent Citizens, and Biographies of Old Settlers and Representative Men* (Chicago: Union Publishing Company, 1887), 498; and *Waseca Herald* (Waseca, MN), January 15, 1904.

1170. Debbie Hemmer and Holli Seehafer, *The Scoop on the* Grant County Review (printed by Grant County Review, CreateSpace, 2016), 8–10; and *Baltimore Sun*, November 28, 1887, accessed October 10, 2018, https://newspaperarchive.com/baltimore-sun-nov-28-1887-p-1/.

1171. Pamela Smith Hill, "The *Pioneer Girl* Manuscripts," in Wilder, *Pioneer Girl*, lxi.

1172. Hill, "The *Pioneer Girl* Manuscripts," lxi.

1173. Hill, "The *Pioneer Girl* Manuscripts," lxi–lxii.

1174. Hill, "The *Pioneer Girl* Manuscripts," lxiii.

1175. Wilder, Manuscript.

1176. Wilder, *The Long Winter.*

1177. Author conversations with John C. Luecke, railroad historian; Ivan Flitter, retired engineer; and Brad Sabin, Vice President, Iowa Northern Railroad.

1178. Laura Ingalls Wilder to Rose Wilder Lane, 23 March 1937, box 13, folder 193, Rose Wilder Lane Papers, Laura Ingalls Wilder Files, Herbert Hoover Presidential Library, West Branch, IA.

INDEX